# Jahresring 63
# SouthEastAsia
# Spaces of
# the Curatorial
# Räume des
# Kuratorischen

# Jahresring 63
# SouthEastAsia
# Spaces of
# the Curatorial
# Räume des
# Kuratorischen

Ute Meta Bauer, Brigitte Oetker (Eds./Hg.)

*SternbergPress*

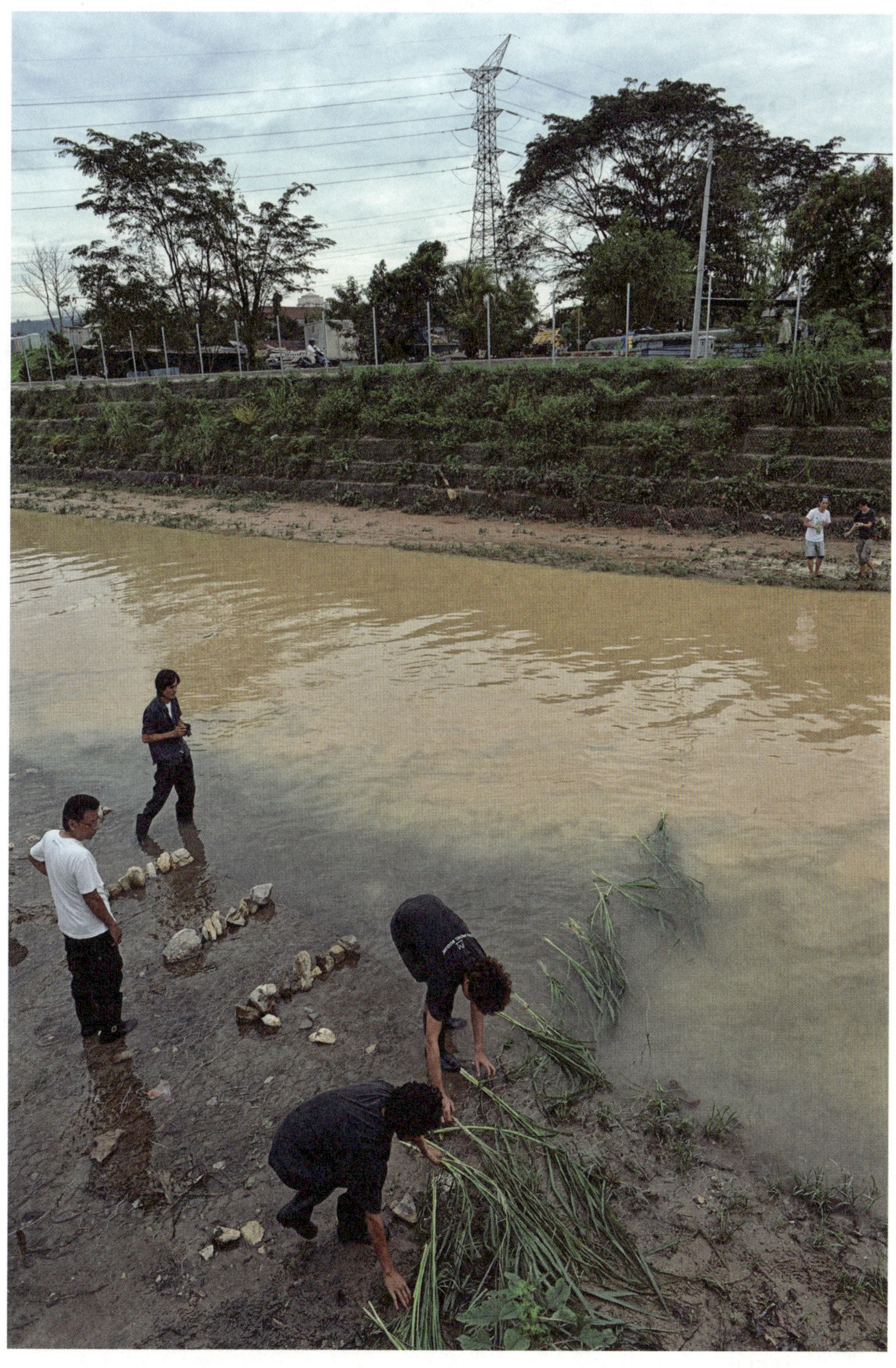

Moelyono Moel, Workshop in Kampung Danda Dalam, 2013
Lostgens' Contemporary Art Space, Kuala Lumpur, Malaysia

# Contents
# Inhalt

# Preface



Contemporary art from Southeast Asia has become increasingly visible in Europe in recent years at biennials, museums, and art fairs. Its contexts of origin and production conditions, however, remain little known. The 63rd issue of the Jahresring sheds light on these contexts, presenting actors and venues that play a crucial role in art-making processes. Authors from Singapore, Malaysia, Indonesia, the Philippines, Myanmar, Thailand, and Vietnam accepted the invitation from Ute Meta Bauer and Lee Weng Choy to offer insights into and discuss the art activities in this region that range from small projects initiated by artists to widely connected international initiatives.

The volume raises the following questions: How can contemporaneity build upon local identities, traditions, and criticalities? How is state repression dealt with? How can one succeed in eluding the tight embrace of the Western art world perceived by some as recolonization?

It shows in a highly impressive way how the production and presentation of art is interconnected with globalization processes, the colonial past, and current power relations.

The texts describe the commitment of curators to create free spaces for art that also integrate the public in the processes of raising historical consciousness and engagement with ecological, social, and geopolitical issues. The Jahresring is honored to present these remarkable initiatives striving for the exploration of new curatorial spaces.

Brigitte Oetker and Isabel Podeschwa

# Vorwort

<br>

Zeitgenössische Kunst aus Südostasien wurde in den letzten Jahren in Europa zunehmend sichtbar, auf Kunstmessen, Biennalen und in Museen. Ihre Entstehungszusammenhänge blieben allerdings weiterhin wenig bekannt. Die vorliegende 63. Ausgabe des Jahresrings beleuchtet diese Zusammenhänge und stellt Orte und Akteure vor, die für die Prozesse künstlerischer Produktion eine wichtige Rolle spielen. Autorinnen und Autoren aus Singapur, Malaysia, Indonesien, von den Philippinen, aus Myanmar, Thailand und Vietnam folgten der Einladung von Ute Meta Bauer und Lee Weng Choy, Einblicke in die Kunstaktivitäten dieser Region zu geben. Lokale, von Künstlern initiierte Projekte werden hier ebenso diskutiert wie weit vernetzte internationale Initiativen.

Dabei treten folgende Fragestellungen hervor: Auf welche Weise kann Zeitgenossenschaft auf lokalen Identitäten, Traditionen und Kritikalität aufbauen? Wie geht man mit staatlichen Repressionen um? Wie kann es gelingen, sich aus der festen Umarmung westlicher Kunstwelten zu lösen, die teilweise als Rekolonialisierung empfunden wird?

Sehr eindrücklich wird geschildert, wie das Entstehen und Zeigen von Kunst mit Globalisierungsprozessen, der kolonialen Vergangenheit und den gegenwärtigen Machtverhältnissen verschränkt sind. Die Texte beschreiben das Engagement von Kuratorinnen und Kuratoren, Freiräume für Kunst zu schaffen, die auch eine Öffentlichkeit in die Prozesse von historischer Bewusstwerdung, in ökologische, sozial- und geopolitische Themen einbindet. Diese wertvollen Ansätze, Räume des Kuratorischen zu schaffen, stellt dieser Jahresring zum ersten Mal vor.

Brigitte Oetker und Isabel Podeschwa

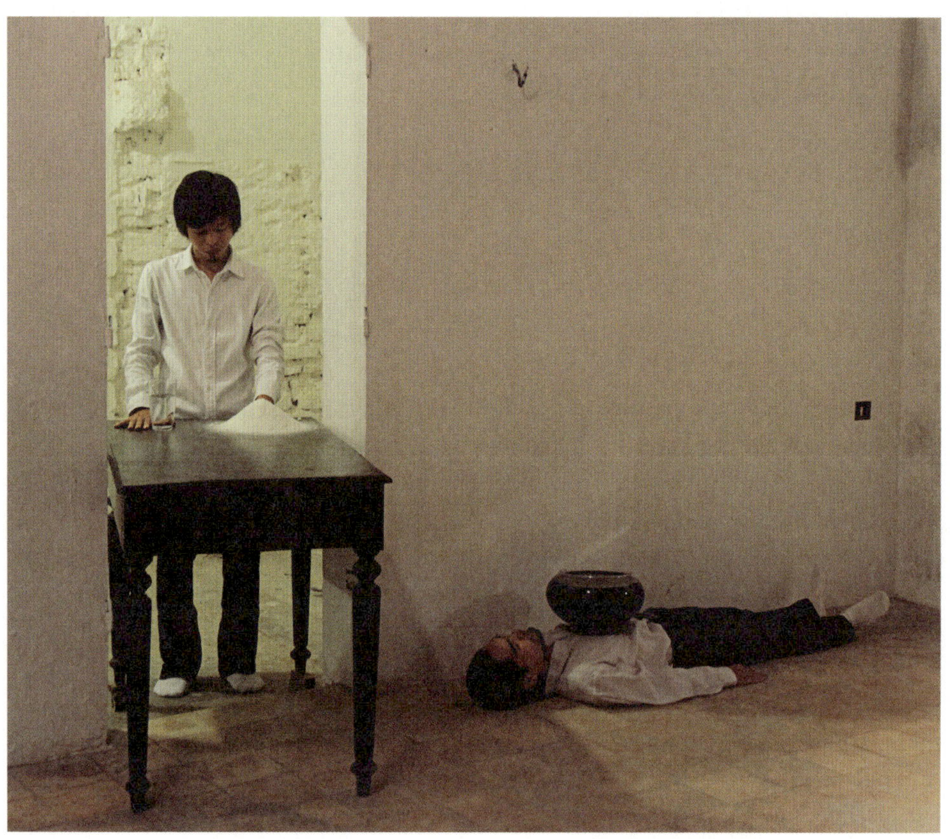

Phu Luc, *Mơ Moi VI (Somniloquy VI)*, 2013
Performance, IN:ACT Art Festival
Nhà Sàn Collective, Hanoi, Vietnam

Ute Meta Bauer

# SouthEastAsia Spaces of the Curatorial

To capture in a single picture the complexity of curatorial processes in a region that does not let itself easily be mapped or defined is an overwhelming task. Subsuming the nation states of the region under the term "Southeast Asia" originates in their colonial and postcolonial histories, and the area today could not be more diverse in terms of economies, infrastructures, and legal frameworks. It can also be futile to attempt to produce a macro narrative about a geopolitical area that is changing so rapidly; we should not pretend that such a publication could keep up with this pace.

As diverse and multilayered as the region itself are its art scenes, infrastructures, and conditions of cultural production. Rather than providing an overview, this publication aims to capture and locate such diversity into the vast range of curatorial spaces throughout Southeast Asia and the multiple critical discourses they generate. Various types of writings mirror the variety of backgrounds and experiences of writers who engage in contemporary art and curatorial practices in the region. The heterogeneity of the material also underlines the diverse contexts in which each curatorial discourse is produced. If the exhibition catalogue was a conventional platform of curatorial articulation in Western art history, the curatorial thinking in Southeast Asia unfolds in new sites and situations. Hence, several selected unpublished texts originate from presentations in symposia, conferences, or workshops, or were commissioned by print and online journals. Yet the curatorial, as art historian and curator Tony Godfrey documents in his excerpt from *Tuesday in the Tropics,* an illustrated weekly letter sent online to those interested, happens also outside the institutional framework, in the artist's studio, or in a welcoming *warung* (small shop). Writing becomes a tool to immerse oneself into a new context to negotiate, understand, and come to terms with ones outsider position.

With this publication, we wish to foster curiosity towards artistic production, but also trigger interest to visit and get familiar with the variety of local spaces where curating takes place, acknowledging how much they contribute in defining what we experience as the art of Southeast Asia. Rather than focusing on the wide range of artists and their practices, which would be an undertaking of several published volumes, we rather explore the curatorial and its spaces as a point of entry. The selection of art spaces matches the range of the texts. Such a selection does not measure up to the density of the regional art spaces, but it gives an insight into the various ways of working, discrepant funding possibilities, and uneven conditions of cultural production. From small to big institutions, artist-run spaces to community-driven projects and galleries, from art fairs to biennials, the various curatorial platforms in the region produce a multi-faceted art ecosystem where the value of each initiative and its unique role needs to be understood. Artist-run spaces such as Cemeti Art House, Yogyakarta, Indonesia, San Art in Ho Chi Minh City in Vietnam, Sa Sa Art Projects and Sa Sa Bassac in Phnom Penh, Cambodia, or the artist-collective Ruangrupa in Jakarta, Indonesia, play a substantial role in supporting the local art scene, fostering exchanges and generating discourse in contexts that experience a lack of public funding, but have wider freedom in terms of approach and content. Larger scale institutions such as the Singapore Art Museum, or the Jorge B. Vargas Museum in Manila contributed to building collections and ensuring that artistic production remains in the public realm and is accessible to a wider public. This publication also captures Southeast Asia in a time of institution building. In 2015 we witnessed the opening of the National Gallery Singapore, which hosts the largest public collection of modern art in Singapore and Southeast Asia in its 64,000 square meters. Such an institution takes on the mission to provide a historical narrative of the region through its collection and exhibition making to the extent that, as art historian Kevin Chua highlighted, "the curatorial has come to replace art history–searching for new critical interpretations, pushing the frontier of artistic knowledge."[1]

While the history of the region is in a process of rewriting, this publication embraces the realm of incongruities attached to Southeast Asia and its past, present, and future. These discrepancies, driven by politics and economy, are deeply embedded within the region and have been addressed both artistically and curatorially. There is no surprise, as Seng Yu Jin points out in his essay "Framing Contemporary Art in Southeast Asia through Exhibitionary Discourse," referencing curators Patrick D. Flores and Apinan Poshyananda, that one of the recurrent themes of exhibitions emerging in the 1990s in this part of the world engaged with the dynamics between "old" and "new." But a "new" that does not replace the "old" as the Western paradigm of progress and linear time preaches; rather a "new" that coexists with the "old." Religions shape the cultural traditions even in the most high-tech environments of many of region's capitals and still play an essential role in everyday life.

Different temporalities emerge simultaneously and overlap rather than succeeding each other.[2] Such a state leads to diverse conditions of cultural production across the region. In his essay "Who Cares a Lot? Ruangrupa as Curatorship," curator and writer David Teh points out the infrastructural differences: while Singapore's art sector is heavily government funded, the art scene of its neighbor, Indonesia, for example, is reliant on a booming art market and bottom-up initiatives.

In "Why Play? An Outsider's Point of View on Making and Seeing Art in Myanmar Today," Singaporean art historian and curator Yin Ker notices the "winds of change blown across the world" from Myanmar to the Middle East and its Arab Spring, only within a year since she wrote the first version of this text in August 2010 and the final version in October 2011. Her comment is even more striking, since very recently Myanmar saw a major political shift in March 2016 with a newly-elected government driven by the former head of opposition, Aung San Suu Kyi.

While the selected texts originate from different contexts of presentation and address various locales in Southeast Asia, there are certain commonalities of ideas and thoughts that weave these narratives together. One important aspect that very much drives the work and energy of our own young center, the NTU Centre for Contemporary Art Singapore, is the belief in artistic production as a form of knowledge on its own. This belief is also articulated in Nora Annesley Taylor's and Kevin Chua's contributions through their focus on two Singaporean artists of different generations, Koh Nguang How and Charles Lim Yi Yong. Taylor's essay, "The *Singapore Art Archive Project* and the Institutions of Memory in Southeast Asia," engages with the *Singapore Art Archive Project* (SAAP), a long-term project of Koh Nguang How. In 2014, SAAP was hosted at Gillman Barracks as part of Koh's residency at NTU CCA Singapore. His project became a point of major interest and a research site for the local, but also international visitors whose access to the archive benefited from Koh's active presence in the space and guidance regarding the materials. The art work and its (re)presentation in Koh's instance is inseparably intertwined. Koh embodies multiple positions from a researcher to a curator, all roles that mirror the various uses to which such an archive opens up. As Taylor points out, SAAP gains legitimacy by operating outside the institutional framework and resisting its appropriation into the official canon, providing alternative, non-authoritative narratives.

In his essay, "The Curatorial as Buoy and Beacon," Kevin Chua focuses on the practice of the artist Charles Lim Yi Yong and his more recent projects *In Search of Raffles' Light* at the NUS Museum (2013–14) and *SEA STATE* (2015, 2016), his project for the 56th Venice Biennale–all collaborations, or one should better say conversations with curator Shabbir Hussain Mustafa. What Lim's work triggers is the ability to translate curiosity into research and to connect practice with theory. His projects develop through an entanglement of various systems of maritime knowledge and acts of transgression, experiments where such knowledge is embodied and contingent on each situation. The exhibited artwork itself generates a space of the curatorial.

As art historian, educator, and and curator Patrick D. Flores highlighted in various essays, the curatorial practice in Southeast Asia is defined by the position of artist-curator. Some of the most visible figures were artists-turned-curators, such as Redza Piyadasa (Malaysia), Jim Supangkat (Indonesia), Raymundo Albano (Phillipines), and Apinan Poshyananda (Thailand), filling the gaps in the art system. However, this overlapping of roles took a new direction of a more conceptual blending between artistic and curatorial positions. This is the case, for example, of the Jakarta-based collective Ruangrupa, as indicated by David Teh. Ruangrupa merges the artistic with the curatorial: it embodies the commitment to a place and specific audience combined with the discursive formats that curating can give shape to. This is illustrated by many of the curatorial platforms established by Ruangrupa such as the "OK Video–Jakarta International Video Festival" or the Jakarta Biennale–all event-driven, discursive manifestations ingrained in the urban fabric of the ever-expanding Indonesian capital.

The politics of care towards an audience and the significance of social connections and affinities are also claimed in Zoe Butt's passionate text "Practicing Friendship: Respecting Time as a Curator." Drawing on her experience leading artist-initiated organizations in China and Vietnam, Butt makes a plea for curatorial and museum networks to acknowledge and respect the need for time, such an approach being crucial when working under conditions of political and cultural restrictions regularly experienced in Vietnam and other parts of Southeast Asia. The value of intimacy, close conversations, and trust as a basis for building knowledge and networks resonates with Tony Godfrey's informal methodology to navigate the art scenes of the Philippines and Indonesia by talking, listening to the artists, and creating a platform to share their thoughts. Such encounters and fragments of conversations that are documented in a diary form provide a raw, unfiltered account of the artists' daily reality in the intimacy of their studio.

On the other hand, researcher and curator Eileen Legaspi-Ramirez addresses the problematics around institutionalized networks in her incisive essay "Southeast Asia in a Crawl Space: Tempering Curatorial Hubris." The author draws attention to the current trend of performing a Southeast Asian identity and how this representation game involves governmental forces alongside cultural agents, whether artists or curators. She highlights how the region is constituted through discourse and networking, with many "peer encounters" running the risk of doing nothing but performing cultural exchange. In his contribution, "Rethinking Curatorial Colonialism," art historian Simon Soon looks into the relation between colonialism and knowledge production as embodied by the curatorial.[3] Such a relation is exemplified through the recent tendency of curating to appropriate acts of activism, a colonizing gesture through which radical politics are flattened and subordinated to hegemonic discourses.

Patrick D. Flores's essay, "Within and Across: Troublesome Propositions," is an attempt to recuperate the power of institutionality and retrace its contribution to knowledge production and artistic formation in the region. While admitting the thin line between institutional critique and its institualization as if they are shadowing each other, Flores also expresses trust and desire to generate change from within. The author overviews current regional institutional models highlighting how their practice can be reformed and transformed to actively contribute in cultural production. Spaces such as the university art museum, artist-run spaces, or archives have the potential to shape the postcolonial contemporary.

Seng Yu Jin's text underlines how the contemporary is constituted through institutions and the "exhibitionary discourses" by focusing on the regional history of exhibitions over a decade (1992–2002), a formative period that shaped ideas on contemporary art and its histories. Tracing art-historically significant exhibitions that mined the emerging field of Southeast Asian contemporary art from the perspectives of Japan, Australia, and within the region, the author examines dominating exhibition narratives. Mapping the critical debate produced through these exhibitions highlights the intersection of cultural politics, art institutions, scholarship, and curating that began to generate different ways of framing contemporaneity.

In the lecture, "The Mekong as a Site of Artistic Production," Gridthiya Gaweewong reflects on a  multi-year project about how regionality can be constituted through artistic and curatorial production. As a curator, she focused on a collective process that addressed the transnational Mekong region shifting from early to current cultural projects that aimed to establish links across nations through exchanges between artists, curators, activists, and other cultural producers.

Yin Ker captures the complexity of self-expression and artistic production in Myanmar, a country subjected to a long-standing military regime and enforcement of severe censorship. The author chose the concept of "play" as a curatorial framework for an exhibition she co-curated alongside Isabel Ching in 2010 at Osage Gallery, Singapore. This marked the first exhibition entirely devoted to contemporary Burmese art organized outside of Myanmar. The concept of play is more than a curatorial device or narrative, it served as a framework for understanding the conditions of production in an authoritarian regime and how humor, hope, imagination, and playing a fool became a means of resistance. Yin Ker brings to the fore the importance of responsibility. In a place where the display and interpretation of an artwork has real life consequences for an artist, curatorial work is pushed towards acting responsibly.

Such attitudes as responsibility, care, and friendship form the basis of the spaces of the curatorial across Southeast Asia. As one can observe from the selected texts, culture in Southeast Asia is strongly performative, theatrical, resilient, resistant, a space defined by individuals, artist collectives' initiatives, but also government-funded institutions. The commitment of artists, curators, collectors, and other supporters create a strong and durable art platform whose growth, visibility, and infrastructural improvements we are currently witnessing.

I would like to express my gratitude towards all those individuals in the region who encouraged me to get engaged with Southeast Asia and who lend their support for this publication. Without Lee Weng Choy's sharing his network and friendship with many of the authors, we could not have achieved such a result in a short time. We thank T. K. Sabapathy, eminent art historian, for his patience in grounding us in the region and facilitating our understanding of the cultural transitions that defined Southeast Asia after colonial times.

I would like to thank all the individuals and institutions that provided us with texts and images and granted permission for use allowing a first glimpse into this very rich fabric of the region: Charles Lim Yi Yong; Agung Hujatnikajennong; Vera Mey; Erin Gleeson; Ong Jo-Lene; *Afterall* and Chicago University Press; Asia Art Archive, Hong Kong; Salon Natasha Archive; Cemeti Art House, Indonesia; Ruangrupa, Indonesia; Jorge B. Vargas Museum, Philippines, Museum of Contemporary Art and Design, Philippines; Nhà Sàn Collective, Vietnam; Sàn Art, Vietnam; Sa Sa Art Projects and Sa Sa Bassac, Cambodia; The Jim Thompson Art Center, Thailand; Lostgens' Contemporary Art Space, Malaysia; Run Amok Collective, Malaysia; National Gallery Singapore, and The Substation, Singapore.

We could have not achieved editing this book in a relatively short time without the support of my colleagues at the NTU CCA Singapore: I thank Cheong Kah Kit for holding threads together, Marc Glöde for his constructive feedback, and Anca Rujoiu for her critical input. My deep appreciation goes to Brigitte Oetker for her curiosity and courage to select this region and introduce it to the community of friends of Jahresring, as well as to a wider public. Our gratitude goes to managing editor Isabel Podeschwa, whose patience and precision in the editorial and translation process are second to none. We would like to thank Aaron Bogart and Nina Köller for their editorial support, Tatjana Günthner and Sternberg Press for their precise work as always; Markus Weisbeck and Victor Kassis of Surface for another collaboration based on mutual understanding. Bringing these diverse texts forward to a German readership would have been impossible without the creative act of translation. On behalf of the authors and myself, I would like to express my appreciation to Anne Breimaier, Barbara Hess, Karl Hoffmann, Danilo Scholz, and Jochen Stremmel. Last but not least, our heartfelt thanks go to the authors for their trust in bringing together the richness of voices: emotional, intense, argumentative, committed perspectives on this region that sees such vast transitions on all levels, hopefully with art and culture as a driving force.

1   Kevin Chua, e-mail correspondence with the editors, July 2016.

2   The experience of "asyncronicities" in Asia marked also the NTU CCA Singapore's inaugural exhibition, "Paradise Lost" (2014) including the works of Fiona Tan, Trinh T. Minh-ha, and Zarina Bhimji. The exhibition served as a way to engage the institution's program with the contrasts and contradictions within the region itself, challenging conventional representations.

3    Kevin Chua also highlighted this connection in an e-mail correspondence with the editors, July 2016: "The curatorial sees itself as doing knowledge production; but what if knowledge production *always had a colonial basis*? Knowledge was the precondition of European global supremacy, and an inherent part of colonial power structures (Sebastian Conrad, *German Colonialism: A Short History* [Cambridge: Cambridge University Press, 2013], 11). In other words, we can't divorce knowledge from power and politics: indeed, knowledge systems, such as cartography, population censuses, or photographic documentation, made colonialism possible."

Timoteus Anggawan Kusno
*Anatomy of (Lost) Memories*, 2015
Cemeti Art House, Yogyakarta, Indonesia

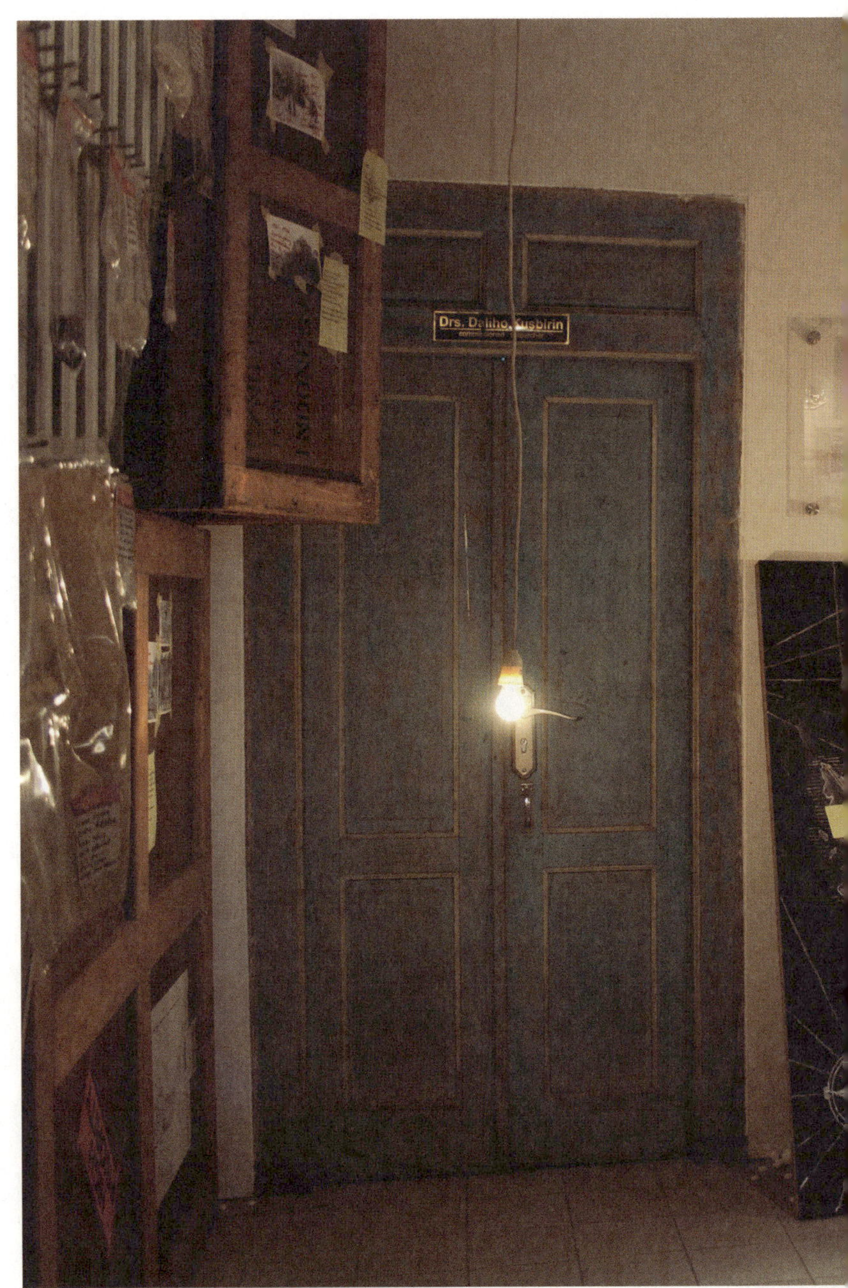

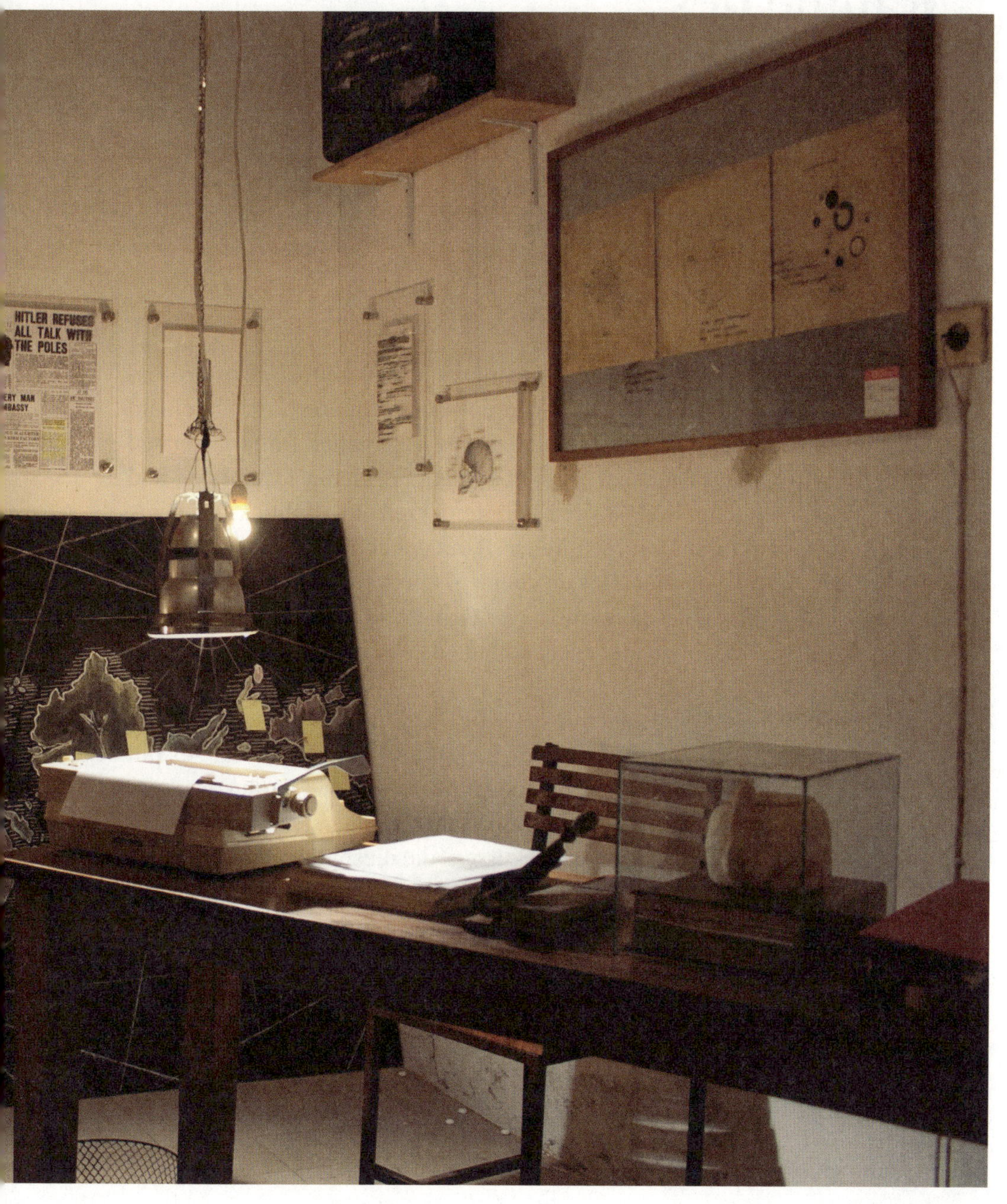
HITLER REFUSES
ALL TALK WITH
THE POLES
ERY MAN
MBASSY

Ute Meta Bauer

# SouthEastAsia Räume des Kuratorischen

Es ist eine enorme Herausforderung, die Komplexität der kuratorischen Prozesse einer Region, die sich nicht einfach kartieren oder definieren lässt, in einem einzigen Bild zu erfassen. Die Zusammenfassung regionaler Nationalstaaten unter dem Begriff Südostasien hat ihren Ursprung in deren kolonialer und post-kolonialer Geschichte. Südostasien könnte derzeit im Hinblick auf seine Ökonomien, Infrastrukturen und rechtlichen Rahmenbedingungen nicht unterschiedlicher sein. Es mag aussichtslos erscheinen, überhaupt erst zu versuchen, ein umfassendes Narrativ eines geopolitischen Gebiets zu produzieren, das sich so schnell verändert; wir wollen also nicht so tun, als ob eine solche Publikation mit diesem Tempo Schritt halten könnte.

So unterschiedlich und vielschichtig wie die Region selbst sind auch ihre Kunstszenen, Infrastrukturen und Bedingungen kultureller Produktion. Anstatt einen Überblick zu bieten, zielt die vorliegende Publikation eher darauf ab, diese Vielgestaltigkeit des breiten Spektrums kuratorischer Räume in ganz Südostasien und in den verschiedenen kritischen Diskursen, die diese Räume hervorbringen, zu erfassen und zu verorten. Die unterschiedlichen Schreibstile spiegeln die Vielfalt der Hintergründe und Erfahrungen von Autorinnen und Autoren wider, die sich mit der zeitgenössischen Kunst und den kuratorischen Praktiken der Region auseinandersetzen. Die Heterogenität des Materials betont auch die unterschiedlichen Kontexte, in denen der jeweilige kuratorische Diskurs entsteht. Während in der westlichen Kunstgeschichte der Ausstellungskatalog eine konventionelle Plattform kuratorischer Überlegungen ist, entwickelt sich das kuratorische Denken in Südostasien an neuen Orten und in neuen Zusammenhängen. Daher stammen einige der ausgewählten, bislang unveröffentlichten Texte aus

Präsentationen anlässlich von Symposien, Konferenzen und Workshops, oder sie entstanden als Auftragsarbeiten für Zeitschriften und Online-Magazine. Doch das Kuratorische findet auch außerhalb des institutionellen Rahmens – im Atelier oder in einem gastfreundlichen *warung*, einem kleinen Laden, – statt, wie der Kunsthistoriker und Kurator Tony Godfrey in seinem Auszug aus „Dienstags in den Tropen" dokumentiert, einem bebilderten Brief, den er wöchentlich an Interessierte mailt. Schreiben wird zu einem Instrument, um sich in einen neuen Kontext zu vertiefen, um die eigene Außenseiterposition zu verhandeln, zu verstehen und zu bearbeiten.

Wir möchten mit dieser Publikation die Neugier auf die künstlerische Produktion in Südostasien fördern, aber auch dazu anregen, Räume, in denen kuratorische Prozesse stattfinden, zu besuchen und in ihrer Vielfältigkeit kennenzulernen. Wir erhoffen uns, dass diese Publikation für den umfassenden Beitrag sensibilisiert, den diese Orte für unsere Wahrnehmung von Kunst aus Südostasien leisten. Anstatt uns mit einem breiten Spektrum von Künstlerinnen und Künstlern und ihren Praktiken zu beschäftigen, was ein Vorhaben für ein mehrbändiges Werk wäre, erforschen wir das Kuratorische und dessen Räume. Die Auswahl der Kunsträume korrespondiert mit der Bandbreite der Texte. Eine solche Auswahl bildet nicht die Dichte der Kunsträume in der Region ab, aber sie bietet einen Einblick in die verschiedenen Arbeitsweisen, unterschiedlichen Finanzierungsmodelle und die uneinheitlichen Bedingungen der kulturellen Produktion. Die diversen kuratorischen Plattformen der Region – von kleinen bis zu großen Institutionen, von selbstorganisierten Orten bis zu gemeinschaftlich getragenen Projekten und Galerien, von Kunstmessen bis zu Biennalen – erzeugen ein facettenreiches Ökosystem der Kunst, in dem der Wert jeder einzelnen Initiative und ihre jeweils einzigartige Rolle verstanden werden muss. Von Künstlerinnen und Künstlern organisierte Räume wie das Cemeti Art House in Yogyakarta, Indonesien, Sàn Art in Ho-Chi-Minh-Stadt, Vietnam, Sa Sa Art Projects und Sa Sa Bassac in Phnom Penh, Kambodscha, oder das KünstlerInnen-Kollektiv Ruangrupa in Jakarta, Indonesien, spielen für die Unterstützung der lokalen Kunstszene eine bedeutende Rolle; sie fördern den Austausch und erzeugen Diskurse in Kontexten, in denen zwar eine öffentliche Finanzierung fehlt, dafür aber bei der Herangehensweise und bei den Inhalten größere Freiheiten bestehen. Größere Institutionen wie das Singapore Art Museum oder das Jorge B. Vargas Museum in Manila, Philippinen, haben dazu beigetragen, Sammlungen aufzubauen und zu gewährleisten, dass die künstlerische Produktion im öffentlichen Besitz bleibt und für ein breites Publikum zugänglich ist. So erfasst die vorliegende Veröffentlichung die Situation Südostasiens in einer Zeit der Institutionsgründungen. 2015 eröffnete die National Gallery Singapore, die auf ihren 64.000 Quadratmetern über die größte öffentliche Sammlung moderner Kunst in Singapur und Südostasien verfügt. Einer solchen Einrichtung kommt die Aufgabe zu, durch ihre Sammlung und ihre Ausstellungspraxis ein historisches Narrativ der Region zu liefern; und sie tut dies, wie der Kunsthistoriker Kevin Chua betont, bis hin zu dem Punkt, an dem „das Kuratorische die Kunstgeschichte ersetzt – auf der Suche nach neuen kritischen Interpretationen, mit denen die Grenzen des Wissens über die Kunst erweitert werden."[1]

In einer Zeit, in der die Geschichte der Region neu geschrieben wird, beschäftigt sich diese Publikation mit den Widersprüchen, die mit Südostasien und seiner Vergangenheit, Gegenwart und Zukunft verknüpft sind. Solche politisch und ökonomisch begründeten Diskrepanzen sind in der Region tief verwurzelt und wurden ebenso künstlerisch wie kuratorisch thematisiert. Wie Seng Yu Jin in seinem Essay „Ausstellungsdiskurse in Südostasien und ihre Wirkung auf die Wahrnehmung des Zeitgenössischen" mit Verweis auf die Kuratoren Patrick D. Flores und Apinan Poshyananda ausführt, ist es nicht überraschend, dass sich Ausstellungen in diesem Teil der Welt in den 1990er Jahren wiederholt mit der dynamischen Beziehung zwischen alt und neu beschäftigt haben. Dieses Neue ersetzt jedoch nicht das Alte, wie es die westlichen Paradigmen des Fortschritts und der linearen Zeit predigen, sondern es koexistiert mit ihm. Religionen prägen kulturelle Traditionen selbst in den avanciertesten High-Tech-Umgebungen vieler Hauptstädte der Region und spielen im Alltag eine zentrale Rolle.

Verschiedene Zeitlichkeiten entstehen simultan und überlagern sich eher, als dass sie aufeinander folgen.[2] Ein solcher Zustand führt zu unterschiedlichen Bedingungen kultureller Produktion in der Region. Der Kurator und Kunsthistoriker David Teh zeigt in seinem Essay „Wen kümmert es wirklich? Das Ruangrupa-Kollektiv als kuratorische Plattform" die infrastrukturellen Unterschiede auf: Während der Kunstsektor in Singapur in hohem Maße staatlich gefördert wird, finanziert sich die Kunstszene im benachbarten Indonesien durch einen boomenden Kunstmarkt und Bottom-up-Initiativen.

In „Why Play? Entstehen und Verstehen von Kunst im heutigen Myanmar – eine Außenseiterperspektive" beobachtet die singapurische Kunsthistorikerin und Kuratorin Yin Ker, dass sich innerhalb nur eines Jahres zwischen der ersten Fassung ihres Textes, die im August 2010 entstanden war und der finalen Fassung von Oktober 2011, die Weltlage von Myanmar bis zum Nahen Osten und seinem Arabischen Frühling erheblich verändert hatte. Ihr Kommentar ist umso bemerkenswerter, da Myanmar erst vor Kurzem einen bedeutenden politischen Umbruch erlebte, als im März 2016 eine neu gewählte Regierung antrat, in der die frühere Oppositionsführerin Aung San Suu Kyi eine zentrale Rolle spielt.

Auch wenn die ausgewählten Texte aus unterschiedlichen Präsentationszusammenhängen stammen und verschiedene Schauplätze in Südostasien thematisieren, gibt es gewisse übereinstimmende Ideen und Überlegungen, die diese Narrative miteinander verknüpfen. Ein wichtiger Aspekt – und zugleich ein starker Antrieb für die Arbeit unseres eigenen neuen Kunstzentrums, des NTU Centre for Contemporary Art Singapore – ist die Überzeugung, dass künstlerische Produktion eine eigenständige Wissensform ist. Diese Gewissheit spricht auch aus den Beiträgen von Nora A. Taylor und Kevin Chua, die sich auf zwei singapurische Künstler verschiedener Generationen, Koh Nguang How und

Charles Lim Yi Yong, konzentrieren. Taylors Essay „Das *Singapore Art Archive Project* und die Institutionalisierung des Erinnerns in Südostasien" beschäftigt sich mit einer langfristig angelegten künstlerischen Arbeit von Koh Nguang How. 2014 war das SAAP im Rahmen von Kohs Residency am NTU Centre for Contemporary Art Singapore im Kunstquartier Gillman Barracks zu Gast. Sein Projekt wurde zu einem wichtigen Anziehungspunkt und einer Forschungsstätte für lokale, aber auch internationale BesucherInnen, deren Zugang zum Archiv von Kohs aktiver Präsenz im Ausstellungsraum und von seiner Unterstützung bei der Nutzung der Materialien profitierte. In Kohs Fall sind das Kunstwerk und seine (Re-)Präsentation untrennbar miteinander verknüpft. Koh verkörpert mehrere Positionen, vom Forscher bis zum Kurator – Rollen, die auch die unterschiedlichen Nutzungsmöglichkeiten eines Archivs widerspiegeln. Wie Taylor ausführt, ist das SAAP so wichtig, weil es außerhalb des institutionellen Systems agiert, dadurch alternative, nicht autoritative Narrative bietet und seiner Aneignung durch den offiziellen Kanon widersteht.

In seinem Essay „Das Kuratorische als Boje und Leuchtfeuer" beschäftigt sich Kevin Chua mit der Praxis des Künstlers Charles Lim Yi Yong und seinen neueren Projekten *In Search of Raffles' Light* im NUS Museum (2013/2014) und *SEA STATE* (2015, 2016), seinem Beitrag für die 56. Venedig Biennale – beides Kooperationen oder, genauer gesagt, Konversationen mit dem Kurator Shabbir Hussain Mustafa. Lims Arbeit triggert die Fähigkeit, Neugier in Forschung zu übersetzen und Praxis mit Theorie zu verbinden. Seine Projekte entstehen durch die Verflechtung verschiedener Systeme maritimen Wissens und durch Überschreitungen: ihnen gehen Experimente voraus, in denen solches Wissen verkörpert und in Abhängigkeit von der jeweiligen Situation begründet ist. Das ausgestellte Kunstwerk erzeugt als solches einen Raum des Kuratorischen.

Wie der Kunsthistoriker, Vermittler und Kurator Patrick D. Flores in mehreren Essays betont hat, ist die kuratorische Praxis in Südostasien von der Position des Künstler-Kurators geprägt. Einige, die besonders hervorgetreten sind und Lücken im Kunstsystem geschlossen haben, waren ehemalige Künstler, die zum Kurator wurden, wie etwa Redza Piyadasa (Malaysia), Jim Supangkat (Indonesien), Raymundo Albano (Philippinen) und Apinan Poshyananda (Thailand). Diese Überlagerung verschiedener Rollen nahm eine neue Richtung und entwickelte sich zu einer eher konzeptuellen Verbindung zwischen künstlerischen und kuratorischen Positionen. Dies gilt beispielsweise, wie David Teh aufzeigt, für das in Jakarta angesiedelte Kollektiv Ruangrupa. Das Künstlerische und das Kuratorische greifen ineinander: Ruangrupa verkörpert das Engagement für einen Ort und ein bestimmtes Publikum und verbindet dies mit diskursiven Formaten, denen das Kuratieren eine konkrete Gestalt verleihen kann. Das zeigt sich an vielen der von Ruangrupa gegründeten kuratorischen Plattformen wie dem *OK Video* Festival oder der Jakarta Biennale – auf Events basierende, diskursive Manifestationen, die mit der urbanen Textur der immer weiter wachsenden Hauptstadt Indonesiens verwoben sind.

Die Politik der Verantwortung für ein Publikum und die Bedeutung sozialer Beziehungen und Affinitäten werden auch in Zoe Butts leidenschaftlichem Statement „In Freundschaft arbeiten. Zeit im kuratorischen Prozess" geltend gemacht. Butt beruft sich auf ihre Erfahrungen als Leiterin von Organisationen, die von KünstlerInnen in China und Vietnam gegründet wurden, wenn sie dafür plädiert, dass kuratorische und museale Netzwerke deren besonderen Zeitbedarf anerkennen und respektieren sollten. Eine solche Herangehensweise ist von entscheidender Bedeutung, wenn man unter den Bedingungen politischer und kultureller Restriktionen arbeitet, die in Vietnam und anderen Teilen Südostasiens an der Tagesordnung sind. Der Wert von persönlichen Beziehungen, offenen Gesprächen und Vertrauen als Grundlage, um Wissen und Netzwerke aufzubauen, findet Widerhall in Tony Godfreys informeller Methode, durch die Kunstszenen der Philippinen und Indonesiens zu navigieren, und in gemeinsamen Gesprächen und Überlegungen eine Plattform zu entwickeln, um diese Einschätzungen mit anderen zu teilen. Diese Begegnungen und Bruchstücke von Konversationen, die er in Form eines offenen Tagebuchs festgehalten hat, bieten eine unmittelbare und ungefilterte Darstellung der Alltagswirklichkeit von Künstlerinnen und Künstlern in der Privatheit ihrer Ateliers.

Die Wissenschaftlerin und Kuratorin Eileen Legaspi-Ramirez hingegen thematisiert in ihrem scharfsinnigen Aufsatz „Südostasien im Zwischenboden. Ein Plädoyer gegen die kuratorische Hybris" die Problematik institutionalisierter Netzwerke. Die Autorin verweist auf die aktuelle Tendenz, eine südostasiatische Identität zu performieren, und zeigt auf, dass in dieses Spiel der Repräsentation, neben kulturellen Akteuren wie KünstlerInnen und KuratorInnen, auch Regierungskräfte involviert sind. Sie unterstreicht, wie die Region durch Diskurse und Netzwerke konstituiert wird, wobei viele „Begegnungen unter Gleichgesinnten" Gefahr laufen, lediglich diesen kulturellen Austausch und nichts darüber hinaus zu vollziehen. Der Kunsthistoriker Simon Soon untersucht in seinem Beitrag „Ein anderer Blick auf den kuratorischen Kolonialismus", inwiefern im Kuratorischen die Beziehung zwischen Kolonialismus und Wissensproduktion bereits angelegt ist.[3] Beispielhaft für diese Beziehung ist die aktuelle Tendenz des Kuratorischen, sich Aktivismus anzueignen – eine kolonialisierende Geste, die radikales politisches Handeln entschärft und hegemonialen Diskursen unterordnet.

Patrick D. Flores' Essay, „Drinnen und draußen. Unbequeme Vorschläge" ist ein Versuch, die Stärke von Institutionalität zurückzugewinnen und ihren Beitrag bei der Wissensproduktion und der künstlerischen Ausbildung in Südostasien nachzuvollziehen. Zwar räumt Flores ein, dass nur ein schmaler Grat die institutionelle Kritik von ihrer Institutionalisierung trennt, als ob das eine der Schatten des anderen ist; gleichzeitig bringt er sein Vertrauen und seinen Wunsch zum Ausdruck, Veränderungen *von innen heraus* anzustoßen. Der Autor gibt einen Überblick über aktuelle Modelle der Gestaltung von Institutionen und betont, wie ihre jeweilige Praxis reformiert und transformiert werden kann, um aktiv zur Kulturproduktion beizutragen. Räume wie das universitäre Kunstmuseum, selbstorganisierte Ausstellungsräume oder Archive haben das Potenzial, die postkoloniale Gegenwart zu gestalten.

Seng Yu Jins Text arbeitet heraus, wie sich das Zeitgenössische durch Institutionen und Ausstellungsdiskurse konstituiert, wobei er sich auf die regionale Ausstellungsgeschichte der Jahre 1992 bis 2002 konzentriert - eine einflussreiche Phase, die das Denken über zeitgenössische Kunst und die Auffassungen ihrer Geschichte nachhaltig geprägt hat. Anhand von historisch bedeutenden Ausstellungen, die das entstehende Feld der zeitgenössischen Kunst Südostasiens aus den Perspektiven von Japan, Australien und der Region selbst erschlossen haben, untersucht der Autor vorherrschende Ausstellungsnarrative. Seine Darstellung der kritischen Debatten, die diese Ausstellungen ausgelöst haben, verdeutlicht die Schnittmengen von Kulturpolitik, Kunstinstitutionen, wissenschaftlicher Forschung und kuratorischer Praxis, die das Zeitgenössische auf unterschiedliche Weise zu formulieren begannen.

Gridthiya Gaweewong untersuchte in ihrem Vortrag „Orte künstlerischer Produktion entlang des Mekong", wie durch künstlerische und kuratorische Produktion Regionalität hergestellt werden kann. Sie konzentriert sich als Kuratorin auf einen kollektiven Prozess, der die transnationale Mekong-Region thematisiert, und behandelt frühe wie auch aktuelle Kulturprojekte, die darauf abzielten, durch den Austausch zwischen KünstlerInnen, KuratorInnen, AktivistInnen und anderen KulturproduzentInnen Beziehungen zwischen den Nationen zu entwickeln.

Yin Ker erfasst die Komplexität künstlerischer Ausdrucksformen in Myanmar, einem Land, das lange unter einer Militärdiktatur stand und in dem strenge Zensur herrschte. Die Autorin wählte das Konzept des Spiels als kuratorischen Bezugsrahmen für eine Ausstellung, die sie 2010 zusammen mit Isabel Ching für die Osage Gallery in Singapur realisierte. Dies war die erste außerhalb von Myanmar organisierte Ausstellung, die ausschließlich zeitgenössischer burmesischer Kunst gewidmet war. Das Konzept des Spiels ist jedoch mehr als nur ein kuratorisches Mittel oder Narrativ; es diente als Bezugspunkt, um die Produktionsbedingungen unter einem autoritären Regime zu verstehen und zeigte, wie Humor und Hoffnung, die Vorstellungskraft und das Verrücktspielen zu Mitteln des Widerstands werden können. Yin Ker betont dabei die Bedeutung von Verantwortung. Dort, wo das Zeigen und Interpretieren eines Kunstwerks Auswirkungen auf das reale Leben eines Künstlers oder einer Künstlerin hat, kann sich kuratorisches Handeln nicht der Verantwortung entziehen.

Haltungen wie Verantwortung, Sorge und Freundschaft bilden die Grundlage der Räume des Kuratorischen in ganz Südostasien. Wie die ausgewählten Texte zeigen, ist die Kultur in Südostasien entschieden performativ, theatralisch, resilient und widerständig. Südostasien ist ein Raum, der von Einzelnen, von Künstlerkollektiven, aber auch von staatlich geförderten Institutionen geprägt wird. Das Engagement von KünstlerInnen, KuratorInnen, SammlerInnen und anderen Förderern bildet eine starke und beständige Plattform für Kunst, deren

Wachstum, zunehmende Sichtbarkeit und infrastrukturelle Verbesserungen wir derzeit erleben.

Ich möchte allen Personen in der Region danken, die mich für Südostasien begeistert haben und die somit diese Publikation mit Rat und Tat unterstützt haben. Wir hätten ein solches Ergebnis nicht erzielen können, wenn nicht Lee Weng Choy sein Netzwerk und seine Freundschaften mit vielen Autorinnen und Autoren mit uns geteilt hätte. Wir danken dem bedeutenden Kunsthistoriker T. K. Sabapathy für seine Geduld, mit der er uns mit der Region vertraut gemacht und unser Verständnis für deren kulturellen Wandel erleichtert hat, der für Südostasien nach der Kolonialzeit so bestimmend war.

Ich möchte allen Personen und Institutionen danken, die uns Texte und Bilder zur Verfügung gestellt und deren Nutzung zugestimmt haben; sie haben uns auf diese Weise einen ersten Einblick in das äußerst dichte Gefüge dieser Region gewährt: Charles Lim Yi Yong; Agung Hujatnikajennong; Vera Mey; Erin Gleeson; Ong Jo-Lene; *Afterall* und Chicago University Press; Asia Art Archive, Hongkong; Salon Natasha Archive, Vietnam; Cemeti Art House, Indonesien; Ruangrupa, Indonesien; Jorge B. Vargas Museum, Philippinen, Museum of Contemporary Art and Design, Philippinen; Nhà Sàn Collective, Vietnam; Sàn Art, Vietnam; Sa Sa Art Projects und Sa Sa Bassac, Kambodscha; Jim Thompson Art Center, Thailand; Lostgens's Contemporary Art Space, Malaysia; Run Amok Collective, Malaysia; National Gallery Singapore, und The Substation, Singapur.

Wir hätten dieses Buch nicht in relativ kurzer Zeit herausgeben können ohne die Unterstützung meiner KollegInnen am NTU CCA Singapore. Mein Dank gilt Cheong Kah Kit dafür, dass er die Fäden in der Hand hielt, Marc Glöde für sein konstruktives Feedback und Anca Rujoiu für ihre kritische Begleitung. Mein aufrichtiger Dank gilt Brigitte Oetker für ihre Neugier und ihren Mut, diese Region auszuwählen und sie der Leserschaft des Jahresrings wie auch einer breiteren Öffentlichkeit vorzustellen. Wir bedanken uns herzlich bei Isabel Podeschwa für ihr inhaltliches Engagement und ihren unermüdlichen Einsatz für diese Publikation. Aaron Bogart und Nina Köller danken wir für das Lektorat, Tatjana Günthner und Sternberg Press für ihre wie immer präzise Arbeit, und Markus Weisbeck und Victor Kassis von Surface für eine weitere Zusammenarbeit, die auf gegenseitigem Verständnis beruht. Ohne den kreativen Akt der Übersetzung wäre es nicht möglich gewesen, diese unterschiedlichen Texte einer deutschen Leserschaft vorzulegen. Dafür möchte ich, auch im Namen der Autorinnen und Autoren, Anne Breimaier, Barbara Hess, Karl Hoffmann, Danilo Scholz und Jochen Stremmel danken. Und nicht zuletzt gilt unser aufrichtiger Dank den Autorinnen und Autoren, die uns das Vertrauen entgegen gebracht haben, die Vielfalt ihrer Stimmen – emotionale, fordernde, analytische, engagierte – und die Unterschiedlichkeit ihrer Perspektiven zusammenzubringen und dadurch einen vielschichtigen Blick auf eine Region zu ermöglichen, die auf allen Ebenen einen tiefgreifenden Wandel erlebt, in dem Kunst und Kultur hoffentlich eine kritische und treibende Kraft darstellen.

1 Kevin Chua, E-Mail-Korrespondenz mit den Herausgeberinnen, Juli 2016.

2 Die Erfahrung von „Asynchronien" in Asien kennzeichnete auch die Eröffnungsausstellung des NTU CCA Singapore, *Paradise Lost* (2014), mit Arbeiten von Fiona Tan, Trinh T. Minh-ha und Zarina Bhimji. Die Ausstellung diente dazu, das Programm der Institution auf die Gegensätze und Widersprüche in der Region zu beziehen und konventionelle Repräsentationen zu hinterfragen.

3 Kevin Chua betonte diesen Zusammenhang auch in einer E-Mail-Korrespondenz mit den Herausgeberinnen im Juli 2016: „Das Kuratorische versteht sich als eine Form von Wissensproduktion; doch was wäre, wenn Wissensproduktion *immer schon* eine koloniale Grundlage hätte? Wissen war eine Voraussetzung für die globale Vormachtstellung Europas und ein Element, das kolonialen Machtstrukturen innewohnte (Sebastian Conrad, *Deutsche Kolonialgeschichte*, München: Beck, 2008, S. 12). Anders gesagt, können wir Wissen nicht von Macht und Politik trennen: Tatsächlich haben Wissenssysteme wie Kartografie, Volkszählungen oder fotografische Dokumentationen den Kolonialismus erst ermöglicht."

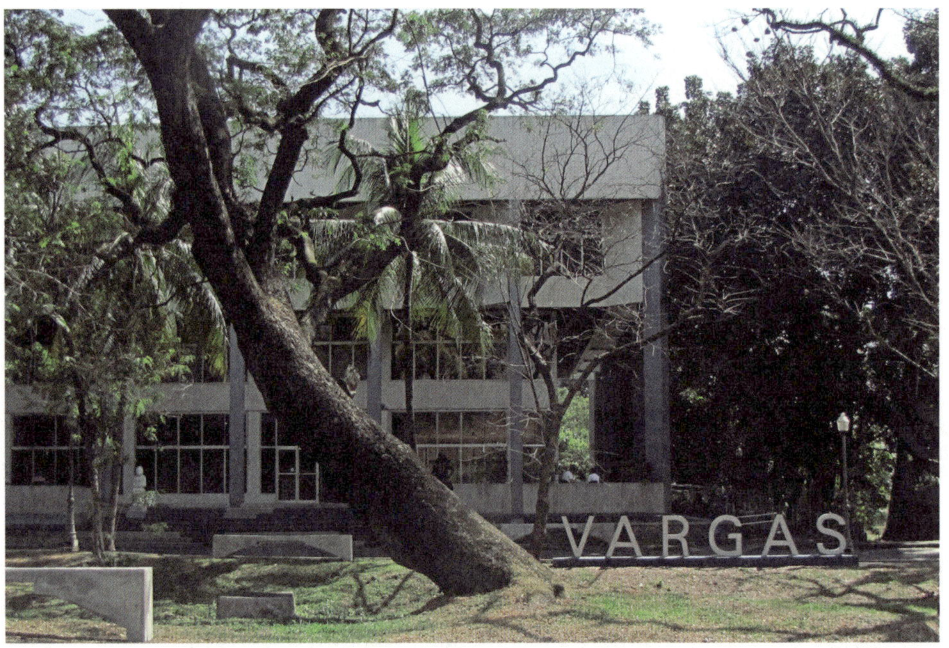

Jorge B. Vargas Museum
University of the Philippines
Quezon City, Philippines

Patrick D. Flores

# Within and Across: Troublesome Propositions

There is much gesture and rhetoric invested in our habits when we find ourselves in the orbit of institutions of so-called "culture." In the National Museum of Cambodia in Phnom Penh, the halls are filled with Buddhist statuary, yet the faithful file in not to see "art," but to offer flowers and incense—prompting us to wonder how the "image in the era of art" residing in the museum actually figures in this sensorium of devotion. When we enter the National Museum in Singapore, the staff tries to interest us in interactive "companions"—audio guides that explain the artifacts to be encountered in a path strewn with annotation. Before a film unreels in a movie house in Bangkok, the audience huddled in darkness rises to sing the King's anthem—testament to the potency of the crown in this society of rather internecine history that reveres the world's longest-reigning living monarch. In the Silpakorn campus, a statue of Silpa Bhirasri, the Italian Corrado Feroci, stands like a sentinel and watches over the students of art; he founded the school under the auspices of King Chulalongkorn in 1943, a lineage that has ensconced the teacher of art in esteem.

It is early evening in Bandung in 2005, and Agus Suwage's exhibition of painted and drawn images of performance art and artists opens to a teeming crowd at the Soemardja Gallery at the Bandung Institute of Technology. Such turnout is not unusual in an art world disposed to *diskusi* in rooms reeking of *kretek*; that Indonesia in the early 2000s would yield the most number of players in the region who called themselves "curator" tells us something about the liberties Indonesians have taken in shaping the "contemporary" through what Slavoj Žižek regards as an exceptional gesture of self-reflexivity: curation, or having things chosen on our behalf. As he clearly puts it:

> Is not the ultimate example of reflexivity in today's art the crucial role of the curator? His role is not limited to mere selection–through his selection, he (re)defines what art is today. [...] Because what we see is the curator's choice. [...] The ultimate artist is not the producer but the curator, his activity of selection.[1]

This essay does not seek to rehearse the rituals of institutional critique and belabor the heroic gesture of a failed conceptualism in the West," or its futile resuscitations in leapfrogging art worlds in the periphery. Rather, it tries to recover the power inherent in institutionality and the desire of artists to participate in its production, whether as a critique of it or as a kind of complicity in its recognition in the guise of negation. This act of recovery may be coincident with the act of offering a reflection on the notion of the "alternative" in art worlds with incommensurate modernities, and how such a category is inserted into Western discourses of supposedly liberating socialities under the sign of, for instance, relationality and related expressions of flux embedded in the infrastructure of the artist-run space, the workshop, collaboration, and so on. Such a fantasy of process may finally be interestingly juxtaposed with the need for centrality in the project of a social movement, a singular modernity, let us say, of class and nation amid neocolonial and neoliberal economic agendas. In other words, the desire for universality or a common humanity must be related to the desire for culture and particularity, giving rise to notions of the "transcultural," or the radical reinterpretation of the "exotic."[2] As Victor Segalen states:

> Exoticism is therefore not an adaptation to something; it is not the perfect comprehension of something outside one's self that one has managed to embrace fully; but the keen and immediate perception of an eternal incomprehensibility.[3]

If we were to meditate on the constitution of knowledge, we might want to chart territories other than those cleared in exceptional ways by the likes of Foucault or Spivak or Bourdieu. We might want to move beyond the imbrication of knowing and naming in power and seek other speculations on knowledge. For instance, we might want to contemplate non-knowledge, or the ways in which the sensible slips away from discourse. We might want to ask if postcolonial knowledge is always ethnographic in nature and if this ethnographic quality is sublime as well.[4] Or, what about the high levels of mixture, such as in the baroque; or the invisible in the Javanese shadow play; or the performance in the Philippine *palabas*?[5] Sarat Maharaj's thoughts on visual art as knowledge production under the rubric of "thinking through the visual" strives to

> eventuate not so much in the well-trodden terrain of the academic disciplines or in the so-called gaps, chinks, and cracks between them or in any

designated "interdisciplinary/transdiciplinary" belt. Rather it is a force in its own right, always incipient in "whatever" spaces—windswept, derelict brownfields and wastelands—where intimations of unknown elements, thinking probes, spasms of non-knowledge emerge, and come into play. It is distinct from the circuits of *know-how* that run on clearly spelled out methodological steel tracks. It is the rather unpredictable surge and ebb of potentialities and propensities—the flux of "no-how." The term is Samuel Beckett's although I intend it here without that shot of bleakness with which he normally imbues it. *No-how embodies* indeterminacy; an "any space whatever" that brews up, spreads, inspissates.[6]

The anthropologist Hugh Raffles interjects with a critical attitude toward "local knowledge" or a "situated knowledge" that is "always in process: emergent in talk, labor, sociality, affect, and many other forms of social practice."[7] This said, such "locality" may drift toward localization, and so he proposes that

> the local of local knowledge requires a radical thinking if it is to stop reproducing a localization that categorizes people as well as knowledge systems. Local knowledge may appear to valorize non-scientific ways of knowing, yet it is trapped by the not-universal of its local into reproducing and reifying the very taxonomy through which knowledges are hierarchized.[8]

In the thoughtful essay "Baroque Curiosity," José Lezama Lima elaborates on the baroque as somehow an underside to Enlightenment omnipotence:

> In Spain and America, it represents the acquisition of a language perhaps unique in the world—furniture for the home, styles of life and curiosity, a mysticism that encompasses new modes of worship, new modes of savoring and preparing delicacies—which exhales a complete way of life, refined and mysterious, theocratic and self-absorbed, errant in form but firmly rooted in its essences.[9]

From the discipline of anthropology, there is talk about the "anthropological laboratory" for the anthropology of the contemporary and its ethical moments in the collaborative process, an instinct verisimilarly current in contemporary art debates.[10]

One way to surface this process of reconsidering authority is to retrace the checkered history of institutions, specifically the museum and the art academy in the formation of the art world and the production of knowledge in Southeast Asia. The loci of the museum and the school are preconditions to coloniality being the site of pedagogy and "culture," and therefore of "corruption," culture being fundamentally an "exploit" and being so, inevitably impure.[11] But they happen to be loci of translation, too, which is constituted by both *doxa* and idiosyncrasy. And so, while there is tutelage in the academy on the one hand there is mastery of the native apprentice on the other as well. In the long term, such mastery may be unrecognizable within the grammar of the so-called "influence." In other words, these sites are laboratories of the modern because they play with the self and generate the "whatever."

Several examples may be cited, and foremost of these is the case of portraiture in Southeast Asia in which representation would be key in creating a space of presence, as if to say: "we are over here." Raden Saleh of Indonesia and Juan Luna of the Philippines are exemplary in this regard, and their achievements in the robust season of the nineteenth century in their homelands and in Europe are well known. The link between academic realism and portraiture was also pivotal in the effort of the Thai Chakri dynasty to belong to the world, with King Mongkut permitting himself to be photographed and his likeness reproduced in painting by Italian painters, whose colleagues in the field of architecture likewise adorned the kingdom with palaces and other grand edifices. This likeness or yearning for likeness, or what the Filipino hero José Rizal would call the "spell of recollection," ought to be read allegorically as a narrative of human progress, both in the facture of art and the consciousness of posing for posterity. It is, moreover, cognate of the allegory of the ethnographic picture that carves out the difference between self and other through, let us say, anthropometry and museology. The collective, that is the nation therefore, coheres into the collection of the details of the colony–people, artifacts, rituals–and the enterprise of collecting can only be foundational; whether it starts off in the mode of the *Wunderkammer* as in Sir Stamford Raffles's trove of flora, fauna, and minutiae in Malaya or the census taken by Dean Worcester in the Philippines who likewise co-founded the country's "national museum." It is important to note that this concatenation of the collection/collective would later be subjected to intense dispute by another incarnation of the "collective" in the form of artists who came together to pursue a vision against the distillation of the multitude into a singularity, the plural into the exceptional, and consequently propose the re-politicization of art[12]–at a time when postwar republics were transfixed on building a "nation," Cold War edition.[13]

The trajectory of this inculcation led to the privileging of nation as the instantiation of identity and difference. While the nation may have been primordial in the contrivance of postcolonial critique and the untranscendability of emancipation, it could not be free from its own politics of consolidation, and thus the tension between the nation-state, the legacy of the postcolonial assertion, and the "contemporary" revision of the entitlement to belong elsewhere in a wider world, so to speak. In Southeast Asia this was most evident in the compelling art movement against the institutions of Suharto's New Order, including the art establishment. It was also clear in the seventies in Thailand and the Philippines that social movements gained momentum against the military governments in Bangkok and Manila. In the Philippines, the arena of contention was the Cultural Center of the Philippines, handiwork of First Lady Imelda Marcos, where experiments in "conceptualism" played out, and to a significant extent refused the social realism against what has been claimed to be a dictatorship. In Thailand the tumult in the seventies animated the Dhamma Group in 1971 and the Artists Front of Thailand in 1974–75, and eventually gave birth to the traditional art program in Silpakorn in 1977. Important in these moments are manifestoes, two of which can be teased out from the Gerakan Seni Rupa Baru Indonesia (New Indonesian Art Movement, 1974–75) and Kaisahan (Solidarity, 1976), and both of which intertwine the political and the aesthetic and advocate a vision that confronted the allure of "development" in the time of the Cold War.[14] Kaisahan, for instance, declared:

> We shall therefore move away from the uncritical acceptance of Western molds, from the slavish imitation of Western forms that have no connection to our national life, from the preoccupation with Western trends that do not reflect the process of our development. We realize that our search will be meaningless if it does not become a collective experience, an experience that is understood and shared by the broadest number of people. In its beginnings, art was not the isolated act that it is now; it was necessary, as integral, a part of the people's lives as the knowledge of when to plant.[15]

The Gerakan, for its part, abided by the following beliefs, among others:

> Diversity is undeniable in Indonesian art, even if such diversity does not by itself signify a desirable development. For the sake of a development that ensures the sustainability of our culture, it is the artist's calling to offer a spiritual direction based on humanitarian values and oriented towards social, cultural, political, and economic realities.[16]

This critique of the West and the invocation of the "diverse" and the "spiritual" may cluster around the "romantic" moment of many manifestoes of avant-garde movements beyond their national origins. In this instance, however, there is a discernible obsession to effect an epistemic break from the "Western." This is most palpable in another manifesto of sorts conceived by Sulaiman Esa and Redza Piyadasa on "mystical reality": "Whereas the Western artist approaches art in terms of the 'spatio/temporal/sensorial' considerations, we are approaching it from a 'mental/meditative/mystical' standpoint."[17]

From the foregoing, we can glean the contemporary through various aspects of sociality, including: curation and the process of gathering; the workshop and the community; criticism and discourse (manifesto, seminal essay, language of the biennial, contemporary discourse and the consumption of the alternative by parachuting cooperators). The "gathering" insinuates a "coming" together of interests, a free play of contradictions, and a ventilation of anxieties. On the other hand, such conjuncture also demands coordination, structure, and representational form. The latter requisite for a norm posits a peregrinate agency to be called "curator," no matter how mistranslated the term may be. It is the curator that accords the coherence on the welter and in the long term a currency on the desire of fragments to be identified as "together," a transcendence of difference and an affirmation of the "collective," which previously was reified, alienated, and instrumentalized as a collection of individuals or individuated entities. This mode of sociality may provoke discussion on the potential fetishization of "process" or the "workshop," which in an earlier time through the *sanggar* in Indonesia turned to a political project for inspiration and not just to the very idea of process itself. That said, it rendered itself prone to the instrumentalization of ideology as a necessary fiction of a cognitive mapping of the totality. The reification of process in the present may, in fact, be in cadence with the neoliberal impulse of production, the customization of preference, the privatization of the reciprocal—in other words, the mechanism of agglomeration.

The "collection/collective" scheme would finally be complicated by the mutation of the artist into a curator, the "avant-garde" agent into an institutionalizing wunderkind who can make the art, pave a path for it, conceptualize a theory for it, and historicize it. The careers of Redza Piyadasa, Jim Supangkat, Raymundo Albano, and Apinan Poshyananda reflect this constellate practice in which kindred initiations that tried to reorder art and its conduct took place nearly simultaneously in Malaysia, Indonesia, the Philippines, and Thailand, respectively.[18] It is through the practice of the artist-curator that certain discourses of the local germinated and conveyed to a global audience. For instance, Albano tried to theorize "installation" as an indigenous form as opposed to painting that is Western:

> *Installations* is a case that should support the fact that painting as art is a purely Western phenomenon and that it speaks a language foreign to the Filipino. If we have paintings today, it is because there is an attempt at exemplifying or competing in this field—in the Western manner. There is no other criteria in judging a painting than those for American or European art, simply because we have no native practice that is equivalent to this art. Purist scholars who love to dig into the indigenous will find no logical precedent for painting, unlike sculpture. It may be that our innate sense of space is not a static perception of flatness but an experience of mobility, performance, body-participation, [and] physical relation at its most cohesive form. Thus installation is akin to *fiestas* and folk rituals, from all our ethnic groups.[19]

If we extend this thesis further, it is this transnationality, or better still, "translocality" of the artist-curator that may be the nexus to the theorization of, first, the contemporaneity of the native as expressive discipline in current time and, second, the aesthetic of the neo-traditional (read: national) as codified in the practices of certain Thai and Balinese artists. The inclusion of Sonabai, a folk artist from a village in India, at the Asia-Pacific Triennial in 1999, and the explanation of her art in the catalogue by the esteemed scholar Jyotindra Jain is instructive. Equally enlightening is Nora Annesley Taylor's use of the phrase "ethnography of Vietnamese Art" in her discussion of painters in Hanoi over the years. According to her:

> Rather than trying to reconstruct a history where historical data is scarce, this book studies the context in which art history is developing in Vietnam based on collective memories and on texts that are recalled and rewritten, spoken, or produced in other ways that stray from a classical Western art history model.[20]

For his part, Apinan Poshyananda forces the mentality for "Thainess" to its extreme servility to orientalism as his thesis for the country's first pavilion at the Venice Biennale in 2003. According to him:

> The journey from the canals in Bangkok to Venice evokes a time dislocation. Thai artists in traditional and contemporary attire are like art pilgrims whose mission is to find their space on the international art arena. To be visible, their endeavor is to construct their own pavilion (*sala*) in Venice despite difficulties and obstacles. Thai artists, like craftsmen, assemble prefabricated Thai house with posts, beams, roof, gable, [and] wall panels transported by boat from Bangkok. In this cultural space Thai artists take on the roles of artisans, master builders, shamans, and performers. They entertain by offering national identities and exotic differences to cultural consumers who experience cultural goods at the First Thai Pavilion in Venice. [...] Despite their exotic displays of painting, video, carpentry, cookery, therapy, massage, and dance, they become messengers and victims of the global trap that causes detriment and destruction. [...] [A] comment on the hierarchy of art internationalism and system of New Art World Order.[21]

The polytropic persona of the artist-curator would later calcify into institutionality, with the individual himself becoming the institution, bearer of knowledge of the local in the global landscape and other characters besides: biennial maker, historian, critic, bureaucrat, and so on. Surely, this power would be resisted, and the most telling case pertained to Supangkat, who in 1995 curated a contemporary exhibition commemorating the alternative axis called the non-aligned movement, which was rearticulated in Bandung, Indonesia in 1955. When he put forward the term "postmodern" to characterize the works at the 1994 Jakarta Biennale, he courted dissent from different fronts. Scholars though it was imprudent, given the fact that Indonesia, they acknowledged, was not yet modern. And it seems that the sheer temerity of a curator to spin a term and fling it onto the fray is in itself an act of audacity worthy of dispute. The career of the artist-curator, therefore, inscribes degrees of institutional critique and institutionalization as he assumed a certain official, authoritative position as arbiter and mediator of complex, discrepant tendencies or dispositions in various circuits in the state and market, hybrid events like biennials and fairs, academia, and even in popular culture. The professional travels and texts of Apinan Poshyananda are exemplary.

These moments of sociality (the gathering of people and the presentation of the gathering to the people) are possibilities that the global holds out, and we see on the horizon stirring instances of emergent modalities that may take them to productive turning points in our knowledge of art in Southeast Asia.

First, there is the university art museum as a platform that nimbly mediates between the state and the market and provides space for contemporary art in relation to an ampler academic discourse and entry points of representation. This space and the interactions within it may provide a salient tangent to the independent curator, trained in the West to curate or commission contemporary art without the requisite rite of passage through art history, connected to the network of mobile peers, and attuned to the cycles of biennials, art fairs, and other curatorial engagements, from off-sites to theaters of spectacle. The university art museum, with its propensity to theorize and refer to the pedigree of knowledge within an interdisciplinary framework, moreover, furnishes a foil to the glibness of the celebrity artistic director, the hipster organizer, the blogger, the event maker, the socialite amateur observer, the stylist, the designer—all of whom have assimilated contemporary art into their happening world that mingles fashion, graphics, street parties, glossy magazines, and the foibles of the ruling class, or the pretenders to its stature. A reconsideration of the university art museum finally references the history of the academy, its pedagogical methods, and its apparatus of scholarship.

Second, there is the modified location of the gallery-*Kunsthalle*-foundation, which has spaces across regions and convenes independent curators, vogue artists, writers, performers, graphic designers, and urban planners in their programs. How it functions as part of a larger sequence of the market and at the same time creates scenographies of the contemporary is a practice worth studying for its political economy and its curious relationship with another solvent entity: the auction, which in Southeast Asia has morphed from a secondary market to a primary one and has superseded the gallery in this commerce at some levels. How does this arrangement thrive and how does it facilitate curation that exists between the state and the market? Does it ultimately feed into the buying and selling, or does it reorganize the antinomies of the contemporary by settling on a liminal terrain all together? This paradigm may be productively seen in relation to a previously privileged platform, the artist-run space. What has happened to it? Has it been rationalized into a system, its unpredictability construed as part of its anticipated dynamic? Has it been made part of the ever-elastic concepts of "development" within a sphere that comprises a gamut of initiatives, from corporate philanthropy to creative industries, from ecological activism to moderate socialisms? At some point, there could be an assemblage.

Third, there is the self-critical institution that tries to activate its past in relation to the "new and the now," or the cult of the young, interspersing the evidence of institutionality with the energy of the contemporary in temporary exhibitions, parasitic projects, and interventions of artists within its conventional spaces (white cube, library, archive). How far can this critique go? Does it strengthen the institution's tenacious modernity by affording it the much-needed reflexivity, or does it undermine its fundamental premises? Does it hasten the institution's decline, or does it defer the already-heralded end of its art history? The opening of a national art gallery in Singapore in the future presents a scenario that prompts us to ruminate on the necessity of such an undertaking in this time of posts: post-museum, post-nation, post-history. Such signals of termination, however, must reckon with the alluring notion of an "Asian century." We may be in an epoch of post-'s, but we are in Asia, the erstwhile timeless Orient, and the "future" of the moment. This raises certain questions, such as: Is this Asia largely Chinese-driven, with museums, hubs, collectors, and exhibitions revolving around China? Is this China interested at all in the rest of Asia?

Fourth, there is the archeology of knowledge. Aside from the usual review of literature on the subject of Southeast Asia or Asia in general, it is high time to examine the "archive" as sedimentation of both naming and knowing. The Asia Art Archive and the Indonesian Visual Arts Archive (expanding the Cemeti Art Foundation) are germinal in this respect. While their efforts must be acknowledged as pioneering, there is also a need for appraisal if they are actually committed as well to analyzing the data they amass through theory and criticism and are accountable to the historiography of its archiving. Related to this archive are critical texts and the journals in which they appeared. These must be collected to posit a bibliography, and the toil of artists themselves who are in the position and are inclined to write the history in ways they think suits their interests of representation. The Comparative Contemporaries project had sought to flesh out this vision, assigning editors who choose texts on which they comment and hopefully create a community of editors and a forest of texts in the long run.[22]

Still under this rubric are the survey exhibitions organized by pioneering institutions like the Fukuoka Asian Art Museum, the Queensland Art Gallery (Asia-Pacific Triennial), Singapore Art Museum, and the Japan Foundation that have proposed models of curation, research, and symposia through the years; even the records of the Association of Southeast Asian Nations or the ASEAN are germane. The coordinates these various commitments have plotted out across the field are indispensable in marking out the latitudes of future practice.

Together with the exhibitionary is the curatorial, which embodies knowledge of art and the ways in which it is disseminated to various publics; implicated here is the "ethical" practice of curators in Southeast Asia, how they work within the constraints of the art world, respond to the ethical standards their peers in more established art systems foist on them, and creatively make do with a structure they helped construct amid compromises without which certain things could not be made possible at all. This everyday relationship with the material condition constitutes local knowledge that must be thought about, alongside terms cast to address realities in art that elude the discursive surveillance of the history of art like "neo-realism" in the Philippines or the "neo-traditional" in Thailand, the hyphenated portmanteau of a theoretical vernacular.

This essay ends on a tangent on the archival: the realization that the archive may actually be rendered more dense and complex if it was to be informed by previous excursions into it by both artists and theorists. We may refer here to the efforts of Walter Benjamin's *Arcades Project* and Aby Warburg's *Mnemosyne Atlas*, on the one hand, and Gerard Richter's *Atlas*, on the other. Foregrounded in these forays are the process of memory and the discourse of the photographic image as well as the distinction between the avant-garde language of the montage, collage, and juxtaposition and the more paratactic perspective in which contiguity of images is privileged. These modalities have implications in our apprehension of the archive as a structure of feeling, an affective milieu, and not merely documentation on our notions of the contemporary and the constellation of the global.[23]

This modest reflection on a possible attitude toward institutions, or the "much-maligned monsters" of the museum or the curator by the intrepid and sometimes well-funded "alternative," some of which are just waiting in the wings, angling for a berth in the scene through staged dramas of criticality, is a challenge to the kind of transformation that the supposed alternative guarantees, the very promise of its political to borrow the phrase from Hannah Arendt. How is this proto-institutionality assured to a certain degree by the legitimization of discourses and concomitant theory proffered by a global curatorium and its exhausted modernism, fatigued by its over investment in art, and in search of vast open spaces in the countryside or the thrill of the helter-skelter city of the third world? How is this responsive to the political history of local social movements that had engaged with socialism in the first half of the twentieth century? What is the theory of the political that calibrates its pressure to make art or to make art that is against itself?

In myriad ways, a contemporary that demands quality in the material and the material in quality, must be forever postcolonial, ceaselessly struggling against inequity and for equivalence, sensitive to the finitude of art, and working toward the aspirations of the impossible sensible.

Again, these are intervals within, preludes to another measure, variations on the theme of the intractable "public" that seems to be always before us.

---

1    Slavoj Žižek, "Whither Oedipus?," in *The Ticklish Subject: The Absent Center of Political Ontology* (London: Verso, 2000), 337.

2   See Wolfgang Welsch, "The Return of Beauty," *Filozofski Vestnik* 28, no. 2 (2007) and Victor Segalen, *Essay on Exoticism: An Aesthetics of Diversity* (Durham: Duke University Press, 2002).

3   Segalen, *Essay on Exoticism*, 21.

4   Matthew Rampley, "The Ethnographic Sublime," *RES: Anthropology and Aesthetics*, no. 47 (Spring 2005).

5   See the exhibition notes "Danas," unpublished (Cultural Center of the Philippines, 2005–6).

6   Sarat Maharaj, "Know-how and No-How: Stopgap Notes on 'Method' in Visual Art as Knowledge Production," *Art and Research: A Journal of Ideas, Contexts and Methods* 2, no.2 (2009).

7   Hugh Raffles, "Intimate Knowledge," *International Social Science Journal* 54, no. 173 (2002): 332.

8   Ibid.

9   José Lezama Lima, "Baroque Curiosity," in *Baroque New Worlds: Representation, Transculturation, Counterconquest,* ed. Lois Parkinson Zamora and Monika Kaup (Durham, NC: Duke University Press, 2010), 213.

10  For further reference see *Designs for an Anthropology of the Contemporary,* eds. Paul Rabinow et al. (Durham, NC: Duke University Press, 2008); Aihwa Ong, *Oikos/Anthropos: Rationality, Technology, Infrastructure* (Berkeley: University of California Press, 2003); and Claire Bishop, "The Social Turn: Collaboration and Its Discontents," in *Right About Now: Art and Theory Since the 1990s,* ed. Margriet Schavemaker and Mischa Rakier (Amsterdam: Valiz, 2007).

11  I was drawn to this idea by way of Alice Sebold.

12  Following Patrick D. Flores, "Collection/Collective: Tracing the Southeast Asian Contemporary," delivered at the CIMAM conference in Shanghai, China (November 9, 2010).

13  See Patrick D. Flores, "Colonial Posterities: Portraiture and the Face of the Modern," *Kasarinlan* 22, no. 2 (2007).

14  Following documentation of the exhibition "Telah Terbit (Out Now)," curated by Ahmad Mashadi, Singapore Art Museum, 2006.

15  See Alice Guillermo, *Protest/Revolutionary Art in the Philippines 1970–1990* (Manila: University of the Philippines, 2001), 243.

16  Sumartono, "The Role of Power in Contemporary Yogyakartan Art," in *Outlet: Yogyakarta within the Contemporary Indonesian Art Scene* (Yogyakarta: Cemeti Art Foundation, 2001), 23.

17  Redza Piyadasa, *Towards a Mystical Reality: A Documentation of Jointly Initiated Experiences by Redza Piyadasa and Suleiman Esa* (Kuala Lumpur: Muzium Seni Negara, 1974), 21.

18  See the documentation of the exhibition "Turns in Tropics: Artist-Curator" for the 7th Gwangju Biennale (2008).

19  Raymundo Albano, "Installations: A Case for Hangings," *Philippine Art Supplement* 2, no. 1 (1981): 3.

20  Nora A. Taylor, *Painters in Hanoi: An Ethnography of Vietnamese Art* (Singapore: National University of Singapore, 2009), 4.

21  Apinan Poshyananda, "Reverie and Phantasm in the Epoch of Global Trauma," in *Thai Pavilion: La Biennale di Venezia, Italia, 2003* (Bangkok: Office of Contemporary Art and Culture, 2003), 63.

22  Comparative Contemporaries is a website anthology project of key texts of art writing in Asia, organized by Lee Weng Choy, and that will be published as a special online project with the Asia Art Archive, http://www.aaa.org.hk (forthcoming).

23  Benjamin Buchloh, "Atlas/Archive," in *The Optic of Walter Benjamin, de-, dis-, ex-,* vol. 3, ed. Alex Coles (London: Black Dog, 1999), 12–35.

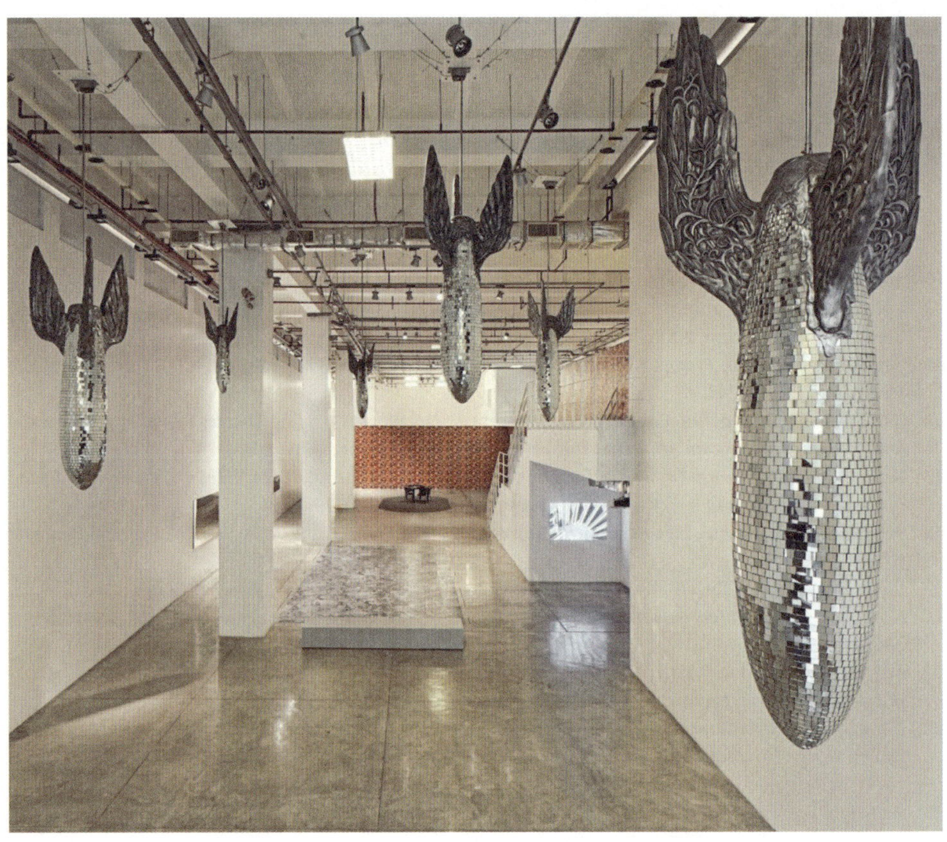

Kawayan De Guia
*Bomba (Fallout)*, 2015
"The Vexed Contemporary"
Museum of Contemporary Art and Design, Manila, Philippines

Patrick D. Flores

# Drinnen und draußen.
# Unbequeme Vorschläge

Wenn wir uns in sogenannten Kulturinstitutionen bewegen, sind unsere Verhaltensweisen stark von erlernten Gesten und Rhetoriken bestimmt. Die Säle des Nationalmuseums von Kambodscha in Phnom Penh sind gefüllt mit buddhistischen Statuen, doch kommen die Gläubigen nicht hier her, um *Kunst* zu sehen, sondern um Blumen und Weihrauch darzubringen. Das bringt mich dazu, darüber nachzudenken, wie sich die Anwesenheit eines Artefakts im Museum in „der Ära des Bildes als Kunst" auf das Empfindungsvermögen von Andacht auswirkt. Wenn wir das Nationalmuseum in Singapur betreten, werden wir von MitarbeiterInnen auf die interaktiven Begleiter aufmerksam gemacht – Audioguides, die uns nahelegen, dass wir uns den Exponaten am besten mit Hilfe vieler Erklärungen nähern sollten. Bevor in einem Kino in Bangkok der Film beginnt, erhebt sich das in der Dunkelheit zusammengedrängte Publikum, um die königliche Hymne zu singen – ein Beleg für die Wirkungsmacht der Krone in der thailändischen Gesellschaft mit ihrer konfliktreichen Geschichte, die den am längsten regierenden, lebenden Monarchen der Welt verehrt. Auf dem Campus der Silpakorn-Universität in Bangkok steht eine Statue von Silpa Bhirasri, der über die Kunststudierenden wacht. Bhirasri wurde in Italien als Corrado Feroci geboren und gründete die Universität 1943 unter dem Patronat von König Chulalongkorn, der einer Herrscherfamilie angehörte, die den Kunstlehrer als geachtete Persönlichkeit unter ihren Schutz stellte.

Es ist noch früh am Abend in Bandung im Jahr 2005, und eine große Menschenmenge strömt in die Soemardja-Galerie am Bandung Institute of Technology zur Eröffnung der Ausstellung von Agus Suwage, in der er Zeichnungen und Malereien von Performances und Performance-KünstlerInnen zeigt. Eine so starke

Resonanz ist nichts Ungewöhnliches für eine Kunstwelt, die gerne *diskusi* in Räumen führt, die nach *kretek*, den indonesischen Nelkenzigaretten duften. Dass Indonesien zu Beginn des dritten Jahrtausends die meisten Akteure in der Region hervorbrachte, die sich als KuratorInnen bezeichnen, sagt etwas über die Freiheiten aus, die sich IndonesierInnen bei der Gestaltung des Zeitgenössischen genommen haben. Slavoj Žižek betrachtet das Kuratieren oder die Tatsache, dass durch den Auswahlprozess eine Ausrichtung definiert wird als einen bemerkenswerten Ausdruck von Selbstreflexivität:

> Stellt nicht die entscheidende Rolle des Kurators im heutigen Kunstbetrieb das beste Beispiel für diese Reflexivität dar? Seine Rolle ist nicht mehr auf die bloße Auswahl beschränkt, sondern er (re-)definiert durch eben diese Auswahl, was heute Kunst ist. [...] Letztlich ist nicht der Produzent der Kunstwerke der Künstler, sondern der Kurator und dessen Auswahltätigkeit.[1]

In diesem Essay soll es weder darum gehen, einmal mehr die Rituale der Institutionskritik durchzuspielen, noch darum, in heroischer Geste dem Westen das Scheitern seines Konzeptualismus vorzuhalten. Auch sollen hier nicht deren Wiederbelebungsversuche thematisiert werden, um die sich hochmotivierte Kunstszenen an der Peripherie vergeblich bemühen. Vielmehr soll es hier um das Potenzial von Institutionalität gehen und soll der Wunsch von Künstlerinnen und Künstlern bestärkt werden, den Prozess der Institutionsbildung mitzugestalten, sei es als Kritik oder als Beteiligung, die als Ablehnung auftritt, durch die aber an der Definition von Institutionalität mitgewirkt wird. Wenn man sich für Institutionalität einsetzt, bedeutet das auch, sich mit Alternativen zu befassen, insbesondere da die Moderne von Kontinent zu Kontinent unterschiedlich definiert wird. Gerade in westlichen Diskursen ist man immer auf der Suche nach emanzipatorischen Formen von Soziabilität und deutet alles im Zeichen relationaler Ästhetik oder verwandter Vorstellungen, die in selbstorganisierten Kunsträumen, Workshops, Kooperationen und Ähnlichem zirkulieren. Eine solche Fantasievorstellung von Prozesshaftigkeit ließe sich auf interessante Weise mit dem Bedürfnis nach einer zentralen Ordnungsstruktur kontrastieren, mit der sich soziale Bewegungen konfrontiert sehen. Auch ist es interessant zu untersuchen, wie die Sehnsucht nach einer singulären Moderne, in der Klasse und Nation Bestand haben, neoliberalen und neokolonialen Strukturen entgegen steht. Oder um es noch einmal anders zu formulieren: Der Wunsch nach Universalität und der Glaube an die Menschheit lässt sich vom Bedürfnis nach Kultur und Partikularität nicht trennen. Aus dieser Verflechtung sind Begriffe wie „transkulturell" entstanden, aber auch die radikale Neuinterpretation des „Exotischen" ist darauf zurückzuführen. Wie Victor Segalen bemerkt:

> Exotismus ist eben keine Angleichung an etwas; es ist kein perfektes Verständnis von etwas, das außerhalb des eigenen Selbst liegt und das man sich

vollständig anzueignen vermochte; es ist vielmehr die eindrückliche, unmittelbare Wahrnehmung einer ewigen Unbegreiflichkeit.[3]

Wenn wir über die Konstituierung von Wissen nachdenken wollen, möchten wir vielleicht nicht unbedingt die Gebiete kartieren, die schon auf beispiellose Weise von DenkerInnen wie Michel Foucault, Gayatri Chakravorty Spivak oder Pierre Bourdieu erschlossen wurden. Vielleicht ist es interessanter, über die Verzahnung von Wissen und Benennen in Machtverhältnissen hinauszugehen und andere Überlegungen über das Wissen anzustellen. Womöglich wollen wir beispielsweise über das Nicht-Wissen nachdenken, oder darüber, wie der Sinn dem Diskurs entgleitet. Vielleicht wollen wir die Frage aufwerfen, ob postkoloniales Wissen immer ethnografischer Natur ist und ob diese ethnografische Qualität auch erhaben ist.[4] Oder wie wäre es, wenn wir uns mit den komplexen Mischungsverhältnissen im Barock oder mit dem Unsichtbaren im javanischen Schattentheater oder mit der Aufführungspraxis im philippinischen *palabas* beschäftigten?[5] Sarat Maharajs Überlegungen zur bildenden Kunst als Wissensproduktion, die unter der Überschrift „Thinking through the visual" [Durch das Visuelle denken/ das Visuelle durchdenken] stehen, zielen nicht so sehr darauf ab,

> auf den ausgetretenen Pfaden akademischer Disziplinen oder in den sogenannten Lücken, Rissen und Brüchen zwischen diesen oder in irgendeiner ausgewiesenen „interdisziplinären/transdisziplinären" Zone zu enden. Sie [Kunst als Wissensproduktion] ist vielmehr eine eigenständige Kraft, die immer in „irgendwelchen" Räumen – sturmumtosten, verlassenen Brachen und Einöden – entsteht, wo Andeutungen von Unbekanntem, gedankliche Sondierungen und Regungen des Nicht-Wissens entstehen und ins Spiel kommen. Sie unterscheidet sich von den Kreisläufen des *Know-how*, die sich auf klar ausgelegten methodologischen Gleisen bewegen. Sie ist ein ziemlich unvorhersehbares Auf und Ab von Potenzialen und Neigungen – ein Fluss des *No-how*. Der Begriff stammt von Samuel Beckett, doch ich verwende ihn hier ohne den Schuss Trostlosigkeit, den er ihm normalerweise beigibt. *No-how* steht für Unbestimmtheit, für „irgendeinen beliebigen Raum", der sich zusammenbraut, sich ausdehnt und verdichtet.[6]

Der Anthropologe Hugh Raffles interveniert mit einer kritischen Haltung gegenüber einem „lokalen Wissen" oder „situierten Wissen", das „immer im Prozess [ist]: Es entsteht im Gespräch, bei der Arbeit, in Gesellschaft mit anderen, im Affekt und in vielen anderen Formen sozialer Praxis."[7] Allerdings kann das „Lokale" [locality] zur Lokalisierung tendieren; daher schlägt er vor, dass

> das Lokale des lokalen Wissens ein radikales Denken erfordert, wenn es nicht weiterhin eine Lokalisierung reproduzieren soll, die Menschen und Wissenssysteme kategorisiert. Es mag so scheinen, dass lokales Wissen

nichtwissenschaftliche Arten von Wissen aufwertet, doch bleibt es durch das Nichtuniverselle seines Lokalen darin gefangen, eben jene Taxonomie zu reproduzieren und zu verdinglichen, durch die Kenntnisse hierarchisiert werden.[8]

In seinem Essay „Baroque Curiosity" beschäftigt sich José Lezama Lima mit dem Barock als einer Art Kehrseite der Omnipotenz der Aufklärung.

> In Spanien und Amerika stellt [der Barock] den Erwerb einer Sprache dar, die weltweit vielleicht einzigartig ist; diese betrifft Einrichtungsgegenstände, Lebensstile und Formen von Neugier ebenso wie einen Mystizismus, der neue Arten von Gottesverehrung, neue Arten des Genießens und der Zubereitung von Delikatessen umfasst, und verströmt einen vollkommen neuen Lebensstil – raffiniert und geheimnisvoll, theokratisch und in sich versunken, formal unruhig, aber tief verwurzelt in dem, was für ihn essenziell ist.[9]

Auf dem Gebiet der Anthropologie spricht man von einem anthropologischen Labor, um die Anthropologie des Zeitgenössischen und die ethischen Aspekte von Kooperationsprozessen zu beschreiben. Dieser Begriff ließe sich auch auf aktuelle Debatten in der zeitgenössische Kunst übertragen.[10]

Um sichtbar zu machen, welchen Einfluss die wechselvolle Geschichte der Institutionen – insbesondere des Museums und der Kunstakademie – auf die Entstehung der Kunstwelt und der Wissensproduktion in Südostasien hat, kommt man nicht umhin, sich erneut mit dem Begriff der Autorität zu befassen. Das Museum und die Akademie sind Voraussetzungen für Kolonialität, weil sie Orte der Pädagogik und der „Kultur" und damit der „Korruption" sind, wobei Kultur grundsätzlich „Ausbeutung" bedeutet und daher zwangsläufig unmoralisch ist.[11] Doch sie sind zugleich Orte der Übersetzung, die ebenso aus der *doxa* wie aus Idiosynkrasie besteht. Und so gibt es an der Akademie einerseits Bevormundung, aber andererseits auch das Können der dort beheimateten Studierenden. Langfristig ist eine solche Vorherrschaft an der Grammatik des sogenannten *Einflusses* möglicherweise nicht ablesbar. Anders gesagt, sind diese Orte Laboratorien des Modernen, weil sie mit dem Selbst spielen und ein *Irgendetwas* hervorbringen.

Hierfür lassen sich verschiedene Beispiele anführen, und an vorderster Stelle das der Porträtkunst in Südostasien, in der die Repräsentation entscheidend zur Entstehung eines Raumes der Präsenz beitrug, als wollte man sagen: „Wir sind hier." Raden Saleh aus Indonesien und Juan Luna von den Philippinen sind in dieser Hinsicht beispielhaft, und ihre Errungenschaften in ihren Heimatländern und in Europa aus der stabilen Phase des 19. Jahrhunderts sind allgemein bekannt. Die Verbindung des akademischen Realismus mit der Kunst des Porträts war auch entscheidend für die Bemühungen der thailändischen Chakri-Dynastie, in der Welt präsent zu sein; König Mongkut ließ sich fotografieren und sein

Abbild von italienischen Künstlern abmalen. Deren Architekten-Kollegen schmückten das Königreich entsprechend mit Palästen und anderen prächtigen Bauwerken. Dieses Abbild beziehungsweise die Sehnsucht nach einem Abbild, oder das, was der philippinische Nationalheld José Rizal als „die Faszination der Erinnerung" bezeichnen würde, sollte allegorisch als Narrativ des menschlichen Fortschritts verstanden werden, sowohl in Bezug auf die Entwicklung der künstlerischen Fähigkeiten als auch auf das Bewusstsein, sich für die Nachwelt abbilden zu lassen. Darüber hinaus ist es verwandt mit der Allegorie des ethnografischen Bildes, das – sagen wir mithilfe von Anthropometrie und Museologie – die Differenz zwischen dem Selbst und dem Anderen herausarbeitet. Das Kollektiv, das von der Nation gebildet wird, verbindet sich zu einer Sammlung von Bestandteilen der Kolonie – Menschen, Artefakte, Rituale –, und das Sammeln wird immer grundlegend sein, ob es nun im Modus der Wunderkammer beginnt, wie in Sir Stamford Raffles' Fundgrube von Flora, Fauna und kleinsten Details auf der malaiischen Halbinsel, oder im Modus der Volkszählung, die Dean Worcester – ein weiterer Mitbegründer des philippinischen Nationalmuseums – in diesem Land durchführte. Es ist wichtig anzumerken, dass diese Verknüpfung von Kollektion und Kollektiv später zum Gegenstand heftiger Debatten seitens einer anderen Verkörperung des *Kollektivs* werden sollte. Dieses entstand durch KünstlerInnen, die sich gemeinsam gegen die Reduktion der Vielfalt auf Singularität und des Pluralismus auf das Exzeptionelle wendeten und stattdessen eine neue Poiltisierung der Kunst vorschlugen,[12] zu einer Zeit, als die Nachkriegsrepubliken wie gelähmt vor der Aufgabe standen, eine *Nation* aufzubauen, und zwar in der Ausgabe „Kalter Krieg".[13]

Diese Prägung führte dazu, dass die Auffassung von Nation als Exemplifizierung von Identität und Differenz vorherrschend wurde. Doch auch wenn die Nation eine grundlegende Voraussetzung für die Herausbildung postkolonialer Kritik und für die Nichttranszendierbarkeit von Emanzipation gewesen sein mochte, war sie nicht frei von einer eigenen Konsolidierungspolitik und damit auch nicht frei von Spannungen zwischen dem Nationalstaat, dem Erbe der postkolonialen Selbstbehauptung und, wenn man so will, der *zeitgenössischen* Revision, Anspruch auf einen anderen Platz in der weiten Welt zu erheben. In Südostasien war dies besonders offensichtlich in der Respekt einflößenden Kunstbewegung gegen die Institutionen der *Neuen Ordnung* der Suhartos, zu denen auch das Kunstestablishment gehörte. Zudem ließ sich in den 1970er Jahren in Thailand und auf den Philippinen nicht übersehen, dass die sozialen Bewegungen gegen die Militärregierungen in Bangkok und Manila stärker wurden. Auf den Philippinen war das von der First Lady Imelda Marcos gegründete Cultural Center of the Philippines Ort der Auseinandersetzungen; dort wurde der *Konzeptualismus* favorisiert, was eine Zurückweisung des sozialen Realismus bedeutete, der sich gegen die Diktatur richtete. Vor dem Hintergrund der Unruhen in Thailand gründete sich 1971 die Dhamma Group und 1975 die Artists' Front of Thailand (AFT); 1977 kam es schließlich zur Gründung des traditionell aufgebauten Kunststudiengangs an der Silpakorn-Universität. Von großer Bedeutung für diese Ereignisse waren Manifeste, unter denen zwei besonders hervorzuheben sind: das von Gerakan Seni Rupa Baru Indonesia (*New Indonesian Art Movement*, 1975) und das von Kaisahan (*Solidarity*, 1976); beide verknüpften das Politische mit dem Ästhetischen und vertraten eine Auffassung, die den Verlockungen von *Entwicklung* in Zeiten des Kalten Krieges kritisch gegenüberstand.[14] So erklärte Kaisahan beispielsweise:

> Wir werden daher von einer unkritischen Akzeptanz westlicher Einflüsse abrücken, von einer sklavischen Nachahmung westlicher Formen, die keine Verbindung zu unserem nationalen Leben haben, und von einer Beschäftigung mit westlichen Trends, die nicht unseren Entwicklungsprozess widerspiegeln. Wir erkennen, dass unsere Suche bedeutungslos sein wird, wenn sie nicht zu einer kollektiven Erfahrung wird – zu einer Erfahrung, die von den meisten Menschen verstanden und geteilt wird. In ihren Anfängen war die Kunst keine isolierte Handlung wie heutzutage; sie war notwendig, ein ebenso integraler Bestandteil des Lebens der Menschen wie das Wissen, wann man etwas anpflanzt.[15]

Auch die Gerakan-Bewegung hielt an ihren Überzeugungen fest:

> Die Vielfalt der indonesischen Kunst ist nicht zu leugnen, auch wenn eine solche Vielfalt an sich noch keine erstrebenswerte Entwicklung ist. Im Sinne einer Entwicklung, die die Nachhaltigkeit unserer Kultur sichert, besteht die Berufung des Künstlers darin, eine spirituelle Richtung aufzuzeigen, die auf humanitären Werten beruht und die sich an sozialen, kulturellen, politischen und wirtschaftlichen Realitäten orientiert.[16]

Eine solche Kritik am Westen und die Beschwörung des „Vielfältigen" und des „Spirituellen" verdichtet sich – unabhängig von nationalen Ursprüngen – immer wieder im *romantischen* Moment zahlreicher Manifeste von Avantgarde-Bewegungen. In diesem Fall lässt sich jedoch eine Obsession erkennen, die einen epistemischen Bruch mit dem „Westlichen" bewirkt. Dies ist deutlich spürbar in einem Manifest anderer Art, das Suleiman Esa und Redza Piyadasa über die „mystische Realität" verfassten: „Während der westliche Künstler gemäß ‚räumlicher/zeitlicher/sensorischer' Überlegungen an die Kunst herangeht, nähern wir uns ihr von einem ‚mentalen/meditativen/mystischen' Standpunkt."[17]

Aus dem weiter oben Gesagten können wir das Zeitgenössische anhand verschiedener Aspekte von Sozialität erfassen; dazu zählen das Kuratorische und der Prozess des Versammelns, der Workshop und die Community, die Kritik und der Diskurs (das Manifest, der einflussreiche Essay, die Sprache der Biennale, der zeitgenössische Diskurs und der Konsum von Alternativen durch die Einbeziehung von Kooperationspartnern). Das *Versammeln* unterstellt ein

Zusammen*treffen* von Interessen, ein freies Spiel der Widersprüche, eine Erörterung dringlicher Anliegen. Auf der anderen Seite erfordert ein solches Zusammentreffen auch Koordination, Struktur und eine Form von Repräsentation. Da Repräsentation nach einer Norm verlangt, braucht sie eine bewegliche Handlungsmacht, die man *KuratorIn* nennt, wie missverstanden dieser Begriff auch sein mag. Der oder die KuratorIn sorgt für eine kohärente Struktur im Durcheinander und langfristig dafür, dass es eine Verständigung über den Wunsch gibt, Fragmente als ein *Miteinander* zu erkennen, die Differenz zu transzendieren und als Bekräftigung des *Kollektivs* zu identifizieren, ein Kollektiv, das zuvor isoliert und entfremdet war, das instrumentalisiert wurde als Sammlung von vereinzelten Individuen. Dieser Modus der Sozialität kann Diskussionen über eine mögliche Fetischisierung des Prozesses oder des Workshops auslösen, der in der Vergangenheit durch den *sanggar* in Indonesien zu einem politischen Projekt der Inspiration wurde und nicht bei der Idee des Prozesses als Selbstzweck stehenblieb. Das heißt, er wurde anfällig für die Instrumentalisierung von Ideologie als einer Fiktion, die notwendig ist, um eine Ganzheit kognitiv zu erfassen. Diese aktuelle Verdinglichung des Prozesses kann durchaus mit dem neoliberalen Produktionsimpuls, mit der Anpassung an Präferenzen, der Privatisierung von Gegenseitigkeit – anders gesagt, mit dem Mechanismus der Agglomeration – zusammenhängen.

Das Schema *Kollektion/Kollektiv* wurde schließlich weiter verkompliziert durch die Mutation des Künstlers zum Kurator und durch die Transformation des Agenten der *Avantgarde* zu einem Wunderkind der Institutionalisierung, das Kunst herstellen, ihr den Boden bereiten, eine Theorie für sie entwerfen und sie historisch einordnen kann. Die Werdegänge von Redza Piyadasa, Jim Supangkat, Raymundo Albano und Apinan Poshyananda zeigen, dass dieses Zusammenführen von Tätigkeiten in Malaysia, Indonesien, auf den Philippinen und in Thailand nahezu zeitgleich verfolgt wurde. Verwandte Initiativen traten mit dem Anspruch an, Kunst und den Umgang mit ihr neu zu ordnen.[18] Diese Praxis des Künstler-Kurators brachte bestimmte Diskurse über das Lokale hervor und vermittelte sie einem globalen Publikum. So versuchte Albano beispielsweise, die Installation – im Unterschied zur Malerei, die westlich ist – theoretisch als eine auf den Philippinen indigene Form zu bestimmen:

> *Installationen* sind ein Beispiel, um die Tatsache zu untermauern, dass die Malerei als Kunstform ein rein westliches Phänomen ist und dass sie zum Philippiner in einer Fremdsprache spricht. Wenn wir heute Gemälde haben, liegt das an dem Versuch, auf diesem Gebiet ein Beispiel zu geben oder zu konkurrieren – auf westliche Art. Zur Beurteilung eines Gemäldes gibt es keine anderen Kriterien als für Gemälde der amerikanischen oder europäischen Kunst, einfach deshalb, weil wir keine indigene Praxis haben, die dieser Kunstform entspricht. Puristische Wissenschaftler, die eine Vorliebe für die Erforschung des Indigenen haben, werden – anders als im Fall der

Skulptur – für die Malerei keinen logischen Vorläufer finden. Es könnte sein, dass unser angeborenes Raumgefühl keine statische Wahrnehmung von Flächigkeit ist, sondern eine Erfahrung von Beweglichkeit, Performance, Beteiligung des Körpers und physischen Beziehungen in ihrer kohärentesten Form. Daher ist die Installation verwandt mit den *fiestas* und den volkstümlichen Ritualen all unserer ethnischen Gruppen.[19]

Wenn wir diese These erweitern, könnte die Transnationalität oder, genauer gesagt, Translokalität des Künstler-Kurators als Bindeglied dienen zwischen der Theoretisierung der Zeitgenossenschaft des Indigenen als einer ausdrucksstarken Disziplin der Gegenwart und der Ästhetik des Neotraditionellen (im Sinne des Nationalen), das in den Praktiken bestimmter thailändischer und balinesischer KünstlerInnen kodiert ist. Dass Sonabai, eine Folk-Art-Künstlerin aus einem Dorf in Indien, 1999 an der Asia Pacific Triennial teilnahm, und dass ihre Kunst im Ausstellungskatalog von der renommierten Wissenschaftlerin Jyotindra Jain erläutert wurde, ist aufschlussreich. Ebenso erhellend ist, dass Nora A. Taylor in ihren Beiträgen über MalerInnen in Hanoi im Lauf der Jahre immer wieder die Formulierung „Ethnografie der vietnamesischen Kunst" verwendete. So behauptet sie:

Anstatt zu versuchen, trotz spärlicher historischer Daten eine Geschichte zu rekonstruieren, untersucht dieses Buch den Kontext, in dem sich die Kunstgeschichte in Vietnam entwickelt, auf der Grundlage von kollektiven Erinnerungen und anhand von Texten, die auf eine Art erinnert und umgeschrieben, ausgesprochen oder produziert werden, die vom klassischen, westlichen Modell der Kunstgeschichte abweicht.[20]

In seiner zugespitzten These über den ersten Länderpavillon auf der Venedig Biennale 2003 reduziert Apinan Poshyananda den Charakter des *Thailändischen* hingegen auf eine extreme Unterwerfung unter den Orientalismus. So bemerkt er:

Die Reise von den Kanälen Bangkoks nach Venedig erinnert an eine Zeitverschiebung. Thailändische Künstler in traditioneller und zeitgenössischer Kleidung gleichen Kunstpilgern, deren Mission darin besteht, in der internationalen Arena der Kunst ihren Platz zu finden. Um sichtbar zu sein, streben sie danach, allen Schwierigkeiten und Hindernissen zum Trotz in Venedig ihren eigenen Pavillon (*sala*) zu errichten. Wie Handwerker bauen thailändische Künstler thailändische Fertighäuser mit Pfählen, Balken, Dach, Giebel und Wandpaneelen zusammen, die mit dem Boot aus Bangkok herangeschafft wurden. In diesem kulturellen Raum spielen thailändische Künstler die Rollen von Kunsthandwerkern, Baumeistern, Schamanen und Darstellern. Sie unterhalten die Kulturkonsumenten, die im ersten thailändischen Pavillon in Venedig Kulturgüter erleben, indem sie ihnen

> nationale Identitäten und exotische Differenzen anbieten. [...] Trotz ihrer
> exotischen Präsentationen von Malerei, Videos, Schreinerarbeiten, Koch-
> kunst, therapeutischen Behandlungen, Massagen und Tanz werden sie zu
> Boten und Opfern der globalen Falle, die Schäden und Zerstörung anrichtet
> [...] [ein] Kommentar auf die Hierarchie des Kunst-Internationalismus und
> auf das System der Neuen Weltordnung der Kunst.[21]

Die höchst anpassungsfähige Rolle des Künstler-Kurators sollte sich später zur Institutionalität verhärten, durch die das Individuum selbst zur Institution, zum Träger des Wissens über das Lokale in einer globalen Landschaft wird, zur Biennale-MacherIn, HistorikerIn, KritikerIn, BürokratIn und so fort. Selbstverständlich stieß solche Macht auf Widerstand. Am deutlichsten zeigt das der Fall von Jim Supangkat, der 1995 eine Ausstellung zeitgenössischer Kunst kuratierte, die an eine alternative Bewegung erinnerte: die 1955 im indonesischen Bandung gegründete, sogenannte *Unangepasste Bewegung*. Als Supangkat den Begriff *postmodern* vorschlug, um die Werke auf der Jakarta Biennale 1994 zu charakterisieren, forderte er gleich mehrere Seiten zum Widerspruch heraus. WissenschaftlerInnen hielten es für unüberlegt, da Indonesien, wie sie behaupteten, noch nicht einmal modern war. Und es scheint, dass die bloße Verwegenheit eines Kurators, einen Begriff zu entwickeln und ihn in die Debatte zu werfen, an sich schon ein mutiger und diskussionswürdiger Akt ist. Die Karriere des Künstler-Kurators schließt also ein gewisses Maß an Institutionskritik und Institutionalisierung ein, sofern sie oder er eine gewisse offizielle, autoritative Position als SchiedsrichterIn und VermittlerIn komplexer, unterschiedlicher Tendenzen oder Haltungen in den verschiedenen Kreisläufen von Staat und Markt, in hybriden Events wie Biennalen und Kunstmessen, an Akademien und selbst in der Populärkultur erlangt hat. Die berufsbedingten Reisen und die Texte von Apinan Poshyananda sind hierfür beispielhaft.

Solche Momente der Sozialität (Menschen zu versammeln und diese Versammlung anderen Menschen zu präsentieren) ergeben sich durch Möglichkeiten, die das Globale mit sich bringt, und wir erkennen am Horizont Beispiele neuer Bedingungen, die Bewegung in die vorhandenen Strukturen bringen und sie zu produktiven Wendepunkten unseres Wissens über die Kunst in Südostasien machen können.

Das erste Beispiel für ein solches Moment der Sozialität ist das Kunstmuseum, das an eine Universität angeschlossen ist, als eine Plattform, die gewandt zwischen dem Staat und dem Markt vermittelt und die der zeitgenössischen Kunst einen Raum bietet, der zu einem umfassenderen akademischen Diskurs in Beziehung steht und Zugänge zur Repräsentation eröffnet. Dieser Raum und die Interaktionen, die darin stattfinden, können eine hervorragende Schnittstelle für freie KuratorInnen darstellen, die im Westen ohne das notwendige Übergangsritual der Kunstgeschichte dazu ausgebildet wurden, zeitgenössische Kunst zu kuratieren oder in Auftrag zu geben, die oder der gedanklich auf ein Netzwerk mobiler KollegInnen fixiert und auf die Zyklen von Biennalen und Kunstmessen sowie auf andere kuratorische Engagements von Off-Schauplätzen bis zu Bühnenspektakeln eingestimmt ist. Darüber hinaus bietet das universitäre Kunstmuseum durch seinen Hang zur Theoriebildung und zum Verweisen auf die Entstehungsgeschichte von Wissen einen Kontrast zur Wendigkeit der berühmten Künstlerischen LeiterInnen, Hipster-VeranstalterInnen, BloggerInnen, Event-ProduzentInnen, prominenten nichtprofessionellen BeobachterInnen, StylistInnen und DesignerInnen; sie alle haben die zeitgenössische Kunst in ihre Happening-Welt einbezogen, in der sich Mode, Grafikdesign, Straßenfeste, Hochglanzzeitschriften und die Eigenheiten der herrschenden Klasse und deren Anwärter miteinander verbinden. Letztlich verweist eine Neubewertung des universitären Kunstmuseums auf die Geschichte der Kunstakademie, ihrer Unterrichtsmethoden und ihrer wissenschaftlichen Apparate.

Das zweite Beispiel ist der veränderte Ort der Galerie/Kunsthalle/Stiftung, der Räume in mehreren Regionen unterhält und in seinen Programmen freie KuratorInnen, angesagte KünstlerInnen, AutorInnen, PerformerInnen, grafische EntwerferInnen und StadtplanerInnen zusammenbringt. Wie dies als Teil eines umfassenderen Marktgeschehens funktioniert und gleichzeitig Szenarien des Zeitgenössischen hervorbringt, ist eine Praxis, die sich zu erforschen lohnt – und zwar im Hinblick auf ihre politische Ökonomie und ihre seltsame Beziehung zu einer anderen solventen Instanz: der Auktion, die sich in Südostasien von einem Sekundärmarkt zu einem Primärmarkt entwickelt und auf bestimmten Ebenen die Galerie in diesem Geschäftsbereich abgelöst hat. Wie floriert dieses Arrangement, und inwiefern erleichtert es das Kuratieren, das sich zwischen dem Staat und dem Markt bewegt? Arbeitet es letztlich dem Kaufen und Verkaufen zu, oder organisiert es die Antinomien des Zeitgenössischen neu, indem es alle zusammen auf einem Grenzgebiet ansiedelt? Man kann dieses Paradigma produktiv im Verhältnis zu einer früher bevorzugten Plattform, dem selbstorganisierten Ausstellungsraum betrachten. Was ist mit diesem Raum geschehen? Wurde er zu einem System rationalisiert, wurde seine Unberechenbarkeit als ein Aspekt seiner erhofften Dynamik interpretiert? Wurde er zu einem Element der endlos dehnbaren Auffassungen von *Entwicklung*, in einem Bereich, der ein breites Spektrum von Initiativen umfasst, die von unternehmerischer Philanthropie bis zur Kreativindustrie, vom Umweltaktivismus bis zu gemäßigten Formen des Sozialismus reichen? An einem bestimmten Punkt könnte es eine Verbindung geben.

Das dritte Beispiel ist die selbstkritische Institution, die versucht, ihre Vergangenheit im Verhältnis zum *Neuen* und zum *Jetzt* oder zum Kult des Jungseins zu aktivieren, indem sie ihre offenkundige Institutionalität durch temporäre Ausstellungen, parasitäre Projekte und künstlerische Interventionen in ihren konventionellen Räumen (White Cube, Bibliothek, Archiv) mit der Energie des Zeitgenössischen durchwirkt. Wie weit kann diese Kritik gehen? Stärkt sie die hartnäckige Modernität der Institution, indem sie ihr eine höchst notwendige Reflexivität liefert, oder untergräbt sie ihre wesentlichen Prämissen?

Beschleunigt sie den Niedergang der Institution, oder zögert sie das bereits verkündete Ende ihrer Geschichte hinaus? Die bevorstehende Eröffnung der Nationalgalerie in Singapur bietet ein Szenario, das uns nahelegt, über die Notwendigkeit eines solchen Unterfangens in dieser Zeit des *Danach*-nach dem Museum, nach der Nation, nach der Geschichte-nachzudenken. Solche Anzeichen eines Endes müssen jedoch der verführerischen Vorstellung eines *asiatischen Jahrhunderts* Rechnung tragen. Wir mögen in einem Zeitalter des *Post-* leben, doch wir befinden uns in Asien, im einstmals zeitlosen Orient und in der derzeitigen *Zukunft*. Dies wirft gewisse Fragen auf, wie zum Beispiel: Wird Asien im Wesentlichen von China vorangetrieben, da sich die Museen, Umschlagplätze, SammlerInnen und Ausstellungen um China drehen? Interessiert sich China überhaupt für den Rest Asiens?

Das vierte Beispiel ist die Archäologie des Wissens. Neben der üblichen Sichtung der Literatur zum Thema Südostasien oder Asien im Allgemeinen ist es an der Zeit, das *Archiv* als eine Sedimentierung des Benennens und des Wissens zu erforschen. Das Asia Art Archive und das Indonesian Visual Arts Archive (vormals Cemeti Art Foundation) stehen diesbezüglich erst am Anfang. Ihre Bemühungen sollten als herausragend anerkannt werden; doch es besteht auch ein Bedarf an Wertung, wenn diese sich tatsächlich der Analyse der von ihnen angehäuften Daten durch Theorie und Kritik widmen und Verantwortung für die Historiografie von deren Archivierung tragen. Dieses Archiv enthält Zeitschriften mit kunstkritischen Texten. Diese müssen in einer Bibliografie erfasst werden, ebenso wie die Anstrengungen jener KünstlerInnen, die willens und in der Lage sind, ihre eigene Geschichte selbst so darzustellen, wie es ihren Interessen entspricht. Das Projekt Comparative Contemporaries hat versucht, diese Vision zu konkretisieren, und RedakteurInnen beauftragt, Texte auszuwählen und zu kommentieren, sodass hier hoffentlich auf lange Sicht eine Gemeinschaft von RedakteurInnen und eine umfassende Textsammlung entstehen.[22]

Dies gilt auch für die Überblicksausstellungen, die von wegweisenden Institutionen wie dem Fukuoka Asian Art Museum, der Queensland Art Gallery (Asia-Pacific Triennial), dem Singapore Art Museum und der Japan Foundation organisiert wurden. Diese haben im Laufe der Jahre verschiedene kuratorische Modelle und Forschungsarbeiten vorgestellt sowie Symposien veranstaltet; selbst das Archiv der Association of Southeast Asian Nations (ASEAN) ist von Relevanz. Die Koordinaten der verschiedenen Einsätze auf diesem Gebiet sind unverzichtbar, um die Grenzen einer künftigen Praxis abzustecken.

Der Aspekt des Ausstellens ist nicht zu trennen von dem des Kuratorischen, der das Wissen über Kunst ebenso einschließt wie die Art und Weise ihrer Verbreitung und Vermittlung an verschiedene Publikumsgruppen. Dies impliziert die *ethische* Praxis von KuratorInnen in Südostasien. Wie arbeiten sie angesichts der Restriktionen der Kunstwelt, wie reagieren sie auf die ethischen Standards, die ihnen ihre KollegInnen in etablierten Kunstsystemen aufnötigen, und wie gehen sie kreativ mit einer Struktur um, die sie auf der Grundlage von

Kompromissen – ohne die gewisse Dinge überhaupt nicht möglich gewesen wären – selbst mit aufgebaut haben? Dieser alltägliche Umgang mit materiellen Bedingungen ist ein lokales Wissen, über das es nachzudenken gilt, ebenso wie über die Begriffe, die geprägt wurden, um Realitäten der Kunst zu thematisieren, die sich der Diskurskontrolle der Kunstgeschichte entziehen, wie etwa der *Neorealismus* auf den Philippinen oder das *Neotraditionelle* in Thailand, *diese* gesetzten Wortkreuzungen des Theoriejargons.

Dieser Essay endet mit einer Randbemerkung zum Archiv – mit der Erkenntnis, dass das Archiv tatsächlich dichter und komplexer würde, wenn es geprägt wäre von den früheren Beschäftigungen mit ihm, sei es durch KünstlerInnen oder durch TheoretikerInnen. Wir verweisen auf die Anstrengungen von Walter Benjamins *Passagen-Werk* und Aby Warburgs *Mnemosyne*-Atlas auf der einen Seite, und auf Gerhard Richters *Atlas* auf der anderen. Diese Vorstöße in das Archiv haben den Prozess der Erinnerung und den Diskurs über das fotografische Bild in den Vordergrund gerückt, aber auch die Unterscheidung zwischen den Verfahren der Avantgarde wie Montage, Collage und Gegenüberstellung, und einer eher parataktischen Perspektive, welche die Nachbarschaft von Bildern privilegiert. Diese Verfahren beeinflussen unser Verständnis des Archivs, das nicht nur eine Dokumentation, sondern auch eine emotionale Struktur und ein affektives Milieu darstellt; zugleich prägen sie unsere Vorstellungen vom Zeitgenössischen und von der Konstellation des Globalen.[23]

Diese Überlegungen zu einer möglichen Haltung gegenüber Institutionen, dem Museum oder KuratorInnen – die von furchtlosen, teils finanziell gut ausgestatteten alternativen Akteuren gelegentlich zu einem *viel gescholtenen Monster* gemacht wurden (wobei einige dieser alternativen Akteure oft nur im Hintergrund darauf warten, durch inszenierte Dramen der Kritikalität in der Szene zu punkten) – sind eine Herausforderung für den Wandel, den der angeblich alternative Akteur garantiert: das *Versprechen* des Politischen, um einen Begriff von Hannah Arendt zu zitieren. Wie wird diese Protoinstitutionalität bis zu einem gewissen Punkt abgesichert durch die Legitimierung von Diskursen und der sie begleitenden Theorien, vorgetragen von einem globalen Kuratorium und seinem erschöpften Modernismus? Welche Rolle spielt hierbei die Ermüdung angesichts eines übermäßigen Engagements für Kunst? Und welche Bedeutung hat dabei die kräftezehrende Suche nach riesigen Freiräumen auf dem Land oder dem Nervenkitzel einer chaotischen Stadt in der Dritten Welt? Inwiefern ist dies eine Reaktion auf die politische Geschichte lokaler sozialer Bewegungen, die sich in der ersten Hälfte des 20. Jahrhunderts mit dem Sozialismus auseinandergesetzt haben? Welche Theorie des Politischen übt Druck aus, Kunst zu machen oder eine Kunst zu machen, die gegen sich selbst ist?

Das Zeitgenössische, das gegenüber den materiellen Bedingungen, also dem Kontext, Anspruch auf Qualität erhebt und von der Qualität verlangt, dass sie sich in den materiellen Bedingungen niederschlägt, muss auf vielfältige Weise immer postkolonial sein und unaufhörlich gegen Ungleichheit und für

Gleichwertigkeit kämpfen; es muss dafür sensibel sein, dass auch Kunst nicht alles leisten kann und dennoch auf eine Sinnhaftigkeit hinarbeiten, die nie ganz erreichbar sein wird.

Das sind, wie gesagt, die Zwischenräume in und der Auftakt von einer anderen Maßstäblichkeit, Variationen zum Thema einer hartnäckigen Öffentlichkeit, die uns immer beobachtet und uns oft einen Schritt voraus ist.


1   Slavoj Žižek, „Oedipus, wohin?", in: ders., *Die Tücke des Subjekts,* aus dem Englischen übersetzt von Eva Gilmer, Andreas Hofbauer, Hans Hildebrandt und Anne von der Heiden, Frankfurt am Main: Suhrkamp, 2001, S. 464.

2   Siehe Wolfgang Welsch, „Wiederkehr des Schönen?", in: Lydia Haustein und Petra Stegmann (Hg.), *Schönheit. Vorstellungen in Kunst, Medien und Alltagskultur*, Göttingen: Wallstein Verlag, S. 39–52; Victor Segalen, *Essay on Exoticism: An Aesthetics of Diversity*, Durham: Duke University Press, 2002.

3   Segalen, op. cit., S. 21.

4   Matthew Rampley, „The Ethnographic Sublime", in: *RES: Anthropology and Aesthetics*, Nr. 47, Harvard University Press, Frühjahr 2005.

5   Siehe die Ausstellungsnotizen *Danas*, Cultural Center of the Philippines, 2005/2006, unveröffentlicht.

6   Sarat Maharaj, „Know-how and No-How: stopgap notes on ‚method' in visual art as knowledge production", www.artandresearch.org.uk/v2n2/maharaj.html, abgerufen am 6. Juli 2016.

7   Hughes Raffles, „Intimate Knowledge", in: *International Social Science Journal*, Bd. 54, Nr. 173, 2002, S. 332.

8   Ibid.

9   José Lezama Lima, „Baroque Curiosity", in: Lois Parkinson Zamora und Monika Kaup (Hg.), *Baroque New Worlds: Representation, Transculturation, Counterconquest*, Durham: Duke University Press, 2010, S. 213.

10  Für weiterführende Hinweise siehe Paul Rabinow, George E. Marcus, James D. Faubion and Tobias Rees (Hg.), *Designs for an Anthropology of the Contemporary*, Durham: Duke University Press, 2008; Aihwa Ong, *Oikos/Anthropos: Rationality, Technology, Infrastructure*, Berkeley: University of California Press, 2003; und Claire Bishop, „The Social Turn: Collaboration and Its Discontents", in: Margriet Schavemaker und Mischa Rakier (Hg.), *Right About Now: Art and Theory Since the 1990s*, Amsterdam: Valiz, 2007.

11  Auf diese Überlegung hat mich Alice Sebold aufmerksam gemacht.

12  Nach Patrick D. Flores, „Collection/Collective: Tracing the Southeast Asian Contemporary", Vortrag im Rahmen der CIMAM-Konferenz, Shanghai, China, 9. November 2010.

13  Siehe Patrick D. Flores, „Colonial Posterities: Portraiture and the Face of the Modern", in: *Kasarinlan*, Bd. 22, Nr. 2, 2007.

14  Vgl. die Dokumentation der Ausstellung *Telah Terbit (Out Now)*, kuratiert von Ahmad Mashadi, Singapore Art Museum, 2006.

15  Siehe Alice Guillermo, *Protest/Revolutionary Art in the Philippines1970–1990*, Manila: University of the Philippines, 2001, S. 243.

16  Sumartono, „The Role of Power in Contemporary Yogyakartan Art", in: Melissa Larner (Hg.), *Outlet: Yogyakarta within the Contemporary Indonesian Art Scene*, Yogyakarta: Cemeti Art Foundation, 2001, S. 23.

17  Redza Piyadasa, *Towards a Mystical Reality: A Documentation of Jointly Initiated Experiences by Redza Piyadasa and Suleiman Esa*, Kuala Lumpur: Muzium Seni Negara, 1974, S. 21.

18  Siehe die Dokumentation der Ausstellung *Turns in Tropics: Artist-Curator* im Rahmen der 7. Gwangju Biennale 2008.

19  Raymundo Albano, „Installations: A Case for Hangings", in: *Philippine Art Supplement*, Bd. 2, Nr. 1, 1981, S. 3.

20  Nora A. Taylor, *Painters in Hanoi: An Ethnography of Vietnamese Art*, Singapur: National University of Singapore, 2009, S. 4.

21  Apinan Poshyananda, „Reverie and Phantasm in the Epoch of Global Trauma", in: *Thai Pavilion: La Biennale di Venezia, Italien 2003*, Bangkok: Office of Contemporary Art and Culture, 2003, S. 63.

22  Comparative Contemporaries ist eine Internet-Anthologie von Schlüsseltexten der Kunstliteratur in Asien, die von Lee Weng Choy organisiert und als spezielles Online-Projekt auf der Webseite des Asia Art Archive veröffentlicht wird.

23  Benjamin Buchloh, „Atlas/Archive", in: Alex Coles (Hg.), *The Optic of Walter Benjamin*, Bd. 3: *de-, dis-, ex-*, London: Black Dog, 1999, S. 12–35.

Singapore Courtyard
National Gallery Singapore

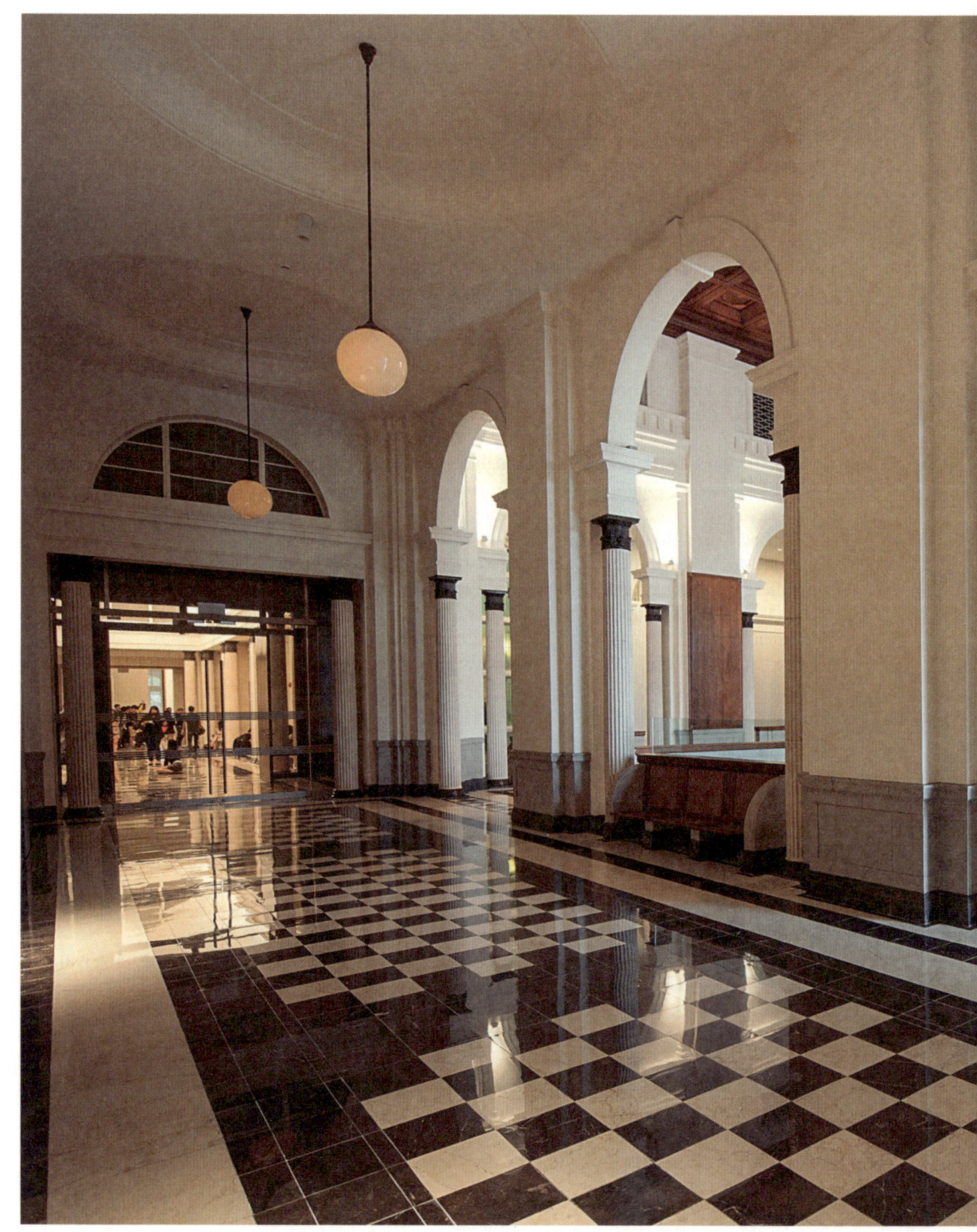

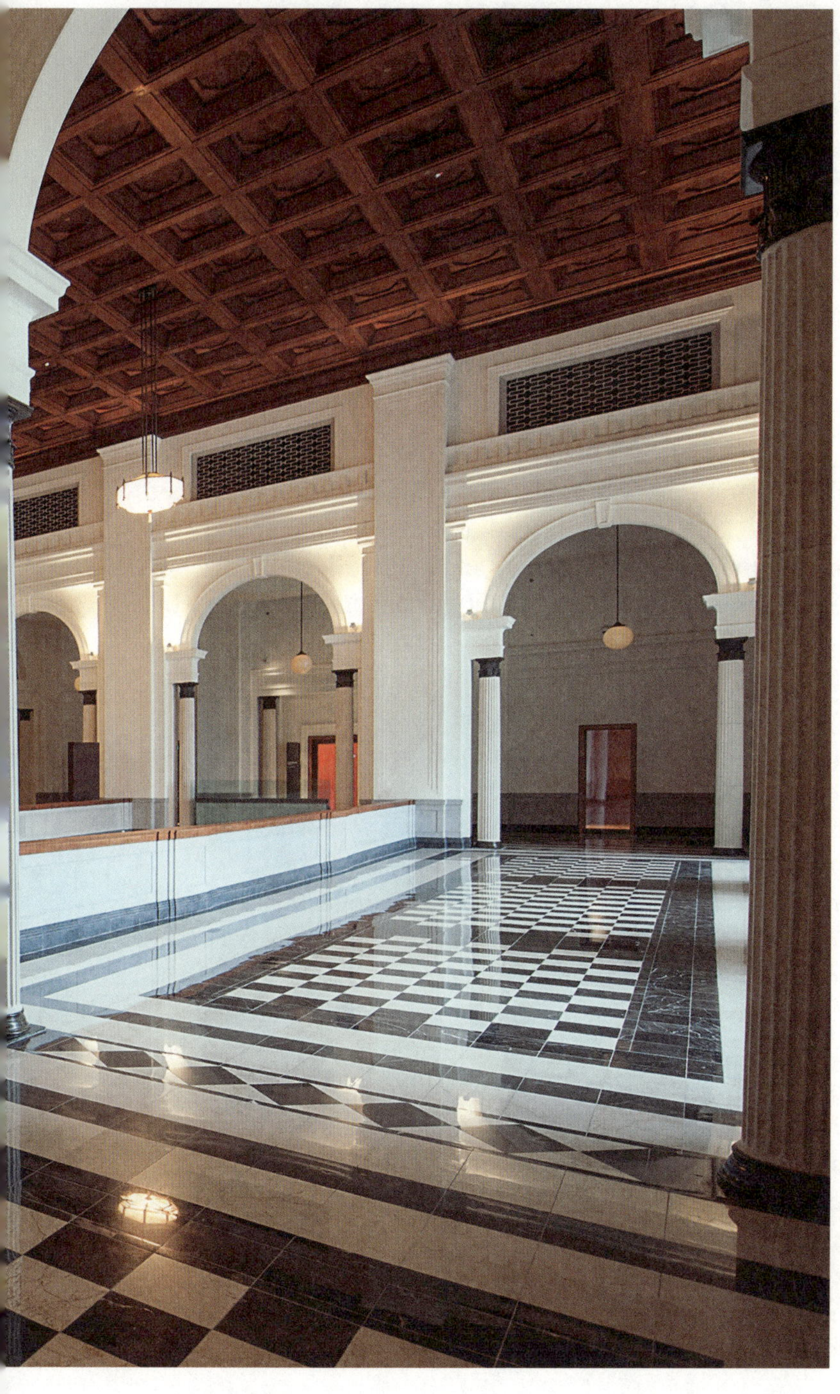

Seng Yu Jin

# Framing Contemporary Art in Southeast Asia through Exhibitionary Discourses

Attempts to locate contemporary art within historical frameworks have gained urgency in the past decade. This is especially so as we see contemporary art making its way into institutions, such as museums and their collections, auction houses, and the academia, as a subject of study. Yet our understanding of what contemporary art is, when aligned along historical perspectives propelled by theories and methodologies, remains elusive. Part of the difficulty in locating this art within historical frameworks stems from the nature of its practices, as they do not (a) conform to significant coherent movements, and (b) deal with dominant mediums, materials, and processes. In these matters we encounter a profound absence of art historical frameworks and criteria with which to organize and structure our understanding of the contemporary in art.

The vexing and apparent resistance of contemporary art to historicization is also played out in Southeast Asia. The challenges to those who are involved with contemporary Southeast Asian art as a field are exacerbated by a struggle to attain critical levels of discursive density necessary for engendering new ways of understanding it. The Comparative Contemporaries anthology project, for instance, which collects texts on Southeast Asian art was cited by Patrick D. Flores when mapping contemporaneity as a self-reflexive awareness and criticality of present conditions in art, with affiliations and affinities that are transient. The brief of Comparative Contemporaries states, "what has not kept pace with the exhibition of contemporary art from Southeast Asia is the art criticism about it. [...] This body of writing remains largely un-collated, insufficiently analyzed, and poorly distributed."[1] Two issues are brought to the fore. The first is the proliferation of exhibitions of contemporary Southeast Asian art in comparison to the paucity of discourse on it, leading to the impression that the exhibition is a significant medium in which this art is displayed, accessed, and interpreted discursively. The second is to unpack the multifarious nature of exhibitions as discursive sites, connected to a constellation of forces bound by institutional, curatorial, scholarly, state, and supranational interests, which are manifested in the exhibition as a medium for display, discursive site, and for the reception of artworks—all of which have been largely unremarked.[2]

This paper examines the exhibition as a prime framer of the history of the contemporary in Southeast Asia over a span of ten years (1992 to 2002). Such a span of time signals the emergence of exhibitions on and about contemporary Southeast Asian art as distinct conceptual categories and destinations. Earlier, the region was submerged in larger encompassing rubrics such as Asia and the Asia Pacific. The focus of this paper is not on the display of artworks or on artworks themselves, but on texts regarded as distinct bodies of writing produced for the purpose of exhibitions that I call *exhibitionary discourse*, which is seen separately from discourse produced from academia. In this respect, exhibitionary discourse includes the curatorial text that frames the exhibition, as well as other writings related to the curatorial objectives of the exhibition. Exhibitionary discourse is a discursive site where academia and museology overlap. The provision of explanations for artworks selected for display in the exhibition also conforms to exhibition discourses in which they engage with selected themes and issues pertinent to the exhibition. This account is a preliminary survey of exhibitionary discourses on the contemporary in Southeast Asian art, paving the way for further scholarship on this topic.

Exhibitions on contemporary art in Southeast Asia emerged in the 1990s; as phenomena they deserve closer scrutiny. Flores cites art historian and curator, Apinan Poshyananda, who outlined how contemporary art in Asia, emerging in the 1990s through exhibitions, was represented and projected along the themes of: (a) Asian Identity, diversity and convergence; (b) binary opposites and the exotic other; (c) the old and the new; (d) migration and diaspora; (e) race, ethnicity, religion, gender; (f) authenticity and appropriation.[3] Such representations in Asia hint at how the contemporary in Southeast Asian art would be represented in the region and how to think about it discursively.[4] Unpacking the exhibitionary discourse is one way in which the history of exhibitions of art in this region can be understood. This is especially so as there is scant or no writing on the contemporary from academia. This situation has arisen, in part, from the relative lack of interest in art history in the region's universities.[5] Academic journals on Southeast Asia such as the *Kyoto Review of Southeast Asian Studies* published by the Centre of Southeast Asian Studies, Kyoto University in 1965, the *Journal of Southeast Asian History* produced by the then University of Singapore in 1960, as well as programs offering Southeast Asian Studies at the Chulalongkorn University, although exceptional, rarely focus on art history.[6] Other journals such as *Philippine Studies* (Ateneo de Manila University) and the *Thai Khadi Journal*

(Thammasat University) specialize in particular disciplines focused on the study of particular countries. T. K. Sabapathy has called the production and circulation of discourse on Southeast Asian art from academia before the new millennia desultory.[7]

The focus on exhibitions as the prime framers of historicizing contemporary art in Southeast Asia stems from their emergence and proliferation in the 1990s; originating from both within and without the region. Three such exhibitions spring to mind, namely: "New Art from Southeast Asia" in 1992 (Japan), "Modernity and Beyond: Themes in Southeast Asian Art" in 1996 (Singapore), and "36 Ideas from Asia: Contemporary Southeast Asian Art" (Association of Southeast Asian Nations, hereafter ASEAN).[8] They have been selected as forerunners of exhibitions on contemporary art that are specific to this region in the 1990s, and along the following three perspectives: from Japan as an outsider looking in, from Singapore looking at the region from within, and from ASEAN, as a regional institutional endeavor seeking to promote economic and political cooperation in the region while attempting to foster regionalism through culture. More importantly, these three exhibitions employ different curatorial premises and frameworks in their exhibitionary discourses for proposing (a) "the new" through the ethnographic; (b) the "beyond" by looking into a postcolonial future framed by shared themes that bind the region; and (c) the conceptual by locating an understanding of the contemporary in the artist as an individual.[9]

An Ethnographic Turn: "The New Art" from Southeast Asia
Emphatic proclamations of the "new," mark the inauguration of exhibitions with specific interests in appraising contemporaneity in Southeast Asian art discursively. The "New Art from Southeast Asia" exhibition, organized by The Japan Foundation (ASEAN Cultural Centre), the Tokyo Metropolitan Government, and the Tokyo Metropolitan Culture Foundation in 1992, is a landmark exhibition in this light. It traveled to the Fukuoka Art Museum, the Hiroshima City Museum of Contemporary Art, and the Kirin Plaza Osaka in Japan. Such interests in the region were concomitant with the founding of the ASEAN Cultural Centre under the Japan Foundation, established in 1990; it registered a significant manifestation of Japan's interest in the region with a mission to introduce its contemporary art to Japan.[10]

Precedents for displaying works from Southeast Asia are traced to three Asian Art Shows organized by the Fukuoka Art Museum; they sparked enough public interest in and initiated research on Southeast Asian contemporary art.[11] The "New Art from Southeast Asia" exhibition was a large project, marking the first conscious attempt to survey and appraise contemporary art from Southeast Asia as a region. Nakamura Hideki, an art historian, Masahiro Ushiroshoji, a curator from the Fukuoka Art Museum, and Tani Arata, an art critic and commissioner for the Japanese Pavilion in the Venice Biennale in 1982 and 1984 and co-curator this exhibition, contributed an essay each in the accompanying publication.

"New Art from Southeast Asia" had a big impact on the Japanese public and their imagination of Southeast Asia. Generally, it signaled a shift in interest from the West towards Asia in Japan.[12] The 1990s witnessed increasing Japanese cultural exports to markets in East and Southeast Asia, most notably its music industry that nearly tripled in volume and value from 5.5 billion yen in 1988 to 14.6 billion yen in 2002.[13] Increased economic trade and cultural exchanges coupled with shifts in Japanese public and government policies, and attitudes towards Asia, formed the geopolitical backdrops for mounting the exhibition.

The choice of the designation "New Art" over contemporary or postmodern art that was current in the 1990s is significant. Nakamura Hideki's essay, titled "The Self Awareness of Human Beings in Flux," sets the tone for the exhibition. He begins by saying,

> In the final decade of the twentieth century, the world is experiencing major changes, as events that upset established notions occur in every region of the globe. The trends in East and Southeast Asia, including dynamic economic growth, represent one of the most noteworthy changes. In the face of new realities, we cannot expect to continue forever to measure Asia in terms of outworn standards.[14]

The standards that Hideki alludes to are Euro-American criteria and frameworks that New Art transcends. Masahiro Ushiroshoji echoes Nakamura's claims when he remarks that

> the changes in the art scene in Southeast Asia, namely, the appearance of a new subject (i.e., changing society), new forms of art (i.e., installation and performance), and the materials (i.e., familiar ones from daily life), come from the desire of artists to engage with societies in which they live and the real world surrounding them.[15]

New Art is synonymous with how artists in this region were dealing with contemporaneity, while engaging with conditions of change in societies and artistic practices. History is evoked in explaining New Art in Southeast Asia. Hideki historicizes Southeast Asian art neatly:

> To put it simply, a generation that adhered to folk traditions was succeeded by one receptive to Western Modernism. Now that the depths of folk culture and the legacy of Western Modernism are taken for granted as a spiritual foundation, a third generation that is trying to forge its own identity is rapidly coming to the fore.[16]

According to Hideki, the second generation of modernist Southeast Asian artists had hybridized folk culture and "Western Modernism" or internationalism; as issues they were observed and discussed by various writers in the three earlier Asian art shows. The "third generation" is the subject of this exhibition, marked by studies of how this generation of artists shifted its preoccupations towards the self and to exploring its own cultural identities. It was therefore historical continuities of New Art with tradition and the folk that defined the interests of artists in Southeast Asia making New Art. This was reaffirmed by Ushiroshoji, who declared that "when Southeast Asian artists took up that difficult challenge, they tried to anchor themselves firmly within the unique and fertile traditions of Southeast Asia."[17]

While history explained the impulses of New Art in the region, it was the ethnographic, evoked through the *folk* and *traditions* of this region that shored up the story of this exhibition. Tani Arata's "Toward an Asian School of Contemporary Art" challenged the linear conception of time, replacing it with a conception of time in Southeast Asia that was primeval, cyclical, and even mythical. For Arata:

> In spite of having been stimulated stimulated by "linear time" and the modern West and metaphors of progress and development, the motifs are not limited to them, but also deal with primeval time that continues to exist. Such motifs include the god of fertility *Buroru*, who emerges from the squashed belly of a naked inverted figure in Agnes Arellano's work. This is a metaphor for the will of the people, who occupy "living" time that exists in myth and experience. It may also express resistance to linear time.[18]

His observation of how "the Postmodern movement began scarcely without any time-lag behind Europe, the United States, and Japan," whereby both modernism and postmodernism occurred simultaneously, was also a condition that shaped the art history of this region, challenging the linear concept of time and replacing it with "primeval time" that exists in the mystical.[19] These proclamations of the primeval, the mystical, and the mythical, mark an ethnographic turn, a return to ethnic traditions as wellsprings from which the new from this region distinguished itself as new art.

## Beyond the Domains of the Modern

Homi Bhabha describes the state of losing one's way amidst the shifting grounds of identity in which once stable paradigms of morality and tradition have been negotiated and re-negotiated incessantly in an attempt to locate grounds and space that are stable enough for the establishment of a new cultural identity, as "the beyond."[20] 1996 was the year that the Singapore Art Museum (SAM) officially opened with its inaugural exhibition, "Modernity and Beyond: Themes in Southeast Asian Art."[21]

While the exhibition adopted a thematic approach the texts in the catalogue were country specific.[22] The six themes allowed for the exhibition to transcend national boundaries, permitting the exploration of relationships, connections, and ruptures in the art history of Southeast Asia as a region.[23] Sabapathy states in the introduction of the exhibition's publication that the thematic approach to "Modernity and Beyond" served to "underscore and enliven studies of modern art and artistic practices in Southeast Asia, as well as tendencies which are cast beyond the domains of the modern."[24] The themes of the exhibition had to do with nationalism, modernity, the real, mythology, self and the other, and urbanization, slipping between the modern and "the beyond," anchoring the exhibitionary discourse in historical contexts particular to the region while opening up speculative entry points into the future leading to the contemporary in Southeast Asian art. Besides the "modest yet significant mark [that] has been registered"[25] by this exhibition in transcending national boundaries that have characterized art writing in Southeast Asia, the prospect of the "beyond" in the exhibition title warrants closer scrutiny. Attention has to be paid to how the term "beyond" has gained currency in postcolonial art discourse in the 1990s and to how it is further advanced by the theme, "Beyond the Future," which was chosen for the "3rd Asia-Pacific Triennial" (APT) in 1999.

What exactly is this new space termed as "the beyond"? Was it intended as a designation, or was it mere coincidence that both the "3rd APT" and SAM's inaugural show employed it in their respective exhibitionary discourses? Thomas McEvilley's fourth phase of identity provides an understanding of the meteoric rise of the word "beyond" in postcolonial discourse. He provides a point of entry into such a domain in his discussion of identity formation by positing a fourth phase in which constructions of identity assume elevated registers. Accordingly, postcolonial artists in the fourth phase of identity "want to get *beyond*"[26] questions of identity and difference, and to move into the future."[27] The word "beyond" thus alludes to the future where artists, now that they are much more secure with their own identities[28] that have been shaped by a complex multitude of factors,

> approach the future not with a determination to re-cohere around a long-lost identity, but with a feeling that that identity (along with the identity of the colonizer) is a thing of the past, and that the future holds new, more interesting identifies for all.[29]

This echoes Homi Bhabha's interest in a new space that he designated as "the beyond," whereby a new cultural identity can take root. The emphasis on the future also signaled a desire to come to terms with colonialism, to get beyond questions of a "pure" identity conceived to resist the hegemonic West, thus indicating symptoms that mark gradual shifts towards McEvilley's fourth (and final) phase, for identity.[30]

<u>The Conceptual Turn: 36 Ideas from Asia</u>

"36 Ideas from Asia: Contemporary South-East Asian Art" was conceived as a traveling exhibition in 2002–03 under the auspices of ASEAN. It sought to present contemporary Southeast Asian art to audiences in Europe. Sabapathy explains in the Curatorial Introduction, that the exposition was underlined by a conscious curatorial effort to re-map Southeast Asian artistically, "as a region to be undertaken along perspectives proposed by individual artists."[31] Such a call signals a possible alternative approach, employing individual artists as microcosms that engage with and are acted upon by an increasingly globalized world, in which the larger macrocosm, patterns, and trends can then emerge if we explore these interactions intelligently. The title of the exhibition was unpacked by Sabapathy and deserves attention. The number 36 in the title denoted the number of artists featured in the exhibition, while "ideas" called "attention to the conceptual aspects in the work."[32]

Curatorially conceptualized in late 1999, when Southeast Asia was perceived as "in the throes of political, economic, and social crisis,"[33] Kwok Kian Chow, then Director of the Singapore Art Museum, explained "36 Ideas"[34] by making reference to a popular song titled "DiobokObok" which, in the Javanese vernacular, "alluded to stirred waters and agitated conditions in a tank, causing the fish within to be unsettled and disoriented."[35] "DiobokObok" as the working title for "36 Ideas" was intentionally designed to capture "poignantly a sense of the tumultuous times and the dramatic events [of the Asian financial crisis] in Southeast Asia in the last years of the latter millennium," with strong allusions to local meanings manifested in the use of an Indonesian idiom to frame the exhibition.[36] The need to map realities of Southeast Asia was also correspondingly articulated by Choo Whatt Bin, the chairman of the ASEAN COCI (Committee on Culture and Information, Singapore) when he recognized that:

> Southeast Asia has witnessed dramatic events in recent years. The regional crisis [1997 Asian financial crisis] was also a catalyst that stirred up dormant sentiments of political, social, and cultural tensions, occasioning dramatic turns of event on political and civil fronts in its wake. The histories and current realities of the countries in the region are reflected in the art histories and the contemporary practices of Southeast Asian artists. The ASEAN COCI proposes to register the varying nature of contemporary art in the region and to surface the concerns of contemporary artists in the region to an international audience.[37]

ASEAN exhibitions sponsored by the COCI in the past had constructed peaceful, beautiful, and untroubled narratives of art in Southeast Asia, framed by national boundaries. "36 Ideas" marked a departure from these by charting new maps that sought to trace the contours of current realities facing the region; realities appraised as simmering with tensions, differences, discontinuities, and heterogeneity from regional rather than national perspectives. Even as Sabapathy points out, the ensuing exhibitionary discourses, wrapped by the polite formalities of cultural diplomacy, continue to manifest themselves.[38] Two other writers, Niranjan Rajah and Patrick D. Flores, contributed essays to the exhibitionary discourse and they deserve close attention.

The underlying premise for this occasion and the exhibitionary discourse may be cast in the following terms: that artists and art works are progenitors of ideas for contemporaneity in Southeast Asian art or that artists and artworks are progenitors of ideas for apprehending contemporaneity in the region's art. Flores's essay, "Homespun Worldwide: Colonialism as Critical Inheritance," surveys the terrain of contemporary art in Southeast Asia, revealing the continuing threads of colonialism that collide and combine in a contingent present. For instance, the aesthetic concept of perspective, as a principal mode of organizing spatiality institutionalized in Southeast Asia by art academies modeled after the Ecole des Beaux-Arts, was resisted by Soe Naing in his painting titled *Village People;* in it, the surface is flattened in a "primitive" manner, shaped by tendencies in folk art. Closer scrutiny of the artworks reveals how aesthetic properties such as space, form, and color are not simply derived from Euro-American ideals. The return to conceptual aspects in artworks in "36 Ideas" privileges ideas consisting of local worldviews and philosophies that particularize contemporary art in Southeast Asia. Artists such as Soeung Vannara and Phy Chan Than conceptualize culture as nature, by tapping into spiritual worlds in which nature, rituals, spirits, and culture are integrated and entwined.

Niranjan Rajah, in his essay, historicizes modern and contemporary art in Southeast Asia by tracing the impulses of modernisms in the various nation-states. In each instance, the impulses are shaped by communism, nationalism, social reform, and ethnicity, and directed towards forging regional, global, and transnational perspectives in art. He locates these conceptual devices in the works by artists in the exhibition. These devices are also historically contingent and form a history of ideas that frame contemporary art making in Southeast Asia. Niranjan Rajah emphasizes "transnational arenas"[39] that go beyond national narratives; he calls for Southeast Asian art to engage with the "cultural challenges posed by globalization and the new suzerainty," entailing the development of new approaches.[40]

"36 Ideas" marked a beginning of a real attempt to forward new approaches and methods for curating and thinking about the region's art and artists, departing from earlier notions and claims of Southeast Asian art as a fixed category. For Niranjan Rajah, the conceptual in the exhibitionary discourse is employed as a device for historicizing the contemporary in Southeast Asian art; it enables him to locate art's sources in the local, in the region's spiritual and natural worlds of artists. The conceptual is the entry point through which one cultivates domains for deep engagement with the contemporary by dealing with the very ideas that embody artworks and by stepping beyond a superficial understanding of them.

<u>Contemporaneity in Southeast Asian Art: The Ethnographic, Thematic, and Conceptual</u>

The span of ten years, from 1992 to 2002, is formative for exhibitionary discourses on the contemporary in Southeast Asian art. The making of exhibitions within these years gave rise to particular discourses that proposed the ethnographic, thematic, and the conceptual terrains for mapping and developing the contemporary as a discursive field in art. The shift towards the conceptual in "36 Ideas" makes possible a provision of theories and concepts on art, requisite for this region.

Much of what is written on Southeast Asian art springs from exhibitionary discourses, initiated by museums, art institutions, and galleries that offer critical but fragmented narratives of the region's art. Art exhibitions remain the primary mode for constructing the region's art; they are invariably driven by diverse agendas. These endeavors construct trajectories that survey the region and its artistic productions. The issues of region and region-ness are engaged with in varying degrees of success by these exhibitions as sites of discourse. Exhibitionary discourses on the contemporary, produced from within and without, are never exclusionary. More often than not, scholars from within the region are active participants in the shaping and mapping of Southeast Asian art outside the region; conversely, scholars from outside the region are vitally involved in developing discourses within it. The constant slippages within exhibitionary discourses of contemporary Southeast Asian art, whereby they bleed into other fields such as Asian art, Asia-Pacific art, and Euro-American art, enrich and deepen knowledge on art, providing further possibilities for exploring notions of the region and region-ness across these areas.

1    Comparative Contemporaries–A Web Anthology Project was a project initiated by art critic Lee Weng Choy; it began with a one day symposium and two days of workshops, titled Comparatives Contemporary, and was organized by The Substation in 2003. The web anthology on Southeast Asian art commenced in late 2012. Please refer to the website http://www.aaa.org.hk/Programme/Details/139 for more details.

2    T. K. Sabapathy, "Regarding Exhibitions," in *The Artists Village: 20 Years On* (Singapore: The Singapore Art Museum, 2008), 7. Sabapathy calls for reviewers to focus not only on the texts produced by exhibitions but also on exhibition displays.

3    Apinan Poshyananda, "Contemporary Southeast Asian Art in the New World Disorder," computer printout, Eugene Tan, Southeast Asian Studies Summer Institute, June 29, 1999.

4    For an insightful account of the history of curation in Southeast Asia, refer to Patrick D. Flores, *Past Peripheral: Curation in Southeast Asia* (Singapore: NUS Museum, 2008), 65.

5    T. K. Sabapathy, *Road to Nowhere: The Quick Rise and the Long Fall of Art History in Singapore* (Singapore: The National Institute of Education, 2010).

6    The *Journal of Southeast Asian History* was renamed *Southeast Asian Studies* in the 1970s.

7    In the last decade, the following art journals on Southeast Asian art have appeared: *Sinlapkorn* (Fine Arts from the Ministry of Arts, Thailand), *SentAp!* (Malaysia), and *C-arts* (Indonesia). Academic publications on Southeast Asian art have surfaced only recently. Patrick D. Flores and Joan Kee, eds., *Third Text: Critical Perspectives on Contemporary Art and Culture* 25, no. 4, July 2011; and Nora A. Taylor and Boreth Ly, eds., *Modern and Contemporary Southeast Asian Art* (USA: Cornell Southeast Asia Program Publications, 2012).

8    The Association of Southeast Asian Nations (ASEAN) was established on August 8, 1967. Its founding members were Singapore, Malaysia, Indonesia, the Philippines, and Thailand. ASEAN's membership

later expanded to include Brunei Darussalam (1984), Vietnam (1995), Laos (1997), Myanmar (1997), and Cambodia (1999). It is politically and culturally diverse. ASEAN serves as a platform to facilitate dialogue and cooperation between its members.

9 Other exhibitions that included contemporary Southeast Asian art under rubrics such as Asia and Asia Pacific are: the "Asia Pacific Triennial of Contemporary Art" in 1993 (Australia), the "4th Asian Art Show" in 1994 (Japan); they have been excluded as this paper focuses on how contemporary art on Southeast Asia was imagined discursively through exhibitionary discourses specifically centered on this region. However, how the conceptual category of Southeast Asia as a contingent category is mediated in other exhibitions adopting different geographical parameters deserves scholarly attention but remains outside the scope of this paper.

10 The ASEAN Cultural Centre was expanded into the Asia Cultural Centre in 1995 to mark the 50th anniversary of the end of the World War II. Interview with Ms. Yasuko Furuich, August 5, 2010 at the Japan Foundation, Tokyo.

11 The Fukuoka Asian Art Shows began with the 1979–80 "Asian Artists Exhibition/Contemporary Asian Art Show," followed by the "2nd Asian Art Show" that was held in 1985. The "3rd Asian Art Show" was organized in 1989. The 4th and final "Asian Art Show" took place in 1994 before it was replaced by the Fukuoka Asian Art Triennial in 1999, marking the opening of the Fukuoka Asian Art Museum. It was also no coincidence that the mayor of Fukuoka City helmed all three "Asian Art Shows" organized by the Fukuoka Art Museum from 1979 to 1989. The Asian Art Shows provided platforms and a "gateway to Asia" for the building of political and economic ties through art, at a time when Japan's trade with Asia was becoming increasingly significant, with Japan at the center.

12 Interview with Ms. Yasuko Furuich, August 5, 2010 at the Japan Foundation, Tokyo.

13 Nissim Otmazgin, "Japanese Government Support for Cultural Export," *Kyoto Review*, Centre of Southeast Asian Studies, no. 3, October 2003.

14 Nakamura Hideki, "The Self Awareness of Human Beings in Flux," in *New Art from Southeast Asia 1992* (Tokyo: Japan Foundation, 1992), 13.

15 Masahiro Ushiroshoji, "The Labyrinthine Search for Self-Identity–The Art of Southeast Asia from the 1980s to 1990s," in *New Art from Southeast Asia 1992* (Tokyo: Japan Foundation, 1992), 21.

16 Ibid.

17 Ibid.

18 Tani Arata, "Toward an Asian School of Contemporary Art," in *New Art from Southeast Asia 1992* (Tokyo: Japan Foundation, 1992), 104.

19 Ibid.

20 Homi Bhabha, "Beyond the Pale: Art in the Age of Multicultural Translation. Figurations for an Alternative Consciousness," in *Cultural Diversity in the Arts: Art, Art Politics, and the Face Lift of Europe*, ed. R. Lavrijsen (Amsterdam: K.I.T. Publications, 1993), 32.

21 The Singapore Art Museum was inaugurated with two exhibitions, namely, "Modernity and Beyond: Themes in Southeast Asian Art and A Century of Singapore Art."

22 The essays in the *Modernity and Beyond: Themes in Southeast Asian Art* catalogue include: "Glimpses into Art in Brunei Darussalam" by Danielle C. W. M. Poppel; "From National Identity to the Self: Themes in Modern Indonesian Art" by Joanna Lee; "Thematic Approaches to Malaysian Art History" by T. K. Sabapathy; "Some Aspects of Nationalism and Internationalism in Philippine Art" by Ahmad Mashadi; "Brief Notes on Traditionalism in Modern Thai Art" by Ahmad Mashadi; and "A Preliminary Thematic Survey of Vietnamese Contemporary Art" by Susie Koay.

23 The six themes are: 1. Nationalism, Revolution, and the Idea of the Modern; 2. Traditions of the Real; 3. Modes of Abstraction; 4. Mythology and Religion: Traditions and Tension, The Self and the Other; and 6. Urbanism and Popular Culture.

24 T. K. Sabapathy, "Introduction," in *Modernity and Beyond* (Singapore: Singapore Art Museum, 1996), 7.

25 Ibid., 7–9.

26 Emphasis added.

27 Thomas McEvilley, *Fusion: West African Artists at the Venice Biennale* (New York: Prestal, 1993), 11.

28 This is in comparison to the state of identity during the first decades after the World War II in which many of the postcolonial countries, newly independent, began to move into McEvilley's third phase of identity.

29 Ibid.

30 In McEvilley, *Fusion: West African Artists at the Venice Biennale*, the fourth phase of identity is based on an acceptance of one's identity as a mosaic of cultural influences that stems from not one source, whether Asian, African, or Western, but from a multitude of sources, thus suggesting both syncretism and eclecticism.

31 T. K. Sabapathy, "Thoughts on an International Exhibition on Southeast Asian Contemporary Art," in *36 Ideas from Asia: Contemporary South-East Asian Art* (Singapore: Singapore Art Museum, 2002), unpaginated.

32 Ibid.

33 Kwok Kian Chow, "Message," in *36 Ideas from Asia: Contemporary South-East Asian Art* (Singapore: Singapore Art Museum, 2002), 10. Kwok is currently the Senior Advisor to The National Art Gallery, Singapore.

34 The Singapore Art Museum, together with the National Heritage Board was tasked with both the project management and art direction of the exhibition. See *36 Ideas from Asia: Contemporary South-East Asian Art* (Singapore: Singapore Art Museum, 2002), 124.

35 Ibid., 10.

36 Ibid.

37 Choo Whatt Bin, "Message," in *36 Ideas from Asia: Contemporary South-East Asian Art* (Singapore: Singapore Art Museum, 2002), 8.

38 T. K. Sabapathy, "Curatorial Introduction," unpaginated.

39 Niranjan Rajah, "Towards a Southeast Asian Paradigm: From Distinct National Modernisms to an Integrated Regional Arena for Art," in *36 Ideas from Asia: Contemporary South-East Asian Art* (Singapore: Singapore Art Museum, 2002), 32.

40 Ibid., 35.

Padang Atrium
National Gallery Singapore

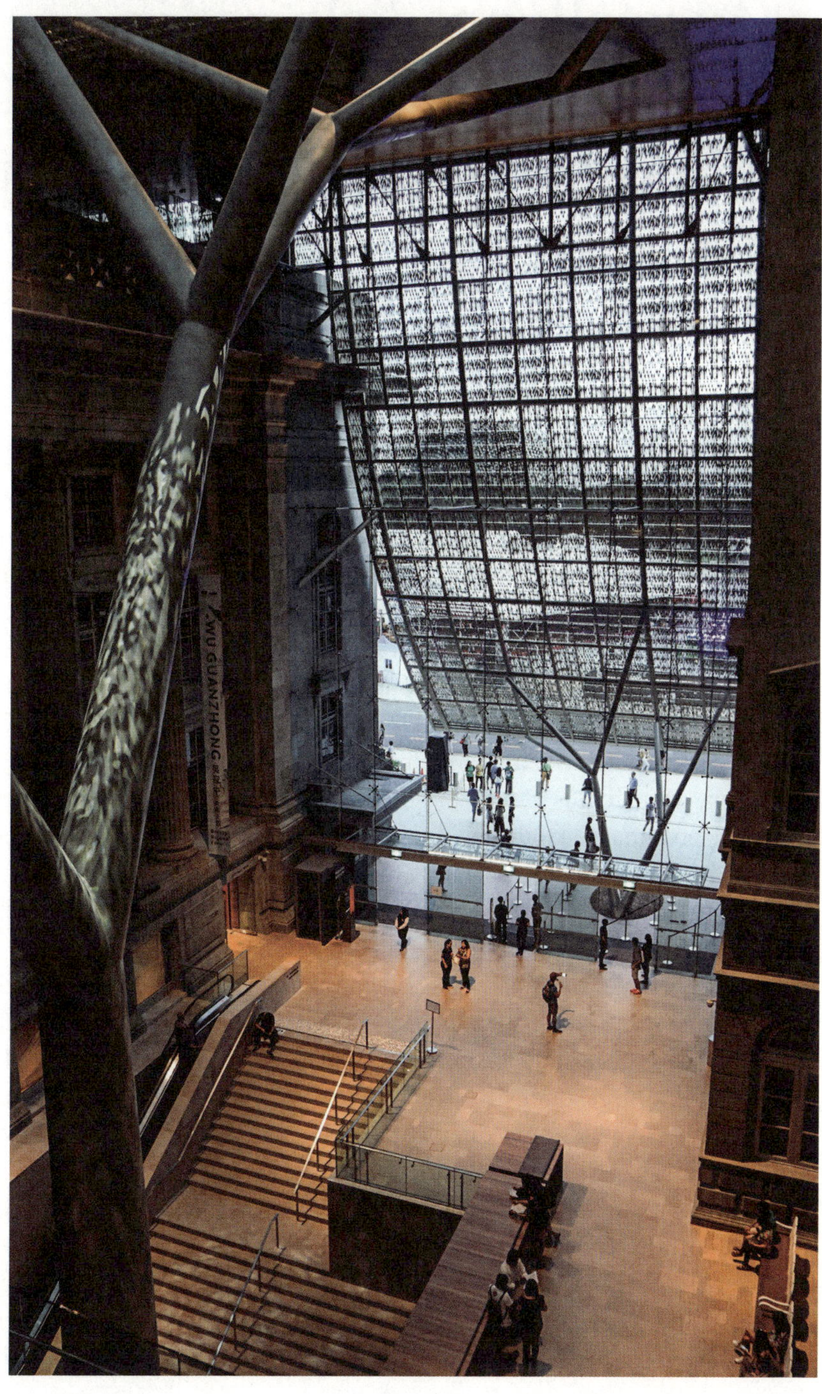

Seng Yu Jin

# Ausstellungsdiskurse in Südostasien und ihre Wirkung auf die Wahrnehmung des Zeitgenössischen

In den Jahren von 1992 bis 2002 wurde zeitgenössische Kunst zunehmend in einem historischen Bezugsrahmen verortet, vor allem in Untersuchungen, die sich auf die zeitgenössische Kunstproduktion und ihren Weg in Institutionen und deren Sammlungen, Auktionshäuser und Universitäten konzentrieren. Und doch bleibt unser Verständnis dessen, was zeitgenössische Kunst ist, schwer fassbar, wenn man versucht, sie entang historischer Linien einzuordnen, die von bestimmten Theorien und Methoden ausgehen. Die Schwierigkeit, diese Kunst in einen historischen Bezugsrahmen zu setzen, beruht teilweise auf der Art ihrer Praktiken, da sich diese (a) nicht an wichtige, miteinander zusammenhängende Bewegungen anpassen und sich (b) mit aktuell vorherrschenden Medien, Materialien und Prozessen beschäftigen. In dieser Hinsicht verfügen wir kaum über kunsthistorische Bezugsrahmen und Kriterien, anhand derer sich unser Verständnis des Zeitgenössischen organisieren und strukturieren ließe.

Der irritierende, offenkundige Widerstand der zeitgenössischen Kunst gegen ihre Historisierung spielt auch in Südostasien eine Rolle. Für diejenigen, die sich mit zeitgenössischer südostasiatischer Kunst beschäftigen, steigt die Herausforderung, weil ein relevantes Niveau diskursiver Dichte erforderlich ist, um neue Wege zu ihrem Verständnis zu erschließen. So charakterisierte Patrick D. Flores das Zeitgenössische als ein selbstreflexives Bewusstsein und eine selbstreflexive Kritik an den aktuellen Bedingungen der Kunst, mit ihren kurzlebigen Verbindungen und Affinitäten, und verwies in diesem Zusammenhang beispielsweise auf das Projekt Comparative Contemporaries, das Texte zur südostasiatischen Kunst in einer Anthologie versammelt. Im Kurztext zu Comparative Contemporaries heißt es, dass das, „was mit dem Ausstellen zeitgenössischer Kunst aus Südostasien nicht Schritt gehalten hat, eine Kunstkritik ist, die sich mit ihr auseinandersetzt. [...] dieser Bestand an Texten bleibt weitgehend verstreut, unzureichend analysiert und wenig verbreitet."[1] Zwei Themen kommen zur Sprache: Zum einen der starke Zuwachs von Ausstellungen zu zeitgenössischer südostasiatischer Kunst, dabei eine vergleichsweise geringe Diskursdichte. Der zweite Aspekt ist folglich, dass es den facettenreichen Charakter von Ausstellungen als diskursiven Ort zu entschlüsseln gilt; dabei sollte die Konstellation von Kräften in den Blick genommen werden, die institutionelle, kuratorische, akademische, staatliche und nationenübergreifende Interessen verfolgt, die sich in der Ausstellung als Medium der Präsentation, als Ort des Diskurses und der Rezeption von Kunstwerken manifestieren – was jedoch bisher weitgehend unbeachtet geblieben ist.[2]

Der vorliegende Essay untersucht das Format der Ausstellung als Bezugsrahmen, in dem die Geschichte der zeitgenössischen Kunst in der Region Südostasien über einen Zeitraum von zehn Jahren (1992–2002) erstmals formuliert wurde. In diesem Zeitraum entstanden Ausstellungen von und über zeitgenössische südostasiatische Kunst als eigenständige begriffliche Kategorie. Zuvor war diese Region aufgrund verallgemeinernder Bezeichnungen wie Asien und asiatisch-pazifischer Raum gewissermaßen nicht sichtbar. Der vorliegende Text richtet den Fokus nicht auf das Ausstellen von Kunstwerken oder auf die Kunstwerke selbst, sondern auf Texte, die sie zum Gegenstand machen. Diese werden als ein eigenständiger Korpus betrachtet, der anlässlich von Ausstellungen entstanden ist und den ich – in Abgrenzung von universitären Diskursen – als *Ausstellungsdiskurs* bezeichne. Der Ausstellungsdiskurs umfasst den kuratorischen Begleittext zur Ausstellung ebenso wie andere Schriften, die sich auf die kuratorische Zielsetzung beziehen. Hier überlagern sich Wissenschaft und Museologie. Auch die Erläuterungen zu den Kunstwerken, die sich mit bestimmten Themen und Fragestellungen der Ausstellung beschäftigen, sind Teil des Ausstellungsdiskurses. Die folgende Darstellung bietet einen vorläufigen Überblick und soll die Grundlagen zu einer weiteren Erforschung dieses Themas legen.

Ausstellungen zur zeitgenössischen Kunst in Südostasien kamen in den 1990er Jahren auf und verdienen als Phänomen eine eingehendere Betrachtung. Flores zitiert den Kunsthistoriker und Kurator Apinan Poshyananda, der in der Vermittlung zeitgenössischer Kunst in Asien in diesem Zeitraum folgende Themen identifiziert: (a) Vielfalt und Übereinstimmung asiatischer Identität; (b) binäre Oppositionen und das exotische Andere; (c) das Alte und das Neue; (d) Migration und Diaspora; (e) Rasse, Ethnizität, Religion, Gender; (f) Authentizität und Appropriation.[3] Diese Kategorisierung asiatischer Kunst läßt sich auch auf südostasiatische Kunst und an sie angeschlossene Diskurse übertragen.[4] Ihr Entschlüsseln bietet eine Möglichkeit, die Geschichte von Kunstausstellungen in dieser Region zu verstehen. Dies gilt umso mehr, als es nur wenige, in manchen Fällen sogar überhaupt keine akademischen Texte zur zeitgenössischen Kunst vorliegen, weil es unter anderem an den Universitäten dieser Region kein ausgeprägtes Interesse an der Kunstgeschichte gibt.[5] Herausragende akademische Zeitschriften zu Südostasien wie etwa die *Kyoto Review of Southeast Asian Studies*, die seit 1965 am Centre of Southeast Asian Studies an der Universität Kyoto erscheint, das *Journal of Southeast Asian History*, das 1960 an der damaligen University of Singapore gegründet wurde, wie auch die Programme für Südostasien-Wissenschaften an der Chualalongkorn University beschäftigen sich nur selten mit kunsthistorischen Themen.[6] Andere Zeitschriften, wie etwa *Philippine Studies* (Ateneo de Manila University) und das *Thai Khadi Journal* (Thammasat University) sind spezialisiert auf bestimmte Disziplinen und konzentrieren sich auf die Erforschung einzelner Länder. T. K. Sabapathy bezeichnet die Produktion und Zirkulation universitärer Diskurse über südostasiatische Kunst vor der Jahrtausendwende insgesamt als schwach.[7]

Betrachtet man Ausstellungen als ersten Bezugsrahmen einer Historisierung von Kunst in Südostasien, so denkt man spontan an drei Beispiele aus den 1990er Jahren in und außerhalb der Region: *New Art from Southeast Asia* (Japan, 1992), *Modernity and Beyond: Themes in Southeast Asian Art* (Singapore, 1996) und *36 Ideas from Asia: Contemporary Southeast Asian Art* (Association of Southeast Asian Nations, kurz ASEAN).[8] Sie gelten als Wegbereiter von Ausstellungen zeitgenössischer Kunst, die für diese Region in den 1990er Jahren charakteristisch sind, und stehen zugleich stellvertretend für drei Perspektiven: Japan steht für den Außenblick auf die Region, Singapur für eine Betrachtung der Region von innen, und ASEAN für eine regionale Organisation, die die wirtschaftliche und politische Zusammenarbeit in der Region stärken und gleichzeitig den Regionalismus mithilfe von Kultur fördern will. Noch wichtiger ist jedoch, dass die drei Ausstellungen von unterschiedlichen kuratorischen Prämissen ausgehen und verschiedene Bezugsrahmen setzen. In ihren Ausstellungsdiskursen richten sie sich auf (a) das *Neue* mithilfe des Ethnografischen; (b) *das darüber Hinausgehende* [the beyond], indem sie den Blick auf eine postkoloniale Zukunft richten, die von gemeinsamen Themen geprägt ist, die die Region zusammenhalten; und (c) das Konzeptuelle, indem man die Auffassung des Zeitgenössischen im Künstler als Individuum verortet.[9]

Eine ethnografische Wende: Neue Kunst aus Südostasien

Die Eröffnungen von Ausstellungen, deren spezifisches Anliegen darin bestand, das Zeitgenössische in der südostasiatischen Kunst diskursiv einzuordnen, waren von emphatischen Proklamationen des *Neuen* begleitet. Die Ausstellung *New Art from Southeast Asia*, die 1992 von der Japan Foundation (ASEAN Cultural Centre), dem Tokyo Metropolitan Government und der Tokyo Metropolitan Culture Foundation organisiert wurde, war in dieser Hinsicht ein Meilenstein. Sie wurde vom Fukuoka Art Museum, dem Hiroshima City Museum of Contemporary Art und dem Kirin Plaza Osaka in Japan gezeigt. Dieses Interesse an der Region ging einher mit der Gründung des ASEAN Cultural Centre unter dem Dach der Japan Foundation im Jahr 1990; Japans Interesse an Südostasien traf auf das Interesse der Region, seine zeitgenössische Kunst in Japan bekannt zu machen.[10]

Vorläufer für Kunstausstellungen aus Südostasien waren die drei *Asian Art Shows*, die das Fukuoka Art Museum organisierte; sie weckten ein ausreichendes öffentliches Interesse und regten eine wissenschaftliche Auseinandersetzung mit zeitgenössischer Kunst aus Südostasien an.[11] *The New Art from Southeast Asia* war ein umfangreiches Projekt und markierte den ersten bewussten Versuch, einen Überblick und eine Bewertung der zeitgenössischen Kunst aus Südostasien als Region zu bieten. Der Kunsthistoriker Nakamura Hideki, Masahiro Ushiroshoji, Kurator am Fukuoka Art Museum, und Tani Arata, Kunstkritiker und Kurator des Japanischen Pavillons der Venedig Biennale 1982 und 1984 sowie Co-Kurator der Ausstellung, verfassten jeweils einen Essay für die begleitende Publikation. *New Art from Southeast Asia* übte einen großen Einfluss auf das japanische Publikum und dessen Bild von Südostasien aus. Die Ausstellung zeigte, dass sich das Interesse Japans generell vom Westen abwandte und in Richtung Asien verlagerte.[12] In den 1990er Jahren exportierte Japan zunehmend Kultur in die Märkte Ost- und Südostasiens, vor allem in der Musikindustrie, deren Volumen und Wert sich von 5,5 Milliarden Yen im Jahr 1988 zu 14,6 Milliarden Yen im Jahr 2002 verdreifachten.[13] Eine veränderte Haltung gegenüber Asien, die Intensivierung der Handelsbeziehungen und des kulturellen Austauschs wie auch Japans Strategiewechsel in seiner Außendarstellung und Politik bildeten den Hintergrund für die Ausstellung *New Art from Southeast Asia*.

Die Bezeichnung *New Art* anstelle von *zeitgenössischer* oder *postmoderner* Kunst, die in den 1990er Jahren gängig waren, ist vielsagend. Nakamura Hidekis Essay „The Self Awareness of Human Beings in Flux" gab den Ton der Ausstellung an. Er beginnt mit der Feststellung:

Im letzten Jahrzehnt des 20. Jahrhunderts erlebt die Welt bedeutende Veränderungen, da in jedem Teil der Erde Ereignisse stattfinden, die unsere gängigen Vorstellungen durcheinanderbringen. Die Entwicklungen in Ost- und Südostasien, einschließlich des dynamischen Wirtschaftswachstums, gehören zu den bemerkenswertesten Veränderungen. Angesichts neuer Realitäten können wir nicht erwarten, Asien für immer nach Maßstäben zu messen, die längst überholt sind.[14]

Die Maßstäbe, auf die Hideki anspielt, sind die euroamerikanischen Kriterien und Bezugssysteme, über welche die *New Art* hinausgeht. Masahiro Ushiroshoji greift Nakamuras Behauptungen auf, wenn er anmerkt, dass

die Veränderungen der Kunstszene in Südostasien, insbesondere das Aufkommen eines neuen Themas (die sich wandelnde Gesellschaft), neuer Kunstformen (Installation und Performance) und neuer Materialien (solche, die uns dem Alltag vertraut sind) vom Wunsch der Künstler herrühren, sich mit den Gesellschaften, in denen sie leben, und mit der realen Welt, die sie umgibt, auseinanderzusetzen.[15]

*New Art* steht für die Art und Weise, wie die KünstlerInnen dieser Regionen mit dem Zeitgenössischen umgingen, wenn sie sich mit den Bedingungen des Wandels in Gesellschaften und künstlerischen Praktiken auseinandersetzten. Neue Kunst in Südostasien wird in Bezug zur Geschichte erklärt, Hideki bietet eine treffende Historisierung an:

> Einfach gesagt, folgte auf eine Generation, die den Traditionen der Volkskunst anhing, eine Generation, die für den westlichen Modernismus empfänglich war. Nun, da die Tiefen der volkstümlichen Kultur und das Erbe der westlichen Moderne als ein sicheres spirituelles Fundament gelten, tritt rasch eine dritte Generation hervor, die versucht, ihre eigene Identität zu formen.[16]

Hideki zufolge hatte die zweite Generation moderner KünstlerInnen in Südostasien die Volkskunst und die westliche Moderne beziehungsweise den Internationalismus hybridisiert; dies wurde von mehreren AutorInnen im Rahmen der drei früheren Ausgaben der Asian Art Shows thematisiert und diskutiert. Gegenstand von *The New Art* ist die dritte Generation; die Ausstellung zeigt, wie diese KünstlerInnengeneration ihre Auseinandersetzung auf das Selbst und auf die Erforschung ihrer eigenen kulturellen Identitäten verlagerte. Das Interesse der KünstlerInnen Südostasiens, die *Neue Kunst* machten, galt also den historischen Kontinuitäten zwischen der *Neuen Kunst*, der Tradition und der Volkskunst. Ushiroshoji unterstrich dies mit der Erklärung: „[A]ls südostasiatische Künstler diese schwierige Herausforderung annahmen, versuchten sie, sich fest in den einzigartigen, fruchtbaren Traditionen Südostasiens zu verankern."[17]

Während die Geschichte eine Erklärung für die Impulse der *Neuen Kunst* in der Region bot, stützte sich das Narrativ dieser Ausstellung auf das Ethnografische, das durch die *Volkskunst* und die *Traditionen* dieser Region hervorgerufen wurde. Tani Aratas Aufsatz „Toward an Asian School of Contemporary Art" stellte die lineare Vorstellung von Zeit infrage und ersetzte sie durch einen Zeitbegriff Südostasiens, der urzeitlich, zyklisch, ja sogar mythisch ist. So bemerkte Arata:

> Auch wenn die Motive von der „linearen Zeit", dem modernen Westen und Metaphern für Fortschritt und Entwicklung inspiriert waren, beschränken sie sich nicht darauf, sondern beschäftigen sich auch mit der Urzeit, die immer noch andauert. Der Fruchtbarkeitsgott *Buroru*, der in Agnes Arellanos Werk aus dem geöffneten Bauch einer an den Füßen aufgehängten Gestalt hervortritt, ist ein solches Motiv. Dies ist eine Metapher für den Willen der Menschen, die in einer „lebendigen" Zeit leben, die es im Mythos und in der Erfahrung gibt. Sie kann auch einen Widerstand gegen die lineare Zeit ausdrücken.[18]

Seine Beobachtung, wie „die postmoderne Bewegung beinahe ohne Verzögerung auf die Entwicklungen in Europa, den Vereinigten Staaten und Japan folgte", wodurch sich Moderne und Postmoderne überlagerten, hat auch die Kunstgeschichte dieser Region beeinflusst, den linearen Zeitbegriff infrage gestellt und ihn durch die *urzeitliche*, mystische Zeit ersetzt.[19] Diese Verkündungen des Urzeitlichen, Mystischen und Mythischen markieren eine Wende und eine Rückkehr zu ethnischen Traditionen als Ursprüngen, die das Neue aus dieser Region als neue Kunst kennzeichneten.

### Über die Gebiete der Moderne hinaus

Homi Bhabha beschreibt den Zustand, sich auf dem schwankenden Terrain der Identität zu verirren, als „das darüber Hinausgehende" [the beyond]. Die vormals unveränderlichen Paradigmen der Moral und der Tradition werden hier immer wieder neu verhandelt, um Grundlagen und Räume zu finden, die für die Gründung einer neuen kulturellen Identität stabil genug sind.[20] Mit einer Ausstellung unter dem Titel *Modernity and Beyond: Themes in Southeast Asian Art* wurde 1996 das Singapore Art Museum (SAM) offiziell eröffnet.[21]

Während die Ausstellung thematisch gegliedert wurde, waren die Katalogbeiträge länderspezifisch angelegt.[22] Die sechs Themen ermöglichten es, nationalstaatliche Grenzen zu überschreiten und die Beziehungen, Verbindungen und Brüche in der Kunstgeschichte Südostasiens als Region zu erforschen.[23] Sabapathy konstatiert in der Einleitung des Katalogs, dass die thematische Herangehensweise von *Modernity and Beyond* dazu diente, „Untersuchungen zur modernen Kunst und zu künstlerischen Praktiken in Südostasien, aber auch zu Tendenzen, die über die Bereiche der Moderne hinausgehen, hervorzuheben und anzuregen".[24] Die Ausstellung beschäftigte sich mit Nationalismus und Moderne, dem Realen und Mythologie, mit dem Selbst und dem Anderen sowie mit Urbanisierung, wobei sie sich zwischen der Moderne und dem „darüber Hinausgehenden" bewegte; sie verankerte den Ausstellungsdiskurs in den historischen Kontexten, die für die jeweilige Region spezifisch sind, und bot zugleich spekulative Ausblicke in die zeitgenössische Kunst Südostasiens. Abgesehen von dem „bescheidenen, aber wichtigen Zeichen",[25] das diese Ausstellung für die Überwindung nationaler Grenzen setzte, die das Schreiben über Kunst in Südostasien bis dahin kennzeichneten, sollte das im Ausstellungstitel in Aussicht gestellte „darüber Hinausgehende" eingehender betrachtet werden. Dabei gilt es besonders zu beachten, wie der Begriff des „darüber Hinausgehenden" im postkolonialen Kunstdiskurs der 1990er Jahre Verbreitung fand und wie er dank des Themas *Beyond the Future*, das 1999 als Titel der 3rd Asia-Pacific Triennial (APT) diente, weiterentwickelt wurde.

Wie genau ist dieser neue Raum beschaffen, der als das „darüber Hinausgehende" bezeichnet wird? Benennt er ein bestimmtes Ziel, oder war es ein bloßer Zufall, dass sowohl die 3rd APT als auch die Eröffnungsausstellung des Singapore Art Museum ihn in ihren jeweiligen Ausstellungsdiskursen verwendeten? Thomas McEvilleys Definition von der *vierten Phase der Identität* liefert eine Erklärung für den kometenhaften Aufstieg dieses Begriffs im postkolonialen kunsttheoretischen Diskurs. Bei der Herausbildung von Identität, behauptet McEvilley, gebe es eine vierte Phase, in der die Konstruktion von Identität höhere Ebenen erreicht. Dies gilt auch für postkoloniale KünstlerInnen, die in der vierten Phase der Identität „über Fragen von Identität und Differenz *hinausgehen*[26] und sich in Richtung Zukunft bewegen wollen".[27] Der Begriff „beyond" spielt daher auf die Zukunft an, in der die KünstlerInnen, die sich nun ihrer eigenen, von vielen komplexen Faktoren geprägten Identitäten viel sicherer sind[28] und die „der Zukunft entgegensehen, ohne einer eigentlich längst verlorenen Identität verhaftet bleiben zu wollen, sondern mit dem Gefühl, dass diese Identität (ebenso wie die des Kolonisators) etwas Vergangenes ist und dass die Zukunft neue, interessantere Identitäten für alle bietet".[29] Darin klingt Homi Bhabhas Interesse an einem neuen Raum an, den er als das „darüber Hinausgehende" [the beyond] bezeichnete und in dem sich eine neue kulturelle Identität verankern kann. Die Betonung der Zukunft signalisierte auch den Wunsch, den Kolonialismus zu verarbeiten und über Fragen einer „reinen" Identität hinauszugelangen, die darauf angelegt war, Widerstand gegen den hegemonialen Westen zu leisten; darin lassen sich Anzeichen eines allmählichen Wandels hin zu McEvilleys vierter (und letzter) Phase der Identität erkennen.[30]

### Die konzeptuelle Wende: *36 Ideas from Asia*

Die Ausstellung *36 Ideas from Asia: Contemporary South-East Asian Art* wurde 2002/2003 als Wanderausstellung unter der Schirmherrschaft der ASEAN organisiert und sollte einem europäischen Publikum zeitgenössische Kunst aus Südostasien vorstellen. In seinem Katalogvorwort erklärt der Kurator Sabapathy, dass die Ausstellung Südostasien im Hinblick auf die bildende Kunst neu kartieren wolle – „als eine Region, die man aus den von einzelnen Künstlern vorgeschlagenen Blickwinkeln betrachten sollte".[31] Damit wurde eine alternative Herangehensweise möglich, wobei die einzelnen KünstlerInnen als Mikrokosmen verstanden werden, die auf eine zunehmend globalisierte Welt reagieren und sich mit dieser auseinandersetzen – Mikrokosmen, in denen der umfassendere Makrokosmos, Muster und Tendenzen zum Vorschein kommen können, wenn die Interaktionen auf intelligente Weise stattfinden. Den Titel der Ausstellung erklärt Sabapathy wie folgt: Die Zahl 36 verweist auf die Anzahl der beteiligten KünstlerInnen, während *Ideas* die „Aufmerksamkeit auf die konzeptuellen Aspekte der Arbeiten" lenkt.[32]

Das kuratorische Konzept der Ausstellung entstand Ende 1999, als man Südostasien „inmitten einer politischen, wirtschaftlichen und sozialen Krise" sah.[33] Kwok Kian Chow, der damalige Direktor des Singapore Art Museum, erläuterte *36 Ideas*[34] mit einem Verweis auf den Popsong *DiobokObok*, dessen Titel im javanischen Dialekt auf „unruhige Gewässer und bewegte Verhältnisse in einem Aquarium anspielt, in dem die Fische unruhig und orientierungslos sind".[35] Als

Arbeitstitel für *36 Ideas* war *DiobokObok* bewusst gewählt worden, um „auf prägnante Weise das Gefühl [zu erfassen], das angesichts der unruhigen Zeiten und der dramatischen Ereignisse [d. h. der Finanzkrise] in Südostasien herrschte"; dass man sich für den Titel einer indonesischen Redewendung bediente, betonte regionale Bezüge.[36] Auch Choo Whatt Bin, der Vorsitzende des ASEAN Committee on Culture and Information, Singapur (COCI), formulierte die Notwendigkeit, die Realitäten Südostasiens zu benennen:

> Südostasien hat in den vergangenen Jahren dramatische Ereignisse erlebt. Die regionale Krise [die asiatische Wirtschaftskrise 1997] war zugleich ein Katalysator, der ein latentes Gefühl politischer, sozialer und kultureller Spannungen an die Oberfläche brachte und dramatische Wendungen auf der politischen und gesellschaftlichen Ebene nach sich zog. Die Geschichten und aktuellen Realitäten der Länder dieser Region spiegeln sich in den Kunstgeschichten und zeitgenössischen Praktiken südostasiatischer Künstler wider. Das ASEAN COCI beabsichtigt, die Wandelbarkeit der zeitgenössischen Kunst in der Region zu erfassen und die Anliegen zeitgenössischer Künstler in der Region einem internationalen Publikum näherzubringen.[37]

Die Ausstellungen des ASEAN, die bis dahin vom COCI gefördert worden waren, hatten friedvolle, schöne und sorgenfreie Narrative über die Kunst Südostasiens konstruiert, die sich innerhalb nationalstaatlicher Grenzen bewegten. *36 Ideas* markierte eine Abkehr hiervon, indem die Ausstellung eine neue Kartografie entwarf, welche die Konturen der aktuellen Gegebenheiten in der Region skizzierte. Man bewertete die Lage eher aus regionalen denn aus nationalen Blickwinkeln und als von schwelenden Spannungen, Differenzen, Brüchen und Heterogenität geprägt, auch wenn sich, wie Sabapathy ausführt, daraufhin Ausstellungsdiskurse manifestierten, die von den höflichen Floskeln der Kulturdiplomatie umrankt waren.[38] Zwei andere Autoren, Niranjan Rajah und Patrick D. Flores, trugen Essays bei, die eine eingehende Betrachtung verdienen.

Ihre Prämisse besagte: KünstlerInnen und Kunstwerke bringen neue Vorstellungen des Zeitgenössischen in der südostasiatischen Kunst hervor, oder KünstlerInnen und Kunstwerke bringen neue Vorstellungen hervor, um das Zeitgenössische der Kunst aus dieser Region zu verstehen. Patrick D. Flores' Essay „Homespun Worldwide: Colonialism as Critical Inheritance" liefert einen Überblick über zeitgenössische Kunst in Südostasien und zeigt dabei die Kontinuitäten der Kolonialität auf, die in der Gegenwart aufeinandertreffen und sich miteinander verknüpfen. So widersetzte sich Soe Naing in seinem Gemälde *Village People* dem ästhetischen Konzept der Perspektive als dem wichtigsten Modus räumlicher Darstellung, der in Südostasien von den Kunstakademien institutionalisiert worden war, die sich am Vorbild der École des Beaux-Arts orientierten; in diesem Gemälde ist der Bildraum verflacht und von Tendenzen der Volkskunst geprägt. Eine genauere Untersuchung der Kunstwerke zeigt, inwiefern ästhetische Eigenschaften wie Räumlichkeit, Form und Farbe nicht einfach von euroamerikanischen Idealen abgeleitet sind. In *36 Ideas* mit seiner Ausrichtung auf konzeptuelle Aspekte werden Ideen bevorzugt, die auf lokalen Weltanschauungen und Philosophien beruhen und die das Spezifische der zeitgenössischen Kunst in Südostasien betreffen. Künstler wie Soeung Vannara und Phy Chan Than entwerfen Kultur als Natur und greifen auf spirituelle Welten zurück, in denen Natur, Rituale, Geister und Kultur integriert und ineinander verflochten sind.

In seinem Essay beschreibt Niranjan Rajah die moderne und zeitgenössische Kunst in Südostasien, indem er den modernistischen Impulsen in den verschiedenen Nationalstaaten historisch nachgeht. Diese Impulse sind in allen Fällen durch den Kommunismus und Nationalismus sowie durch soziale Reformen und Ethnizität geprägt und wollen regionale, globale und transnationale Perspektiven in der Kunst entwickeln. Er verortet diese konzeptuellen Verfahren in den Werken von KünstlerInnen, die an der Ausstellung beteiligt waren. Diese Verfahren sind auch historisch bedingt und bilden eine Ideengeschichte, die die Entstehung zeitgenössischer Kunst in Südostasien beeinflusst. Niranjan Rajah hebt die Bedeutung „transnationaler Arenen"[39] hervor, die über nationale Narrative hinausgehen; er fordert dazu auf, dass sich die Kunst Südostasiens mit „den kulturellen Herausforderungen durch die Globalisierung und die neue Oberherrschaft" auseinandersetzt und so neue Herangehensweisen entwickelt.[40]

*36 Ideas* markierte den Beginn eines ernsthaften Versuchs, neue Herangehensweisen und Methoden des Kuratierens und des Nachdenkens über die Kunst und die KünstlerInnen der Region zu fördern, und ließ dabei frühere Vorstellungen und Vereinnahmungen von südostasiatischer Kunst als einer festgeschriebenen Kategorie hinter sich. Aus Niranjan Rajahs Sicht wird das Konzeptuelle in Ausstellungsdiskursen genutzt, um das Zeitgenössische der südostasiatischen Kunst zu historisieren; es ermöglicht ihm, die Quellen der Kunst im Lokalen, in den regionalen spirituellen und natürlichen Welten der KünstlerInnen zu verorten. Das Konzeptuelle ist ein Zugang, um Gebiete für eine tiefgehende Auseinandersetzung mit dem Zeitgenössischen zu erschließen, indem man sich mit den zugrundeliegenden Ideen beschäftigt, die die Kunstwerke verkörpern, und so ein oberflächliches Verständnis überwindet.

### Das Zeitgenössische in der Kunst Südostasiens: Ethnografische, thematische und konzeptuelle Herangehensweisen

Die Dekade von 1992 bis 2002 war prägend für die Ausstellungsdiskurse über das Zeitgenössische in der südostasiatischen Kunst. Die drei hier besprochenen Ausstellungen schlugen ethnografische, themenbezogene und konzeptuelle Herangehensweisen vor, um das Zeitgenössische als ein diskursives Feld der Kunst zu kartieren und weiterzuentwickeln. Die Hinwendung zum Konzeptuellen in *36 Ideas* lieferte die Theorien und Konzepte zur Kunst, die in dieser Region benötigt werden.

Vieles von dem, was über Kunst aus Südostasien geschrieben wird, beruht auf Ausstellungsdiskursen, die von Museen, Kunstinstitutionen und Galerien initiiert wurden und die wichtige, aber nur bruchstückhafte Narrative der Kunst dieser Region bieten. Ausstellungen bleiben auch weiterhin die vorrangige Ausdrucksform, um Kunst der Region vorzustellen. Sie sind mit vielfältigen Interessen verknüpft. Diese Ausstellungen beschäftigen sich als Orte des Diskurses mehr oder weniger erfolgreich mit Fragen der Region und Regionalität. Ausstellungsdiskurse über das Zeitgenössische, die innerhalb oder außerhalb der Region produziert werden, sind nie ausschließend. Meistens sind WissenschaftlerInnen aus der Region aktiv daran beteiligt, die südostasiatische Kunst außerhalb der Region zu vermitteln und zu kartieren; WissenschaftlerInnen, die von außerhalb kommen, spielen ihrerseits eine zentrale Rolle innerhalb der Region. Die ständigen Verschiebungen in den Ausstellungsdiskursen über zeitgenössische südostasiatische Kunst, durch die diese Diskurse in andere Felder wie asiatische Kunst, asiatisch-pazifische Kunst und euroamerikanische Kunst hineinwirken, bereichern und vertiefen das Wissen über Kunst und eröffnen weitere Möglichkeiten, geografisch übergreifende Vorstellungen von der Region und von Regionalität zu erforschen.

1    Comparative Contemporaries – A Web Anthology Project wurde vom Kritiker Lee Weng Choy initiiert; es begann mit einem eintägigen Symposion, an das sich ein zweitägiges Programm mit Workshops unter dem Titel Comparatives Contemporary anschloss, und wurde 2003 von The Substation organisiert. Die Web-Anthologie über südostasiatische Kunst wurde im Mai 2013 gelauncht. Siehe http://www.aaa.org.hk/Programme/Details/139 für weitere Details.

2    T. K. Sabapathy, „Regarding Exhibitions", in: *The Artists Village: 20 Years On*, Ausst.-Kat. The Singapore Art Museum, Singapur, 2008, S. 7. Sabapathy fordert RezensentInnen auf, sich nicht nur auf die Texte, die zu Ausstellungen produziert werden, sondern auch auf die Ausstellungspräsentationen zu konzentrieren.

3    Apinan Poshyananda, „Contemporary Southeast Asian Art in the New World Disorder", Computer-Ausdruck, Eugene Tan, Southeast Asian Studies Summer Institute, 29. Juni 1999.

4    Für eine aufschlussreiche Darstellung der Geschichte des Kuratierens in Südostasien, siehe Patrick D. Flores, *Past Peripheral: Curation in Southeast Asia*, Singapur: NUS Museum, 2008, S. 65.

5    T. K. Sabapathy, *Road to Nowhere: The Quick Rise and the Long Fall of Art History in Singapore*, Singapur: The National Institute of Education, 2010.

6    Das *Journal of Southeast Asian History* wurde in den 1970er Jahren in *Southeast Asian Studies* umbenannt.

7    In der zurückliegenden Dekade erschienen folgende Zeitschriften über südostasiatische Kunst: *Silpakorn University Journal* (Bildende Kunst, Ministerium der Künste, Thailand), *SentAp!* (Malaysia) und *C-arts* (Indonesien). Akademische Veröffentlichungen zur südostasiatischen Kunst sind ein relativ neues Phänomen; siehe Patrick D. Flores und Joan Kee (Hg.), *Third Text: Critical Perspectives on Contemporary Art and Culture*, Bd. 25, Nr. 4, Juli 2011; Nora A. Taylor und Boreth Ly (Hg.), *Modern and Contemporary Southeast Asian Art*, Southeast Asia Program Publications, Cornell: Cornell University Press, 2012.

8    Die Association of Southeast Asian Nations (ASEAN) wurde am 8. August 1967 gegründet. Ihre Gründungsmitglieder waren Singapur, Malaysia, Indonesien, die Philippinen und Thailand. Als weitere Mitglieder kamen später Brunei Darussalam (1984), Vietnam (1995), Laos (1997), Myanmar (1997) und Kambodscha (1999) hinzu. ASEAN ist politisch und kulturell heterogen und dient als Plattform, um den Dialog und die Zusammenarbeit zwischen ihren Mitgliedern zu erleichtern.

9    Andere Ausstellungen, in denen zeitgenössische südostasiatische Kunst unter Kategorien wie „Asien" und „Asien-Pazifik" subsummiert wurde, waren die Asia Pacific Triennial of Contemporary Art 1993 (Australien) und die 4th Asian Art Show 1994 (Japan); sie werden hier nicht behandelt, da sich der vorliegende Text darauf konzentriert, wie Vorstellungen von zeitgenössischer Kunst über die Region Südostasien in Ausstellungsdiskursen entwickelt wurden, die sich spezifisch auf diese Region konzentrierten. Die Frage, wie die konzeptuelle Kategorie Südostasien als kontingente Kategorie in anderen

Ausstellungen vermittelt wird, denen andere geografische Parameter zugrunde liegen, verdient durchaus eine wissenschaftliche Betrachtung, kann jedoch im Rahmen des vorliegenden Aufsatzes nicht untersucht werden.

10 Das ASEAN Cultural Centre wurde 1995 zum Asia Cultural Centre erweitert; Anlass war der 50. Jahrestag des Endes des Zweiten Weltkriegs. Interview mit Frau Yasuko Furuich am 5. August 2010 in der Japan Foundation, Tokio.

11 Die Fukuoka Asian Art Shows begannen mit der Asian Artists Exhibition/Contemporary Asian Art Show (1979/1980); 1985 folgte die zweite Asian Art Show; die dritte Asian Art Show wurde 1989 organisiert. Die vierte und letzte *Asian Art Show* fand 1994 statt, bevor sie 1999, mit der Eröffnung des Fukuoka Asian Art Museum, von der Fukuoka Asian Art Triennial abgelöst wurde. Es war auch kein Zufall, dass der Bürgermeister von Fukuoka City die Leitung der drei Asian Art Shows übernahm, die zwischen 1979 und 1989 vom Fukuoka Art Museum organisiert wurden. Als Plattformen und „Tor nach Asien" dienten die Asian Art Shows dem Aufbau politischer und wirtschaftlicher Beziehungen mithilfe der Kunst, in einer Zeit, als Japans Handel mit dem restlichen Asien zunehmend an Bedeutung gewann, wobei Japan das Zentrum bildete.

12 Interview mit Frau Yasuko Furuich am 5. August 2010 in der Japan Foundation, Tokio.

13 Nissim Otmazgin, „Japanese Government Support for Cultural Exports", in: *Kyoto Review of Southeast Asia*, Centre of Southeast Asian Studies, Nr. 4, Oktober 2003.

14 Nakamura Hideki, „The Self Awareness of Human Beings in Flux", in: *New Art from Southeast Asia 1992*, Ausst.-Kat. Japan Foundation, Tokio, 1992, S. 13.

15 Masahiro Ushiroshoji, „The Labyrinthine Search for Self-Identity – The Art of Southeast Asia from the 1980s to 1990s", in: *New Art from Southeast Asia*, 1992 (wie Anm. 14), S. 21.

16 Ibid.

17 Ibid.

18 Tani Arata, „Toward an Asian School of Contemporary Art", in: *New Art from Southeast Asia*, 1992 (wie Anm. 14), S. 104.

19 Ibid.

20 Homi Bhabha, „Beyond the Pale: Art in the Age of Multicultural Translation. Figurations for an Alternative Consciousness", in: Ria Lavrijsen (Hg.), *Cultural Diversity in the Arts: Art, Art Politics, and the Face Lift of Europe*, Amsterdam: K.I.T. Publications, 1993, S. 32.

21 Das Singapore Art Museum eröffnete eigentlich mit zwei Ausstellungen: *Modernity and Beyond: Themes in Southeast Asian Art* und *A Century of Singapore Art*.

22 Der Band *Modernity and Beyond: Themes in Southeast Asian Art* umfasst folgende Beiträge: Danielle van Poppel, „Glimpses into Art in Brunei Darussalam"; Joanna Lee, „From National Identity to the Self: Themes in Modern Indonesian Art"; T. K. Sabapathy, „Thematic Approaches to Malaysian Art History"; Ahmad Mashadi, „Some Aspects of Nationalism and Internationalism in Philippine Art"; ders., „Brief Notes on Traditionalism in Modern Thai Art"; Susie Koay, „A Preliminary Thematic Survey of Vietnamese Contemporary Art".

23 Die sechs Themen sind: 1. Nationalismus, Revolution und die Idee der Moderne, 2. Traditionen des Realen, 3. Modi der Abstraktion, 4. Mythologie und Religion: Traditionen im Spannungsverhältnis, das Selbst und der Andere, 6. Urbanismus und Populärkultur.

24 T. K. Sabapathy, „Introduction", in: *Modernity and Beyond* (wie Anm. 21), S. 7.

25 Ibid., S. 7-9.

26 Hervorhebung des Verfassers.

27 Thomas McEvilley, *Fusion: West African Artists at the Venice Biennale*, New York: Prestel, 1993, S. 11.

28 Dies im Vergleich zum Zustand ihrer Identität in den ersten Jahrzehnten nach dem Zweiten Weltkrieg, in denen viele postkoloniale Länder mit dem Beginn ihrer neuen Unabhängigkeit allmählich in McEvilleys dritte Phase der Identität eintraten.

29 McEvilley, op. cit.

30 Laut McEvilleys *Fusion: West African Artists at the Venice Biennale* beruht die vierte Phase der Identität darauf, dass die eigene Identität als ein Mosaik kultureller Einflüsse akzeptiert wird, das sich nicht aus einer einzigen (asiatischen, afrikanischen oder westlichen) Quelle, sondern aus einer Vielzahl von Quellen speist, und daher ebenso Synkretismus wie Eklektizismus nahelegt.

31 T. K. Sabapathy, „Thoughts on an International Exhibition on Southeast Asian Contemporary Art", in: *36 Ideas from Asia: Contemporary South-East Asian Art*, Ausst.-Kat. Singapore Art Museum, Singapur, 2002, unpaginiert.

32 Ibid.

33　Kwok Kian Chow, „Message", in: *36 Ideas from Asia* (wie Anm. 31), S. 10. Kwok ist derzeit Senior Advisor an der National Art Gallery, Singapur.

34　Das Singapore Art Museum wurde zusammen mit dem National Heritage Board mit dem Projektmanagement und der künstlerischen Leitung der Ausstellung beauftragt; siehe *36 Ideas from Asia* (wie Anm. 31), S. 124.

35　Ibid., S. 10.

36　Ibid.

37　Choo Whatt Bin, „Message", in: *36 Ideas from Asia* (wie Anm. 31), S. 8.

38　Sabapathy, „Curatorial Introduction", in: *36 Ideas from Asia* (wie Anm. 31), unpaginiert.

39　Niranjan Rajah, „Towards a Southeast Asian Paradigm: From Distinct National Modernisms to an Integrated Regional Arena for Art", in: *36 Ideas from Asia* (wie Anm. 31), S. 32.

40　Ibid, S. 35.

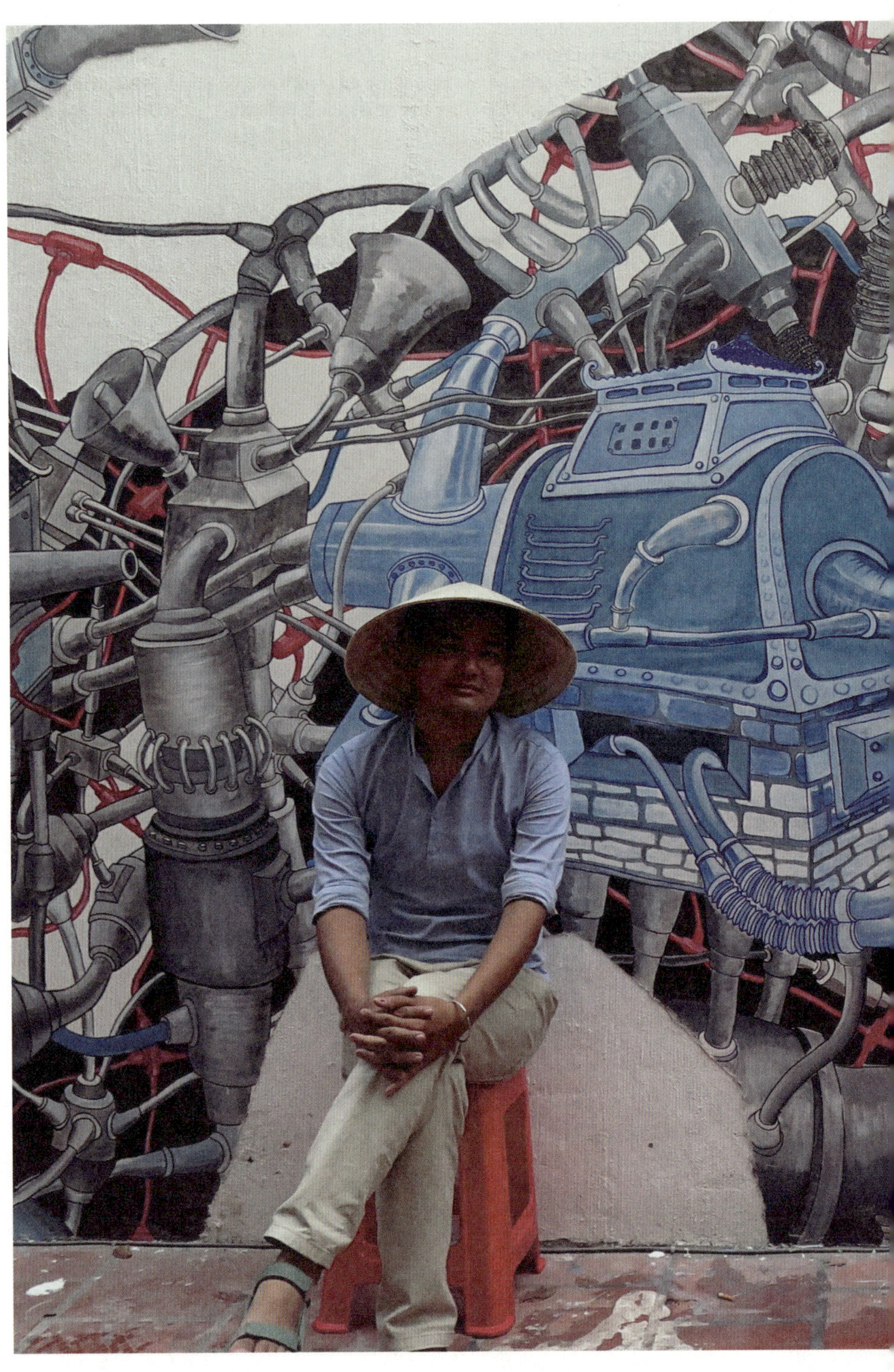

Bui Cong Khanh and friends in front of their mural
*The Puzzle of History*, 2015
Sàn Art, Ho Chi Minh City, Vietnam

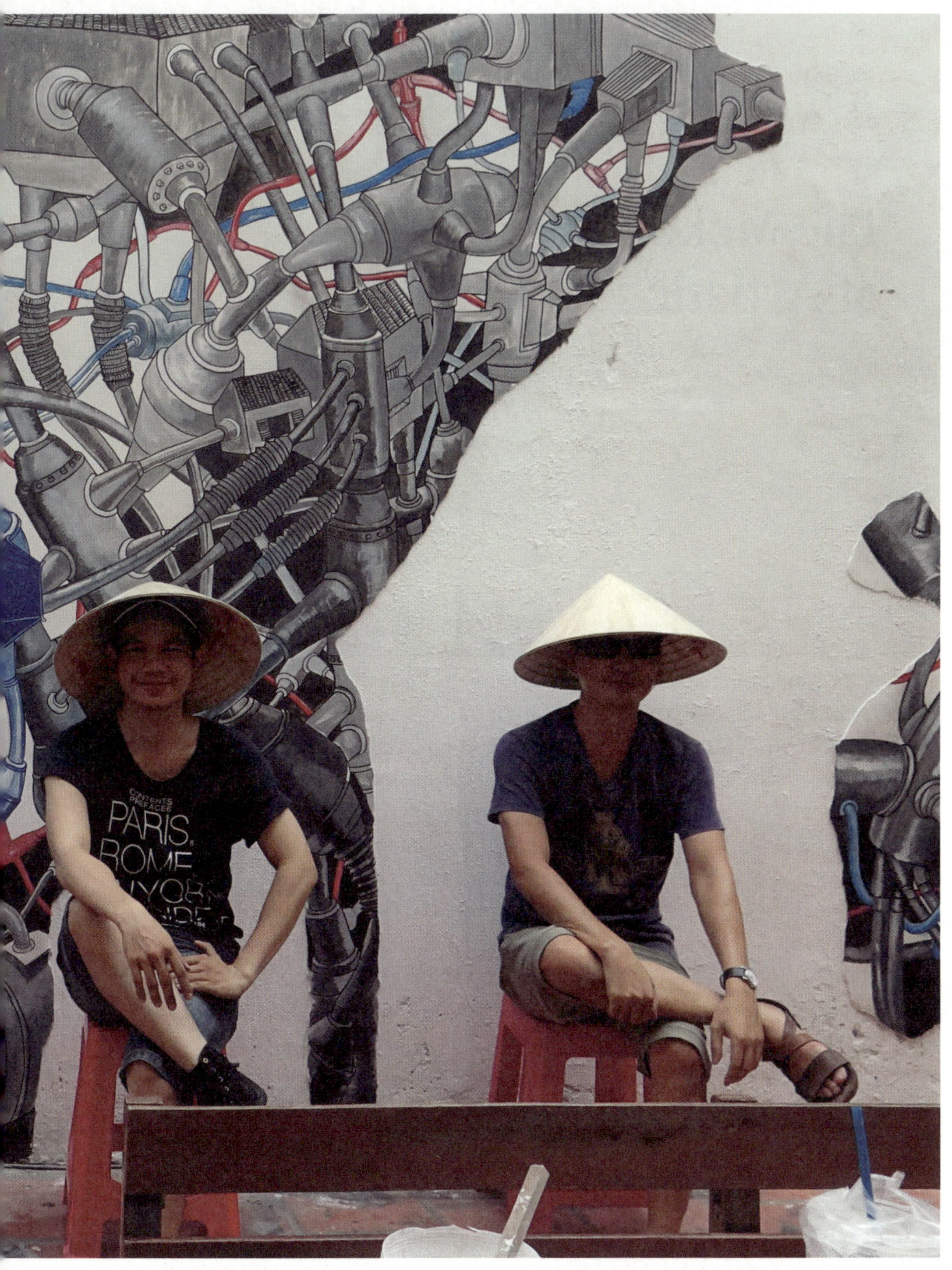

Gridthiya Gaweewong

# The Mekong as a Site of Artistic Production

There have been many different levels of artistic engagement and cultural exchange within Southeast Asia over the last decades, especially during the Cold War. These were facilitated mostly through the Association of Southeast Asian Nations (ASEAN). But the gatherings were conducted in a top-down manner and did not reach out to wider audiences. Few projects were implemented at the grassroots level and most were instigated by international agencies. At the end of the Cold War, funding from the United States—mostly from the Asian Cultural Council (ACC), the Rockefeller Foundation, and the Ford Foundation—generated many art and cultural programs related to Greater Mekong.

In 2000, the ACC, in collaboration with the Rockefeller Foundation, organized its first Forum on Arts and Culture in the Mekong Region, inviting academics, artists, and cultural workers to meet in Manila, Bangkok, and Siem Reap, respectively. I joined the Siem Reap meeting in 2003, right after a massive protest by Khmer activists against Thai pop star Kop Suwanan, whose controversial statement, "Angkor belonged to Thailand," provoked so much anger that the Thai embassy in Phnom Penh fell victim to an arson attack. During this conference, the ACC tried to figure out how to promote collaboration and cultural exchange between American artists and artists from Greater Mekong.

This initiative led to grants being given to researchers, curators, and artists in order to travel around the region and to try to find a way to work with each other, looking for "communal sharing" or senses of communitas among us. The notion of the communal later required a rethink in order to encompass differences, given that Southeast Asia is fragmented and multicultural. Since 2003, there have been many art-related projects focusing on Greater Mekong in Thailand, including the Mekong Art and Cultural Collaboration Project: Brainstorming Session, conducted in December 2003 and funded by the Heinrich Böll Stiftung in Thailand and their Southeast Asia regional office.

My preliminary research was funded by ACC: I spent about six months traveling around the region, also visiting the Kunming, Yunnan, area. Other types of projects were implemented within the Mekong subregion, mostly in the form of workshops and exhibitions. The yearlong Continuum Asia Project (CAP), directed by Ong Keng Sen of TheatreWorks, focused on people-to-people collaboration. Based on the principle of capacity building, it brought together elders from the Ramayana dance tradition of Laos, youths from the ancient palace town of Luang Prabang, and artists of Asia. Keng Sen then developed a multidisciplinary project, Continuum: Beyond the Killing Fields, a collaboration between Khmer traditional dancers and a puppet master, who narrated stories of survival during the Khmer Rouge regime. This project traveled around the United States and Europe.

I would like to look at the history of exhibitions that focus on Greater Mekong, most of which took place in the region's capitals. One example is the Mekong Art and Culture Project's exhibition entitled "Underlying." Curated by young curators from four countries—Cambodia, Laos, Thailand, and Vietnam—it toured the area from 2007 to 2008. The Faculty of Painting, Sculpture, and Graphic Arts, Silpakorn University, Thailand organized the project. They focused on nurturing young regional curators such as Vollak Kong, Misouda Heuangsoukhoun, Penwadee Nophaket Manont, and Le Ngoc Thanh from Cambodia, Laos, Thailand, and Vietnam, respectively. The project was designed to expand and encourage regional contemporary art and culture as well as provide valuable community-based learning experiences. It aimed to strengthen participating art institutes in the region in order to improve their theoretical and practical capacity, to create new knowledge, apply new approaches to art and arts education, open new avenues of exchange, transfer the results in order to facilitate cooperation among regional art institutions, and encourage members of the public and the greater arts communities within the region to be part of this collaborative movement. The conclusions of the curators' meetings were summarized in their unified exhibition concept, "Underlying," as well as the exhibition's sub-themes, and the choice of artists and venues in each country. The selected local curators interpreted the main theme based on their respective contexts.

The same year, France Morin, a Canadian curator based in New York, launched her long-term community art project "The Quiet in the Land," which used the artists-in-residence and exhibition format and invited international artists to work with the various communities in Luang Prabang on the banks of the Khang and Mekong rivers. This project expanded the geographical approach by using the Mekong River as a point of departure for collaboration and cultural exchange between artists and the arts community, making the Mekong a site of production and having artists work directly with the community.

The project in which I was involved was the brainchild of the late Montien Boonma, who returned from the Johannesburg Biennale wanting to create a regional art project. He started to talk about making the Mekong Biennale. Boonma was on the curatorial committee of Project 304, an alternative space that I co-founded and directed in the late 1990s, and we talked about how to get this concept off the ground. After his death, I continued to explore the possibilities of realizing this project. I received a grant from the ACC to conduct research in the Greater Mekong Subregion, which incorporates South China and the Kunming area. Based on my trips and a review of different biennials around the world, I looked into an alternative approach that was not a biennial nor was it tied to a specific country, rather it consisted of rotating projects within the region. During this period, however, many regional nations were experiencing political, economic, and cultural problems, which presented both drawbacks and challenges.

After the research trip I invited key people from each country to Chiang Mai for a brainstorming session aimed at conceptualizing the upcoming rotating Mekong Cultural Collaborative project within the Greater Mekong Subregion. The workshop took place over two days at Chiang Mai University. The idea was to create a platform for regional art and cultural workers to exchange information, strategies, and resources in order to come up with a new approach to artistic practice, to identify the issues related to the Mekong with regards to Thailand, and to define the relationships and significance to each community's country of origin. I also invited local partners from the cultural, political, and social arenas, as well as core members of Chiang Mai Social Installation (one of the important artist-initiated community and public art projects from the early 1990s) and activists from Chiang Rai to present the ecological system of the Mekong River. Many programs emerged from that brainstorming session including exhibitions, residencies, workshops, and capacity-building and educational programs that allowed local artists to collaborate with regional artists. We called this project Mekong Lab. After the brainstorming session and more research, I came to the conclusion that we were not ready to launch this project for various reasons—economics and politics, to be particular. The status of this project is thus pending, and I have kept the report and plan in my desk drawer ever since.

During this period, I also organized residency programs in Chiang Mai, inviting five artists from the region to stay for one month. This small, short-term, ad-hoc residency program was made possible through a grant from Arts Networks Asia, headed by Ong Keng Seng. The role of Arts Networks Asia as a supporter of the mobilization of artists within Asia has been enormous, but rarely credited and acknowledged in the wider context.

Singaporean artist Charles Lim was one of the first artists who participated in this brainstorming session as an observer and had the chance to meet many young artists from the area. Lim later started to develop his seminal series that explores the geobody of Singapore, *SEA STATE*, which focuses on the infrastructural, economic, and security system of Singapore, and the connectedness of the sea territory. Another resident, Saigon-based Vietnamese American artist Richard Streitmatter-Tran was interested in the Mekong to the point that he continued his research on the region with a grant from Asia Art Archives. This grant allowed him to get to know the region sufficiently in order to make "Mekong Platform," a project co-curated with Russell Stores at the 6th Asia Pacific Triennial of Contemporary Art in 2009.

### Shifting from a Metaphor and Source of Inspiration to the Site of Production

In more recent decades, as international funding to support the arts and cultural activities in the Mekong area subsided, the number of art programs fell. Regional exhibitions have continued, but they have become more institutionalized, and grassroots and artists-initiated projects have diminished. The Mekong region as a topic also became less present, however, though some artists and curators began looking at the Mekong again, but in a different way.

Art historian Pamela Corey's essay about international representation of Southeast Asian art, "Metaphor as Method: Curating Regionalism in Mainland Southeast Asia," raised important questions about curatorial approaches to particular geographic areas. She pointed out that the Mekong was used as a metaphor in major international shows, such as Streitmatter-Tran's "Mekong Platform" and the collaborative "Long March Project: Ho Chi Minh Trail in Vietnam and Cambodia."[1] This kind of regional approach in the exhibition helped elevate the area, but at the same time it also presented problems when the projects were executed, presented, and represented within the region and beyond. Corey questioned the use of metaphor:

> However, as regional metaphors—like the territories they speak for—are always in flux, the nuances of their meanings need to be historicized and further deconstructed as they are integral to apparatuses of knowledge production. For this discussion, I want to expand on the question of how—and for whom—a geographical metaphor endures, and the embeddedness of such metaphors in curatorial projects particular to mainland Southeast Asia.[2]

She referred to exhibitions in the region, and how the region was "represented" in different periods (colonial, Cold War, postcolonial, and the present). The "Mekong Platform" drew criticism from the Australian artist and critic Sue Hajdu, who pointed out that two things were missing: the role of China in dam building and regional border conflicts.

Some artists who did not romanticize the Mekong by drawing on the nostalgia of French Indochina or the Hollywood representation of the river during the Cold War tackled the critical points raised by Hajdu. They shifted from representation of the Mekong to presenting its reality as a site of artistic production. In the 2000s, the Mekong again became a hot topic, with many regional artists starting to reexamine the area in terms of its significance as a site of memory, its relationship to the Cold War, as well as its current situation as a source for water resources and energy through the construction of hydropower dams in China. The nostalgic and romantic idea and perception about Mekong as the battlefield, a border in the Cold War period, started to shift from memory to daily reality. A few regional artists have shown concern for the ecological problems of the Mekong River. Their recent works have focused particularly on the threat of dam construction on the upstream Mekong and its consequences for biodiversity as well as future water resource management.

In Vietnam, artist Tiffany Chung addressed the issue of flooding around the Mekong Delta and in Saigon. Drawn from her memories of war, Chung's *Floating Town* was constructed as a model proposal of floating houses and survival tools for future disaster relief and shown at the Singapore Biennale in 2011. She wrote:

> This work is based on a personal narrative that for years I had completely forgotten. After the fall of Saigon many families had to move to locations in the middle of nowhere. My mother also had to move because my father was in prison. We moved to the middle of the Mekong Delta and happened to be there during the historic flood in 1978. As a very young child, the only memory I had of this was of an enormous sea of water. Growing up I could never seem to get rid of this image of rising water. However I forgot about this story until last year when there was considerable media attention in Vietnam about China building eight hydropower dams in the upper reaches of the Mekong River and how that might affect the lower regions of the Mekong Delta. That's when I started to remember.[3]

Two years later at the 2013 Singapore Biennale, Laotian artist Bounpaul Phothyzan's installation *We Live* (2013) explored issues of ecological death and destruction on the riverbank. This work highlighted the changes made to the environment as a result of human action. He investigated changes spurred by severe drought during dry seasons and flooding during rainy seasons in the central area of the country. Fish skeletons not only acted as a reminder of the passing of sea life, but also served as a sign of human mortality.

On the other side of the Mekong River, opposite Vientiane, Laos, internationally acclaimed filmmaker and artist Apichatpong Weerasethakul started to work with the river. In his short film *Luminous People* (2007), he reenacted the ritual after his father's cremation when the family sailed along the Mekong and scattered the ashes down river. From that moment, he felt attached to the site, because it was where his beloved father's spirit remained. Coincidentally, Jenjira, his muse, also relocated to her hometown, the border town of Nong Khai, on the Mekong River.

During his research for *Uncle Boonmee Who Can Recall His Past Lives* (2010), Weerasethakul traveled around Thailand's northeast to look for Uncle Boonmee and visited many different villages. The research process was transformed into a video installation, *The Primitive Project* (2009), which was shown in the Haus der

Kunst, Munich. On the research trip, he noticed that along the river some areas were flooded while others were suffering from drought. This was at a time when the Mekong River Commission was dealing with water management on the Mekong River and there was considerable controversy about the proposed construction of dams along the river, with several dams to be built in China and a few in Laos. Thai environmental activists protested against the dam construction in Xayaburi, Laos, but without success.

While continuing to excavate the memories of the villages from ex-comrade farmers, monks, and fortunetellers in order to locate the real Uncle Boonmee, he went to Nabua, a small village in Sakon Nakhon that was the site of the first battle between the military and the comrade farmers in September 1965. But the ecological issues remained in his mind and he went back to the area again to visit Jenjira and to work on short film, video, and photography projects, which were articulations of his concerns surrounding the Mekong's ecological system.

During a trip to Nong Khai he produced the photographic series *For Tomorrow for Tonight* (2011). The Power Boy is part of this photography project. The series reveals the ecological system of the Mekong River and the paradox within the relationship between Thailand and Laos in the construction of the Xayaburi Dam, which is designed to produce electricity for Laos and the region. Thailand is the main consumer of this power, but even while Thai protestors demonstrated against its construction, they continued to use the electricity it generated. Thailand's hypocrisy in water resource management and dam construction was repeated on the Western side of the country, where a dam was built on the Salaween River in Myanmar rather than in Thailand.

In *Cactus River* (2012), a diary of Weerasethakul's visit to newlyweds Jenjira and a retired soldier from New Mexico, who live near the river, Weerasethakul reflects on the drought and low level of the river. That same year, he also produced *Mekong Hotel* (2012), a feature film based on the unrealized project "Ecstasy Garden," which was inspired by the Pob ghost,[4] folklore, animism, and the river's ecological system. *Mekong Hotel* is a portrait of a hotel near the Mekong River in Thailand's northeast, which marks the border between Thailand and Laos. The film shuffles different realms, fact and fiction, expressing the bonds between a vampire-like mother and her daughter, the young lovers and the river. The film, which was shot during severe flooding in Thailand, also weaves in layers of demolition, politics, and a drifting dream of the future.

Critics have praised the last six minutes of this film, commenting on the director's use of a long take of the river and its surroundings that invites viewers to contemplate the fact that slowness operates differently. It is less atomizing, as duration triggers a more interpersonal mode of spectating.[5] In the film, Weerasethakul invites viewers to study and ponder the Mekong River; he allows us to let us see the river as a thing in itself. Even though the artist now lives in Chiang Mai, the north of Thailand, Isan, along the Mekong, is still his primary location, his site of production.

These above-mentioned projects demonstrate how the artists in Greater Mekong gradually shifted their interest to look at the present condition and the reality of the river. They deconstructed the myth of the Mekong River as the Mighty Mekong and a Hollywood representation into something that is no longer a metaphor or fantasy.

In her essay, Pamela Corey mentions the river project launched by the Goethe Institut, Hanoi, in the early 2010s, which worked directly with the Mekong as a site and explored environmental issues. The Goethe Institut organized the "River Scapes in Flux," an international eco-cultural exhibition on the river landscapes in Southeast Asia and took it on tour in 2012–13 to Hanoi, Ho Chi Minh City, Bangkok, Phnom Penh, Jakarta, and Manila. Seven curators and seventeen artists participated in the project. Using the river as the main resource for transportation and economy, and the effects of the economy and climate change as the points of departure, the artists, who came from different river regions in Southeast Asia, demonstrated their concerns about the ecological system in works of art in an multidisciplinary manner. The exhibition sought to create a discourse on the key ecological issue in a new context and shifted the practice to the next level by encouraging artists and curators to think about the reality of the riverine system in the region in general. Although the production and research site was on the river, the show was held in the capitals—not all of which are situated on the banks of a river, especially the Mekong, but on the Red River, Chao Phraya, and Irrawaddy.[6]

Indeed, no exhibition on Greater Mekong has been held in which artists have worked and exhibited on site. The exception is "The Quiet in the Land," which brought international artists to Luang Prabang for a month's residency and focused on producing site-specific works. The exhibition was displayed at the National Gallery, Luang Prabang, and long-term community-based projects and workshops with schools and temples were held. In terms of artistic production, Jun Nguyen-Hatsushiba, Rirkrit Tiravanija, Vong Phaophanit, and Ann Hamilton dealt directly with the river. Phaophanit, a Laotian artist based in London, made a short film commenting on the transformation of his native country. More than twenty years after fleeing to Europe, Phaophanit came back to explore his country through different eyes, offering critical observation on the town that was once the royal capital of Laos and its metamorphosis to a tourist destination full of Chinese visitors.

The presentation and narratives of the Mekong that emerged in "The Quiet in the Land" included the artists' projections and perceptions—nostalgia for the mighty Mekong River, the serenity of Buddhism, and portraits of a slow and sleepy town. However, Phaophanit presented the harsh realities of today's Mekong. There is more to be seen in the projects by local artists, who transcend such exotic images of the Mekong and dived directly into the core problems posed by environmental issues.

In retrospect, it's still impossible to reinvoke the unrealized Mekong Lab project now, for many of the same reasons as before. Such situations remind us that this region still lacks the infrastructure and the capacity to initiate our own projects. We still need international support, and even though the region's economies have improved, our current political and social conditions does pose a challenge and do prevent us to collaborate more often with each other. The future of the Association of Southeast Asian Associations Nations (ASEAN) Economic Community (AEC) is still unknown and impossible to predict.

Suppression of rights and freedom of speech under the recent shift back to military rule in Thailand is a drawback for the AEC. If we want to realize a Mekong project that will be more appropriate for the situation and context, we must learn from past initiatives and exhibitions. This is quite urgent and we need to look more closely into the matter, as no one knows how much time we have. We have to be aware that the river and its ecological problems will not wait for us to react.

1    In 1999, the Chinese artist and curator Lu Jie launched the Long March Project out of a need to visualize social developments and changes in Chinese contemporary art. The project involving a number of artists, curators, and scholars made reference to Mao's Long March and the ideological and utopian notions associated with it. Long March Ho Chi Minh Trail is an expansion of the project initiated in 2008. "The Ho Chi Minh Trail is historically understood as a logistical supply route created during the Second Indochina War (1969-74), forming a vast network of passageways across China, Vietnam, Laos, and Cambodia. This rhizomic map offers useful reflection on the nature of overlapping histories of the region, providing strong metaphors and departure points for critical discussion. The area was the strategic battleground between the two Communist powers of China and the Soviet Union during the Second Indochina War, with China's decision to support Vietnam during this time being integral to Mao Zedong's domestic argument to gather the masses against Imperialist forces encroaching on its national borders (e.g. USA). This cunning decision not only announced China's support for revolutionist forces in Vietnam, but also encouraged Mao's grand plans for The Great Proletarian Cultural Revolution. The 'Ho Chi Minh Trail (Duong Truong Son)' project seeks to analyse the metaphorical legacy of this trail, engaging pertinent comparisons with broader international movements of social thought, strategy and intervention." (Zoe Butt, "Collapsing the Bilateral: Creating Conciousness," *Artlink* 29, no. 2 [June 2009], www.artlink.com.au/articles/3242/collapsing-the-bilateral-creating-consciousness. Editor's note)
2    Pamela N. Corey, "Metaphor as Method: Curating Regionalism in Mainland Southeast Asia," *Yishu, Journal of Contemporary Chinese Art*, no. 13 (March/April 2014): 72.
3    Tiffany Chung, artist talk "The River Project," August 28, 2010, Campbelltown Arts Centre, Sydney. See *Broadsheet* 39, no. 4 (2010): 284–88.
4    Pob ghost (ปอบ) is a kind of ghost in Thai folklore that exists in the Isan area. It is believed that this ghost likes to eat fresh flesh and is always hungry. A person who becomes a Pob ghost would have had magical power and shamanistic ability in life. Unable to protect their magical powers, they become Pob ghosts in death. Of either gender, the ghost possesses the body that will become a medium, eating the medium's organs, especially the liver and stomach, until they die. The explanation of this phenomenon notes that the Pob is the mechanism constructed by the villagers who wish to alienate others, whether strangers or community members who behave strangely. In the ancient times, such a person would be marginalized, alienated, and excommunicated from the village. (Translated by the author from the Thai Wikipedia page).
5    To understand this difference, we must unpack how the film presents its final shot as a vista. Vistas are views made possible by outlooks: a riverbank, the edge of a hill, a hotel balcony, and here, cinema. In Weerasathakul's filmmaking, a vista is not just a panoramic expanse; it is a shared view, a vision seen together and shared over time. See Karl Schoonover, "Slowness as Intimacy in Apichatpong's Mekong Hotel," *In Media Res*, http://mediacommons.futureofthebook.org/imr/2012/12/04/slowness-intimacy-apichatpong-s-mekong-hotel.
6    Available at http://blog.goethe.de/riverscapes, accessed on September 11, 2016.

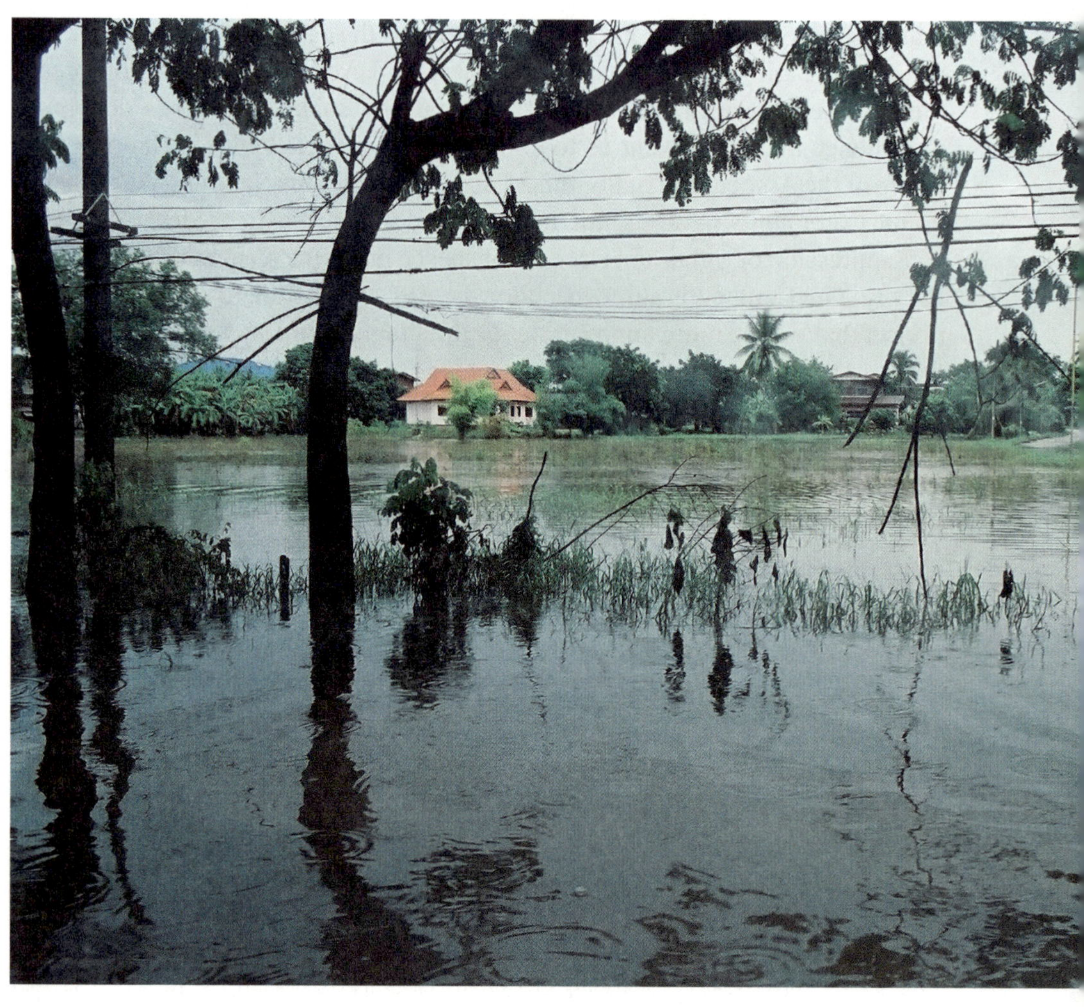

Apichatpong Weerasethakul
Nong Khai Flood, Research trip to Isan, Thailand, 2009

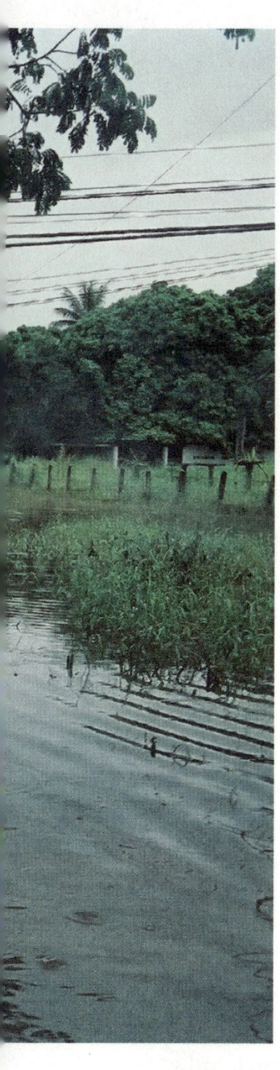

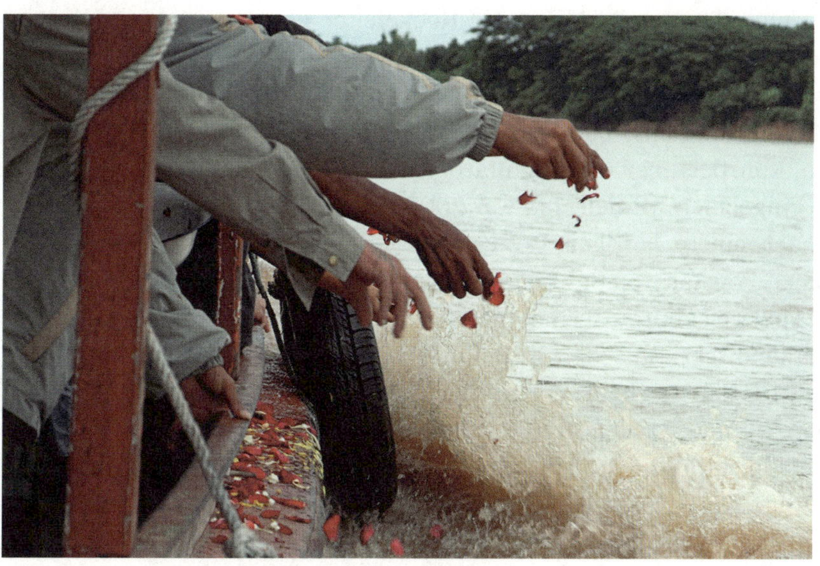

Apichatpong Weerasethakul
*Luminous People*, 2007
Film still

Gridthiya Gaweewong

# Orte künstlerischer Produktion entlang des Mekong

Südostasien hat in den letzten Jahrzehnten und vor allem während des Kalten Krieges unterschiedliche Initiativen zur Förderung von künstlerischem Engagement und kulturellem Austausch hervorgebracht. Die meisten dieser Initiativen wurden von der Association of Southeast Asian Nations (ASEAN) angestoßen. Die Treffen waren hierarchisch strukturiert und es war kein Interesse zu erkennen, eine größere Öffentlichkeit einzubeziehen. Nur wenige Projekte setzten an der Basis an – diese waren dann meistens von internationalen Initiativen angeregt. Gegen Ende des Kalten Krieges wurden viele Kunst- und Kulturprojekte in der Mekong-Region durch Fördergelder aus den USA ermöglicht, vor allem des Asian Cultural Council (ACC), der Rockefeller Foundation und der Ford Foundation.

Im Jahr 2000 organisierte das ACC zusammen mit der Rockefeller Foundation das erste Forum für Kunst und Kultur in der Mekong-Region, zu dem AkademikerInnen, KünstlerInnen und KulturarbeiterInnen nach Manila, Bangkok und Siem Reap eingeladen wurden. Ich war 2003 beim Teffen in Siem Reap dabei, das kurz nach einem heftigen Protest von Khmer-AktivistInnen gegen den thailändischen Popstar Kop Suwanan stattfand, der mit seiner umstrittenen Bemerkung „Angkor gehört zu Thailand" für so viel Verärgerung gesorgt hatte, dass die thailändische Botschaft in Phnom Penh Opfer eines Brandanschlages wurde. Das ACC hatte sich auf der Konferenz der Fragestellung gewidmet, wie Zusammenarbeit und Austausch zwischen KünstlerInnen aus Amerika und der Mekong-Region gefördert werden könnte.

In der Folge wurden Reisestipendien an ForscherInnen, KuratorInnen und KünstlerInnen vergeben, um neue Möglichkeiten der Zusammenarbeit zu suchen und ein stärkeres Gemeinschaftsgefühl zu entwickeln. Da Südostasien eine multikulturelle Region ist, erforderte dieses Programm ein starkes Umdenken aller Beteiligten, da kulturelle Differenzen offensiv einzubeziehen waren. Seit 2003 gibt es mittlerweile viele Kunstprojekte in Thailand, die sich mit der Mekong-Region auseinandersetzen, unter anderem das Mekong Art and Cultural Collaboration Project: Brainstorming Session, das im Dezember 2003 stattfand und von der Heinrich-Böll-Stiftung und deren regionalem Büro in Südostasien finanziert wurde.

Meine vorbereitenden Recherchen wurden vom ACC gefördert. Ich reiste etwa sechs Monate lang durch die Region und besuchte auch die chinesischen Provinz Yunnan mit ihrer Hauptstadt Kunming. Andere Projekte wurden direkt in der Mekong-Region realisiert, meistens in Form von Workshops oder Ausstellungen. Das Continuum Asia Project (CAP) etwa, das auf ein Jahr angelegt war und von Ong Keng Sen von TheatreWorks in Singapur geleitet wurde, kreiste um Fragen der Zusammenarbeit und war als eine Art Fortbildung durch Gruppenarbeit konzipiert. Es brachte die erfahrensten AkteurInnen der *Ramayana*-Tanztradition in Laos mit Jugendlichen aus der historischen Palaststadt Luang Prabang und KünstlerInnen aus Asien zusammen. Keng Sen entwickelte mit allen ein interdisziplinäres Projekt mit dem Titel *Continuum*: *Beyond the Killing Fields*, in dem traditionelle Tänzer der Khmer und ein Puppenspieler vom Überleben während des Regimes der Roten Khmer erzählten. Das Projekt tourte anschließend durch die USA und Europa.

Ich werde mich im Folgenden auf die Ausstellungen mit Fokus auf die Mekong-Region konzentrieren, die vor allem in den Hauptstädten der Region zu sehen waren. Beispielsweise entstand im Rahmen des Mekong Art and Culture Project die Ausstellung mit dem Titel *Underlying*. Das Projekt wurde von der Fakultät für Malerei, Skulptur und Grafik der thailändischen Silipakorn-Universität organisiert, von jungen KuratorInnen aus den vier Ländern Kambodscha, Laos, Thailand und Vietnam kuratiert und in den Jahren 2007 und 2008 an verschiedenen Orten der Region gezeigt. Die Initiative sollte vor allem regionale KuratorInnen aus Kambodscha, Laos, Thailand und Vietnam, wie Vollak Kong, Misouda Heuangsoukhoun, Penwadee Nophaket Manont und Le Ngoc Thanh unterstützen. Es ging außerdem darum, zeitgenössische Kunst und Kultur über die regionalen Grenzen hinaus zu fördern, bekannt zu machen und gemeinsame Erfahrungen zu sammeln. Darüber hinaus sollten die Kunstinstitutionen in den einzelnen Regionen dabei unterstützt werden, ihr theoretisches und praktisches Potenzial zu entfalten, neues Wissen zu generieren und neue Ansätze für die Kunstproduktion und Kunstvermittlung anzuwenden. Ziel war, die Ergebnisse der Projekte in die Kooperation zwischen regionalen Kunstreinrichtungen einzubringen und die Öffentlichkeit zu ermutigen, Teil dieser kollektiven Entwicklung zu werden. Die Ergebnisse mehrerer dieser Treffen flossen in das erwähnte Ausstellungskonzept von *Underlying* ein. Gemeinsam wurde über die untergeordneten Themen der jeweiligen Ausstellungen in jedem Land, die

Ausstellungsorte und die Auswahl der KünstlerInnen entschieden. Jeder KuratorIn war es letztendlich aber selbst überlassen, das Hauptthema der Ausstellung dem Kontext des eigenen Landes gemäß zu interpretieren.

Im selben Jahr startete das Langzeit-Projekt der in New York lebenden kanadischen Kuratorin France Morin *The Quiet in the Land*. Es sah Aufenthaltsstipendien und Ausstellungen vor. Internationale KünstlerInnen wurden eingeladen, mit verschiedenen Gruppen in Luang Prabang am Rande der Flüsse Kang und Mekong zu arbeiten. Die Flüsse waren geographische Ausgangspunkte für die Zusammenarbeit und den kulturellen Austausch zwischen KünstlerInnen und Künstler-Communities. So wurde die Mekong-Region zu einem Ort künstlerischer Produktion, und KünstlerInnen von außerhalb konnten mit den dort ansässigen Gruppen in unmittelbaren Kontakt treten.

Die Idee für dieses Projekt hatte der verstorbene Montien Boonma, der von der Johannesburg Biennale mit dem Wunsch zurückkehrte, eine in der Region angesiedelte Kunstinitiative zu entwickeln. Er sprach davon, eine Mekong Biennale ins Leben zu rufen. Montien Boonma war Mitglied des kuratorischen Kommittees von Project 304, einem alternativen Ort, den ich mitgegründet und in den 1990er Jahren geleitet hatte. Boonma und ich sprachen darüber, wie man die Idee einer Mekong Biennale in die Realität umsetzen könnte und nach seinem Tod arbeitete ich an dem Projekt weiter. Ich erhielt Fördergelder vom ACC, um in einem Teilgebiet der Mekong-Region zu recherchieren, die Südchina und die Kunming-Region umfasste. Meine Reisen und die Auseinandersetzung mit vielen verschiedenen Biennalen auf der ganzen Welt führten dazu, dass ich mich letztlich für ein alternatives Format entschied, das weder eine Biennale, noch an ein einzelnes Land gebunden war. Stattdessen sah es Einzelprojekte vor, die durch die Region wandern würden. Da viele der beteiligten Nationen zu dieser Zeit mit politischen, ökonomischen und kulturellen Problemen zu kämpfen hatten, waren wir im Planungsprozess mit einigen Herausforderungen und Hindernissen konfrontiert.

Nach der Rückkehr von meiner Forschungsreise lud ich wichtige Akteure jedes Landes nach Chiang Mai zu einem Brainstorming in Form eines zweitägigen Workshops ein, um mit ihnen gemeinsam das Mekong Cultural Collaborative Project zu planen. Es wurde unter anderem diskutiert, das Projekt in der Mekong-Region im Rotationsprinzip von Ort zu Ort wandern zu lassen. Bei dem Treffen sollten sich die eingeladenen Kunst- und KulturarbeiterInnen über Strategien und vorhandene Ressourcen austauschen, um neue Zugänge zu Fragen der Kunstproduktion zu ermöglichen. Zudem ging es um die Beziehung zwischen der Mekong-Region und Thailand und das Verhältnis der dort Lebenden zu ihrem Heimatland. Ich hatte auch Akteure der lokalen kulturellen, politischen und sozialen Szenen aus Chiang Mai eingeladen, sowie Mitglieder der Chiangmai Social Installation (einer wichtigen, in den 1990er Jahren von KünstlerInnen initiierten Gruppe, die öffentliche Kunstprojekte organisiert). Darüberhinaus waren UmweltaktivistInnen aus Chiang Rai dabei, die über das ökologische System des

Mekong-Flusses sprachen. Aus dem Brainstorming gingen viele Ausstellungen, Künstleraufenthalte, Workshops, Initativen für *capacity-building* und Bildungsprogramme hervor, die lokal angesiedelten KünstlerInnen die Möglichkeit boten, mit KünstlerInnen aus anderen Regionen zusammen zu arbeiten. Das Ganze tauften wir Mekong Lab. Nach dem Workshop und weiteren Recherchen war ich mir jedoch sicher, dass das Mekong Lab aus ökonomischen und politischen Gründen noch nicht reif für eine direkte Umsetzung wäre. Seitdem wartet das Projekt in meiner Schreibtischschublade darauf, realisiert zu werden.

Während dieser Zeit organisierte ich außerdem ein Residenzprogramm in Chiang Mai, das mir die Möglichkeit gab, fünf KünstlerInnen für einen Monat in die Stadt einzuladen. Es wurde durch ein Stipendium vom Arts Networks Asia ermöglicht, das von Ong Keng Seng geleitet wird. Die Bedeutung von Arts Networks Asia für die Mobilität von KünstlerInnen in Asien wird in größeren Zusammenhängen viel zu wenig gewürdigt.

Charles Lim aus Singapur, der als Beobachter am Brainstorming teilgenommen hatte, war einer der ersten Künstler, der auf diese Weise viele junge KünstlerInnen aus der Region kennenlernen konnte. Lim begann später seine wegweisende Projektreihe *SEA STATE*, die sich der Untersuchung des sogenannten *geobody* von Singapur widmet, einem Geflecht von infrastrukturellen, ökonomischen und sicherheitspolitischen Faktoren, anhand dessen sehr unterschiedliche Zusammenhänge in dieser vom Meer geprägten Region deutlich gemacht werden können. Richard Streitmatter-Tran, ein in Saigon lebender vietnamesisch-amerikanischer Künstler, der auch am Residenzprogramm teilgenommen hatte, fand die Mekong-Region so interessant, dass er seine anfänglichen Forschungen mithilfe eines Stipendiums des Asia Art Archives fortsetzte. Daraus ging die *Mekong Platform* hervor, ein mit Russell Stores kuratiertes Projekt, das 2009 auf der 6. Asia Pacific Triennial of Contemporary Art gezeigt wurde.

Von einer Metapher und Inspirationsquelle zum Ort künstlerischer Produktion
In den letzten Jahrzehnten gab es insgesamt weniger Kunstprojekte in der Mekong-Region, was unter anderem auf den Rückgang der internationalen Fördergelder für Kunst und Kultur zurückzuführen ist. Regionale Ausstellungsaktivitäten gab es zwar weiterhin, allerdings setzte eine stärkere Institutionalisierung ein und kleinere, privat initiierte KünstlerInnenprojekte wurden seltener. Das Thema Mekong-Region ist mittlerweile weniger präsent, einige KünstlerInnen und KuratorInnen scheinen jedoch auf neue und andere Weise auf den Mekong zu blicken.

In ihrem Aufsatz „Metaphor as Method: Curating Regionalism in Mainland Southeast Asia" spricht die  Kunsthistorikerin Pamela Corey über die Repräsentation von Kunst aus Südostasien im internationalen Kontext und weist auf wichtige Fragen zum kuratorischen Umgang mit einzelnen geographischen Regionen hin. Corey hebt hervor, dass der Begriff Mekong in großen internationalen Ausstellungen, wie Richard Streitmatter-Trans *Mekong Platform* und dem in Kollaboration entstandenen *Long March Project: Ho Chi Minh Trail in Vietnam and Cambodia*, als Metapher benutzt wurde.[1] Diese Art des Umgangs mit dem Mekong als Region in Ausstellungen führte einerseits zu einer Aufwertung, andererseits resultierten daraus auch konkrete Probleme für die Umsetzung solcher Projekte und ihre regionale und überregionale Vermittlung. Pamelas Kritik eines metaphorischen Gebrauchs von Mekong lautet:

> Da regionale Metaphern – genau wie die Territorien, für die sie stehen – in Zusammenhänge eingebunden sind, die sich ständig verändern, muss auch ihre Bedeutung historisiert und kontinuierlich dekonstruiert werden, da sie einen wesentlichen Teil der Wissensproduktion ausmachen. Im Rahmen dessen würde ich die Diskussion gerne auf die Frage lenken, wie und vor allem für wen geographische Metaphern tatsächlich Bestand haben, und wie sie in kuratorische Projekte eingebunden wurden, die in Südostasien stattfanden.[2]

Sie bezog sich damit auf Ausstellungen in der Mekong-Region und ihre Darstellung verschiedener historischer Abschnitte (Kolonialismus, Kalter Krieg, Postkolonialismus und Gegenwart). Das Projekt *Mekong Platform* etwa, wurde von der australischen Künstlerin und Kunstkritikerin Sue Hajdu in diesem Zusammenhang für zwei Auslassungen kritisiert: die Rolle Chinas beim Bau von Dämmen und die Grenzkonflikte in der Region.

Diese Kritik Hajdus rief einige KünstlerInnen auf den Plan, die sich einer romantisierenden Sicht auf den Mekong verweigerten und die mit nostalgischen Projektionen der ehemaligen Kolonie Französisch-Indochina oder verklärenden Repräsentationen Hollywoods während des Kalten Krieges nichts zu tun haben wollten. Die KünstlerInnen thematisierten den Mekong in ihren Arbeiten stattdessen als Ort künstlerischer Produktion. In den 2000er Jahren wurde der Mekong erneut ein heftig diskutiertes Thema unter ortsansässigen KünstlerInnen, die die Region als Ort der Erinnerung und ihre Rolle im Kalten Krieg neu beleuchteten und ihre aktuelle Bedeutung für die Wasser- und Energieversorgung durch Chinas Staudamm-Politik aufzeigten. Der nostalgisch und romantisch inspirierte Blick auf den Mekong als Kriegsschauplatz und Grenze im Kalten Krieg verschob sich von der Erinnerungskultur hin zu einer Wahrnehmung als Ort der Gegenwart. Einige der dort ansässigen KünstlerInnen waren angesichts der massiven ökologischen Probleme der Region sehr besorgt. Ihre künstlerischen Arbeiten konzentrierten sich vor allem auf die Bedrohung, die der Bau von Dämmen in den höher gelegenen Abschnitten des Flusses darstellt und die Konsequenzen, die sich daraus für die biologische Vielfalt und die Verteilung der Wasserressourcen in der Region ergeben.

In Vietnam hat sich die Künstlerin Tiffany Chung mit Überschwemmungen im Mekong-Delta und in Saigon beschäftigt. Ausgehend von ihren Kindheitserinnerungen an den amerikanischen Krieg, konzipierte sie die Arbeit *Floating Town*,

Modelle von schwimmenden Häusern und Notausrüstungen zum Überleben bei Überschwemmungskatastrophen. Zu ihrer Arbeit, die 2011 auf der Singapur Biennale zu sehen war, schreibt sie:

> Diese Arbeit geht auf ein persönliches Erlebnis zurück, an das ich mich viele Jahre lange nicht erinnert hatte. Nachdem Saigon gefallen war, mussten viele Familien an Orte ziehen, die im Nirgendwo lagen. Auch meine Mutter musste wegziehen, weil mein Vater im Gefängnis war. Wir zogen ins mittlere Mekong-Delta und waren dort, als 1978 die historische Überschwemmung passierte. Als kleines Kind war die einzige Erinnerung, die ich an diese Zeit hatte, ein riesiges Wassermeer. Während meiner ganzen Kindheit konnte ich das Bild eines ständig steigenden Wasserpegels nie ganz vergessen. Schließlich vergaß ich es doch, bis ich letztes Jahr durch ein gesteigertes Interesse der Medien in Vietnam auf die acht Staudämme aufmerksam wurde, die China am oberen Teil des Mekong-Flusses bauen wollte. Es wurde darüber spekuliert, welche Auswirkungen die Dämme auf die unteren Regionen des Mekong-Deltas haben würden. Das war der Moment, in dem ich mich wieder erinnerte.[3]

Zwei Jahre später war die Installation *We Live* (2013) des Künstlers Bounpaul Phothyzan auf der Biennale in Singapur zu sehen, mit der die ökologische Zerstörung am Mekong-Ufer thematisiert wurde. Die Arbeit wies auf die Folgen menschlicher Eingriffe in die Umwelt der Region hin. Bounpaul Phothyzan untersuchte insbesondere die Veränderungen, die sich im Innern des Landes abzeichneten: extreme Dürren in Trockenphasen und Überschwemmungen in Regenzeiten. Die in der Installation ausgestellten Fischskelette erinnerten nicht nur an das Meeressterben, sie standen auch für menschliche Sterblichkeit.

Auf der anderen Seite des Mekong-Flusses bei Vientiane in Laos begann der bereits international bekannte Künstler Apichatpong Weerasathakul seine Arbeit. Sein Kurzfilm *Luminous People* (2007) ist ein Re-enactment der Beerdigung seines Vaters, dessen Asche von der Familie während einer Bootsfahrt im Fluss verstreut wurde. Seitdem fühlt sich Apichatpong Weerasathakul diesem Ort verbunden, weil hier der Geist seines Vaters ruht. Jenjira Pongpas, Darstellerin in fast allen seiner Filme, zog es ebenfalls zurück in ihren Heimatort Nong Khai, eine Grenzstadt am Rande des Mekong-Flusses.

Während der Recherchen für *Uncle Boonmee Who Can Recall His Past Lives* (2010) reiste Weerasathakul durch Thailands Nordosten und besuchte viele Dörfer. Die Videoinstallation *The Primitive Project* (2009), die im Haus der Kunst in München gezeigt wurde, dokumentiert diese Recherchereise, bei der auch Weerasathakul feststellen mußte, dass manche Regionen entlang des Mekong von Überschwemmungen betroffen waren, andere von Dürren. Genau zu dieser Zeit verhandelte die Mekong River Commission über den Umgang mit Wasser am Mekong, was von heftigen Kontroversen begleitet wurde, die sich vor allem am geplanten Bau weiterer Staudämme in China und Laos entzündeten. Es gab Proteste von thailändischen UmweltaktivistInnen gegen den Bau des Damms in Xayaburim, Laos, die jedoch erfolglos blieben.

Als Apichatpong Weerasathakul seine Reise fortsetzte, um die Erinnerungen von Dorfbewohnern, ehemals kommunistischen Bauern, von Mönchen und Wahrsagern aufzuzeichnen – immer auf der Suche nach Onkel Boonmee – gelangte er in ein kleines Dorf in Sakon Nakhon, das im September 1965 Schauplatz der ersten Schlacht zwischen Militär und Genossen aus der Landwirtschaft gewesen war. Aber auch die ökologischen Themen beschäftigten Weerasathakul weiterhin und er kehrte in die Gegend, in der Jenjira Pongpas wohnte, zurück, um an Kurzfilmen, Videos und Fotografien zum Ökosystem des Mekong zu arbeiten.

Während einer Reise nach Nong Khai stellte er die Fotoserie *For Tomorrow for Tonight* (2011) fertig, deren Protagonist die fiktive Person The Power Boy ist. Mit dieser Arbeit weist Weerasathakul auf die Probleme des Ökosystems Mekong hin und zeigt die Spannungen im Verhältnis zwischen Thailand und Laos, die sich zuspitzten, als der Xayaburi-Damm gebaut wurde: Obwohl der Damm für die Stromversorgung in Laos errichtet wurde, bezieht Thailand den größten Teil der dort produzierten Energie. Und obwohl thailändische AktivistInnen gegen den Bau protestiert hatten, bezogen auch sie die Elektrizität von dort. Thailands Scheinheiligkeit bei der Verteilung von Wasserressourcen wurde auch im westlichen Teil des Landes sichtbar. Ein Staudamm, der im angrenzenden Myanmar am Salaween-Fluss gebaut wurde, kommt vor allem Thailands Stromversorgung zu Gute.

In *Cactus River* (2012), ein filmisches Tagebuch von Weerasathakuls Besuch bei der frisch verheirateten Jenjira und ihrem Mann, einem Militärveteran aus Mexiko, mit dem sie zusammen am Rande des Mekong lebt, beschäftigt sich Weerasathakul mit dem niedrigen Wasserpegel des Mekong zur Zeit einer Dürre. Im selben Jahr produzierte er auch *Mekong Hotel* (2012), einen Film, der auf dem nie realisierten Projekt *Ecstasy Garden* basiert, das vom thailändischen Pob-Geist[4] inspiriert ist, von Folklore, und Animismus. *Mekong Hotel* ist das Portrait eines Hotels in der Nähe des Mekong-Flusses im Nordosten Thailands, nahe der Grenze zu Laos. Der Film wurde während einer schweren Überschwemmung in Thailand gedreht, stellt Bezüge zwischen Faktischem und Fiktionalem her und erzählt die Geschichte der Beziehungen einer vampirhaften Mutter zu ihrer Tochter, zweier junger Liebender und ihrer Bindung zum Fluss. Auf einer anderen Ebene erzählt der Film auch von Zerstörung, von politischen Zusammenhängen und Zukunftsträumen, die der Fluss mit sich nimmt.

KritikerInnen haben vor allem die letzten sechs Minuten des Films gelobt. Die lange Kameraeinstellung, die den Fluss und seine Umgebung zeigt, lädt die BetrachterInnen ein, darüber nachzudenken, dass Langsamkeit eigenen Gesetzen folgt. Sie zergliedert Erfahrungen weniger in einzelne Momente und unterstützt eine Betrachtung, die stärker an Zusammenhängen und Zwischenmenschlichem interessiert ist.[5] Weerasathakul lädt die BetrachterInnen ein, über den

Mekong nachzudenken und ihn genauer zu untersuchen, damit sie den Fluss als eigenständigen Organismus wahrnehmen. Obwohl der Künstler jetzt in Chiang Mai, im Norden Thailands lebt, ist Isan am Mekong weiterhin der Ort, an dem seine künstlerische Produktion stattfindet.

Die geschilderten Projekte zeigen, wie das Interesse der KünstlerInnen in der Mekong-Region sich langsam verändert und auf ihre aktuelle Lebenssituation und die Realitäten des Flusses richtet. Der Mythos des Mekong-Flusses als Sinnbild des Mächtigen und seine Hollywood-Repräsentation wurde dekonstruiert und in etwas umgewandelt, das nicht mehr nur Metapher oder Fantasieprodukt ist.

In ihrem Essay erwähnt Pamela Corey ein Projekt über den Mekong und seine ökologischen Bedingungen, das in den frühen 2010er Jahren vom Goethe-Institut in Hanoi initiiert wurde. *River Scapes in Flux* war eine Ausstellung mit internationaler Ausrichtung. Sie thematisierte Ökologie und Kultur in Flusslandschaften Südostasiens und war von 2012 bis 2013 in Hanoi, Ho-Chi-Minh-Stadt, Bangkok, Phnom Penh, Jakarta und Manila zu sehen. Am Projekt nahmen sieben KuratorInnen und siebzehn KünstlerInnen teil, die aus verschiedenen Flussregionen Südostasiens kamen. Ihr gemeinsamer Ausgangspunkt war der Fluss als Verkehrsader, ökonomische Ressource und Ort, an dem sich der Klimawandel besonders folgenreich auswirkt. Ihr Anliegen mündete in genreübergreifende Arbeiten zum Ökosystem des Flusses. Die KünstlerInnen und KuratorInnen wurden aufgefordert, neu über den Fluss als eigenständigen Organismus in der Region und damit verbundene wichtige ökologische Themen nachzudenken. Obwohl die Recherche und Produktion der ausgestellten Arbeiten an den Flüssen stattgefunden hatte, waren die Ausstellungen in den Hauptstädten zu sehen, die zum Teil weit von den Flüssen Mekong, dem Roten Fluss, Chayo Phraya oder Irrawaddy entfernt liegen.[6]

Es gibt bisher tatsächlich keine Ausstellung in der Mekong-Region, bei der KünstlerInnen vor Ort produziert *und* ausgestellt haben. Die Ausnahme stellt das Projekt *The Quiet in the Land* dar, das internationale KünstlerInnen für einen Monat in Luang Prabang versammelte, die dort ortsspezifische Arbeiten schufen. Ausstellungsort war die Nationalgalerie in Luang Prabang, außerdem wurden Langzeitprojekte in Gemeinden initiiert und Workshops in Schulen und Tempeln abgehalten. Jun Nguyen-Hatsushiba, Rirkrit Tiravanjia, Vong Phaophanit und Ann Hamilton bezogen sich in ihren künstlerischen Arbeiten direkt auf den Fluss. Phaophanit, ein Künstler aus Laos, der in London lebt, drehte einen Kurzfilm, der sich mit Veränderungen in seinem Heimatland auseinandersetzte. Mehr als zwanzig Jahre nach seiner Flucht nach Europa kehrte Phaophanit nach Laos zurück, um kritisch festzustellen, dass die Stadt, die einst königliche Hauptstadt war, eine Metamorphose durchlebt hatte und zur Touristenattraktion für chinesische Urlauber geworden war.

Die Arbeiten und Narrative, die im Rahmen von *The Quiet in the Land* entstanden waren, machten mentale Projektionen und konkrete Eindrücke sichtbar, die die eingeladenen KünstlerInnen mit der Mekong-Region verbanden – eine Gewisse Nostalgie für den mächtigen Fluss, Gleichmut, der im Buddhismus zu finden ist, und Portaits verschlafener Städte am Fluß. Phaophanit hingegen entschied sich für die Darstellung einer harschen Realität in der heutigen Mekong-Region. Auch lokale KünstlerInnen lassen exotisierende Darstellungen des Mekong hinter sich und beschäftigen sich konkret mit zentralen Problemen der Umwelt.

Rückblickend scheint es noch immer unmöglich, das Mekong Lab umzusetzen. Die Vergangenheit zeigt, dass es uns als Region immer noch an Infrastrukturen und Möglichkeiten mangelt, eigene Projekte zu initiieren. Wir benötigen nach wie vor internationale Unterstützung und obwohl sich unsere ökonomische Situation verbessert hat, erlaubt unsere aktuelle politische und soziale Realität noch keine intensivere Zusammenarbeit. Es ist schwer vorhersehbar, wie sich die Association of Southeast Asian Associations Nations (ASEAN) Economic Community (AEC) weiterentwickeln wird.

Die Unterdrückung der Bevölkerung und ihrer Rechte, die mit der derzeitigen Rückkehr zur Militärregierung in Thailand verbunden ist, bedeutet auch für die AEC einen Rückschlag. Wenn wir in Zukunft Projekte in der Mekong-Region realisieren wollen, die sich sinnvoll mit unserer Situation und den gegebenen Realitäten auseinandersetzen, müssen wir aus den Initiativen und Kunstprojekten der Vergangenheit lernen. Wir wissen nicht, wie viel Zeit uns noch bleibt. Wir müssen uns darüber im Klaren sein, dass die ökologische Situation des Flusses keinen weiteren Aufschub erlaubt.

1   1999 initiierte der chinesische Künstler und Kurator Lu Jie das Long March Project aus dem Bedürfnis heraus, gesellschaftliche Entwicklungen und sozialen Wandel in der zeitgenössischen Kunst Chinas Sichtbarkeit zu verschaffen. Das Projekt, in das viele KünstlerInnen, KuratorInnen und WissenschaftlerInnen involviert waren, nahm Bezug auf Maos langen Marsch und die damit verknüpften ideologischen und utopischen Vorstellungen. Long March Ho Chi Minh Trail ist eine Erweiterung des Projekts, die im Jahr 2008 angestoßen wurde. „Historisch betrachtet war der Ho-Chi-Minh-Pfad eine logistische Versorgungsroute, die während des zweiten Indochinakriegs (1969–1974) entstanden ist und ein weit verzweigtes Wegenetz durch China, Vietnam, Laos und Kambodscha bildete. Diese rhizomatische Karte regt dazu an, der miteinander verwobenen Geschichte der Region nachzugehen und bietet starke Metaphern und Ausgangspunkte für eine kritische Diskussion. Die Region war während des zweiten Indochinakriegs ein strategisches Schlachtfeld zwischen den beiden kommunistischen Mächten China und der Sowjetunion, wobei Chinas Entschluss, Vietnam zu unterstützen, ein wesentlicher Bestandteil von Mao Zedongs innenpolitischem Argument war, die Massen gegen die imperialistische Gefahr an Chinas Grenzen (z.B. die USA) zu mobilisieren. Diese Entscheidung kündigte nicht nur Chinas Unterstützung der revolutionären Kräfte in Vietnam an, sondern stützte auch Maos hochfliegenden Pläne für die Große Kulturrevolution. Das Projekt Ho Chi Minh Trail (Duong Truong Son) versucht das metaphorische Vermächtnis des Pfads zu analysieren, indem relevante Vergleiche mit allgemeineren internationalen Bewegungen im Bereich gesellschaftlicher Theorien, Strategien und Interventionen angestellt werden." (Zoe Butt, „Collapsing the Bilateral: Creating Consciousness", in: *Artlink*, Bd. 29, Nr. 2, Juni 2009; www.artlink.com.au/articles/3242/collapsing-the-bilateral-creating-consciousness.)

2   Pamela N. Corey, „Metaphor as Method: Curating Regionalism in Mainland Southeast Asia," in: *Yishu, Journal of Contemporary Chinese Art*, Nr. 13, März/April 2014, S. 72.

3   Tiffany Chung, Künstlergespräch zu The River Project, 28. August 2010, Campbelltown Arts Centre, Sydney. Vgl. *Broadsheet* 39, Nr. 4, S. 284-288.

4	Der Pob-Geist (ปอบ) ist eine Art Geistwesen in der thailändischen Folklore, die in der Region Isan im Nordosten verbreitet ist. Es wird geglaubt, dass der Geist gerne frisches Fleisch isst und immer hungrig ist. Eine Person, die zum Pob-Geist wird, hat magische Kräfte und schamanistische Fähigkeiten. Weil es als Lebender jedoch nicht möglich ist, diese Kräfte abzuschirmen und zu behalten, ist der Tod unvermeidlich. Der Pob-Geist nimmt dann Besitz vom Körper des Mediums, das Mann oder Frau sein kann, und isst die Organe, besonders die Leber und den Magen, bis der Tod eintritt. Die Erklärung, die sich zu diesem Phänomen des Aberglaubens finden lässt, lautet, dass *Pob* als Mechanismus verstanden werden kann, mit dem die Dorfbewohner Einzelne ausgrenzen konnten, sowohl Fremde als auch Mitglieder der Gemeinschaft, die durch merkwürdiges Verhalten auffielen. In früheren Zeiten wurde eine solche Person ausgegrenzt und aus dem Dorf vertrieben. (Übersetzung aus dem thailändischen Wikipedia durch die Autorin)

5	Um diesen Unterschied zweier Betrachterperspektiven besser zu verstehen, muss man sich genauer ansehen, wie der Film seine letzte Einstellung als Aussicht (vista) präsentiert. Eine Aussicht ist eine Betrachterperspektive, die durch den Blick von etwas herab oder aus etwas heraus ermöglicht wird: ein Ufer, der Grat eines Berges, ein Hotelbalkon oder, wie in diesem Fall, ein Kino. In Weerasathakuls Film ist eine Aussicht nicht nur eine Panorama-Einstellung, sondern ein gemeinsamer Blick auf etwas, eine Vision von etwas, die über einen längeren Zeitraum hinweg geteilt wird. Vgl. Karl Schoonover, „Slowness as Intimacy in Apichatpong's Mekong Hotel," in: *In Media Res*, 4. Dezember 2012, http://mediacommons.futureofthebook.org/imr/2012/12/04/slowness-intimacy-apichatpong-s-mekong-hotel, abgerufen am 31. Juli 2016.

6	http://blog.goethe.de/riverscapes, abgerufen am 11. September 2016.

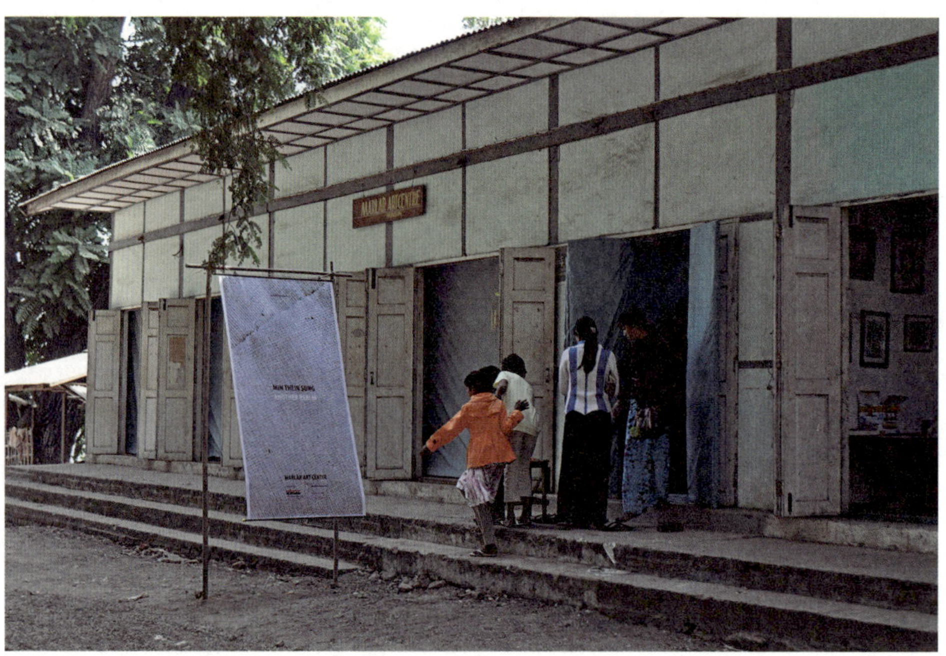

Marlar Art Centre
Mingun, Sagaing, Myanmar

Yin Ker

# Why Play? An Outsider's Point of View on Making and Seeing Art in Myanmar Today

Public space in Myanmar is a monitored one.[1] It is not a condition that is unique to the country, but witnesses do suggest that Big Brotherism is comparatively pervasive in at least its densely populated areas. In the most extreme of cases, shared space is a stage on which the individual lives out his or her days in perpetual performance before the scrutiny of other individuals. There are the eyes of parents, the eyes of siblings, the eyes of teachers, the eyes of friends, the eyes of neighbors, the eyes of strangers, the eyes of rivals, the eyes of the government–themselves no less subjected to the probing eyes of those they track or mind. Eyes watch at every corner of the street, in every space beyond the walls of a bathroom, with consequences ranging from the innocuous to the precarious, depending on who is watching and what is being watched. Is it any coincidence that Min Thein Sung makes the toilet the seat of respite in *Restroom* (2008-10)? For the artist or writer seeking to exhibit or publish, there is a more ominous end: censorship. Even though not all eyes seek to censure and punish–apart from the authorities' henchmen, there are the watchful neighbor, the caring teacher, and the anxious parent who watch out of curiosity, concern, and love even–they add to the intensity of the glare like small spotlights. They swathe the individual and weigh down his or her every thought and movement.

Of the above outsider's impressions of public space in Myanmar, what is significant apropos an enquiry into contemporary Burmese artistic production is how the Orwellian setting of urban Myanmar, which impact the artists' personal and professional lives in ways more than one, might shape their stratagems to circumvent the pressures and obstacles encountered on a daily basis, whether deliberately or unconsciously. Implicated by extension are the ways of curating contemporary Burmese art–if the relatively unexplored terrain of Burmese art's contextual significances are to be respected in spite of its mounting affiliation with international narratives, as the preliminary survey that is "plAy: Art from Myanmar Today"[2] sought to. By "contextual significances," we mean the aggregate of factors conditioning its experience today. It is an approach to Myanmar that finds faint echo in the one-dimensional narrative perpetuated in international media, which has made politics the principal lens for interpreting almost every aspect of the country. The military government has been conveniently cited as the single cause of all woes ranging from the humanitarian to the psychiatric and the moral, independently of the complications of the colonial legacy in Myanmar, and the common assumption that politics alone can *and* must define Burmese art is but one of the many collateral misfortunes.

Admittedly, a military government since 1962 has ruled Myanmar; an entire generation of artists has grown up–or grown old–under it. The men in green command and the others obey. An open society has never been on the horizon, and this has been the country's incident music for close to half a century. Still, it would be too facile–spurious even–to give the military government full credit for the country's deviant situation, just as it would be ludicrous to deny its hand in Myanmar's state of affairs today. Clearly, as for many other aspects of her society, the roots of the observed surveillance phenomenon are neither purely institutional nor cultural; realities on the ground are infinitely more complex than the media's dichotomic partition of Burmese politics. As much as we cannot turn a blind eye to the country's politico-social particularities, without which it is impossible to fathom the contexts in which the artists operate, politicized paradigms fail to reflect the full complexity of Burmese artistic practice. In fact, they obscure any constructive discussion of Myanmar. In other words, without undermining the implications of Myanmar's political situation, is there not much more going on in the country than politics, from which meaningful frameworks for looking at, presenting, and discussing contemporary art in Myanmar may be derived?

The steady supply of reports and analyses on the human rights abuses and humanitarian disasters endured by Myanmar's pious citizenry whose woes seem to know no end do not constitute breaking news anymore, and it would be blasé and vulgar to harp on the country's political fiasco or to dwell on the brutal punishments meted out for the mildest defiance on the pages of a publication. Idle chatter that sensationalizes the system's transgressions would be an insult to the many who have sacrificed beyond measure for expressing an opinion or for speaking what they value above their life even. Indeed, what good is there in fueling darkling perspectives on the country, intensifying the demonization of the persecutor along with the glorification of victimhood, or disseminating the fear on which the torturer feeds by reiterating the self-evident, if the situation cannot be mitigated in the process? Besides, is the demystification of the political impasse, which has captivated dilettantes, scholars, and activists for decades, not best left to pundits more qualified who hopefully know better than the curator and art historian? There is nothing new that the chicken can tell the duck about the pond.

Until a firmer grasp of the matrix of Burmese society is arrived at through studies extending beyond the stalemate of politics, it is perhaps a ludic interpretation of her artists' strategies that would allow for the least biased and most comprehensive experience of her very eclectic artistic production. It permits an entry point imposing minimal preconceived notions on what constitutes contemporary Burmese art, allowing the nuances of her realities to surface without excessive manipulation. In engaging with Myanmar's contemporary art through a relatively universal concept, the curators seek to unshackle it from the politicization of Myanmar and to bring it into the folds of international art–not only so that the Burmese artists might benefit from the exposure and conversations, but also for the purpose of enriching contemporary art discourses eventually. The conscious decision to reject politicized takes in "plAy" is moreover out of consideration for the safety and interests of all individuals involved in the project, whose stakes in the country are professional as well as affective. Indeed, the decision to adopt "play" as the theme for the largest platform to date for Burmese contemporary creation is motivated by reasons both ideological and pragmatic. Its pertinence merits a brief exposition.

For an artist, alongside Myanmar's surveillance culture, but graver still, would be censorship. The literary arts were perhaps the first and hardest hit. As swiftly as a year after the coup in 1962, editors were arrested and publishing houses closed down. The dos-and-don'ts on printed matter explicitly spelt out since 1975–Anna Allott's *Inked Over, Ripped Out: Burmese Storytellers and the Censors* (1993) provides a succinct overview of its genesis–have challenged writers to no end: how does one stay true to one's art without sacrificing personal freedom or losing one's life? In the case of the visual arts, no set of clear-cut guidelines exists. There is also a distinction between public exhibitions and private shows which are not subjected to the same censorship procedure. While it is quite certain that works liable to be interpreted as expressing violent emotions will be suppressed, along with nudes or works in primarily black and red, for example, there is no set of hard and fast regulations known to artists. To the bewilderment of the art community, strikingly provocative works have been approved while relatively innocuous ones have been banned. Indeed, in tandem with the margin of maneuver is arbitrariness, which keeps even the most seasoned artists on their toes. The fate of an exhibition whose preparation spans an entire year or more is decided within a couple of hours over refreshments by censorship representatives whose worth has been proven in any field but art, and whose justification for censoring an artwork may be as artless as "too much black and not enough pink." This is not a hypothetical.

Fear eats into the soul. It is dread for that which has no name. Burmese artists walk a tightrope between maximizing their creative potential and bypassing censorship laws whose criteria can be truly enigmatic. When playing ball in the dark, one imagines a shadow when there really is none. The stress can be overwhelming. So far, there is no known record of any human being from anywhere in the world who has succumbed to the pressures of uncertainty, scrutiny, and censorship, but it should be no a surprise that they are more difficult to live with than to die from. It is in this climate of surveillance and trepidation that "play" is particularly salutary: if to live means no more than a performance according to the rules, expectations, and whims of others, there must be means of respite and refuge so that the trial that is life is not renounced en masse. According to Dutch cultural historian Johan Huizinga in *Homo Ludens: A Study of the Play-Element in Culture* (1938), man is not just one who makes (*Homo Faber*) but also a "playing man" (*Homo Ludens*).[3] Play can be as straightforward as a child's game or much more; it is laughter and the comic, but exceeds them, for it is seriousness of a primeval expression. Donning the garb of paradox beyond logic, it operates in defiance of reason (though not wisdom), and transcends conventional truths. As such, through play, it becomes possible for an individual's mind to operate from an exalted sphere without physically leaving the stage that is one's duty or damnation. This state of mind embraces alternative paradigms whose boundaries are defined by the player alone, ergo bypassing established order. Without doubt, Burmese artists know all too well that head-on confrontations with the authorities will not get them far. They have also learnt that there are always multiple ways to articulate each issue, that equivocality is power. "All roads lead to Rome" and "there is always more than one way to skin a cat"; these two phrases are best appreciated by the dispossessed but resourceful.

The thirst for self-expression is universal, and the need for it real, no matter how narrow the leeway for expression and the luxury of it. It is every sentient being's prerogative to exercise his or her will and to act as he or she deems fit. While the Burmese people's perception of normality, their threshold for pain, their aspirations, etc., understandably deviate from those who live beyond the country's borders, axiomatically, their fundamental needs and hopes are common to all humanity. In times characterized by the prevalence of public inspection and censorship—of which we are all prey, though some more than others—play, which is akin to an oasis of liberty, hence functions as a metaphor for resilience and resistance too, with possibly subversive overtones depending on the intent and interpretation. MPP Yei Myint's *Playing with Three Numbers* (2009), Nyein Chan Su's *Who Is It?* (2009), and Aung Myint's *The Intruders* (2010) are examples of works that purposefully engage play at levels both explicit and implicit: play and game in their literal sense become the means to express a desolation so profound and complex that it cannot be spoken of in plain terms. Instead of polemics, they resort to irony, to jest and to play. Indeed, the fiercer the repression, the greater the relevance of play that is the very antithesis of fear; it becomes the weapon of resistance and the vehicle of the unabated quest for panacea. In the words of Romano Guardini in *The Spirit of Liturgy,* first published almost a century ago, during the World War I, like liturgy, play is "pointless but significant."[4] It is all the more crucial in moments of darkness and confusion, for play muffles thunders' roars, alleviates tensions, and is a bridge to sunrise as in Wah Nu's lyrical *Aung Zeya Light Project No. 1* (2004–08). In play, hope abides.

If Huizinga's argument that poetry, like play, "lies beyond seriousness, on that more primitive and original level where the child, the animal, the savage, and the seer belong, in the region of dream, enchantment, ecstasy, laughter" were to be extrapolated, the Burmese people's legendary love for poetry, which has a far longer history than art in Myanmar—"art" being a modern construct whose implantation is inextricable from the colonial enterprise—can be at least partially explained by its ability to extract one from quotidian dolor too.[5] It would be likewise for wordplay, one of the country's favorite pastimes. It is certainly not significant that contemporary Burmese artists often meld poetry with art, as does The Maw Naing in *Gently Immerse Like an Oar, Like Its Blade that Circles Above Water* (2004–10).[6] Alongside are artists that explore "the region of dream, enchantment, ecstasy, laughter" away from the bleakness or impossibility of reality using visual metaphors: Zar Min Htike's *Portrait of an Artist as a Goblin, Nos. 1–22* (2009–10), Min Thein Sung's *They and Another Realm* (2009–10), and Soe Naing's *Play* (2010) in this exhibition, for example. In comparison, Ko Z's *Room* (2010), an intimate account of the artist's internal struggles between freedom and restraint, the extraordinary and the mundane, resides on the fringe of this "region of dream." In these works, play becomes a makeshift asylum that synchronously translates itself into a stratagem against the context of a severely compromised freedom.[7]

Undeniably, together with fortitude springing from the faith of many in Buddhist teachings advocating mental deliverance in the face of material bondage, the spirit of play has been a dynamo behind contemporary creation in Myanmar.[8] While censorship has in general proven itself to be feeble in the face of creative impulses of a primordial order, artists in Myanmar remain nonetheless very vulnerable in the matter of exhibiting their works—at this point in history in 2010 of the Common Era at least. Burmese artists living and working within the country are compelled to answer for any exhibition or performance held locally or overseas, unlike others based abroad and have no obligation back home. Even when their works are shown outside of the country, any work (mis)interpreted as a challenge to the regime's legitimacy can result in the artist being barred from returning to Myanmar, among other punitive measures. Neither are they protected in any way by or against the foreign private or public institutions hosting their works. Most artists hence retaliate by honing their versatility and inventiveness so as to trump censorship restrictions through ingenious means of expression. It is probably why they have been quick to embrace a wide range of media and approaches, with cost-free and non-collectable performance art being one of the most popular modes of expression.[9] There is no straightforward solution and the combat takes place on all fronts.

The aberrant situation in which Burmese artists find themselves obliges foreign professionals and institutions of art collaborating with them to operate in a similar manner. Both the curator and writer of Burmese art are responsible for the fortune of the artists with whom they work, since any contentious interpretation of the exhibited works can have threatening consequences. The matter is of concern to any artist residing in Myanmar or has loved ones in similarly vulnerable positions. An exhibition presenting works that lend to interpretations of political activism is a ticking time bomb, for it suffices for an ignorant or self-serving journalist or activist to appropriate any of them or any aspect of the curatorial proposition in favor of his or her personal agenda to cause the entire group of artists immense distress back home. Any foreigner involved in a purportedly political exhibition also risks being blacklisted by the Burmese government. To be sure, it is way too convenient and irresponsible for armchair critics who have never set foot in Myanmar and have no plans to do so to exhort political content and criticism in making and staging contemporary Burmese art; courage and foolhardiness are quite distinct. As such, the curator and writer walk a tightrope similar to that of the artist: to provide the artist with the most conducive conditions to develop and to present his or her works on the one hand, and to guard the interests of the team against accusations of political involvement, among other flights of fancy, on the other. With Burmese art and artists, there are responsibilities beyond mounting exhibitions that inspire, challenge assumptions, and spur critical discourses.

Until the cause of fear is doused, Myanmar's artists and curators will continue to court paradox and allusion. Under this scenario, "play" remains as relevant for the former as it does for the latter as a viable approach to framing and presenting contemporary Burmese art. In addition to its cathartic properties, play absolves in the same way that ignorance exonerates children and the mad. In the context of an authoritarian society, there is indeed wisdom in passing off or being passed off as "mad," as is the case of some of modern Myanmar's most illustrious artists like Bagyi Aung Soe and Po Po: the mad on its fringe thinks and acts unfettered by the dictates of acceptable behavior. Similarly, "play" as a curatorial concept camouflages and exempts, whether it is with respect to the works of art's conception, realization, display or reception; it encapsulates the mettle of Burmese artists and art without putting them in a quandary. Its fluidity and open-endedness moreover accommodate a wide spectrum of subject matter and methods. Most importantly, it resists the flattening of complexity imposed by politicized frameworks: Myanmar is neither the golden land, nor the sob story whose only actors are child soldiers, underage prostitutes, tortured intellectuals, and dispossessed farmers. Yes, Myanmar is problem-ridden with grievances untold but it is not all that she is: she has been first and foremost the site of utmost human resilience, where grace is possible amidst despair, as Myat Kyawt asserts in *People of Grace* (2009). It is neither desolation nor self-pity that pulls one through the darkest hour, but hope, humor, and the ability to imagine and to devise through play in the face of adversity. It is precisely this buoyancy that has borne them through many a vicissitude. To quote Huizinga again, "in play we move below the level of the serious, as the child does; but we can also move above it–in the realm of the beautiful and the sacred."[10]

Play is considered innate to Man and some animals. Yet, there is no pretending that the construct of "play," like that of "art," is arguably a foreign one. At the heart of Burmese culture molded by Buddhism, there is no place for it. The Burmese Theravādin Buddhist's ideal of existence is devoted to the cultivation of constant mindfulness through insight meditation (*vipassanā*). This round-the-clock awareness does not advocate the suspension of attentiveness–however momentarily–and leaves little room for diversion of any kind, let alone play. In fact, "play" is a word that has no equivalent in the scriptures, not because it is condemned, but because it is a notion that is alien to an ideology whose end is karmic deliverance. Indeed, that which an outsider reads as "play" in a work of art can very well be intended to embody something else altogether; that which dialectics can argue with brio and reason establish with seeming certainty is not necessarily true or right. For example, while Myat Kyawt's *Energy* (2010) is presented and experienced as a game, its rationale is in fact rooted in Buddhist philosophy: the profound Law of Dependent Origination (*Paṭiccasamuppāda*). Even if an artist chooses not to disagree with interpretations of his or her work, it could be due to his or her understanding of audience reception as inevitably variable, since the phenomenal world are mere projections of the capricious mind, conforming to Buddhist teachings; the artist's taciturnity does not necessarily denote endorsement of any interpretation as consistent with his or her intention. To be sure, in order to fully experience and appreciate the works gathered in "plAy," "play"–or any other curatorial concept for that matter–is the seed coat that must ultimately fall off. "Play" is merely one among many possible ways of engaging with Burmese art today, and its weaknesses and merits lessons for future endeavors.

For many from the supposedly free world of presumably free press, there is much to learn from a people who, after close to half a century of controlled press, excel in irony and subtext. The Burmese artist is not necessarily inclined to employ explicit symbols or tortured acts to make a statement, and likewise, the curator of Burmese art. Its tenor is seldom writ large: it is mellow, discreet, and internalized; it seeps forth by degrees.[11] A rose sitting in a chipped vase placed in the middle of a busy road in Yangon fades into the city's anonymity. Yet, it can be the very incarnation of resistance, just as play is in the face of authoritarianism. The beholder who understands sees, just as Johann Wolfgang von Goethe, a figure eons away from the consciousness of contemporary art, wrote, "You only see what you know." ("*Man sieht nur das, was man weiß.*") Regrettably, in the current bedlam of misapprehensions, Burmese art's understated mode has yet to prove itself coherent and palatable to players of the international art world, whose approval many Burmese artists nonetheless covet. Detractors who neither understand nor care to, yet persist in regurgitating stereotypes and trumpeting prejudices trapped in a simplistic bipolar paradigm of good versus evil, democracy versus dictatorship, political versus propaganda art, etc. are unfortunately many. What is to be done in order to be seen and heard above the cacophony of politicized or exoticized discourses? To be accepted into the White Cube, must Burmese artists play to a new tune in disaccord with that which has been time-honored at home? What about their contextual significances? Does "Myanmar" still matter to those who have become diligent citizens of Facebook, Twitter, YouTube, and Google? What might be the purpose of making art in Myanmar today in the first place, if it is not only to join the bandwagon of international art professionals and to become a fixture in the circuit of biennials, triennials, and art fairs? Why play in the first place?

1   In this paper, we will be referring to Burma as Myanmar, conforming to her appellation within ASEAN. "Myanmar" is generally used to mean the people and language too, but for the purpose of grammatical distinction, "Burmese" is used here to denote the nationality and national language, which is more specifically that of the Bamars, Myanmar's largest ethnic group.

2   "Why Play? An Outsider's Point of View on Making & Seeing Art in Myanmar Today" was written for the exhibition catalogue of "plAy: Art from Myanmar Today," which took place at Osage Singapore under the auspices of the Osage Foundation. Held from May 8 to June 20, 2010, six months prior to the reforms underway in Myanmar since November 2010, it is to our knowledge the first exhibition entirely devoted to contemporary Burmese art organized outside of Myanmar. "plAy" was co-curated by Isabel Ching and the author, and featured commissioned new media installations, performances, sculptures, and paintings by thirteen Burmese artists based in Yangon and Bagan: Aung Myint, Emily Phyo, Ko Z, Min Thein Sung, MPP Yei Myint, Myat Kyawt, Nyein Chan Su (NCS), Po Po, Soe Naing, The Maw Naing, Tun Win Aung, Wah Nu, and Zar Min Htike. The fruit of multiple studio visits and discussions in Myanmar, preparations for "plAy" spanned over a year, beginning with brainstorming sessions in Singapore during the second quarter of 2008. "plAy" as a working title was conceived on a research trip in Yangon in December 2008. The original curatorial essay was written in August 2010 and revised in October 2011. In this time, winds of change had blown across the world; the Arab Spring and the then ongoing Occupy Wall Street protests held out possibilities of alternative futures. In Myanmar, Aung San Suu Kyi had been released from house arrest in November 2010, and less than a year later on September 30, 2011, Myanmar's new president stood up against China on the Myitsone Hydropower Project on the Irrawaddy River. Thousands of prisoners were freed the following month, among other positive changes on the home front. Hope was reignited in the hearts of many; pundits argued that a political watershed was in the making and that real change was on the horizon. In the art scene, there was a surge of nudes and portraits of the Lady, which would have never passed the scrutiny of the censorship board in former times. For the curators and artists of "plAy," instead of "art from Myanmar *today*," it became possible to speak of "contemporary art," a term which had been interpreted by the military government as synonymous with politically critical positions and could not be used without risking reprisal from the authorities. More than half a decade on, the issues presented in this essay offer insights into a phase in the practice of contemporary art in Myanmar. These challenges are however not entirely absent from the art scene today. The promises of sustained change for the better can neither erase overnight the scars sustained over decades, nor suppress that which might be ingrained into the psyche of a people. It is hence with awareness of this country's protean modern history that a reading of "Why Play? An Outsider's Point of View on Making and Seeing Art in Myanmar Today," which was conceived within another political matrix, might be most meaningful; it is by staying mindful of the inevitable negotiations between transformations and anachronisms that the perspectives elaborated in this essay might best serve further investigations into contemporary Burmese art, a nascent practice and discipline built on the shifting sands that has been Myanmar.

3   The author begs to differ from Huizinga's conclusion that play cannot be present in plastic arts due to "their being bound to matter and to the limitations of form inherent in it," and their exhibition being "necessarily part of some rite or other festival, entertainment or social event." Johan Huizinga, *Homo Ludens: A Study of the Play-Element in Culture* (London: Routledge, 2002), 166–67.

4    Ibid., 19.

5    Ibid., 117.

6    Art festivals and events where participants juxtapose new media and performance art with poetry recitals accompanied by guitar ballads are not uncommon. The intimate relationship between poetry and the fine arts in Myanmar merits further research.

7    It is also this aspect of the play element that has led many Burmese artists and amateurs of art to equate art with freedom. When asked why and how they started to paint, to make installations, or to engage in performance art, Burmese artists' answers seldom stray far from the association of art with "freedom" and virtues like sincerity, truth, and selflessness, as if art were synonymous with all things wholesome.

8    Time and again, artists have cited Buddhist teachings as a source of strength. To maintain their morale in this arbitrary milieu, many look to religion and moral virtues like patience and faith for spiritual grounding.

9    The association of moral virtues with avant-garde forms of artistic expression like installation and performance art in Myanmar rests upon the opinion that ephemeral works promising no financial gain are better aligned with the altruistic ideal of engaging with society.

10    Huizinga, *Homo Ludens*, 19.

11    Possibly a cultural propensity exacerbated by the country's repressed political climate, only further research can ascertain its mechanisms and dynamics.

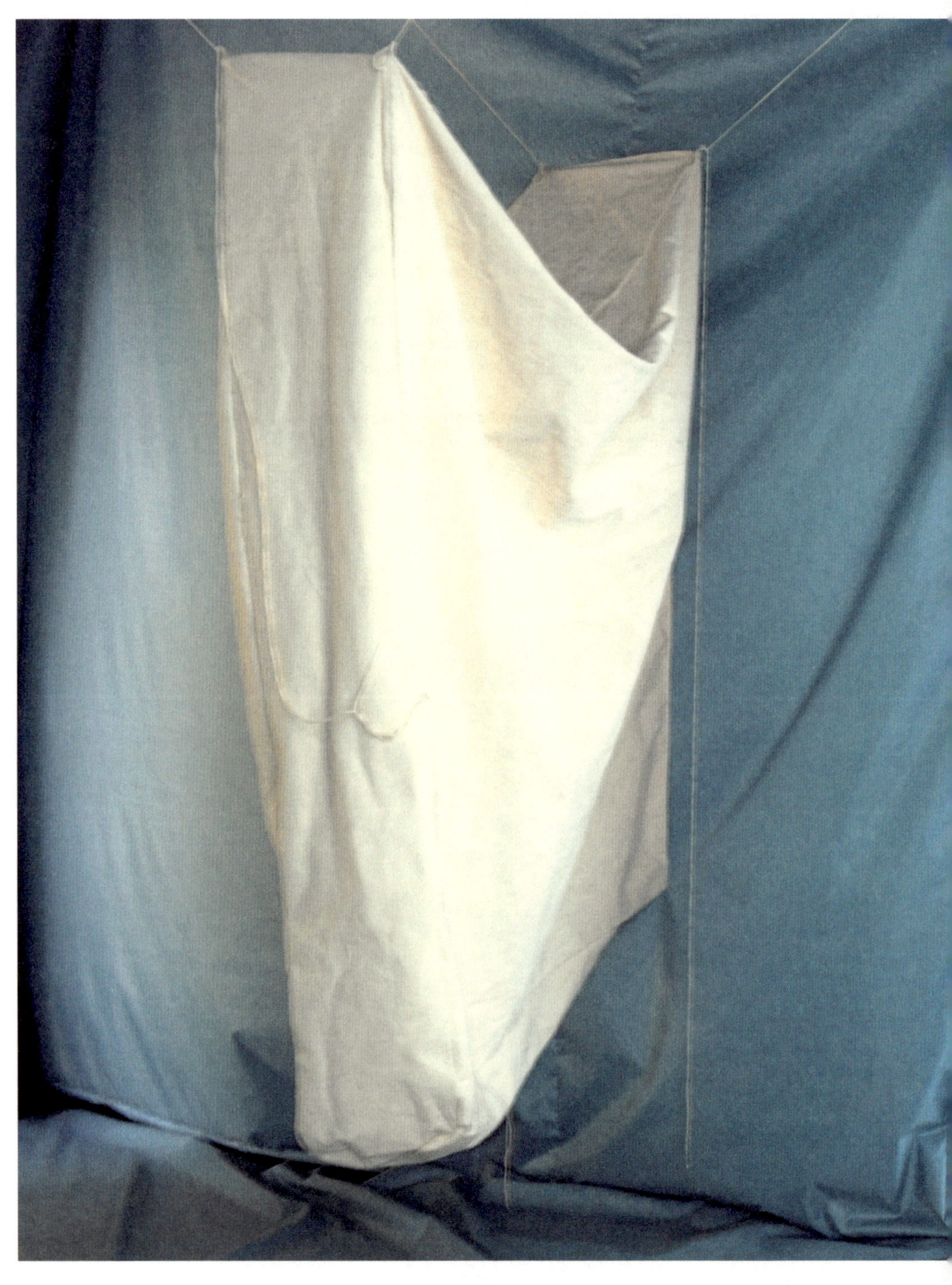

Min Thein Sung
*Another Realm*, 2013
Marlar Art Centre, Mingun, Sagaing, Myanmar

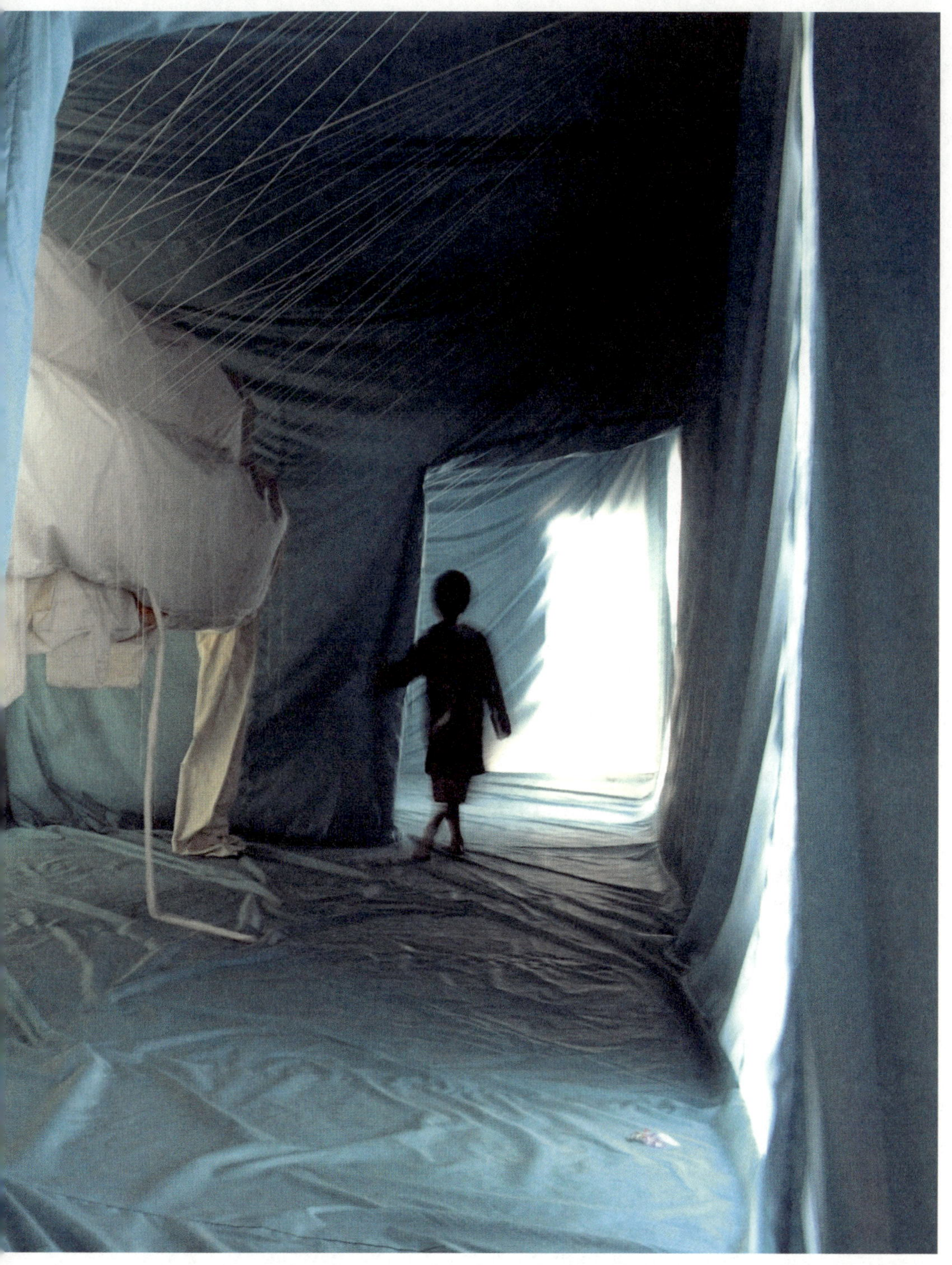

Yin Ker

# Why Play? Entstehen und Verstehen von Kunst im heutigen Myanmar – eine Außenseiterperspektive

In Myanmar wird der öffentliche Raum überwacht.[1] Ähnliches geschieht auch in anderen Staaten, aber Zeugenberichten zufolge hat die staatliche Kontrolle zumindest in den dichtbesiedelten Gebieten des Landes Auswüchse ähnlich wie Big Brother erreicht. In solchen Extremfällen wird die Öffentlichkeit zur Bühne, auf der einzelne Leben ständig dem prüfenden Blick anderer Personen ausgesetzt sind. Man wird von Eltern, Geschwistern, LehrerInnen, FreundInnen, Fremden, KonkurrentInnen und der Regierung observiert. Und sie alle werden selbst wiederum misstrauisch von denjenigen beäugt, die sie doch eigentlich beaufsichtigen sollen. An jeder Straßenecke erwarten einen skeptisch umherwandernde Augen. Sobald man die Toilette verlässt, wird man gemustert. Das hat Folgen, die mal harmlos, mal schwerwiegend sind, je nachdem wer gerade wen wobei beobachtet. War es Zufall, dass Min Thein Sung in *Restroom* (2008–2010) ausgerechnet die Toilette zu einem Rückzugsort erklärte? KünstlerInnen, die ausgestellt, und AutorInnen, die veröffentlicht werden wollen, haben noch etwas anderes zu befürchten: Zensur. Nicht jedes Augenpaar ist auf Zensur und Bestrafung aus. Neben dem Behördenspitzel gibt es den umsichtigen Nachbarn, den aufmerksamen Lehrer, die besorgten Eltern. Sie alle passen auf, sie beobachten uns aus Neugier, aufgrund ihrer Aufsichtspflicht oder weil sie uns lieben. Es ist, als ob sich zum grellen Licht der Observierung das Leuchten kleiner Taschenlampen gesellte. Die Helligkeit hüllt das Individuum vollständig ein, Scheinwerfer sind auf jeden Gedanken und jede Bewegung gerichtet.

Das sind die Eindrücke einer Außenseiterin. Es wäre interessant, näher zu untersuchen, inwiefern sich die Orwell'sche Atmosphäre in den Städten Myanmars auf die künstlerische Praxis auswirkt. Kunstschaffenden werden im Privaten wie im Beruflichen Steine in den Weg gelegt. Man versucht beinahe täglich, Druck auf sie auszuüben. Es braucht großes taktisches Geschick, damit umzugehen. Das betrifft unweigerlich auch die kuratorische Praxis in der burmesischen Gegenwartskunst, die nur aus dem ihr eigenen Bedeutungszusammenhang heraus verstanden werden kann – zumindest war das unser Ansatz bei der Ausstellung *plAy: Art from Myanmar Today* –, auch wenn sie zunehmend an internationale Debatten in der Kunstwelt anknüpft. Zu diesem Bedeutungszusammenhang gehören sämtliche Aspekte, die das Leben in Myanmar heute prägen. Die internationalen Medien hingegen fokussieren sich ausschließlich auf die Politik, wenn sie über das Land schreiben. Die Militärregierung gilt als Grund allen Übels, sie stecke hinter den humanitären, psychischen, moralischen Missständen, so als ob es in Myanmar kein komplexes Kolonialerbe gäbe. Dass man daraus schließt, burmesische Kunst ist politisch und müsse das auch sein, ist ein bedauerlicher Kollateralschaden dieser Haltung.

Natürlich ist es eine Tatsache, dass in Myanmar seit 1962 eine Militärregierung an der Macht ist. Eine ganze Generation von KünstlerInnen wuchs in ihrem Schatten auf; sie wurde mit der Junta alt. Die Männer in Uniform befehlen, alle anderen haben zu gehorchen. Eine offene Gesellschaft stand niemals zur Debatte. Und so geht das schon ein halbes Jahrhundert. Trotzdem wäre es voreilig – und falsch –, sich die Militärregierung als alleinigen Schuldigen an dieser Misere herauszugreifen, genauso wie es voreilig und falsch wäre, sie von ihrer schwerwiegenden Verantwortung für die Situation freizusprechen. Dass sich eine burmesische Überwachungsgesellschaft herausbilden konnte, hat weder rein institutionelle noch rein kulturelle Gründe. Die Wirklichkeit vor Ort ist unendlich viel komplizierter als die Welt von Gut und Böse, der man in den Medien begegnet. Man kann die sozialen Besonderheiten des Landes nicht einfach außer Acht lassen. Sie sind Teil des Kontexts, in dem KünstlerInnen arbeiten. Die überpolitisierten Deutungsmuster werden der tatsächlichen Vielfalt und Komplexität künstlerischer Praxis in Myanmar nicht gerecht. Mehr noch: Sie erschweren konstruktive Diskussionen. Ich will die politischen Probleme hier nicht kleinreden, aber es stellt sich doch die Frage, ob es im Land noch etwas anderes gibt als Politik, ob es vielleicht nicht noch andere Ansätze gibt, um burmesische Kunst zu begreifen, zu präsentieren und zu besprechen.

An Meldungen über Menschenrechtsverletzungen und humanitäre Katastrophen herrscht wahrlich kein Mangel. Die tiefgläubigen BürgerInnen Myanmars, deren Schrecken kein Ende zu kennen scheint, lassen all das tapfer über sich ergehen, so liest man. Auf die Titelseiten der internationalen Presse schaffen sie es jedoch nicht mehr. Und doch wäre es genauso verfehlt und geschmacklos, ständig die missliche politische Lage des Landes zu betonen und sich darin zu ergehen, die drakonischen Strafen aufzuzählen, die verhängt werden, wenn sich jemand nur die kleinste Verfehlung auf einer Seite einer Publikation erlaubt hat. Effekthascherische Leitartikel verhöhnen mit ihrem Geschwätz über das System der Unterdrückung nur diejenigen, die teuer dafür bezahlen mussten, dass sie es wagten, ihre Stimme zu erheben und sich für Dinge einzusetzen, die sie für wichtiger erachten als Leib und Leben. Was bringt es denn, jedes Mal aufs Neue düstere Szenarien für das Land zu entwerfen, welche die Täter dämonisieren und die Opferrolle fetischisieren? Ein solches Vorgehen verstärkt die Angst, die den Folterern in die Hände spielt. Man schreibt, was ohnehin alle wissen, an der Lage ändert sich dadurch rein gar nichts. Und sind ExpertInnen nicht eher dazu imstande, die politische Situation zu entwirren, in der sich Myanmar befindet und die ForscherInnen, BürgerInnen und AktivistInnen schon seit Jahrzehnten umtreibt, als es KuratorInnen und KunsthistorikerInnen sind? Das will ich doch stark hoffen. Nicht umsonst heißt es: Schuster, bleib' bei deinem Leisten.

Bis gründlichere Studien zur Struktur der burmesischen Gesellschaft vorliegen, die über den Tellerrand der Politik hinausblicken, wäre es vielleicht angezeigt, sich den oft spielerischen Strategien der KünstlerInnen zuzuwenden. So könnte ein unvoreingenommeneres und zugleich weniger partielles Verständnis der künstlerischen Produktion in Myanmar entstehen. Es wäre ein Ansatz, der die Präsenz der vorgefassten Meinungen zur burmesischen Gegenwartskunst auf ein absolutes Minimum zu reduzieren versucht und stattdessen die zahllosen Facetten der ästhetischen Wirklichkeit zum Vorschein kommen lässt, ohne sie zwanghaft den eigenen (politischen) Vorlieben anzupassen. Der Begriff des Spiels, über den wir uns der burmesischen Gegenwartskunst nähern, ist relativ universell angelegt und gestattet uns als KuratorInnen, diese Kunst aus den Fesseln der Überpolitisierung zu befreien und einen größeren Austausch mit KünstlerInnen aus anderen Ländern anzuregen. Zum einen könnten burmesische KünstlerInnen von der Öffentlichkeit und den Debatten profitieren, zum anderen würden dadurch letzten Endes auch die internationalen Kunstdiskurse bereichert. Es gibt einen weiteren Grund, der erklärt, warum wir uns bewusst dafür entschieden haben, dem rein politischen Zugriff auf Kunst in *plAy* eine Absage zu erteilen: aus Rücksichtnahme auf die Sicherheit und die Interessen der an diesem Projekt Beteiligten, die ansonsten um ihre berufliche Zukunft im Land bangen müssten, von den affektiven Belastungen ganz zu schweigen. Die Entscheidung, mit dem Oberbegriff *Spiel* eine Plattform für Kunst aus Myanmar zu schaffen, war also pragmatischer und ideologischer Natur. Daher verdient sie eine Erklärung.

Für KünstlerInnen aus Myanmar ist die Zensur eine größere Gefahr als die allgegenwärtige Kultur des Überwachens. Literarische AutorInnen waren davon zuerst – und am härtesten – betroffen. Kaum ein Jahr war nach dem Staatsstreich vom März 1962 vergangen, als LektorInnen verhaftet und Verlage geschlossen wurden. Was bei Buchveröffentlichungen zulässig ist und was nicht, wird seit 1975 feinsäuberlich in Dokumenten aufgeführt, wie man in Anna Allots 1993 erschienenen Studie *Inked Over, Ripped Out: Burmese Storytellers and the Censors* nachlesen kann. AutorInnen sahen sich einem Dilemma gegenüber: Wie kann man sich und seiner Kunst treubleiben, ohne dabei die individuelle Freiheit und das eigene Leben aufs Spiel zu setzen? Für die bildenden Künste gibt es derartige

Leitlinien nicht. Zudem muss man unterscheiden zwischen öffentlichen Ausstellungen und privaten, die einer weniger strengen Zensur unterliegen. Werke, in denen heftige Emotionen zum Ausdruck kommen oder die zumindest in diese Richtung gedeutet werden könnten, und Arbeiten, die Nacktheit darstellen oder die überwiegend in Schwarz und Rot gehalten sind, werden häufig mit einem Verbot belegt. Doch es gibt keine eindeutig festgelegten Regeln in diesem Bereich. Zum Erstaunen der burmesischen Kunstwelt durften einige über die Maßen provokative Werke ausgestellt werden, während relativ unverfängliche Arbeiten aus dem Verkehr gezogen wurden. Schon diese Willkür und Unvorhersehbarkeit schränken den Bewegungsspielraum ein und machen den KünstlerInnen das Leben schwer. Über das Schicksal einer Ausstellung, an der man über ein Jahr lang intensiv gearbeitet hat, entscheiden Vertreter der Zensurbehörde, die sich auf allen möglichen Feldern Kompetenzen erworben haben, nur nicht auf dem der Kunst, auf einer kurzen Sitzung, bei der Snacks und Erfrischungsgetränke gereicht werden. Die Begründungen für das Verbot klingen dann so kunstsinnig wie „zu viel Schwarz, zu wenig Rosa". Das ist leider kein Witz.

Die Angst frisst sich in die Seele. Es ist die Furcht vor etwas, für das es keinen Namen gibt. Burmesische KünstlerInnen vollführen ständig einen Drahtseilakt. Wie kann man sein künstlerisches Potenzial ausschöpfen und gleichzeitig die Zensurvorgaben umgehen, wenn man nicht einmal nachvollziehen kann, welche Maßstäbe angelegt werden? Wer im Dunkel stochert, sieht irgendwann Schatten, wo gar keine sind. Einigen wird der Stress zu viel. Bislang gibt es kaum statistische Nachweise darüber, dass Menschen irgendwo auf der Welt vor lauter Ungewissheit, Schikane und Spitzelei zugrunde gegangen sind. Entscheidend ist doch, dass es schwieriger ist, damit zu leben als daran zu sterben. In dieser von Furcht und Überwachung geprägten Atmosphäre erweist sich gerade das *Spiel* als heilsam. Wenn es im Leben nur noch darum geht, Regeln zu befolgen, Erwartungshaltungen gerecht zu werden und mögliche Stimmungsschwankungen vorauszuahnen, braucht man dringend Ruhe und die Möglichkeit, sich zurückzuziehen, sonst verzweifelt man völlig an dieser qualvollen Existenz und hat nur noch den Wunsch, sie zu beenden. Der niederländische Kulturhistoriker Johan Huizinga schrieb 1938 in *Homo Ludens*, dass der Mensch nicht nur ein Homo faber sei, sondern auch ein „spielendes" Wesen, ein Homo ludens eben.[3] Das Spiel kann so einfach sein wie Sachen, die sich Kinder ausdenken. Es kann komisch sein, zum Lachen bringen. Und doch geht es über all dies hinaus. Es ist ein zutiefst ernster Ausdruck von etwas Ursprünglichem. Oft gibt sich das Spiel willentlich dem Paradox hin und scheint jede Logik auszuschalten. Es widerstrebt der Vernunft (aber nicht der Weisheit) und überschreitet unseren konventionellen Wahrheitsbegriff. Im Spiel gelingt es dem Geist, sich in exaltierte Höhen zu katapultieren, ohne die physische Bühne des individuellen Körpers verlassen zu müssen, auf der wir unseren Pflichten oder unserem verdammten Schicksal gemäß agieren. Dieser Gemütszustand erschließt alternative Denkweisen. Es obliegt allein dem Spieler, Grenzen zu ziehen – oder die bestehende Ordnung zu unterlaufen. Burmesischen KünstlerInnen muss niemand erzählen, dass direkte Konfrontationen mit der Staatsmacht wenig bringen. Sie mussten lernen, dass es mehr als einen Weg gibt, um ein Problem anzugehen. Mehrdeutigkeit ist Macht. „Alle Wege führen nach Rom". Die findigen Machtlosen verstehen, was damit gemeint ist.

Den Wunsch nach Selbstentfaltung teilen alle, er entspricht einem allgemeinen Bedürfnis - egal wie entbehrlich dieser Wunsch manchen vorkommen mag, egal wie gering die Spielräume sind, um dieses Bedürfnis auszuleben. Jedes empfindungsfähige Wesen hat das Vorrecht, seinem Willen zu folgen und im Einklang mit den eigenen Vorstellungen zu handeln. Was in Burma als *normal* gilt, welche Ziele sich die Leute dort setzen und wo die Schmerzgrenze liegt - all das mag sich von der Situation in anderen Ländern unterscheiden. Doch die Bedürfnisse und Hoffnungen, die diesen Vorstellungen zugrunde liegen, sind allen Menschen gemein. In Zeiten, in denen die Öffentlichkeit beaufsichtigt und zensiert wird - und wir alle sind davon betroffen, wenn auch in unterschiedlichem Ausmaß - wird das Spiel zu einer Oase der Freiheit und zu einer Metapher der Unbeugsamkeit und Widerständigkeit, die je nach Intention und Interpretation durchaus politische Konnotationen haben kann. MPP Yei Myints *Playing with Three Numbers* (2009), Nyein Chan Sus *Who Is It?* (2009) und Aung Myints *The Intruders* (2010) gehören zu den Arbeiten, die sich auf mehr als einer Ebene mit dem Spiel auseinandersetzen. Das Spiel dient hier buchstäblich als Mittel, um einer Trostlosigkeit Ausdruck zu verleihen, die so tief sitzt und so komplex strukturiert ist, dass sie sich nicht in Worte fassen lässt. Statt zu polemisieren, greifen die KünstlerInnen lieber auf Ironie, Spiel und Scherz zurück. Je schlimmer die Repression, desto wichtiger ist das Spiel als Antwort auf die Angst. Das Spiel ist ein Werkzeug des Widerstands und ein Übermittler des unauslöschlichen Strebens nach etwas Besserem. Vor fast hundert Jahren schrieb Romano Guardini in *Vom Geist der Liturgie* (1918), noch unter dem Eindruck der Schrecken des Ersten Weltkriegs, das Spiel sei „zwecklos, aber sinnvoll".[4] Das Spiel erweist sich als unabdingbare Ressource in Zeiten der Wirren. Es dämpft das Donnergrollen, löst Spannungen auf und weist den Weg in den Sonnenaufgang, wie Wah Nuhs poetische Arbeit *Aung Zeya Light Project No. 1* (2004–2008) veranschaulicht. Wo gespielt wird, bleibt Hoffnung.

Entwickelt man Huizingas Argument weiter, wonach die Dichtung, wie auch das Spiel, „jenseits vom Ernst" steht, „auf jener ursprünglichen Seite, wo das Kind, das Tier, der Wilde und der Seher hingehören, im Felde des Traums, des Entrücktseins, der Berauschtheit und des Lachens", könnte man daraus schlussfolgern, dass die Liebe der Burmesen zur Dichtung, deren Geschichte in Myanmar viel weiter zurückreicht als die der Kunst - *Kunst* ist ein moderner Begriff, der mit dem Kolonialismus im Land Einzug hielt -, sicher auch mit dem Verlangen zu tun hat, sich den täglichen Strapazen wenigstens zeitweilig zu entziehen.[5] Gleiches gilt für die Wortspiele, die sich in Myanmar großer Beliebtheit erfreuen. Es ist sicher kein Zufall, dass zeitgenössische burmesische KünstlerInnen oft

Dichtung und bildende Kunst vermischen, wie The Maw Naing bereits im Titel seiner Arbeit unterstreicht: *Gently immerse like an oar, Like its blade that circles above water* (2004-2010).[6] Dazu kommen in dieser Ausstellung KünstlerInnen, die im Feld „des Traums, des Entrücktseins, der Berauschtheit und des Lachens" umherstreifen, um einer desolaten und unwirklichen Wirklichkeit visuelle Metaphern abzutrotzen: Zar Min Htikes *Portrait of an Artist as a Goblin, Nos. 1-22* (2009-2010), Min Thein Sungs *They and Another Realm* (2009-2010) und Soe Naings *Play* (2010). Ko Z verortet seine Arbeit *Room* (2010), eine äußerst intime Darstellung seiner inneren Zerrissenheit, zwischen Freiheit und Zurückhaltung, dem Außergewöhnlichen und dem Banalen, am Rande des Traumfelds. Diese Werke präsentieren das Spiel als behelfsmäßigen Zufluchtsort, der zugleich als Basislager fungiert, von dem aus der nächste spielerische Schlag gegen eine Struktur geplant werden kann, die Freiheiten erheblich beeinträchtigt.[7]

Es steht außer Frage, dass das Spielerische, begünstigt von der Kraft, die viele aus einem buddhistischen Glauben schöpfen, der die geistige Erlösung von materieller Knechtschaft verspricht, eine wichtige Triebfeder des künstlerischen Schaffens in Myanmar ist.[8] Die ursprünglichen schöpferischen Impulse vermag auch die Zensur nicht zu ersticken, doch selbst im Jahr 2010 machen sich KünstlerInnen, die ihre Werke ausstellen, schnell angreifbar. Im Gegensatz zu ausgewanderten KünstlerInnen, müssen diejenigen, die im Land geblieben sind, über jede Performance und jede Ausstellung im In- und Ausland Rechenschaft ablegen. Selbst internationale Sichtbarkeit bietet keinen Schutz, wenn die Behörden (nicht immer zurecht) meinen, eine Arbeit untergrabe die Legitimität des Regimes. Dann kann dem Künstler sogar die Rückkehr ins Land untersagt werden – und das ist nur eine der möglichen Sanktionen. Proteste privater oder öffentlicher AusstellungsmacherInnen im Ausland verhallen ungehört. Umgekehrt können burmesische KünstlerInnen kaum auf staatliche Unterstützung zählen, falls ihnen außerhalb der Landesgrenzen Unrecht widerfährt. Die KünstlerInnen rächen sich auf ihre Weise: Der Einfallsreichtum und die Vielgestaltigkeit ihrer Werke sind den Restriktionen stets einen schöpferischen Schritt voraus. Vielleicht haben sich burmesische KünstlerInnen auch deshalb früh mit neuen Medien und Methoden befasst; besonders populär ist die Performance Art, denn sie kostet nichts und ist nichts für Sammler.[9] Wo es keine einfachen Lösungen gibt, wird der Kampf an allen ästhetischen Fronten geführt.

Die aberwitzige Situation, mit der sich burmesische KünstlerInnen konfrontiert sehen, lässt für ausländische Institutionen und KuratorInnen, die mit ihnen zusammenarbeiten, ein ähnlich vorsichtiges Vorgehen ratsam erscheinen. KuratorInnen und KritikerInnen sind in gewisser Weise verantwortlich für das Schicksal der KünstlerInnen, die sie ausstellen oder über die sie schreiben, denn jede missliebige Auslegung von Behördenseite kann schwerwiegende Konsequenzen haben. Alle in Myanmar lebenden KünstlerInnen kennen diese oder ähnliche Situationen oder jemanden, der in Gefahr schwebte. Eine Ausstellung, die politisch sensible Werke präsentiert oder Anlass dazu gibt, hinter der Kunst einen

irgendwie gearteten politischen Aktivismus zu vermuten, ist eine tickende Zeit-
bombe, denn es braucht nur einen unfähigen Journalisten, nur einen eigennützi-
gen Aktivisten, der sich auf diese oder jene Arbeit beruft, um sie für seine Zwecke einzuspannen, und schon steht zu befürchten, dass allen an der Ausstellung
beteiligten KünstlerInnen bei ihrer Rückkehr nach Myanmar Unheil droht. Aus-
länderInnen, die an einer vermeintlich politischen Ausstellung mitgewirkt haben, werden von der burmesischen Regierung schon mal auf eine schwarze Liste
gesetzt. Natürlich ist es einfach, sich als internationaler Kritiker, der noch dazu
nie in Myanmar gewesen ist, hinzustellen und von burmesischen AusstellungsmacherInnen politischere Inhalte einzufordern. Einfach – und unverantwortlich
ist es auch. Mut ist nicht dasselbe wie Leichtsinn. Nicht nur die KünstlerInnen,
auch die KuratorInnen vollziehen einen Drahtseilakt. Einerseits sind sie dazu
aufgerufen, Rahmenbedingungen zu schaffen, in denen KünstlerInnen produktiv arbeiten können. Andererseits müssen sie ihre MitarbeiterInnen vor möglichen Verdächtigungen, Anschuldigungen und unterstellten – und zumeist imagi-
nären – politischen Verwicklungen in Schutz nehmen. Wer mit burmesischen
KünstlerInnen arbeitet, ist für mehr verantwortlich als nur das Gelingen einer
Ausstellung, die inspirieren, den kritischen Diskurs voranbringen und Gewohnheiten in Frage stellen soll.

Solange die eigentliche Ursache der Angst nicht verschwunden ist, müssen
Myanmars KünstlerInnen und KuratorInnen mit Anspielungen und Paradoxien
Vorlieb nehmen. Auch deshalb erscheint das *Spiel* im Kontext burmesischer
Kunst als vielversprechende Leitkategorie. Neben den bereits erwähnten kathar-
tischen Eigenschaften schützt das Spiel auf die gleiche Weise, wie das Unwissen
Kinder und psychisch kranke Menschen vor Strafe bewahrt. In einer autoritären
Gesellschaft kann es durchaus von Vorteil sein, als *Wahnsinniger* abgestempelt
zu werden oder sich selbst dazu zu erklären, wie einige der bekanntesten KünstlerInnen des Landes, darunter Bagyi Aung Soe und Po Po vorgemacht haben.
Psychisch Kranke denken und handeln außerhalb des Diktats des gesellschaft-
lich Akzeptablen. Als kuratorische Kategorie dient das *Spiel* nicht zuletzt der
Tarnung, denn es schafft Freiräume bei der Konzeption, Umsetzung, Ausstellung und Rezeption eines Kunstwerkes. Es erweist der Standhaftigkeit der burmesischen Kunst die Ehre, ohne die KünstlerInnen in Schwierigkeiten zu bringen. Dass dieser Begriff sich so offen und fluide ausnimmt, heißt auch, dass sich
die unterschiedlichsten Themen und Ansätze mit ihm vereinen lassen. Politische
Lesarten führen hingegen häufig zu einer künstlichen Verflachung, zu einem
Weniger an Komplexität. Myanmar ist kein Paradies, aber es ist auch mehr als
eine einzige Horrorgeschichte mit ihren Kindersoldaten, minderjährigen Prosti-
tuierten, gefolterten Intellektuellen und Bauern, denen man Grund und Boden
weggenommen hat. Ja, Myanmar wird von unzähligen Krisen geplagt, über viele
Missstände wird gar nicht berichtet. Aber das Land ist eben auch mehr als die
Summe seiner einzelnen Probleme. Es ist ein Hort der Widerständigkeit, immer
wieder kommt inmitten all der Verzweiflung Anmut zum Vorschein, wie Myat

Kyawt in *People of Grace* (2009) beteuert. In schwierigen Stunden helfen weder Verzagen noch Selbstmitleid, sondern Hoffnung, Humor, Vorstellungskraft und spielerischer Trotz im Angesicht all der Widrigkeiten. Heitere Gelassenheit hilft, Rückschläge zu verkraften. Der Mensch „spielt als Kind", um noch einmal Huizinga zu zitieren, „unterhalb des Niveaus ernsthaften Lebens." Doch er „kann auch über diesem Niveau spielen: Spiele der Schönheit und Heiligkeit"[10]

Das Spielen ist dem Menschen und einigen anderen Tieren eigen. Allerdings lässt sich nicht leugnen, dass der Begriff des *Spiels* für BurmesInnen wohl genauso fremd ist wie der Begriff der *Kunst*. In der vom Buddhismus geprägten Kultur Myanmars existierte er lange nicht. Der burmesische Theravada-Buddhismus kultiviert mithilfe der auf Einsicht ausgerichteten Vipassana-Meditation vielmehr das Ideal der Achtsamkeit. Diese Form ständiger Bewusstheit kann mit jeder Unterbrechung der Aufmerksamkeit, mag sie auch noch so kurzzeitig sein, nur wenig anfangen. Sich abzulenken, ja einfach nur zu spielen – dafür wird kaum Raum gelassen. In den buddhistischen Schriften gibt es kein Pendant zur Kategorie des Spiels, nicht unbedingt, weil diese Tätigkeit ausdrücklich verurteilt würde, sondern weil dieser Begriff einer auf karmische Erlösung ausgerichteten Ideologie zutiefst fremd sein muss. Was Außenstehende für den spielerischen Ansatz eines Kunstwerkes halten, steht oft für etwas ganz anderes. Was die Dialektik siegesgewiss als Postulat der Vernunft aufzeigt, muss nicht unbedingt wahr oder richtig sein. Auf den Betrachter wirkt Myat Kyawts *Energy* (2010) wie ein Spiel, doch das Grundprinzip dieser Arbeit entstammt der buddhistischen Philosophie. Es ist eine Auseinandersetzung mit dem *Paṭ iccasamuppāda*, dem Gesetz des Entstehens in Abhängigkeit. Unterlässt es ein Künstler, einer bestimmten Interpretation seiner Werke zu widersprechen, kann auch dies der Einsicht geschuldet sein, dass der Rezeptionsprozess sich nicht steuern lässt, da aus buddhistischer Sicht die Welt der Erscheinungen lediglich eine Projektion unseres wankelmütigen Geistes ist. Die Schweigsamkeit des Künstlers sollte ihm nicht als Zustimmung zu einer bestimmten Interpretation ausgelegt werden, die meint, seine tieferen Absichten durchdrungen zu haben. Eine Ausstellung wie *plAy*, die das weite Feld des Spielens erkundet, sollte – wie das bei jeder anderen kuratorischen Leitkategorie auch geboten wäre –, nicht darauf bestehen, den einzig gültigen begrifflichen Schlüssel zum Verständnis der Werke in den Händen zu halten. Das *Spiel* bietet lediglich einen möglichen Zugang zur burmesischen Gegenwartskunst unter vielen. Das Ausstellungskonzept hat Stärken und Schwächen, aus denen sicher Schlüsse für die Zukunft gezogen werden können.

Auch die ach so freie Welt mit ihrer ach so freien Presse kann vielleicht noch etwas von einem Volk lernen, das es nach fast einem halben Jahrhundert staatlicher Überwachung zu wahrer Meisterschaft gebracht hat, wenn es darum geht, Ironie einzusetzen und einen Subtext zu entziffern. Burmesische KünstlerInnen verwenden vielleicht nicht unbedingt Symbole mit hohem Wiedererkennungswert oder schockierende Folterbilder, die ihr politisches Anliegen herausstellen sollen. Und burmesische KuratorInnen arbeiten ähnlich zurückhaltend. Burmesische Kunst ist in ihrem Gehalt selten plakativ, sondern abgeklärt und unaufdringlich. Sie folgt einer innerlichen Dynamik, sie gibt sich erst nach und nach zu erkennen.[11] Eine Rose, die in eine rissige Vase gestellt und dann mitten auf einer vielbefahrenen Straße stehengelassen wurde, verliert sich allmählich in der Anonymität der Stadt. Ist sie möglicherweise der Inbegriff des Widerstands, so wie das Spiel sich als widerständig im Angesicht des Autoritarismus erweist? Die BetrachterInnen, die verstehen, werden die Blume sehen. Johann Wolfgang Goethe, der mittlerweile Lichtjahre vom Kunstdiskurs entfernt zu sein scheint, schrieb einst: „Man sieht nur das, was man weiß." Gegenwärtig ist es schwer, sich im Lärm der Fehl- und Schnellschüsse Gehör zu verschaffen. Die Behutsamkeit der burmesischen Kunst stößt, wenn sie denn überhaupt als solche wahrgenommen wird, bislang kaum Türen in jene internationale Kunstwelt auf, von der sich zahlreiche KünstlerInnen in Myanmar Anerkennung erhoffen. Stattdessen werden die immer gleichen Stereotype wiederholt. Vorurteile gedeihen prächtig, da sie mit einem einfachen Schema diametraler Gegensätze operieren: Gut gegen Böse, Diktator gegen Demokratie, politische Kunst gegen Propaganda – die Liste ließe sich fortsetzen. Wie kann man in dieser Kakophonie der orientalisierend-überpolitisierten Stimmen überhaupt seine eigene Stimme finden? Müssen burmesische KünstlerInnen, um in den inneren Zirkel der internationalen Kunstwelt vorzudringen, sich von alten Gewohnheiten verabschieden? Aus welchem Bedeutungszusammenhang heraus lassen sich ihre Werke dann erschließen? Welchen Stellenwert hat *Myanmar* überhaupt noch, wenn sich die meisten doch eher als engagierte BürgerInnen in den digitalen Ländereien von Facebook, Twitter, YouTube und Google verstehen? Und welche Rolle käme der Kunst in Myanmar zu, wenn das einzige Ziel darin bestünde, die nötige Aufmerksamkeit von KunsthändlerInnen und KuratorInnen zu bekommen, um endlich im internationalen Zirkus der Biennalen, Triennalen und Messen vertreten zu sein? Dann kann man sich das Spiel auch sparen.

1    Im vorliegenden Beitrag wird Burma dem offiziellen, im ASEAN-Wirtschaftsraum üblichen Sprachgebrauch gemäß als Myanmar bezeichnet. Mit Myanmar ist in der Regel auch das dort lebende Volk und die Sprache gemeint. Der Einfachheit halber wird im Folgenden jedoch von der burmesischen Nationalität und Sprache die Rede sein, die vor allem von den *Bamar*, der größten Volksgruppe im Land, gesprochen wird.

2    Dieser Text wurde für den Katalog der Ausstellung *plAy: Art from Myanmar Today* verfasst, die vom 8. Mai bis zum 20. Juni 2010 unter der Schirmherrschaft der Osage Foundation in der Osage Galerie in Singapur stattfand – also unmittelbar bevor im November 2010 zaghafte demokratische Reformen in Myanmar begannen. Es war meines Wissens die erste Ausstellung außerhalb Myanmars, die sich ausschließlich burmesischer Gegenwartskunst widmete. Gemeinsam mit Isabel Ching kuratierte ich *plAy*. Neben Medienkunst waren Performances, Skulpturen und Gemälde von dreizehn burmesischen KünstlerInnen aus Rangun und Bagan zu sehen: Aung Myint, Emily Phyo, Ko Z, Min Thein Sung, MPP Yei Myint, Myat Kyawt, Nyein Chan Su (NCS), Po Po, Soe Naing, The Maw Naing, Tun Win Aung, Wah Nu und Zar Min Htike. Vorausgegangen waren dem Ganzen ausgiebige Atelierbesuche und Diskussionen. Insgesamt nahmen die Vorbereitungen in Myanmar über ein Jahr in Anspruch. Die Idee für *plAy* kam erstmalig in der zweiten Jahreshälfte 2008 bei Diskussionen in Singapur auf. Auf den Titel legten wir uns dann im Dezember 2008 während eines Forschungsaufenthaltes in Rangun fest. Eine erste Fassung des Essays

war im August 2010 fertig, eine überarbeitete Version lag im Oktober 2011 vor. In der Zwischenzeit hatte sich die Weltlage erheblich verändert. Der Arabische Frühling und die Bewegung Occupy Wall Street ließen eine andere, bessere Zukunft möglich erscheinen. In Myanmar selbst wurde Aung San Suu Kyi im November 2010 aus dem Hausarrest entlassen. Ein knappes Jahr später, am 30. September 2011, widersetzte sich der neue Präsident Myanmars den chinesischen Plänen für den Bau des Myiotsone Wasserkraftwerkes am Irrawaddy-Fluss. Tausende Gefängnisinsassen wurden im folgenden Monat begnadigt. Das waren nur einige der positiven Veränderungen im Land. Bei vielen keimte Hoffnung auf, KommentatorInnen sprachen gar von einem historischen Wendepunkt, tiefgreifende Veränderungen schienen greifbar nahe. In der Kunstszene tauchten plötzlich überall Akte auf. Porträts von Aung San Suu Kyi hingen an den Wänden, ohne dass die Zensurbehörden deswegen eingeschritten wären. KuratorInnen und KünstlerInnen sprachen nun nicht länger von *Kunst aus dem heutigen Myanmar*, sondern von *Gegenwartskunst*, die der Militärregierung früher als gleichbedeutend mit politischen unlauteren Positionen galt und oft Repressalien nach sich zog. Mehr als fünf Jahre sind seit seitdem vergangen. Der Essay vermittelt einen Einblick in eine bestimmte Phase der burmesischen Gegenwartskunst. Einige der darin angesprochenen Punkte haben bis heute nichts von ihrer Gültigkeit für die Kunstszene verloren. Das Versprechen echter Veränderungen reicht nicht aus, um alte Wunden zu heilen oder Haltungen zu überwinden, die sich der Psyche eines ganzen Volkes eingeprägt haben. Der vorliegende Essay, der in einem völlig anderen politischen Kontext entstand, ist nun selbst zum Zeugnis der wechselhaften Geschichte Myanmars geworden. Einiges mag anachronistisch anmuten, anderes kann vielleicht nach wie vor zum besseren Verständnis einer burmesischen Gegenwartskunst beitragen, deren Umrisse noch nicht deutlich erkennbar sind, da sie sich erst allmählich vor dem Hintergrund der jüngsten Ereignisse abzeichnen.

3   Ich stimme Huizinga jedoch nicht zu, wenn er behauptet, dass das spielerische Element in den bildenden Künsten abwesend sei, da sie „der Materie und all den Begrenzungen, die daraus resultieren, verhaftet bleiben". Ausstellungen sind dann auch Huizinga zufolge „zwangsläufig Teil eines Ritus", sie sind „Feierlichkeit, Vergnügen oder gesellschaftliches Ereignis". Johan Huizinga, *Homo Ludens: A Study of the Play-Element in Culture*, London: Routledge, 2002, S. 166f.

4   Romano Guardini, *Vom Geist der Liturgie*, Mainz/Paderborn: Grünewald Verlag, 1997, S. 59.

5   Johan Huizinga, *Homo Ludens. Vom Ursprung der Kultur im Spiel*, Reinbek: Rowohlt, 1956, S. 133.

6   Kunstfestivals und -veranstaltungen, auf denen die TeilnehmerInnen neue Medien, Performance Art und Poesielesungen, die von Gitarrenmusik begleitet werden, zusammenbringen, sind keine Seltenheit. Es würde sich lohnen, dem engen Verhältnis von Dichtkunst und bildender Kunst in Myanmar eine eingehendere Untersuchung zu widmen.

7   Aus diesem Grund ist für viele burmesische KünstlerInnen Spiel gleichbedeutend mit Freiheit. Auf die Frage, warum sie mit der Malerei begonnen haben, sich für die Installationskunst entschieden oder der Performance Art den Vorzug gegeben haben, antworten viele burmesische KünstlerInnen, dass Kunst für sie eine *Freiheit* verheiße, die mit Tugenden wie Aufrichtigkeit, Wahrhaftigkeit und Selbstlosigkeit assoziiert wird – ganz so, als ob Kunst dem guten Leben zuträglich wäre und einem ethischen Gebot folgte.

8   Immer wieder betonen KünstlerInnen, dass ihnen die buddhistische Lehre in einer von Willkür gekennzeichneten Gesellschaft Mut macht. Religiöse Überzeugungen und moralische Tugenden wie Geduld und Vertrauen schaffen eine gewisse Stabilität.

9   Dass Tugendethik und avantgardistische künstlerische Praktiken wie Installationen und Performance Art in Myanmar oft zusammengehen, hat sicher mit der dort verbreiteten Vorstellung zu tun, dass vergängliche Werke, von denen man sich keinen finanziellen Gewinn verspricht, sich leichter in Einklang mit altruistischen gesellschaftlichen Idealen bringen lassen.

10  Huizinga, op. cit., S. 26.

11  Was, das muss dazu gesagt werden, durchaus eine Langzeitfolge des Klimas politischer Unterdrückung sein kann. Auch hier wären weitergehende Untersuchungen kultureller Mentalitäten in Myanmar wünschenswert.

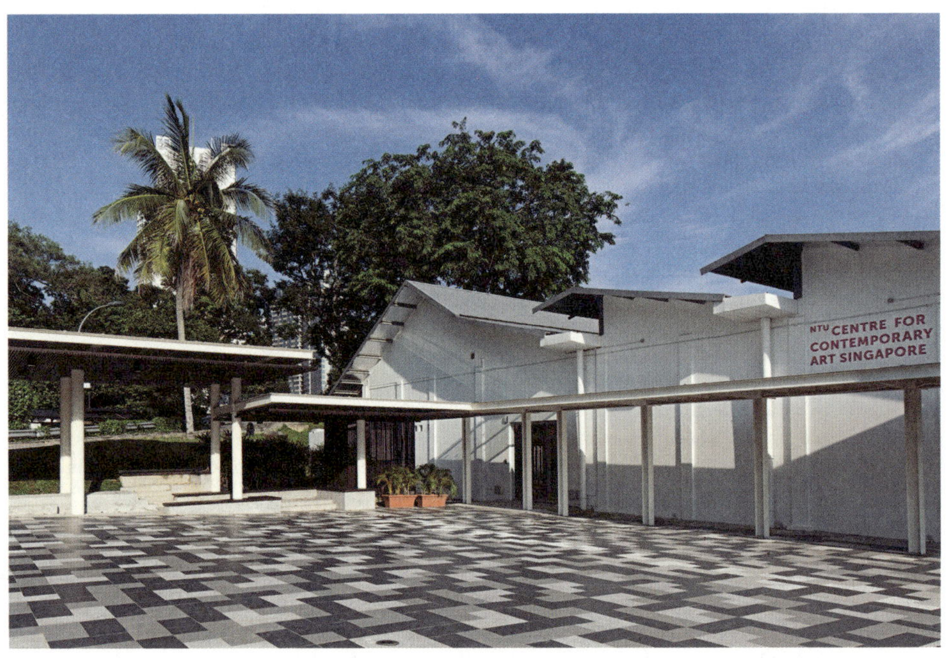

Exhibition hall
NTU Centre for Contemporary Art Singapore

Nora A. Taylor

# The *Singapore Art Archive Project* and the Institutions of Memory in Southeast Asia

On March 25, a day after Singapore's first Prime Minister Lee Kuan Yew passed away at the age of 91, I paid a visit to artist Koh Nguang How at his studio in the arts compound known as Gilman Barracks. Koh, as his friends know him, had been in residence there since July 2014 as part of Nanyang Technological University's Center for Contemporary Art's artist residency program. Since July, Koh has been displaying a portion of the archival material that he owns, arranging it according to various current events and exhibitions taking place at the NTU CCA Singapore or elsewhere in town. That day, I inquired if he had any special material on Lee Kuan Yew, or if he had been asked, as he often is, to supply photographs or newspaper clippings about the man to journalists or writers reporting on the events of the day. He admitted that he had been asked but he did not have anything to offer. Surprisingly, among the press and exhibition documents in his possession spanning over thirty years, there are hardly any references to the former Prime Minister. According to him, this was, in fact, not so surprising because Lee Kuan Yew rarely made pronouncements about art and culture. The neglect on the part of government institutions toward contemporary art practices, partially explains why someone like Koh has taken it upon himself to taking photographs and collecting exhibition materials pertaining to art events in Singapore taking place since 1986.

The subject of this paper is not Singapore government policy toward the arts per se, but rather Koh's project in particular. Although they are related, what interests me more is the very existence of—and that an artist should see the need for—an extensive archive of Singapore art outside of an institutional framework. Beyond its ontology, or the essential nature of the Singapore Art Archive Project, as he calls it, the question is: what are its contents, what story does it tell, what kind of narrative does it represent and how does it relate to other constructions of Singapore art history in the nation's cultural institutions? The archive as a work of art is nothing new. In 2004, Hal Foster described the tendency in post-war art to use appropriated images and accumulations of found objects, and he includes the practices of situationists and feminist artists in his classification, as evidence of an "archival impulse."[1] Foster's list of art works that can be qualified as archival, however, does not include actual physical archives but rather art works that recall moments in history by using elements from existing archives. By archive, I mean a collection of historical records and primary source documents stored in libraries or data banks. In the case of Koh Nguang How's Singapore Art Archive Project, the word archive can be used in a Foucauldian sense, as a trace object of a historical moment that has now passed.[2] It also represents two kinds of objects: a body of photographs taken by the artist of various art events taking place in Singapore, mostly in independent art spaces, and printed matter consisting of exhibition opening invitations, flyers, catalogues and newspapers, primarily the *Chinese Daily Paper*, *Lianhe Zaobao*, and the *Straits Times*. The archival impulses Hal Foster describes are instances where artists use archival material as ready-mades, thus, in his words, appropriating, interrogating, and reconfiguring the archive. This approach to the archive was also taken up by Okwui Enwezor in his exhibition at the International Center of Photography in 2008: "Archive Fever: Uses of the Document in Contemporary Art." Enwezor selected artists who use photographs as a field of inquiry into history. The artist then becomes an agent of memory and the archive, according to Enwezor "emerges as a place in which concerns with the past are touched by the astringent vapors of death, destruction, and degeneration."[3] The artists that both Foster and Enwezor refer to are not in the business of creating archives, but rather they act as archaeologists, excavating history. Koh is a retriever as well, but also a creator. The difference between Koh's archive and the works described by Foster and Enwezor is that the archival material that Koh presents is both deeply personal and public. It pertains as much to him as to the artists who figure in his archive. Koh is not calling for the viewer to interpret his photographs, nor does he manipulate them. They are what they are, both document and documentary evidence of an event that he attended. Another difference is that Koh's archive is about the art world and thus directly about art history.

Koh's profile has shifted in definition from that of a researcher to an artist and vice-versa. And his project has vacillated, depending on one's viewpoint, from a stack of papers to an archive to an artwork and back again. Its mutable quality is what makes it interesting. These are his photographs but they pertain to the greater narrative of Singaporean contemporary art history. Beyond its physical form or objecthood, Koh's archive has a performative component that is activated when he shows it to viewers. It is its function as an ongoing durational oral history project based on primary source documents the artist has collected for nearly three decades that is also what makes it appealing to those who come to seek him out. Koh offers a service to researchers, curators, and artists looking for documents or trips down memory lane. His archive is a storytelling device and the paradox lies in that its narrative is unfixed. It is neither authoritative nor ideological. It relates to a history that has yet to be written. It is the source material for an invisible art history.

In October 2014, the National Gallery of Singapore made an offer to Koh to acquire the bulk of his archive. The proposed contract described the "work" as photographs, film, negatives, 35 mm slides, books, posters, brochures, exhibition invites and artists' documents dated from 1988 to 2000. The title of the work was identified as *Singapore Art Archive Project @ NGS* and the author was listed as Koh Nguang How. The contract did not state the number of documents nor did it list them individually. The "work" therefore was relatively loosely defined and open-ended. It was potentially up to the artist to define it. However, in the negotiations for acquiring the work, the curators at the National Gallery also had their editorial say. For example, the National Gallery could not acquire Koh's collection of newspapers for several reasons. One was a lack of storage space, but also potential copyright issues with the newspaper companies in question. At one point in the discussion, the museum stated that it needed to limit the acquisition to material dated prior to 1990 due to an agreement with the National Heritage Board, the government body that oversees collections at the state-owned museums, and the Singapore Art Museum. Koh's archive straddled that decade and in the process of discussing the terms of the acquisition, Koh decided not to sell the work to the museum. He cited being overly attached to it, but I suspect he was also concerned about losing his role in animating it and guiding visitors through it.

When I first started meeting with Koh in early September, I was very interested in the museum's acquisition of the "work" and the whole issue of an archive as a work of art. In my mind, the archive was going to a new home and was therefore undergoing a kind of symbolic and indexical transformation, from a personal to a public archive, from a roomful of ephemeral documents or memorabilia to a veritable academic institution. In its displacement from the artist's house to the museum, the archive would become not only sanitized but also become finally the history that it told, both an object of research and an object *for* research. It would become, in essence, a primary source for art historians to examine and validate their own research. Its museumization would give it authority. Until it entered the storerooms or display cases of the museum, it could only be an artist's project, an amateur venture, an independent resource outside of the parameters of official discourse. It would become a work of art on display in a museum that would lend itself to engaging in dialogue with other works of art held in the same museum and thus become part of a narrative. Such a work would invite the public to read it alongside or against other histories known to the viewer. Putting Koh's archive on display in the museum would have, I believed, elevated it to a status beyond its materiality. It would become art history.

It turns out that I was wrong. Koh turned down the National Gallery's offer, but this did not mean that the archive returned to its primal state, as Koh's personal hoard of papers, photographs, and documents. In the eight or nine months of his residency at the Center for Contemporary Art, over eight thousand people visited his studio to pour through his material and listen to him tell the stories behind each documented event. His residency generated discussion among artists, curators, and art historians that led to a greater conversation about Singapore art history. Several talks by art historians that took place at the CCA borrowed images from Koh's archive. More importantly, during its time on display in his studio at the CCA, the archive became activated and animated by Koh's interactions with visitors to the space. Since it was exhibited in a studio space rather than a museum, it resisted the kind of fumigation, conservation, sanitization, and thus fossilization that would have been necessary had it been acquired by the museum, but it still served the kind of service that it would have had it been on display in the museum, for it encouraged its viewers to think about history and the story of Singapore contemporary art. That Koh declined the National Gallery's offer did not prove detrimental to the status of his archive. On the contrary, by virtue of being open for view for nearly a full-year at the CCA, its recognition and need only grew.

I don't have time to go into Koh's life story in this short presentation, but after becoming the unofficial chronicler of Singapore art events in the 1980s, during the course of the 90s, Singapore's cultural institutions underwent a series of changes. In 1991, the National Arts Council was founded; in 1993, the National Heritage Board created three museums out of the National Museum: The Singapore History Museum, the Asian Civilizations Museum, and the Singapore Art Museum. All three were located within a few hundred meters of one another in Singapore's Civic District. With the arrival of these institutions, Koh's archiving methods also began to change, as did the purpose of his endeavor. With the dawn of the Internet age, his quest for material documents increased and he became a scavenger, perusing abandoned sites around Singapore, a documenter of a "lost" Singapore and a salvager of newspapers discarded from press companies' storage houses. By 2000, he also stopped systematically taking pictures of art exhibitions and performances as the accessibility of digital cameras enabled artists to record their events with their own devices. With the material that he had accumulated, he took on the role of a researcher, the go-to person for information about Singapore art history. But he also became a fact-checker. In 2004, he presented a work as part of an exhibition organized by the independent curatorial collective p-10, to showcase some of the knowledge that he had accumulated. Titled "Errata …," curator Woon Tien Wei described the exhibition as "inspired by Koh's brand of empirical formula in his research of Singapore art, the exhibition is based on an error in print or in writing (to be contested) in the book *Channels & Confluences: A History of Singapore Art* by Kwok Kian Chow, published by the National Heritage Board/Singapore Art Museum in 1996." The impetus for the show was an error that Koh spotted, a misattributed date for a key painting in the history of Singapore art. The painting in question, *National Language Class* by Chua Mia Tee was erroneously dated 1950 when it was in fact painted in 1959. He titled his work *Errata: Page 71, Plate 47. Image Caption. Change Year: 1950 to Year: 1959; Reported September 2004 by Koh Nguang How*. p-10 deliberately omitted the title of the book, according to Woon Tien Wei, to give it a bit of ambiguity. In the brochure printed by p-10 on the occasion of the exhibition, Tien Wei further states that the exhibition "charts the unraveling of (Singapore Art) History as we know it, as a result of Koh's 'archaeological finds' as he excavates the 'ruins' left behind or forgotten. The status of this erratum is pending but not final. History needs the confluences of dialogues and perpetual re-orderings to maintain its relevance to the times."[4]

In pointing out such a seemingly minute error in what essentially was the first book on Singapore art history to be published since the opening of the Singapore Art Museum, written by the director of that institution no less, *Errata* undermined the authority of the Museum and its ability to write an authoritative art history. *Errata* gave Koh the opportunity to legitimize his archiving process and classify it as a work of art. It gave his archive a name, the Singapore Art Archive Project (SAAP) in 2005, and a purpose: to construct a meta-narrative of Singapore art history. In my discussion with him, Koh also stated that *Errata* showed that archival materials can speak for a work, but he admits that they can also speak wrongly; they simply provide another view. But, more importantly, it drew attention to the painting in question *National Language Class*, as it prompted an opportunity for a public discussion about the artist and the subject of the work, the language education policies in post-independence Malaya. The error in the date was by no means trivial. 1959 was a far more important date in Singapore history as it marked the election of Lee Kuan Yee as Prime Minister.

In May of this year, Koh opened an exhibition at the Jendela (Visual Arts Space), Esplanade, Singapore. Titled "Art Places," it consisted of a display of over 164 photographs that Koh took since 1987 of various locations in Singapore where art events, performances, or exhibitions took place. The display diverged from previous ones, at the Singapore Biennale of 2011 and "Errata …," in that he chose to reprint and enlarge the photographs so that they appeared to stand on their own as individual images rather than part of a series of snapshots. This prompted the viewer to look at the photographs in a different light, and in my opinion opened them up to additional possibilities for interpretation. As he recounted, walking through the exhibition, he purposefully focused on the places, the locations where art events took place, and the audience in attendance, rather than the artists or their works. "If I showed pictures of the artists' works without the context," he told me, "then it would be a copyright infringement and no longer be my work, but theirs. Artists should take responsibility for documenting their own work." As such, they do become intriguing to look at for one begins to see the events and places from his perspective, as an observer, rather than a participant. At times, however, he seemed to have taken the pictures from the air, or from no particular place at all. For example, the images of Hong Bee Warehouse which was scheduled for demolition and that artists took over as a site for staging performances and installations, are taken from a more distant location from above, as the building can be seen in its entirety rather than close up. The building itself becomes the focus of the image, the relic of mid-century architecture. There are other examples of structures that have since been destroyed or renovated and repurposed such as St. Joseph's Institution, now the Singapore Art Museum. The exhibition deliberately makes visible the ad hoc nature of art spaces prior to the institutionalization of Singapore and Southeast Asian art under the government's Renaissance City Plan (RCP) in the late 1990s. It is as if Koh wants to make clear that contemporary art did not need those newer institutions to thrive and be legitimated.

The photographs provide minimal information on actual events. They offer hints or clues for those familiar with those moments in art history. There is a photograph of artists and friends of Josef Ng that would otherwise simply look like a gathering of people, outside of the Singapore Subordinate Court. Those in the know would immediately identify the scene as Josef Ng's judicial hearing after he was fined for obscenity in the aftermath of his New Year's Eve performance from December 1993 to January 1994 as part of the AGA event in the corridor of the Fifth Passage mall. Although Koh witnessed the performance, for this exhibition, he chose not to display a photograph of Ng's piece *Brother Cane*. In a way, the photograph of those who came to support Ng at his trial is more telling of the event. That is, it tells a different kind of story, one of the consequences of an art event rather than the artist's work itself. And, still to this day, it is Ng's arrest and the subsequent ban on funding for performance art over the following decade that is most remembered by the art community—and not the character or nature of his actual performance piece.

This recent exhibition makes clear to me that Koh's practice goes beyond the archive proper or a particular definition of an archive. The selection of photographs is integral to the work and demonstrates how his life-long archival practice can be variously displayed, reconfigured, and  analyzed, in other words curated. It also legitimizes and affirms his identity as an artist whose practice is to show and narrate art history. His oral history, the accompanying narrative, his performance, is still integral to the work but he has also, paradoxically, subdued or repressed the indexical qualities of the photographs by enlarging them and offering the viewer a way of experiencing the past on the viewer's terms by testing the viewer's own ability to remember certain moments in Singapore art history and certain places on the island. They move beyond the events themselves, beyond their historical baggage, and enter into a realm of memory. His photographs, although he avails them to all of those who are interested, in my view, do not merely speak of the Singaporean past or past art spaces, events, and happenings. They are also *his* past: a past seen through his own eyes. As archival objects, they are therefore inherently flawed, or overly personalized. But, isn't he saying that that is the point of all and any archive? Since I wrote the longer version of this paper, I began to consider the Singapore Art Archive Project as a site of memory in Pierre Nora's sense—one that resists history. "Memory," he writes, "is life, borne by living societies founded in its name. It remains in permanent evolution, open to the dialectic of remembering and forgetting, unconscious of its successive deformation, vulnerable to manipulation and appropriation, susceptible to being dormant and periodically revived. History, on the other hand, is the reconstruction, always problematic and incomplete, of what is no longer. Memory is a perpetually actual phenomenon, a bond tying us to the eternal present: history is a representation of the past."[5]

1    Hal Foster, "An Archival Impulse," *October* 110 (Fall 2004): 3–22.
2    Michel Foucault, *The Archaeology of Knowledge (L'archéologie du savoir)* (Paris: Éditions Gallimard, 1971).
3    Okwui Enwezor, *Archive Fever: Uses of the Document in Contemporary Art* (New York: International Center of Photography, 2008), 46.
4    Text for brochure accompanying the exhibition, "Errata: Page 71, Plate 47. Image Caption. Change Year: 1950 to Year: 1959; Reported September 2004 by Koh Nguang How," p-10, September 15–October 14, 2004.
5    Pierre Nora, "Between Memory and History: Les Lieux de Mémoire," *Representations* 26 (Spring 1989): 8.

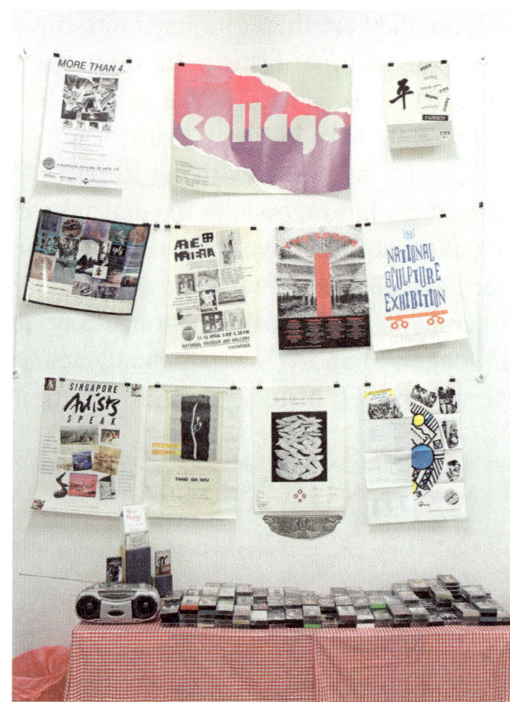

Koh Nguang How
*Singapore Art Archive Project
(SAAP@CCA)*, 2014
Residency studios
NTU CCA Singapore

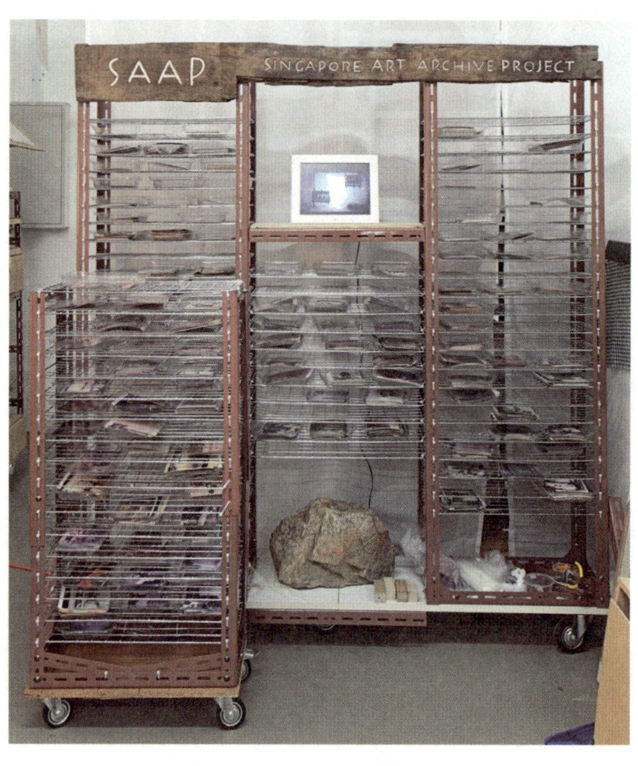

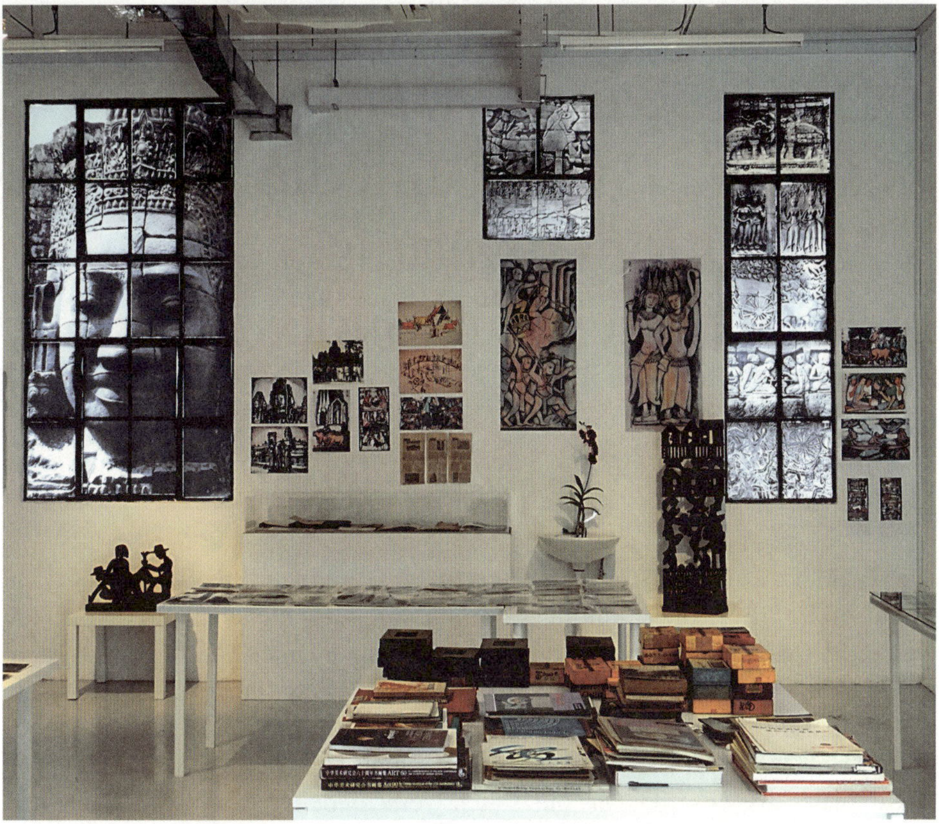

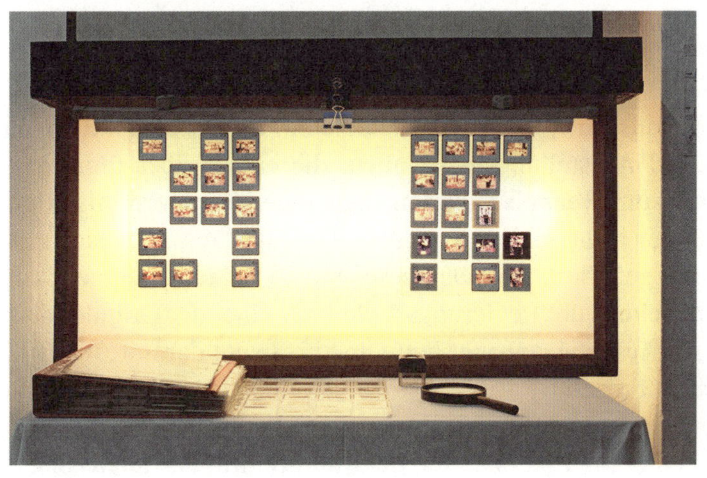

Nora A. Taylor

# Das *Singapore Art Archive Project* und die Institutionalisierung des Erinnerns in Südostasien

Am 25. März 2015, ein Tag, nachdem Singapurs erster Premierminister Lee Kuan Yew im Alter von 91 Jahren gestorben war, besuchte ich den Künstler Koh Nguang How in seinem Atelier in den Gillman Barracks, einem Kunstareal in Singapur. Koh, wie ihn seine Freunde nennen, hatte dort seit Juli 2014 ein Aufenthaltsstipendium des Center for Contemporary Art der Nanyang Technological University. Im Rahmen dieses Stipendiums stellte er Teile seines eigenen Archivmaterials aus, das er anlässlich verschiedener Veranstaltungen und Ausstellungen im NTU CCA Singapore oder anderswo in der Stadt jeweils neu arrangierte. An diesem Tag fragte ich ihn, ob er spezielles Material zu Lee Kuan Yew hätte und – was häufig vorkommt – von JournalistInnen oder anderen AutorInnen, die über aktuelle Ereignisse berichten, gebeten worden sei, Fotos oder Zeitungsausschnitte zur Verfügung zu stellen. Man hätte ihn gefragt, antwortete er, er habe aber nichts Entsprechendes anzubieten. Es war erstaunlich, dass es in den Presse- und Ausstellungsmaterialien, die er aus über dreißig Jahren gesammelt hatte, kaum Verweise auf den ehemaligen Premierminister gab. So erstaunlich sei es gar nicht, meinte Koh, denn Lee Kuan Yew hätte sich selten zu Kunst und Kultur geäußert. Gerade diese Nichtbeachtung zeitgenössischen Kunstgeschehens seitens der Regierungsstellen war einer der Gründe, warum es sich Koh 1986 zur Aufgabe gemacht hatte und bis heute daran festhält, Kunstveranstaltungen in Singapur fotografisch zu dokumentieren und Ausstellungsmaterial zu sammeln.

Es geht mir in diesem Text nicht um die Kulturpolitik der Regierung Singapurs, sondern speziell um Kohs Projekt. Obwohl sie miteinander zusammenhängen, interessiert mich eher die Tatsache, dass ein umfangreiches Archiv zur singapurischen Kunst außerhalb eines institutionellen Rahmens überhaupt existiert und ein Künstler es als notwendig erachtet, ein solches Archiv aufzubauen. Jenseits der Ontologie oder des Wesens des *Singapore Art Archive Project*, wie Koh es nennt, stellen sich folgende Fragen: Welche Inhalte hat es, welche Geschichten erzählt es, welches Narrativ wird vermittelt und in welchem Verhältnis steht es zu den Konstruktionen der Kunstgeschichte Singapurs, die in den staatlichen Kultureinrichtungen entworfen werden? Das Archiv als Kunstwerk ist nichts Neues. 2004 beschrieb Hal Foster die Tendenz in der Kunst der Nachkriegszeit, angeeignete Bilder und gefundene Objekte zu verwenden, und sah Praktiken von Situationisten und feministischen Künstlerinnen als Zeichen eines „archivalischen Impulses".[1] Allerdings umfasst Fosters Aufzählung von Kunstwerken, die als archivalisch bezeichnet werden, nicht wirkliche, physische Archive, sondern Werke, die mit Elementen aus bestehenden Archiven an historische Momente erinnern. Mit Archiv meine ich eine Sammlung historischer Aufzeichnungen und primärer Quellendokumente, die sich in Bibliotheken befinden oder die in Datenbanken gespeichert sind. Im Fall von Koh Nguang Hows *Singapore Art Archive Project* kann der Begriff Archiv im Foucault'schen Sinne verwendet werden, als materialisierte Spur eines vergangenen Augenblicks.[2] Kohs Archiv repräsentiert zwei Arten von Objekten: Fotografien, die der Künstler bei verschiedenen Kunstveranstaltungen vor allem in freien Kunsträumen in Singapur gemacht hat und gedrucktes Material wie Einladungskarten, Flyer, Kataloge und Zeitungen, darunter in erster Linie die *Chinese Daily Paper*, *Lianhe Zaobao* und *The Straits Times*. Wenn Hal Foster von archivalischen Impulsen spricht, bezieht er sich auf Projekte, bei denen KünstlerInnen Archivmaterial als Readymades nutzen und – in seinen Worten – sich das Archiv aneignen, es befragen und neu konfigurieren. Diese Herangehensweise an das Archiv wurde auch von Okwui Enwezor bei seiner Ausstellung *Archive Fever: Uses of the Document in Contemporary Art* im International Center of Photography in New York im Jahr 2008 aufgegriffen. Enwezor lud KünstlerInnen ein, die in ihre Arbeit Fotografien einbeziehen und sie als Mittel historischer Befragung nutzen. Die KünstlerInnen werden zu Agenten der Erinnerung und laut Enwezor wird das Archiv zu einem Ort, „an dem das dringliche Interesse an der Vergangenheit von den beißenden Dämpfen des Todes, der Zerstörung und des Zerfalls berührt wird".[3] Den KünstlerInnen, auf die sich sowohl Foster als auch Enwezor beziehen, geht es nicht um den Aufbau von Archiven als Tätigkeit an sich, sie handeln vielmehr wie ArchäologInnen, die Geschichte ausgraben. Koh ist ebenfalls jemand, der Dinge zurückholt, aber er schafft auch etwas Neues. Der Unterschied zwischen Kohs Archiv und den von Foster und Enwezor beschriebenen Arbeiten besteht darin, dass das von ihm präsentierte Material sowohl zutiefst persönlich als auch öffentlich ist. Es ist ebenso ein Teil seiner Geschichte wie der KünstlerInnen, die in seinem Archiv zu finden sind. Koh verlangt von den Betrachtern nicht, dass sie seine Fotos interpretieren, noch manipuliert er sie. Sie sind das, was sie sind, sowohl Dokumente als auch dokumentarische Belege der Veranstaltungen, die er besucht hat. Ein weiterer Unterschied besteht darin, dass sich sein Archiv auf die Kunstwelt bezieht und somit unmittelbar auf die Kunstgeschichte.

Kohs Position hat sich von der eines Forschers zu der eines Künstlers entwickelt, aber auch umgekehrt, und sein Projekt könnte man je nach Betrachtungsweise als Unmengen von Papier, als Archiv oder als Kunstwerk bezeichnen – und diese Wandelbarkeit macht es so interessant. Es sind zwar Fotografien, die er gemacht hat, doch gehören sie dem umfassenderen Narrativ der zeitgenössischen Kunstgeschichte Singapurs an. Jenseits seiner physischen Form oder Objekthaftigkeit besitzt Kohs Archiv eine performative Komponente, die aktiviert wird, wenn er es Menschen zeigt. Was das Archiv für die Besucher so reizvoll macht, ist seine Funktion als fortlaufendes Projekt der *Oral History* basierend auf Quellendokumenten, die der Künstler seit beinahe dreißig Jahren sammelt. Er bietet eine Dienstleistung für ForscherInnen, KuratorInnen und KünstlerInnen, die nach Dokumenten suchen oder eine Reise in die Vergangenheit unternehmen möchten. Sein Archiv kann viele Geschichten erzählen und das Paradoxe daran ist, dass sein Narrativ in keiner Weise festgelegt ist. Es ist weder offiziell noch ideologisch. Es bezieht sich auf eine Geschichte, die noch geschrieben werden muss und ist das Quellenmaterial für eine bisher nicht verfügbare Kunstgeschichte.

Im Oktober 2014 bot die National Gallery of Singapore Koh an, einen Großteil seines Archivs zu kaufen. Der vorgelegte Vertrag beschrieb das Werk als Sammlung von Fotografien, Filmen, Negativen, 35mm-Dias, Büchern, Plakaten, Broschüren, Einladungskarten und Dokumenten von KünstlerInnen aus den Jahren 1988 bis 2000. Der Titel des Werks lautete *Singapore Art Archive Project @ NGS* und als Autor wurde Koh Nguang How angeführt. Allerdings bestimmte der Vertrag weder die Anzahl der Dokumente noch listete er die Dokumente einzeln auf. Das Werk war daher nicht genau definiert oder greifbar; letztlich lag es am Künstler, zu bestimmen, was dazu gehörte, wobei die KuratorInnen der National Gallery bei den Verhandlungen zum Erwerb der Arbeit natürlich auch inhaltlich mitzureden hatten. Beispielsweise konnte die National Gallery das Konvolut an Zeitungen aus Kohs Archiv nicht erwerben, weil dazu die Lagerkapazitäten fehlten und Urheberrechtsfragen mit den Zeitungsherausgebern Schwierigkeiten hätten bereiten können. Während der Verhandlungen wurde von Museumsseite geäußert, in Absprache mit dem National Heritage Board, der Regierungsstelle, die für die Sammlungen staatlicher Museen zuständig ist, und dem Singapore Art Museum, müsse sich der Erwerb auf Material vor 1990 beschränken. Kohs Archiv umfasste dieses Jahrzehnt, aber ging auch weit darüber hinaus. Im Zuge der Verhandlungen über die Kaufbedingungen entschied Koh dann, das Werk nicht an das Museum zu verkaufen. Er sagte, er würde zu sehr daran hängen, aber ich vermute, dass er auch die Sorge hatte, seine Rolle zu verlieren, als derjenige der das Archiv lebendig hält und mit den Besuchern in Kontakt tritt.

Als ich mich Anfang September die ersten Male mit Koh traf, war ich sehr an dem Erwerb des Werks durch das Museum und dem Thema des Archivs als Kunstwerk interessiert. In meiner Vorstellung hätte das Archiv durch den Ankauf ein neues „Zuhause" gefunden und so eine Art symbolische und indexikalische Veränderung erfahren – von einem persönlichen zu einem öffentlichen Archiv, von einem Raum voller vergänglicher Dokumente und Erinnerungsstücke zu einer veritablen akademischen Institution. Durch den Umzug von der Wohnung des Künstlers ins Museum würde das Archiv nicht nur geordnet, sondern endlich Teil der Geschichte werden, die es erzählt; sowohl Forschungsgegenstand als auch Gegenstand *für* die Forschung. Es würde im Wesentlichen eine primäre Quelle für KunsthistorikerInnen zur Untersuchung und Überprüfung ihrer eigenen Forschung werden. Seine Musealisierung würde ihm Autorität verleihen. Käme das Archiv nicht in die Lagerräume und Vitrinen des Museums, würde es nur das Projekt eines Künstlers bleiben, die Unternehmung eines Laien, eine unabhängige Quelle außerhalb der Parameter des offiziellen Diskurses. Im Museum hingegen würde es zu einem ausgestellten Kunstwerk, das mit anderen Kunstwerken in Dialog treten und somit Teil eines Narrativs würde. Die Öffentlichkeit wäre eingeladen, es neben oder gegen andere bekannte Geschichten zu lesen. Ich war der Meinung, dass die Präsentation von Kohs Archiv im Museum ihm einen Status jenseits seiner Materialität verleihen würde – es würde Teil der Kunstgeschichte werden.

Es stellte sich aber heraus, dass ich falsch lag. Koh lehnte das Angebot der National Gallery ab, was aber nicht bedeutete, dass das Archiv zu seinem ursprünglichen Zustand zurückkehrte – als Kohs persönliche Sammlung von Zeitungen, Fotos und Dokumenten. Während seines acht- oder neunmonatigen Residenzaufenthaltes im Center for Contemporary Art besuchten mehr als achttausend Menschen sein Atelier, um im Material zu stöbern und seine Geschichten zu jedem dokumentierten Ereignis zu hören. Dieser Aufenthalt regte Diskussionen zwischen KünstlerInnen, KuratorInnen und KunsthistorikerInnen an, die zu einem umfassenderen Diskurs über die singapurische Kunstgeschichte führten. Mehrere KunsthistorikerInnen liehen sich Material aus Kohs Archiv für Vorträge im CCA. Noch wichtiger war, dass während der Dauer der Ausstellung in seinem Atelier im CCA das Archiv durch Kohs Interaktionen mit den BesucherInnen lebendig wurde. Da es in einem Atelier und nicht in einem Museum präsentiert wurde, entging das Archiv der Konservierung, Säuberung und letztendlich „Versteinerung", die unabwendbar gewesen wäre, wenn das Museum es erworben hätte. Dennoch leistete es das, was es auch im Museum geleistet hätte, denn es ermutigte die BesucherInnen, über die Geschichte der zeitgenössischen Kunst Singapurs nachzudenken. Dass Koh das Angebot der National Gallery abgelehnt hatte, erwies sich für den Status seines Archivs nicht als Nachteil, ganz im Gegenteil: Da es beinahe ein ganzes Jahr lang im CCA ausgestellt war, gewann es an Bedeutung und es zeigte sich, wie notwendig es war.

Ich kann in diesem Text nicht ausführlicher auf Kohs Lebensgeschichte eingehen, aber nachdem er in den 1980er Jahren zum inoffiziellen Chronisten der Kunstereignisse in Singapur wurde, erfuhren die Kulturinstitutionen des Landes in den 1990er Jahren einige Veränderungen. 1991 wurde das National Arts

Council gegründet; 1993 wurde durch den National Heritage Board das National-museum in drei Museen aufgeteilt: das Singapore History Museum, das Asian Civilizations Museum und das Singapore Art Museum. Alle drei befanden sich wenige hundert Meter voneinander entfernt in Singapurs Civic District. Durch die Etablierung dieser Institutionen veränderten sich auch Kohs Methoden der Archivierung und die Zielsetzung seines Projekts. Mit dem Aufkommen des Internets nahm seine Suche nach materiellen Dokumenten zu und er wurde zu einem Sammler: er durchkämmte verlassene Orte der Stadt, dokumentierte das *verlorene* Singapur und rettete Zeitungen, die Verlage aus ihren Depots ausmisteten. Um das Jahr 2000 hörte er auf, systematisch Fotos von Kunstausstellungen und Performances zu machen, da die Verbreitung von Digitalkameras es KünstlerInnen erlaubte, ihre Veranstaltungen selbst zu dokumentieren. Mit dem gesammelten Material wurde er nun zum Forscher, zu der Person, die man aufsucht, wenn man Informationen zur Kunstgeschichte Singapurs benötigte. Er wurde aber auch zu einem „Fact-Checker". 2004 präsentierte er seine Arbeit als Teil einer vom unabhängigen Kuratorenkollektiv p-10 organisierten Ausstellung, um etwas von dem Wissen, das er gesammelt hatte, weiterzugeben. Die Ausstellung unter dem Titel *Errata …* beschrieb der Kurator Woon Tien folgendermaßen: „Inspiriert von Kohs empirischer Herangehensweise an die Erforschung der singapurischen Kunst, basiert die Ausstellung auf einem (angefochtenen) Druckfehler oder fehlerhaften Text in dem Buch *Channels & Confluences: A History of Singapore Art* von Kwok Kian Chow, 1996 herausgegeben vom National Heritage Board/Singapore Art Museum." Die Schau wurde angeregt durch einen Fehler, den Koh bemerkt hatte: die falsche Jahresangabe eines bedeutenden Gemäldes der Kunstgeschichte Singapurs. Das betreffende Bild, *National Language Class* von Chua Mia Tee, wurde fälschlicherweise auf das Jahr 1950 datiert, statt auf 1959. „Errata: Page 71, Plate 47. Image Caption. Change Year: 1950 to Year: 1959; Reported September 2004 by Koh Nguang How". p-10 ließ den Titel des Buchs bewusst weg, um laut Woon Tien Wei die Sache im Unklaren zu lassen. In der von p-10 anlässlich der Ausstellung herausgegebenen Broschüre schreibt Tien Wei, die Ausstellung „kartografiert als Ergebnis von Kohs ‚archäologischen Funden' die Auslöschung der Geschichte (der singapurischen Kunst) wie wir sie kennen, da er hinterlassene oder vergessene ‚Ruinen' ausgräbt. Der Status dieses Erratums ist schwebend, aber nicht endgültig. Die Geschichte benötigt das Zusammenfließen von Dialogen und eine permanente Neuordnung, um für die heutige Zeit relevant zu bleiben."[4]

Indem auf einen solchen, scheinbar winzigen Irrtum im allerersten Buch zur Kunstgeschichte Singapurs seit Eröffnung des Singapore Art Museums, geschrieben von dessen Direktor, aufmerksam gemacht wurde, unterminierte *Errata …* die Autorität des Museums und seine Kompetenz, eine offizielle Kunstgeschichte zu verfassen. *Errata …* gab Koh die Gelegenheit, seinen Prozess des Archivierens als Kunstwerk zu legitimieren. Sein Archiv erhielt 2005 einen Namen, das *Singapore Art Archive Project* (SAAP), und eine Zielsetzung: die

Bildung eines Meta-Narrativs der Kunstgeschichte Singapurs. In unserem Gespräch sagte Koh, *Errata* … habe gezeigt, dass Archivmaterial für eine Arbeit sprechen könne, räumte aber ein, dass es auch Falsches aussagen könne – es biete schlicht eine andere Perspektive. Wichtiger war, dass die Aufmerksamkeit auf das fragliche Gemälde *National Language Class* gelenkt wurde und sich so eine Gelegenheit bot, öffentlich über die Künstlerin und das Thema ihrer Arbeit, die Spracherziehungspolitik in Malaysia nach der Unabhängigkeit zu diskutieren. Die falsche Datumsangabe war ganz und gar nicht trivial. 1959 war ein bedeutendes Jahr in der Geschichte Singapurs, es markierte die Wahl von Lee Kuan Yee zum Premierminister.

Im Mai 2015 eröffnete Koh die Ausstellung *Art Places* in der Jendala Gallery, die im Kulturzentrum Esplanade in Singapur ihre Räume hat. Die Ausstellung bestand aus 164 Fotos, die Koh seit 1987 bei verschiedenen Kunstveranstaltungen, Performances und Ausstellungen in Singapur aufgenommen hatte. Die Präsentation unterschied sich von den früheren Ausstellungen auf der Singapur Biennale 2011 und bei *Errata* …, da er die Fotos dieses Mal vergrößert hatte und als eigenständige Drucke, nicht als Serie von Schnappschüssen zeigte. Das regte die BetrachterInnen an, die Fotografien anders wahrzunehmen und eröffneten meiner Meinung nach zusätzliche Interpretationsmöglichkeiten. Koh berichtete, durch die Ausstellungen gelaufen zu sein und sich bewusst auf den Ort und das jeweilige Publikum konzentriert zu haben, weniger auf die Künstler und ihre Arbeiten. „Hätte ich Bilder der Werke der Künstlerinnen ohne Kontext gezeigt", sagte er, „hätte ich damit das Urheberrecht verletzt und es wären nicht mehr meine Arbeiten, sondern ihre. Für die Dokumentation ihrer Arbeit aber sollten KünstlerInnen selbst Verantwortung übernehmen." In dieser Hinsicht sind sie tatsächlich faszinierend, denn man beginnt, die Veranstaltungen und Orte aus seiner Perspektive als Beobachter und nicht als Teilnehmer zu betrachten. Manchmal scheint Koh die Fotos aus der Luft aufgenommen zu haben oder von einer völlig unklaren Position. So sind die Bilder der Hong Bee Lagerhalle, die abgerissen werden sollte und von KünstlerInnen als Ort für Performances und Installationen besetzt wurde, von einer erhöhten Position aufgenommen und man überblickt das gesamte Gebäude. Ein Relikt der Architektur aus der Mitte des letzten Jahrhunderts steht also im Mittelpunkt. Es gibt weitere Beispiele von Gebäuden, die seitdem zerstört oder renoviert und umfunktioniert wurden, etwa das St. Joseph's, eine Institution, aus der inzwischen das Singapore Art Museum geworden ist. Die Ausstellung macht das Improvisierte und Temporäre der Kunsträume vor der Institutionalisierung der singapurischen und südostasiatischen Kunst im Zuge des Renaissance City Plans (RCP) in den späten 1990er Jahren sichtbar. Es ist, als wollte Koh verdeutlichen, dass die zeitgenössische Kunst diese neueren Institutionen gar nicht gebraucht hat, um sich zu entfalten und sich zu legitimieren.

Die Fotos liefern nur wenig Information zu den eigentlichen Veranstaltungen. Sie geben Hinweise für diejenigen, die sich mit den gezeigten Momenten der

Kunstgeschichte auskennen. Da ist beispielsweise ein Foto, das Josef Ng mit Freunden und anderen KünstlerInnen vor dem Singapore Subordinate Court zeigt. Man könnte es einfach für eine Ansammlung von Menschen halten. Eingeweihte wissen natürlich sofort, dass das Bild nach der Gerichtsverhandlung von Josef Ng entstanden sein muss, der wegen „Obszönität" zu einem Bußgeld verurteilt worden war, in Folge seiner Performance am Silvesterabend 1993 bei der AGA Veranstaltung in der Fifth Passage Mall. Obwohl Koh die Performance gesehen hatte, zeigte er in dieser Ausstellung keine Fotos von Ngs *Brother Kane*. In gewisser Hinsicht sagt das Foto der Menschen, die Ng beim Verfahren unterstützten, weit mehr über die Veranstaltung aus. Es erzählt eine andere Geschichte: die der Folgen eines Kunstereignisses und nicht die der Arbeit des Künstlers selbst. Und bis heute ist es die Verhaftung von Ng und das darauffolgende, ein Jahrzehnt während Verbot von Performancekunst das, was der Kunstszene am meisten in Erinnerung geblieben ist, nicht der Charakter oder die Art seiner eigentlichen Performance.

Diese jüngste Ausstellung macht für mich deutlich, dass Kohs Praxis über das Archiv an sich oder eine bestimmte Definition des Archivs hinausgeht. Die Auswahl der Fotografien ist ein integraler Bestandteil der Arbeit und zeigt, wie seine lebenslange archivalische Praxis auf unterschiedliche Weise ausgestellt, neustrukturiert und analysiert – mit anderen Worten kuratiert – werden kann. Sie legitimiert und bestätigt auch seine Identität als Künstler, dessen Praxis darin besteht, Kunstgeschichte zu zeigen und zu erzählen. *Oral History*, das begleitende Narrativ und Kohs Präsentationen sind immer noch feste Bestandteile der Arbeit, doch die indexikalischen Eigenschaften der Fotos hat er paradoxerweise unterdrückt oder verdrängt, indem er sie vergrößert hat und den BetrachterInnen damit die Möglichkeit gegeben hat, die Vergangenheit zu ihren eigenen Bedingungen zu erleben. Er forderte sie heraus, sich an bestimmte Momente der singapurischen Kunstgeschichte zu erinnern und an Orte der Insel, die es so nicht mehr gibt. Sie werden über die konkreten Anlässe hinausgetragen, überwinden ihren historischen Ballast und treten ein in den Bereich der Erinnerung. Meiner Ansicht nach erzählen seine Fotografien – obwohl er sie allen Interessierten zur Verfügung stellt – nicht nur von der Vergangenheit Singapurs und den Kunsträumen, Veranstaltungen und Happenings, sondern auch von seiner Vergangenheit – einer Vergangenheit durch seine Augen betrachtet. Als Objekte eines Archivs sind sie daher immanent defizitär oder vielleicht zu persönlich. Aber sagt er uns damit nicht auch, dass das genau das Wesen jedes Archivs ist? Während der Arbeit an der längeren Version dieses Vortrags habe ich begonnen, das *Singapore Art Archive Project* als Ort der Erinnerung im Sinne von Pierre Nora zu begreifen, als Ort, der sich gegen die Geschichte wehrt:

Erinnerung ist Leben, von lebendigen Gesellschaften hervorgebracht, die in ihrem Namen gegründet wurden. Sie entwickelt sich ständig weiter, der Dialektik von Erinnern und Vergessen zugewandt, sich ihrer sukzessiven

Verformung nicht bewusst, anfällig für Manipulation und Aneignung, schlafend und in unregelmäßigen Abständen geweckt. Geschichte hingegen ist die immer problematische und unvollständige Rekonstruktion dessen, was nicht mehr ist. Erinnerung ist ein immerwährend präsentes Phänomen, das uns an die ewige Gegenwart bindet; Geschichte ist eine Darstellung der Vergangenheit.[5]

1    Hal Foster, „An Archival Impulse", in: *October*, Bd. 110, Herbst 2004, S. 3–22.

2    Michel Foucault, *Die Archäologie des Wissens (L'archéologie du savoir)*, Frankfurt am Main: Suhrkamp, 1973.

3    Okwui Enwezor, *Archive Fever: Uses of the Document in Contemporary Art*, New York: International Center of Photography, 2008, S. 46.

4    Text aus dem Begleitheft der Ausstellung *Errata: Page 71, Plate 47. Image Caption. Change Year: 1950 to Year: 1959; Reported September 2004 by Koh Nguang How*, p-10, 15. September–14. Oktober 2004.

5    Pierre Nora, „Between Memory and History: Les Lieux de Mémoire", in: *Representations*, Nr. 26, Frühjahr 1989, S. 7–24, hier S. 8.

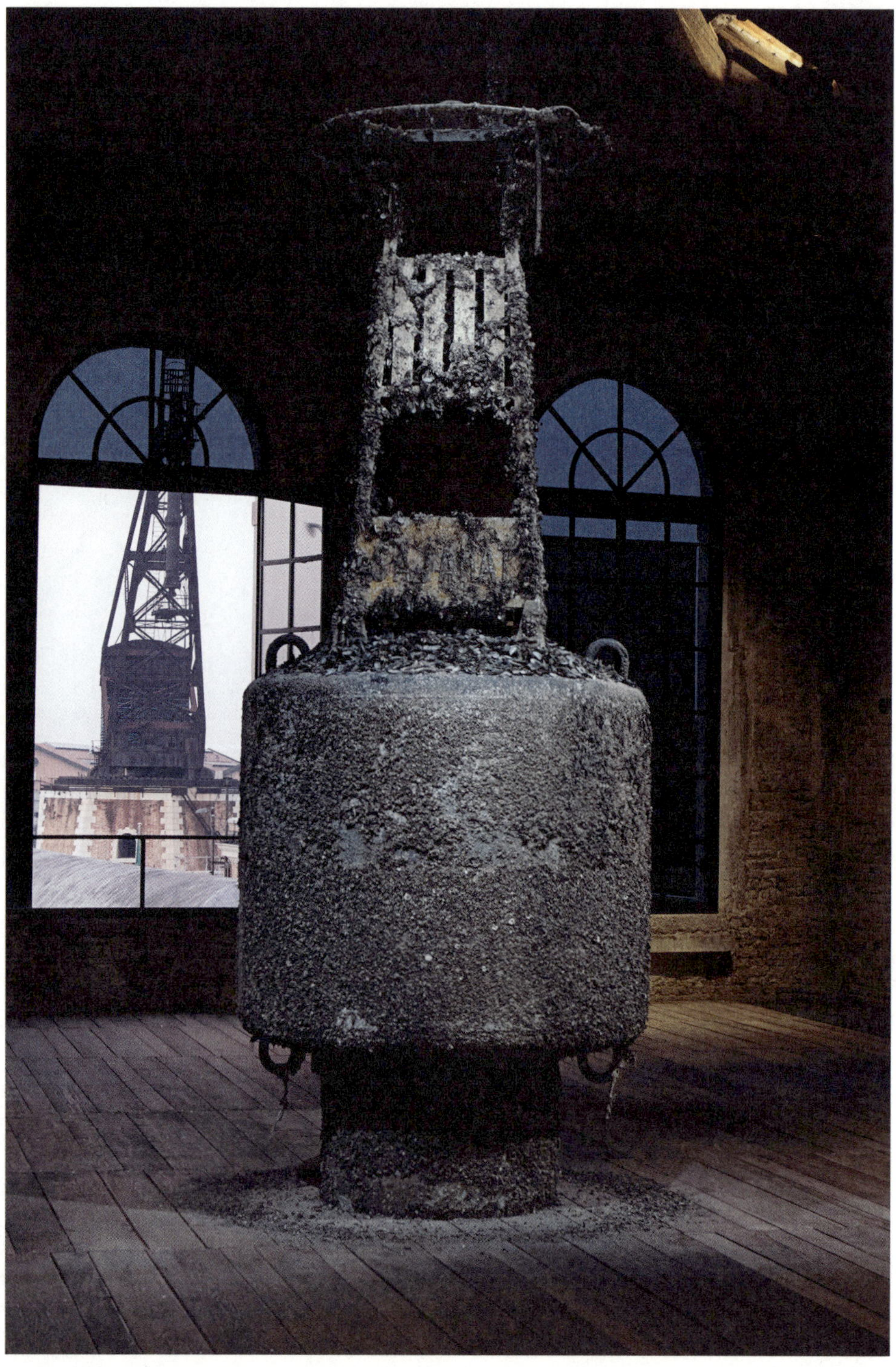

Charles Lim Yi Yong
*SEA STATE 2: As Evil Disappears (Sajahat Buoy)*, 2015
Singapore Pavilion, 56th Venice Biennale

Kevin Chua

# The Curatorial as Buoy and Beacon

There is a belief held by people along the east coast of England from Northumberland to Kent that most deaths happen at the receding of the tide. Shakespeare must have been familiar with it when he made Falstaff die "just between twelve and one, e'en at the turning of the tide."[1] The Malays of the Singapore-Malaysia region, too, used to send out "disease boats," loaded with offerings, into the sea as a way to expurgate disease, sickness, and death.[2] Walter William Skeat, no stranger to stories of Malay magic, recounts the following tale:

> The *kramat* [sacred place[3]] about which I am now writing is a very remarkable one. It is situated on the extreme point of land at the mouth of the river Selangor, close to where the new lighthouse has been erected. A magnificent *kayu ara* (a kind of fig tree) forms a prominent feature of the *tanjong* (point or cape), and at the base of this tree, enveloped entirely by its roots, is an oblong-shaped space having the appearance of a Malay grave, with the headstones complete. [...] To this sacred spot constant pilgrimages are made by the Malays, and the lower branches of the tree rarely lack those pieces of white and yellow cloth which are always hung up as an indication that some devout person has paid his vows." After Raja Abdullah died, he was buried there. Skeat's informant adds: "When walking along the *pantai* (shore), if you chance to meet a very large tiger let him pass unharmed. It is only Raja Abdullah's ghost, and in proof thereof you will see it leaves no footmarks on the sand.[4]

At the center of the Singapore Pavilion's exhibition space at the 2015 Venice Biennale is a giant buoy, towering over ten feet. Looking at this buoy that disappeared off the southern coast of Singapore around 2008, I think of such watery deaths.

While many writers have written about Charles Lim's artistic practice–which combines filmmaking, archival research, artifact sleuthing, and experiments in digital media with his broad, professional interest in the sea–few have asserted the stakes of his practice within national, regional, and global scales. Though many of his works are allusively political–seeming to place their wager on the open-endedness of archival practice–a more interesting approach, as I see it, is to tie formal aspects of his work to his maritime politics. It is, essentially, to find his politics of form.

"In Search of Raffles' Light" was a multi-dimensional archival project and exhibition that opened in October 2013 at the National University of Singapore (NUS) Museum in Singapore. The project concerned the Raffles Lighthouse, situated on Pulau Satumu, one of several islands south of Singapore. Built by Indian convicts and completed in 1855, it was named after Sir Stamford Raffles, "founder" of modern Singapore, and subsequently functioned as the southernmost marker of Singapore's territorial waters.[5] The project was a collaboration between Lim and Shabbir Hussain Mustafa, then-curator at the NUS Museum. They investigated the site, gathered information about the lighthouse, dug up objects and relics from storerooms, filmed the lighthouse and its environs, and talked to various people connected with the lighthouse over the years–seamen, lighthouse keepers, collectors, sea enthusiasts, and museum professionals, including Eric Alfred, former curator of Zoology at the Raffles Museum from 1957-72. All these individuals had stories to tell. One slowly realized that the lighthouse was less a monument than an absent center for a series of archival traces.

Lim has been conducting an interrelated series of investigations about the sea known as *SEA STATE*. The title alludes to the paradox that while Singapore has been so defined by its relations with the sea–think of the country's identity as a port, which dates back to the colonial era from 1819[6]–the country has an existential denial of its surrounding waters. The sea is everything hidden and invisible; it is danger, flux, and chaos. It is what we don't want to admit into the light of consciousness.[7] Indeed, the title of the exhibition, not "Raffles Lighthouse" but "Raffles' Light," alludes to the light of the Enlightenment brought by Raffles and company.[8] Where exactly is the sea, and how do we think of it more as *limit* than entity?

In the exhibition, we saw maps, diagrams, and model lighthouses (intriguingly displayed above shoulder-level, to give the illusion of looking upwards at the lighthouse, the same viewpoint from which one would come upon it at sea). Didactic paintings illustrated proper buoy maintenance, while a set of light boxes showed water light levels at various locations around Singapore (indicating levels of pollution, it cleverly alluded to the mixing of color paints). This last object played especially into the exhibition's theme: for does not the longing for clean and clear water derive from a concomitant desire for purity–the clarity and promise of light? Instead of knowledge of the sea, what we were being exposed to and challenged with was the sea as a process of knowledge.

One story that emerged from the "Raffles' Light" archive told how Port of Singapore Authority employees would come to these outlying islands in the 1950s, including Pulau Satumu, for picnics.[9] Because the lighthouse was in a restricted area, these picnics were, strictly speaking, illegal–hence the activity had a transgressive appeal. This particular story echoed the central video in the exhibition: a nighttime view of Raffles Lighthouse, taken from a boat circling Pulau Satumu. Lim, we learn, had to film precisely at the legal limits of the island (which extended out onto the water by several meters). To have gone farther would have been considered trespassing.[10]

Several of Lim's works flirt with trespassing, or engage in subtle forms of border breaching. In the film *It's Not that I Forgot, but that I Chose not to Mention* (2009–10), a man swims from one end of a pool. Moving rather slowly, we soon realize he is wiping algae off the floor. Back and forth he goes, and what results is a curious, yet elegant, line drawing (we are given a bird's-eye view of the pool, which flattens the visual plane). The swimmer's motion metaphorizes an erasure that's mental, maybe historical, which seems recuperated by the work's sinuous aesthetic. Then we find out that Lim's access to the pool involved a bit of trespassing: the pool, disused, had been boarded up.[11] One question is whether the languid tone of the film, its expansiveness and sense of ease, *required* that initial trespassing. Lim's work treads on a host of actions designed to thwart the material appropriation of a peasant's labor, such as foot-dragging, poaching, pilfering, dissimulation, sabotage, desertion, absenteeism, squatting, and flight. Anthropologist James Scott terms "infrapolitics" such "low-profile forms of resistance that dare not speak in their own name."[12] Though infrapolitical acts are often considered futile as a form of resistance, perhaps they are less defensive than at first appears. In certain circumstances and contexts, I would argue, they can be *constitutive* of politics.

In the film *All the Lines Flow Out* (2011), a boat languidly moves down several of Singapore's *longkangs*. Though these storm drains remove water, waste, and effluvia from the island interior, we don't think about them–they've become naturalized in the city's imagination. The film is at one level, then, an allegory of forgetting. In a beguiling early scene, a man crafts a makeshift fish trap out of a plastic water bottle (which also slyly allegorizes the do-it-yourself nature of Lim's aesthetic). During the course of the making of the film, Lim was intrigued by the recent capture of the thief Mat Selamat. But, more fascinating than the stories of how he escaped using storm drains, was the myth that he simply *drew a doorway* in order to escape. Such an act taps into a long history of Malay magic.[13] Lim's aesthetic has a topological continuity between inside and outside, containment and release. One cannot be reduced to the other. It is as though every scene of a boat drifting downward simultaneously produces a feeling of being trapped. Rupture and continuity circle around each other.

Speckled with rust, barnacles gripping its bottom, seawater almost dripping from its sides, a buoy formed one component of the installation assembled by Lim, with curatorial assistance from Shabbir Hussain Mustafa, for the Singapore Pavilion at the 56thVenice Biennale in 2015.[14] For the installation, Lim recreated a buoy that had mysteriously disappeared off Singapore's southern coast around 2008. Examining marine charts of the area, Lim noticed that an entire island, Pulau Sejahat, had disappeared, absorbed into the surrounding landmasses that had been filled in with sand. The Sejahat Buoy was located off the island, and may have been removed by the Marine and Port Authority of Singapore during the course of the filling-in of the land, or (more likely) been buried under layers of sand. No trace of it remains; nor do maps do the work of mourning. But why recreate and display this buoy?[15] Indeed, the process of artificially growing barnacles on the buoy in the sea, and its subsequent removal and transportation, hints at *ritual*—as though some object was being buried and exhumed.[16]

Buoy and island disappeared because of Singapore's program of land expansion, which has not been without controversy. Since the 1960s, the country's land area has grown from 581.5 to 710 square kilometers.[17] Land reclamation has accelerated over the last ten years or so. By 2030, the country plans to expand by another seventy square kilometers—an increase in land area of thirty percent from its original size. (One recent project built on reclaimed land is the aptly named Marina Bay Sands, a five-star hotel and casino, with clear views of the southern sea.[18] This complex curiously resembles the leisure resorts for nineteenth-century colonial elites, often built on frontier hill stations.[19] Of course Singapore thinks of itself not simply as the center of Southeast Asia, but at the frontier of global capitalism. Since at least the 1960s, leisure has occupied the forefront of the military-industrial-financial complex.) What's troubling is the scale of the state's land reclamation, and the illegalities that lurk behind the entire endeavor. Singapore's importation of more than 273 million US dollar worth of sand in 2008 alone, for instance—and these are the government's own figures—only accounts for the *legal* trade in sand. Because of the sheer volume, no one country can provide enough to quench Singapore's thirst for sand. Some of it has thus come from Malaysia, some from Indonesia. "Many of Indonesia's islands that lie within easy reach of Singapore have few or no inhabitants," writes journalist Chris Milton, "and Singapore has taken advantage of this geography, going so far as to wipe some places entirely off the map."[20] In 2003, Nipah island, which lay on the Singapore-Indonesia border, disappeared. Between 2005–10, a further twenty-four islands are believed to have disappeared under the waves. Though a number of illegal sand excavation activities have been traced back to companies in Singapore, the Singapore government flatly denies that it condones the importation of illegal sand. And yet it continues: in 2003, smugglers excavated and shipped an estimated 300 million cubic meters of sand, worth 2.5 billion dollars.[21] Recent governmental prohibitions on the exportation of sand have had the effectiveness of an open sieve.

Yet the land reclamation that has been taking place *around* the island is re-playing a colonial history, of the clearing and opening up of land *on it*.[22] While the geo-strategic importance of Singapore within the region–linking the all-important Malacca Straits to the trade routes to China and Indonesia–is familiar, few acknowledge that a concomitant process of expansion occurred *into* the is-land. Inward extension preceded outward expansion. The surveying of territory in mid-to-late nineteenth-century Singapore re-enacted a whole history of enclosure in Britain.[23] The genre of landscape painting produced in nineteenth-century Singapore was, then, cruelly ironic: land became mapped and gridded, ready for consumption. Pushing out the internal frontier was the first step in the bolting down of national sovereignty.

The Singapore state's expansion–less a "reclaiming" than a "claiming" of land–also involved a taming of the Southern Islands and the surrounding sea. Pirates roamed these waters in the first half of the nineteenth century–or at least that was when they *became* a problem. The line between pirates and privateers was razor thin; often one couldn't tell whether the small ships that frequented these waters were being used for trade or something more nefarious. The many coves and inlets in the region along with their fast boats allowed "pirates" to escape detection. Though the late-eighteenth century shift in British policy favored trade over dominion, policy makers did want to establish settlements in the region that could become bases for commerce.[24] So, aware of Dutch attempts to reassert supremacy in the Malay Archipelago, Stamford Raffles used a piracy argument to urge the British to make settlements and sign precautionary treaties with the native princes. A settlement would impose, he said, a

> wholesome restraint [...] upon the conduct of our own countrymen trading in the Archipelago. Our duty to other nations, and to the cause of justice, no less than a regard for our national character, requires that *the peaceable natives of the islands* should not be kept at the mercy of every mercantile adventurer of our own nations. The inducements and facilities to rapine are too numerous in that quarter to be overlooked.[25]

Phrasing British activity as protective of "peaceable" natives–he means future merchant settlers–as privateers were turned into pirates, strengthened the Brit-ish case for being in the region.

As sovereignty was unclear, Raffles and the British had to find a way to le-gally justify their encroachment.[26] Over the course of the 1810s and 20s, piracy came more and more to be seen as ingrained in a particular group of people in this region.[27] If ingrained, the British would have a moral duty to provide pater-nal regulation by imposing control. Also employed during these decades was the language of property, which was yet another way to shift the responsibility of piracy onto these native peoples. Rear Admiral Sir Edward Owen, for instance, wrote:

> A great portion of the robberies complained of are it is said, committed by the Praus [i.e., *prahus* or sailing boat] belonging to the Southern Islands now under Dutch protection in their progress to the Bird Nests Islands to the Northward. These islands, all belonging either to our Government or that of Siam, are farmed out to traders for their profit, and these visits are not less an infringement of the property of those who rent them than of the territorial right of the Country they belong to.[28]

The process resembles what I have elsewhere called "garden logic": the British liberal political imagination shifts blame and agency onto an Other, creating a gap in the law that justifies their own action and intervention.[29] In many ways, the British are "forced" into action.[30] We should also recall that the determination of lines of sovereignty in the sea goes back to the seventeenth century, when Hugo Grotius defended the Dutch seizure of the cargo of the Portuguese vessel Santa Catarina, near the Malacca Straits, by arguing that it was not an act of piracy.[31] Out of the legal scuffle emerged his treatise *The Freedom of the Seas* (1609), which justified freedom of trade in international waters for the centuries to come. But, of course, "freedom" was reserved to those who could give the name to "piracy."

Like a lighthouse or a storm drain, the buoy is a piece of infrastructure. Electrical, heating and cooling systems, waste systems, roads and traffic systems: infrastructure is what undergirds society and allows it to function.[32] Because it is often unnoticed, or blithely appreciated, infrastructure can be a more potent means of state power.[33] Indeed, the provision of infrastructure can be a way to get *around* politics. That infrastructure is often seen to subtend the political and in fact expresses the ability of the state to control the political *frame* of the economic (e.g., the repeal of the British Corn Laws in 1846 enabled free trade around the world, including the Southeast Asian region). Infrastructure can be said to be the complement of infrapolitics: if infrastructure allows for the creation of a new politics, so too can a disruption of infrastructural flows interfere with it (one thinks of the barricades set up in the streets of Paris during the Revolution of 1848, and the wide boulevards built by Baron Georges-Eugène Haussmann in the 1850s and 60s in order to thwart such disruption). Small acts of transgression may even keep infrastructural systems in play. What is striking about Singapore's maritime history—once one disabuses oneself of the triumphalist story of national "progress" and "development"—is the extraordinary role played by infrastructure. Infrastructure was crucial to Singapore's "rise" as an international port, its nodal position in a series of networks.[34] (Governmental rhetoric of Singapore being a regional "hub" occludes this more tangled history.) Yet the politics of infrastructure runs deep, and often lies hidden. Historian Eric

Tagliacozzo has argued that the late-colonial (i.e., 1880s–1910s) border between Singapore and Indonesia emerged in relation to smuggling and piracy in the region.[35] In other words, the border didn't pre-exist politics; it was formed in relation to it. Infrastructure–buoys, lighthouses, communication networks–was directly involved in the border's production. (The 1880s and 90s saw a shift from free trade to a more coercive form of commerce, with increasing attempts to tax and control trade flows.)[36] Infrastructure is now at the heart of the Singapore state's emergency politics: instead of being at the mercy of accident and disaster, the challenge for the state is to manage such risk, to program accident into the material foundations of infrastructure.[37]

The buoy's light once served as a metaphor of knowledge and consciousness. But it also connotes state policing. Infrastructure is how a state "sees"; surveillance is on the other side of safety.[38] The disappearance of the Sejahat Buoy, even the outmoding of Raffles Lighthouse, mark the trading-in of one form of infrastructure (buoys, lighthouses) for another (machine-like vision, the "sight" of digital networks). But the nature of sovereignty, I think, has stayed the same. One question is whether the Singapore state *needs* to trade with these so-called sand "smugglers": it is as though the state needs to perform that original land theft, over and over again.[39] The founding of territory must properly be exceptional. Sovereignty is never a given, it continually needs to be reattained. If political foundation requires a constitutive lie, the Sejahat Buoy may be our primordial vanishing.

One intriguing detail is that Sejahat means "evil" in Malay. Sejahat Island was so named because of the dangerous reefs around it, or the presence of dark spirits on it. In a way, the island's disappearance announces the triumph of secular modernity.[40] No more spirits around these waters. Sand itself conjures up an image of purity. But land reclamation has also bolstered the rise of the Singapore state, one bent on territorial expansion and secretive trading practices–perhaps a different kind of evil (or better, beyond good and evil).

For many, Lim's work has been exemplary for attempts to think the "curatorial" in Singapore and Southeast Asia. But this is not because of the epic scale of many of his exhibitions, nor due to the fact that these exhibitions take Southeast Asia as their subject matter. It is, rather, because these exhibitions push at the limits of curating as a process of knowledge production.[41] Indeed, Lim often deploys various systems of maritime knowledge–navigational, cartographic, oceanographic, sailing–to figure exhibition structure and process. Often, as in the film *SEA STATE 6: Capsize* (2015), in which Lim flips his sailboat, over and over again, theory is entwined with practice, with neither reduced to the other. In fact, material acts (in this case, flipping) may be said to produce theory. Many of the tropes or figures in his works enact a *learning* process, or stage some kind of (possible) failure. Learning/failing is built into exhibition and display; the exhibition becomes a *staging* of embodied knowledge, rather than a beacon of certainty. What do artifacts know, and do? Lim's exhibitions have been characterized by a sense of precariousness or impending ruin. This is not an effort to theatrically wring out drama, but rather is an effect of his emphasis on the precariousness and contingency of knowledge. For Lim, the process of knowing, and the testing of material conditions, is as important as the acquired knowledge; indeed, Lim "knows" processually, in and through mediation, theoretical artifacts, reflexive exhibitions. And rather than be "historical," I would say that Lim's method, in pushing at the limits of exhibitional practice and knowledge, necessarily opens up history, allows the past to face the present.

I imagine the buoy, with its hypnotic, swirling light, looking back at us. No longer a safety device crucial for ships to safely pass through the region's waters, it has passed into a larger system of maritime infrastructure and transportation. What was once a reassuring light for the desolate seaman has turned into the blip and flicker of a port authority control terminal. If, in ages past, one sent out disease boats, it was to propitiate the gods. Modernity, in contrast, involves calling *ourselves* gods—but the joke may ultimately be on us, with risk only increasing, and more and more systems going out of control. Marking a dangerous area, the Sejahat Buoy once facilitated passage into Singapore's waters. Now, let it stand as an index to a secret history of state expansion and sovereignty—a signal of dark things to come.

1    James Frazer, *The Golden Bough* (London: Penguin, 1996; first published 1922), 42. Parts of his book draw from Walter William Skeat (see below).

2    Walter William Skeat, *Malay Magic, being an Introduction to the Folklore and Popular Religion of the Malay Peninsula* (London: Macmillan, 1900), 433–34.

3    Malay for "holy place, place of pilgrimage, or shrine; not necessarily a grave."

4    Skeat, *Malay Magic*, 68. Parts of this section were drawn from *The Selangor Journal: Jottings Past and Present* 2 (1894): 90–92.

5    Over the course of about a century and a half, the lighthouse has become a research area for marine biologists, a work place for lighthouse keepers, and a haven for treasure hunters. Visible for twenty nautical miles, the lighthouse beacon long consisted of kerosene lamps, and was finally automated in 1988. With automation, the lighthouse keeper's role changed, turning him into more of a caretaker. Raffles Lighthouse is one of five lighthouses maintained by the Maritime and Port Authority of Singapore, and continues to guide ships away from rocky waters.

6    This familiar notion, that Singapore's port history began in 1819, is being rewritten: see *Early Singapore 1300s–1819: Evidence in Maps, Text and Artifacts*, eds. John N. Miksic and Cheryl-Ann Low Mei Gek (Singapore: Singapore History Museum, 2004); John N. Miksic, *Singapore and the Silk Road of the Sea, 1300-1800* (Singapore: NUS Press, 2013).

7    For Singapore's "forgetting of the sea," see Paul Rae, "Singapore on Sea," in *ISSUE: Art Journal*, 1: LAND (2012): 46-50. Allan Sekula's *Fish Story* (1989-95) provided an exemplary model for Lim's practice. Lim, then with the group Tsunami.net, exhibited at documenta 11 (Kassel, Germany, June 8–September 15, 2012) along with Sekula.

8    Historians have criticized an older model of the "Enlightenment" based on secular rationality and science, finding that reason is shot through with irrationality and the unconscious. In this newer model, Enlightenment mind or history is constituted by aberration and error.

9    Newspaper articles point to picnics for school children on the islands in 1954 and '56. (Note that residents of Singapore were not allowed on the islands.)

10   Though Lim and Mustafa had requested permission from the Maritime and Port Authority of Singapore to visit the lighthouse, permission was denied. The idea to film the lighthouse at night emerged at this point, also because most publicized photographs show the island during the day.

11   The swimming pool was at the former Singapore Airlines Country Club in Changi.

12 James C. Scott, *Domination and the Arts of Resistance: Hidden Transcripts* (New Haven: Yale University Press, 1990), 19.

13 For example, "It has been observed by the author (pp. 71, 153, 163) that *kramat* animals generally have some physical peculiarity, such as a shrunken foot or stunted tusk; it may be added that they are sometimes white [...], and thus marked out from their fellows by the characteristic sacred colour. I remember reading in the local Straits newspaper some years ago that a white mouse-deer, which was caught somewhere in the Negri Sembilan, was regarded by the Malays as *kramat*: very soon after its capture, I believe on the same evening, it escaped from its cage overnight, a fact which no doubt further corroborated the natives in their belief as to its sacred character." (Skeat, 674).

14 Conversations for this essay began on a sailing trip off Singapore's southern coast with Lim, Mustafa, and the author in August 2014. The novelty of this "studio visit" lay in the fact that Lim often seeks to *enact* the process of knowledge, which helps investigators gain a better understanding of his art projects.

15 Lim's process, which involves a combination of archival and artifact research, and conversations with various individuals, crucially requires a "testing" of material conditions. Hence the attempt to grow barnacles on the buoy as a way to simulate—and hence understand—actual conditions of environment and history within a specific framework. One thing that results from Lim's months-long process of artificially growing barnacles on the recreated buoy is that the object is inscribed with time. The barnacles, in a sense, embed the buoy back in a specific time and place, against its relocation to a more virtual exhibition space. Mustafa has pointed out how the temperature of Singapore's surrounding waters is highly suitable for barnacle growth. More barnacles appear on ships' hulls here, than in any other part of the world. This current reality of calm waters and stable temperature, however, contrasts with the myth of rough waters off Singapore's southern coast: Sang Nila Utama was believed to have thrown his crown into the sea to quell a storm—in order to found Singapura. The point on "choppy waters" comes from "THE GRID, intimations of a chart: Captain Wilson Chua in conversation with Charles Lim and Shabbir Hussain Mustafa," in *SEA STATE 8 Seabook: An Art Project by Charles Lim* (Singapore: National Library Board, 2015).

16 Lim's process, which involves a combination of archival and artifact research, and conversations with various individuals, crucially requires a "testing" of material conditions. Hence the attempt to grow barnacles on the buoy as a way to simulate—and hence understand—actual conditions of environment and history within a specific framework.

17 Chris Milton, "The Sand Smugglers," *Foreign Policy* (August 4, 2010), available at http://foreignpolicy.com/2010/08/04/the-sand-smugglers, accessed on January 20, 2015.

18 The conflation of "casino" and "desert" in "Marina Bay Sands" is not a coincidence: one of the partners of this "integrated development" is the Las Vegas Sands Corporation. "Desert" metaphorizes a *tabula rasa* or blank space, and is often associated with postmodernist capitalism of the 1970s–'90s: see Robert Venturi, *Learning from Las Vegas: The Forgotten Symbolism of Architectural Form* (Cambridge, MA: MIT Press, 1977); Fredric Jameson, *Postmodernism, or, the Cultural Logic of Late Capitalism* (Durham, NC: Duke University Press, 1991). The critical history of these edifices of global casino capitalism has yet to be written; but see, for starters, Jeff Sallaz, *The Labor of Luck: Casino Capitalism in the United States and South Africa* (Berkeley, CA: University of California Press, 2009).

19 See for instance Eric T. Jennings, "From Indochine to Indochic: The Lang Bian/Dalat Palace Hotel and French Colonial Leisure, Power and Culture," *Modern Asian Studies* 37, no. 1 (2003): 159–94.

20 Milton, "The Sand Smugglers."

21 It is a question how far these "smugglers" are simply individuals trying to eke out a living. They are "illegal" from the point of view of the state.

22 Joshua Comaroff touches on this point in his "Built on Sand: Singapore and the New State of Risk," *Harvard Design Magazine*, no. 39 (2015), available at http://www.harvarddesignmagazine.org/issues/39/built-on-sand-singapore-and-the-new-state-of-risk, accessed on January 20, 2015.

23 For a counter-history of land expansion in Singapore, see Kevin Chua, "The Tiger and the Theodolite: George Coleman and the Dream of Extinction," *FOCAS: Forum on Contemporary Art and Society* 6 (2007): 124–49. For the history of enclosure in Britain, see J. M. Neeson, *Commoners: Common Right, Enclosure, and Social Change in England, 1700–1820* (New York: Cambridge University Press, 1993).

24 Nicholas Tarling, *Piracy and Politics in the Malay World* (Melbourne: F. W. Cheshire, 1963), 11.

25 D. C. Boulger, *The Life of Sir Stamford Raffles* (London, 1897), 272–73; cited in *Tarling, Piracy and Politics in the Malay World*, 16–17 (emphasis mine). He continued: "But there is also a particular circumstance which requires our immediate vigilance. An extensive marine is fitting out at Batavia, ostensibly for the suppression of piracy. Unless we go hand in hand in maintaining the *general security* of the Eastern Seas,

and show ourselves immediately as a party interested, so as to share the influence which the display of this armament is calculated to produce on the minds of the native chiefs, it will easily be made the means of resuming that absolute sovereignty over the Archipelago which is the object of the Dutch policy, and which is so highly important to our honour and interest to prevent." (Tarling, 17, emphasis mine).

26  Fullerton: "It appears to me that the Islands south of the Singapore Straits and within the political limits of the Netherlands Government form the great seat and centre of the mischief." Minute, October 22, 1823, *Straits Settlements Factory Records* 125 (November 3, 1828) and 157. Quoted in *Tarling, Piracy and Politics in the Malay World*, 35.

27  Owen: "by such means only very little can be done to check a practice which is so deeply rooted in the habits and the cherished predilections of these people [...]" Owen to Ibbetson, October 24, 1830, Board's Collections 52586 (East India Company and India Board Records, Commonwealth Relations Office), 119. Quoted in *Tarling, Piracy and Politics in the Malay World*, 53.

28  Ibid.

29  For "garden logic," see Kevin Chua, "Simryn Gill and Migration's Capital," *Art Journal* 61, no. 4 (Winter 2002): 4-21. For "gap in the law," see Tracy McNulty, "The Gap in the Law and the Border-Breaching Function of the Exception," *Konturen* (2008): 1-26.

30  There is also a *tabula rasa* move at work—a constitutive or original erasure, often of agency of the indigenous group(s) involved, that is very common to colonial ideology.

31  See Jennifer L. Gaynor, "Piracy in the Offing: The Law of Lands and the Limits of Sovereignty at Sea," *Anthropological Quarterly* 85, no. 3 (Summer 2012): 824; Laura Benton, "Legal Spaces of Empire: Piracy and the Origins of Ocean Regionalism," *Comparative Study of Society and History* 47, no. 4 (2005): 700-24. For new work on Grotius, see Martine Julia van Ittersum, *Profit and Principle: Hugo Grotius, Natural Rights Theories, and the Rise of Dutch Power in the East Indies, 1595-1615* (Leiden: Brill, 2006); and Peter Borschberg, *Hugo Grotius, the Portuguese, and Free Trade in the East Indies* (Singapore: NUS Press, 2011).

32  For infrastructure, see Brian Hayes, *Infrastructure: A Guide to the Industrial Landscape* (New York: W. W. Norton & Company, 2014); *Infrastructure as Architecture: Designing Composite Networks*, ed. Katrina Stoll and Scott Lloyd (Berlin: Jovis Verlag GmbH, 2010).

33  For the politics of infrastructure, see Joseph W. Westphal, "The Politics of Infrastructure," *Social Research* 75, no. 3 (Fall 2008): 793-804.

34  See for instance, Anthony Reid, "Singapore between Cosmopolis and Nation," in *Singapore from Temasek to the 21st Century: Reinventing the Global City*, ed. Karl Hack and Jean-Louis Margolin (Singapore: NUS Press, 2010), 37-54.

35  Eric Tagliacozzo, *Secret Trades, Porous Borders: Smuggling and States along a Southeast Asian Frontier, 1865-1915* (New Haven: Yale University Press, 2005). For buoys and lighthouses, see 82ff.

36  Ibid., 88.

37  For emergency politics, see Bonnie Honig, *Emergency Politics: Paradox, Law, Democracy* (Princeton, NJ: Princeton University Press, 2011); and Carl Schmitt, *The Concept of the Political* (1932), trans. George Schwab, expanded edition (Chicago: University of Chicago Press, 2007).

38  By the early twentieth century, "Lighthouses became imposing, efficient structures, floating panopticons where crews could remain self-sufficient for months at a time. It was much more difficult now for people to cross over unseen into the Indies, as a necklace of watchtowers—fully able to see, even at night— stretched all across the frontier" (Tagliacozzo, *Secret Trades, Porous Borders*, 84). He also notes the "steady eye kept on commercial shipping movements [...] especially in the border residencies" (ibid., 86). See also Tagliacozzo, "The Lit Archipelago: Coast Lighting and the Imperial Optic in Insular Southeast Asia, 1860-1910," *Technology and Culture* 46, no. 2 (April 2005): 306-28. My phrase echoes James C. Scott, *Seeing Like a State* (New Haven: Yale University Press, 1998).

39  The British "persuasion" of local Malay princes to hand over the island of Singapore between 1819-1823 is well known. See C. M. Turnbull, *A History of Singapore 1819-1975* (London: Oxford University Press, 1977), 23.

40  There may be a racial component to all this: Chinese whiteness (the color of sand) displaces a Malay-named island. But this displacement of Malays had happened before: while imagining the recreation of the once-great port city of Temasek (which had thrived in the fourteenth and fifteenth centuries), Raffles shunted the actual Malays living on Singapore in *his* present. (For Raffles's mythmaking, see Christina Skott, "Imagined Centrality: Sir Stamford Raffles and the Birth of Modern Singapore," in *Singapore from Temasek to the 21st Century: Reinventing the Global City*, ed. Hack and Margolin, 155-84.)

41  See the anthology *The Curatorial*, ed. Jean-Paul Martinon (London: Bloomsbury, 2013).

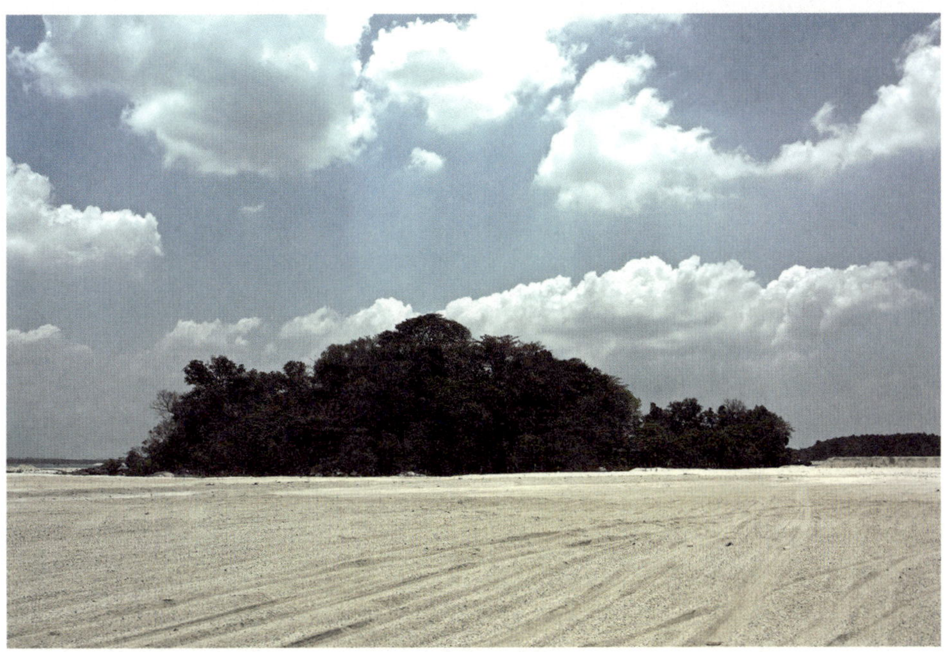

Charles Lim Yi Yong
*SEA STATE 2: As Evil Disappears (Pulau Sajahat)*, 2012
C-print

Kevin Chua

# Das Kuratorische als Boje und Leuchtfeuer

An der Ostküste Englands von Northumberland bis Kent ist der Glaube verbreitet, dass der Tod die meisten Menschen bei Ebbe ereilt, wenn das Meer zurückweicht. Mit diesem Volksglauben muss Shakespeare vertraut gewesen sein, als er Falstaff „just zwischen zwölf und eins" sterben ließ, „grade wie es zwischen Flut und Ebbe stand".[1] Die Malaien der Region Singapur-Malaysia sandten mit Opfergaben beladene *Boote des Leids* ins Meer, um Hinfälligkeit, Krankheit und Tod abzuwehren.[2] Walter William Skeat, dem Geschichten malaiischer Magie bekannt waren, gibt folgende Erzählung wieder:

Der *kramat* [heiliger Ort[3]], über den ich nun schreiben will, ist ausgesprochen bemerkenswert. Er liegt am äußersten Ende der Küste an der Mündung des Flusses Selangor, in der Nähe der Stelle, wo der neue Leuchtturm errichtet worden ist. Ein markantes Merkmal am *tanjong* (Landspitze oder Kap) ist ein prächtiger *kayu ara*, eine Art Feigenbaum, und am Fuß dieses Baums, völlig von seinen Wurzeln umschlossen, befindet sich ein rechteckiger Raum, der ein malaiisches Grab samt Grabstein sein könnte. […] Zu diesem heiligen Ort unternehmen die Malaien häufig Pilgerreisen, und in den unteren Zweigen des Baums fehlen selten jene weißgelben Tücher, die immer als Zeichen dafür aufgehängt werden, dass ein gläubiger Mensch seine Gelübde abgelegt hat. […]" Raja Abdullah war nach seinem Tod dort begraben worden. Skeats Gewährsmann fügt hinzu: „Wenn du am *pantai* (Ufer) entlang gehst und zufällig einem sehr großen Tiger begegnest, lass' ihn unversehrt passieren. Es ist nur Raja Abdullahs Geist, und zum Beweis dessen wirst du sehen, dass er keine Fußspuren im Sand hinterlässt.[4]

Im Zentrum des Singapurer Pavillon auf der Venedig Biennale 2015 stand eine riesige Boje, die mehr als drei Meter hoch war. Es handelte sich um die Nachbildung einer Boje, die 2008 vor der Südküste Singapurs verschwand, und die mich an all die Tode im Wasser denken lässt.

Über Charles Lims künstlerische Praxis wurde viel geschrieben – sie verbindet sein breit angelegtes, professionelles Interesse am Meer mit dem Filmemachen, der Archivforschung, dem Aufspüren von Artefakten und auch dem Experimentieren mit digitalen Medien. Doch nur wenige AutorInnen haben die Anwendung seiner Praxis innerhalb nationaler, regionaler und globaler Maßstäbe herausgestellt. Viele seiner Werke enthalten politische Anspielungen und er scheint auf die prinzipielle Unbegrenztheit archivalischer Praxis zu setzen. Ich halte es aber methodisch für interessanter, formale Aspekte seines Werks mit seinem meerespolitischen Engagement zu verknüpfen. Es geht im Grunde genommen darum, seine Politik der Form zu verstehen.

*In Search of Raffles' Light* war ein multidimensionales archivalisches Projekt, das im Oktober 2013 im Museum der National University of Singapore (NUS) ausgestellt wurde. Das Projekt bezog sich auf Raffles Lighthouse, einen Leuchtturm auf Pulau Satumu, einer von mehreren Inseln im Süden Singapurs. Der Leuchtturm, der von indischen Sträflingen gebaut und 1855 fertiggestellt worden war, wurde nach Sir Stamford Raffles, dem „Gründer" des modernen Singapur, benannt und markierte den südlichsten Punkt von Singapurs Hoheitsgewässern.[5] *In Search of Raffles' Light* ist eine Zusammenarbeit zwischen Lim und Shabbir Hussain Mustafa, dem damaligen Kurator am Museum der NUS. Gemeinsam untersuchten sie den Ort, sammelten Informationen über den Leuchtturm und seine Umgebung, beförderten Objekte und Relikte aus Magazinen zu Tage, filmten den Leuchtturm und seine Umgebung und sprachen mit verschiedenen Menschen, die im Laufe der Jahre mit dem Leuchtturm in Verbindung gestanden hatten – mit Seeleuten, Leuchtturmwärtern, Sammlern, Meeresliebhabern und Museumsmitarbeitern, darunter Eric Alfred, der ehemalige Kurator für Zoologie am Raffles Museum, der von 1957 bis 1972 dort tätig war. All diese Personen hatten Geschichten zu erzählen. Man begriff allmählich, dass der Leuchtturm weniger ein Monument als ein bisher fehlendes Zentrum für eine Reihe archivalischer Spuren war.

Lim hat Untersuchungen über das Meer durchgeführt, die als zusammenhängende Reihe unter dem Namen *SEA STATE* bekannt wurde. Der Titel spielt auf das Paradoxon an, dass der Staat die ihn umgebenden Gewässer grundsätzlich negiert, obwohl Singapur weitgehend durch seine Beziehungen zum Meer definiert ist – man denke nur an seine Identität als Hafenstadt, die in die Kolonialzeit zurückreicht.[6] Das Meer steht für alles Verborgene und Unsichtbare; es ist Gefahr, Wandel, Chaos. Es ist alles das, was wir nicht wahrhaben, nicht ins Licht des Bewusstseins dringen lassen wollen.[7] Tatsächlich spielt der Titel der Ausstellung, nicht Raffles Lighthouse, sondern *Raffles' Light* auf das Licht der Aufklärung an, das von Raffles und Gleichgesinnten mitgebracht wurde.[8] Wo genau liegt das Meer, und wie kommen wir dazu, es eher als *Begrenzung* denn als Ganzes zu denken?

In der Ausstellung waren Landkarten, Diagramme und Leuchtturmmodelle zu sehen (die faszinierenderweise mehr als schulterhoch ausgestellt waren, um die Illusion zu vermitteln, man schaue zum Leuchtturm hinauf, die Perspektive also, aus der man sich ihm auf dem Meer nähern würde). Didaktische Malereien beispielsweise illustrierten die ordnungsgemäße Bojenwartung, während eine Reihe von Leuchtkästen Lichtstärken unter Wasser an verschiedenen Stellen im Umkreis Singapurs zeigten (die Angabe von Verschmutzungsgraden war eine intelligente Anspielung auf das Mischen von Malfarben). Dieses Objekt passte besonders gut zum Titel der Ausstellung: Leitet sich denn die Sehnsucht nach sauberem und klarem Wasser nicht von einem damit einhergehenden Wunsch nach Reinheit ab, der Klarheit und Verheißung des Lichts? An die Stelle der Kenntnis des Meeres war das Meer als Erkenntnisprozess getreten, dem wir ausgesetzt, mit dem wir herausgefordert wurden.

Aus dem Archiv von *Raffles' Light* geht beispielsweise hervor, dass Angestellte der Port of Singapore Authority in den 1950er Jahren zu den abgelegenen Inseln, unter anderem Pulau Satumu, zum Picknicken kamen.[9] Weil der Leuchtturm sich in einem Sperrgebiet befand, waren diese Picknicks im Grunde genommen illegal – was einen Teil ihrer Attraktivität ausgemacht haben wird. Diese spezielle Geschichte findet ihr Echo im zentralen Videofilm der Installation: eine nächtliche Ansicht von Raffles Lighthouse, aufgenommen von einem Schiff, das Pulau Satumu umkreist. Lim musste beim Filmen die legale Grenze der Insel (die mehrere Meter vom Ufer entfernt verläuft) genau einhalten. Wäre er näher herangefahren, hätte man das als widerrechtliches Betreten angesehen.[10]

Mehrere von Lims Arbeiten beschäftigen sich mit subtilen Formen der Grenzüberschreitung oder kokettieren mit Übertretungen. Im Film *It's Not that I Forgot, but that I Chose not to Mention* (2009–2010) schwimmt ein Mann in einem Swimmingpool. Er bewegt sich ziemlich langsam, und mit der Zeit wird klar, dass er Algen vom Boden wischt. Er schwimmt auf und ab, und seine Bewegungen ergeben eine merkwürdige und doch elegante Strichzeichnung (wir sehen den Pool aus der Vogelperspektive, was die optische Ebene flach macht). Die Bewegung des Schwimmers ist die bildhafte Umschreibung einer Auslöschung, die einen mentalen, vielleicht auch historischen Ursprung hat, der durch die gewundene Ästhetik der Arbeit zurückgewonnen scheint. Dann finden wir heraus, dass Lims Zutritt zum Pool nicht ganz legal war: der nicht mehr genutzte Pool war zuvor mit Brettern vernagelt.[11] Es stellt sich die Frage, ob nicht genau diese anfängliche Übertretung den lakonischen Ton des Films, seine meditative Ruhe und seine Leichtigkeit überhaupt erst ermöglicht. Lims Arbeit beruft sich auf all die widerständigen Handlungen der LandarbeiterInnen, die dazu gedacht sind, der Ausbeutung ihrer Arbeitskraft durch Andere Grenzen zu setzen: Zeitschinden, Wilderei, Diebstahl, Heuchelei, Sabotage, Desertieren, Blaumachen, Hausbesetzung. Der Anthropologe James Scott bezeichnet diese „unauffälligen

Formen des Widerstands, die nicht in ihrem eigenen Namen zu sprechen wagen" als „Infrapolitik".[12] Obwohl oft behauptet wird, Handlungen im Rahmen der bestehenden Verhältnisse seien als Form des Widerstands zum Scheitern verurteilt, sind sie doch weniger defensiv, als es zunächst scheinen mag. Unter bestimmten Umständen und in gewissen Zusammenhängen können sie nämlich durchaus eine Grundlage für Politik bilden.

Im Film *All the Lines Flow Out* (2011) fährt ein Boot gemächlich durch mehrere von Singapurs *longkangs*. Obwohl diese Regenkanäle Wasser, Abfall und üble Gerüche aus dem Inneren der Insel abführen, denken wir nicht über sie nach – sie sind Teil unserer Vorstellung von Stadt geworden. Der Film ist auf einer gewissen Ebene eine Allegorie des Vergessens. In einer amüsanten Szene zu Beginn des Films baut ein Mann aus einer Plastikflasche eine improvisierte Fischreuse (was auch eine kluge Parallele zum Do-it-yourself-haften von Lims Ästhetik ist). Während der Dreharbeiten für den Film interessierte sich Lim sehr für die nicht lange zurückliegende Festnahme des Diebs Mat Selamat. Aber faszinierender als der Bericht, wie er über die Regenkanäle entkam, war für ihn der Mythos, dass er einfach *eine Tür zeichnete*, um zu entkommen. Dieses Element der Erzählung ist aus der langen Geschichte malaiischer Magie zu verstehen.[13] Lims Ästhetik hat eine topologische Kontinuität zwischen Innen und Außen, Zurückhaltung und Öffnung. Sie kann nicht auf eines von beiden reduziert werden. Es ist so, als ob jede Szene eines ruhig dahin treibenden Boots gleichzeitig auch das Gefühl auslöst, man säße in der Falle. Bruch und Kontinuität umkreisen einander.

Eine rostbefleckte Boje, an deren Boden sich Rankenfußkrebse klammerten und von der fast noch Meerwasser tropfte, war ein Bestandteil der von Lim mit kuratorischer Hilfe von Shabbir Hussain Mustafa konzipierten Installation für den Pavillon Singapurs bei der Venedig Biennale 2015.[14] Für die Installation baute Lim eine Boje nach, die um das Jahr 2008 auf mysteriöse Weise vor Singapurs Südküste verschwand. Als Lim Seekarten des Gebiets überprüfte, stellte er fest, dass eine ganze Insel fehlte, Pulau Sejahat, verschluckt vom Sand, der aufgeschüttet worden war, um Land zu gewinnen. Die Sejahat-Boje befand sich vor der Insel und war vielleicht im Verlauf der Landgewinnungsmaßnahme von der Marine and Port Authority of Singapore entfernt oder (wahrscheinlicher) unter mehreren Schichten von Sand begraben worden. Keine Spur von ihr blieb zurück, und auch Landkarten leisten keine Trauerarbeit. Aber warum sollte man diese Boje nachbauen und ausstellen?[15] Tatsächlich hat das Verfahren, Rankenfußkrebse künstlich auf der Boje im Meer nachwachsen zu lassen und diese Boje anschließend zu demontieren und abzutransportieren, etwas von einem *Ritual* – als wäre irgendein Objekt begraben und exhumiert worden.[16] Boje und Insel verschwanden im Zuge des Landgewinnungsprogramms, das viele Kontroversen auslöste. Seit den 1960er Jahren ist die Landfläche Singapurs von 581,5 auf 710 Quadratkilometer angewachsen.[17] Die Landgewinnung hat sich im Laufe der letzten zehn Jahre beschleunigt. Bis 2030 plant Singapur, sich um weitere 70 Quadratkilometer zu vergrößern – eine Zunahme an Landfläche von 30 Prozent gemessen an der ursprünglichen Größe. (Ein Projekt aus jüngerer Zeit, das auf neu gewonnenem Land gebaut wurde, ist das treffend benannte Marina Bay Sands, ein Fünf-Sterne-Hotel mit Casino und direktem Blick auf die Südsee.[18] Dieser Komplex ähnelt merkwürdigerweise den Erholungsorten für die kolonialen Eliten im 19. Jahrhundert, die oft nahe der Grenzstationen in den Bergen gebaut wurden.[19] Natürlich hält sich Singapur nicht nur für das Zentrum Südostasiens, sondern auch für das Grenzgebiet des globalen Kapitalismus. Seit den späten 1960er Jahren steht Freizeit an der vordersten Front des militärisch-industriell-finanziell geprägten Komplexes.) Beunruhigend sind die Größenordnung der Neulandgewinnung und die Rechtsübertretungen, die mit ihnen einhergehen. Singapurs Einfuhr von Sand im Wert von mehr als 273 Millionen Dollar allein im Jahr 2008 zum Beispiel – und das sind die offiziellen Zahlen der Regierung – erfasst nur den legalen Handel mit Sand. Wegen der schieren Menge kann kein Land allein genug Sand liefern, um Singapurs Durst danach zu stillen. Deshalb stammt der Sand zum Teil aus Malaysia, zu einem anderen Teil aus Indonesien. „Viele indonesische Inseln, die von Singapur aus leicht zu erreichen sind, haben wenige oder keine Einwohner", schreibt der Journalist Chris Milton, „und Singapur hat sich diese geografische Situation zunutze gemacht, indem es so weit gegangen ist, manche Orte völlig von der Landkarte wegzuwischen."[20] Im Jahr 2003 verschwand die Insel Nipah, die an der Grenze zwischen Singapur und Indonesien lag. Man nimmt an, dass zwischen 2005 und 2010 weitere vierundzwanzig Inseln unter den Wellen verschwunden sind. Obwohl eine Reihe illegaler Sandabgrabungen bis zu Unternehmen in Singapur zurückverfolgt wurden, streitet die Regierung Singapurs kategorisch ab, die Einfuhr illegalen Sands stillschweigend zu dulden. Und trotzdem wird der Sandabbau fortgeführt: 2003 gruben Schmuggler geschätzte 300 Millionen Kubikmeter Sand im Wert von 2,5 Milliarden Dollar aus und verschifften ihn.[21] Verbote der Sandausfuhr, die von der Regierung in jüngster Zeit verhängt wurden, hatten die Wirksamkeit eines sehr groben Siebes.

Doch die Landgewinnung um die Insel herum wiederholt die Kolonialgeschichte und die mit ihr einhergehenden Rodungen und Erschließungen von Land *auf* der Insel.[22] Während die geostrategische Bedeutung Singapurs innerhalb der Region nicht neu ist – da sie die überaus wichtige Straße von Malakka mit den Handelsrouten nach China und Indonesien verbindet –, erkennen nur wenige an, dass ein damit verbundener Prozess der Ausdehnung *in* die Insel hinein stattfand. Ausdehnung nach innen ging der Expansion nach außen voraus. Die Vermessung von Territorien im Singapur der zweiten Hälfte des 19. Jahrhunderts wiederholt die Geschichte der Einfriedung in Großbritannien.[23] Das Genre der im Singapur des 19. Jahrhunderts produzierten Landschaftsmalerei war von grausamer Ironie: Land wurde kartografiert, in Planquadrate aufgeteilt und bereit gemacht, um wirtschaftlich genutzt zu werden. Das Hinausschieben der inneren Grenze war der erste Schritt zur Sicherung der nationalen Souveränität.

Die Expansion des Stadtstaates Singapur – weniger eine *Wiedergewinnung* als eine *Gewinnung* von Land – brachte auch eine Domestizierung der südlichen

Inseln und des sie umgebenden Meeres mit sich. Piraten durchstreiften diese Gewässer in der ersten Hälfte des 19. Jahrhunderts – oder zumindest war das die Zeit, als sie zum Problem wurden. Die Grenze zwischen Piraten und Freibeutern war äußerst dünn; man konnte oft nicht erkennen, ob die kleinen Schiffe, die sich in diesen Gewässern aufhielten, für den Handel oder für etwas Ruchloseres genutzt wurden. Die vielen Buchten und Meeresarme der Region erlaubten es Piraten, mit ihren schnellen Schiffen unentdeckt zu bleiben. Da der Wechsel in der britischen Politik gegen Ende des 18. Jahrhunderts dem Handel vor der Herrschaft den Vorzug gab, wollten die Politikstrategen in der Region Niederlassungen gründen, aus denen Handelsstützpunkte werden konnten.[24] Stamford Raffles, der von Versuchen der Niederländer wusste, ihre Oberherrschaft im Malaiischen Archipel wieder geltend zu machen, benutzte das Argument der Piraterie, um die Briten zur Gründung von Niederlassungen und zum Abschluss vorsorglicher Verträge mit den eingeborenen Fürsten zu bewegen. Eine Niederlassung, meinte er, würde

> dem Benehmen unserer Landsleute, die im Archipel Handel treiben, eine wohltuende Zurückhaltung auferlegen. Unsere Pflicht gegenüber anderen Nationen und die Sache der Gerechtigkeit, ebenso wie die Rücksicht auf unseren Nationalcharakter machen es erforderlich, dass *die friedlichen Eingeborenen der Inseln* nicht jedem kaufmännischen Abenteurer unserer Nationen ausgeliefert sind. Die Verlockungen und Gelegenheiten zur Raubwirtschaft sind in dieser Gegend zu zahlreich, um übersehen zu werden.[25]

Britischen Aktivitäten als schützend für „friedliche Eingeborene" zu bezeichnen – er meint zukünftige Handelskolonisten – lieferte den Briten eine Begründung für ihre Anwesenheit in der Region. Da die Hoheitsgewalt unklar war, mussten Raffles und die Briten eine Möglichkeit finden, ihre Übergriffe legal zu rechtfertigen.[26] Im Lauf der 1810er und 1820er Jahre wurde Piraterie mehr und mehr als etwas angesehen, das einer Gruppe von Menschen in dieser Region in Fleisch und Blut übergegangen war.[27] Wenn die Piraterie also drohte sich zu etablieren, hatten die Briten eine moralische Verpflichtung, für eine paternalistische Ordnung zu sorgen, indem sie Kontrollfunktionen wahrnahmen. Was außerdem während dieser Zeit zum Einsatz kam – noch eine weitere Methode, die Verantwortung für die Piraterie den indigenen Völkern zuzuschieben –, war die Sprache des Eigentums. Konteradmiral Sir Edward Owen schrieb beispielsweise:

> Ein großer Anteil der Räubereien, über die man klagt, werden, so sagt man, von den Prauen [d.h. *prahus*, Segelschiff] begangen, die zu den Südlichen Inseln gehören. Sie stehen seit ihrem Vordringen zu den Bird Nests Islands im Norden unter dem Schutz der Holländer. Diese Inseln, die alle entweder unter unserer Regierung oder der von Siam stehen, sind kommerziellen Händlern in Pacht gegeben worden, und diese Besuche sind nicht weniger

ein Verstoß gegen die Eigentumsrechte derjenigen, die sie gepachtet haben, als gegen die Gebietshoheit des Landes, dem sie gehören.[28]

Der Vorgang erinnert daran, was ich an anderer Stelle als „Gartenlogik" bezeichnet habe: die interpretatorische Kreativität der Briten hinsichtlich politischer Prozesse schiebt einem Anderen Schuld und bestimmte Taten in die Schuhe, wodurch eine Lücke im Gesetz geschaffen wird, die Interventionen rechtfertigt.[29] In mancherlei Hinsicht sind die Briten zum Handeln *gezwungen*.[30] Wir sollten auch daran denken, dass die Festlegung von Hoheitsgrenzen im Meer in das 17. Jahrhundert zurückreicht, als Hugo Grotius die Beschlagnahmung der Ladung des portugiesischen Schiffs *Santa Caterina* in der Nähe der Straße von Malakka durch die Niederländer mit dem Argument verteidigte, dass es sich nicht um einen Akt der Piraterie handele.[31] Aus dem juristischen Handgemenge ging seine Abhandlung *Mare Liberum* (Das freie Meer; 1609) hervor, das für die kommenden Jahrhunderte die Freiheit der Handelsschifffahrt in internationalen Gewässern rechtfertigte. Aber *Freiheit* war natürlich denjenigen vorbehalten, die *Piraterie* definieren konnten.

Wie ein Leuchtturm oder ein Regenkanal ist die Boje ein Stück Infrastruktur. Elektroanlagen, Heiz- und Kühlsysteme, Abfallsysteme, Straßen und Verkehrssysteme: Infrastruktur ist das, was Gesellschaft unterstützt und ihr das Funktionieren ermöglicht.[32] Weil sie oft unbemerkt bleibt oder für selbstverständlich gehalten wird, kann Infrastruktur ein umso wirksameres Mittel der Staatsmacht sein.[33] Tatsächlich kann die Bereitstellung von Infrastruktur eine Möglichkeit sein, Politik zu *umgehen*. Dass Infrastruktur oft das Politische und das Ökonomische zu unterstützen scheint, bringt vielmehr die Fähigkeit des Staates zum Ausdruck, den politischen Rahmen des Ökonomischen zu kontrollieren (z. B. ermöglichte die Abschaffung der britischen Getreidegesetze 1846 Handelsfreiheit auf der ganzen Welt, einschließlich Südostasiens). Infrastruktur kann als Ergänzung der Infrapolitik bezeichnet werden: So wie Infrastruktur die Gestaltung einer neuen Politik ermöglicht, kann diese zugleich durch eine Unterbrechung infrastruktureller Ströme behindert werden (man denke an die während der Revolution von 1848 in den Straßen von Paris errichteten Barrikaden-und an die breiten Boulevards, die von Haussmann in den 1850er und 1860er Jahren gebaut wurden, um diese zu verhindern). Kleine Akte von Überschreitungen könnten sogar dazu beitragen, die infrastrukturellen Systeme am Laufen zu halten. Das Auffallende an Singapurs maritimer Geschichte-wenn man sich von der Triumphgeschichte nationalen *Fortschritts* gedanklich verabschiedet-ist die außergewöhnliche Rolle, die die Infrastruktur dabei gespielt hat. Infrastruktur war für Singapurs *Aufstieg* als internationaler Hafen als Knotenpunkt verschiedener Netzwerke von entscheidender Bedeutung.[34] (Die Regierungsrhetorik, dass Singapur ein regionales *Drehkreuz* sei, verdeckt diese etwas verwickeltere Geschichte.) Doch die Politik der Infrastruktur ist nicht immer durchschaubar und liegt oft im Verborgenen. Der Historiker Eric Tagliacozzo hat behauptet, dass die Grenze zwischen Singapur und Indonesien, spätkolonial, also in der Zeit zwischen den 1880er und den 1910er Jahren, vor dem Hintergrund der Schmuggelei und Piraterie entstanden sei.[35] Mit anderen Worten: die Grenze existierte nicht vor der Politik; sie wurde in Relation zu ihr gezogen. Und die Infrastruktur – Bojen, Leuchttürme, Kommunikationsnetzwerke – war direkt in die Grenzziehung eingebunden. (In den 1880er und 1890er Jahren kam es zu einem Übergang vom Freihandel zu einer stärker eingeschränkten Form des Handels, mit zunehmenden Versuchen, Handelsströme zu besteuern und zu kontrollieren.[36]) Heute steht die Infrastruktur im Mittelpunkt der Katastrophenschutzpolitik des Staates Singapur: Die Herausforderung für den Staat, der Unglücksfällen und Katastrophen nicht mehr hilflos ausgeliefert sein will, liegt darin, solche Risiken einzuplanen und Unglücksfälle in die Ausstattung von Infrastrukturen miteinzuberechnen und die entsprechenden finanziellen Grundlagen bereitzustellen.[37]

Das Licht der Boje diente früher als Metapher für Erkenntnis und Bewusstsein. Aber es steht auch für staatliche Überwachung. Infrastruktur ist die Art und Weise, wie ein Staat *sieht*; Überwachung ist die Kehrseite der Sicherheit.[38] Das Verschwinden der Sejahat-Boje sowie die Tatsache, dass Raffles Lighthouse nicht mehr zeitgemäß ist, bezeichnen den Tausch einer Form von Infrastruktur (Bojen, Leuchttürme) gegen eine andere (maschinenunterstütztes Sehen, der „Blick" digitaler Netzwerke). Aber das Wesen der Herrschaft ist, glaube ich, gleich geblieben. Eine Frage, die sich in diesem Zusammenhang aufdrängt, lautet, ob der Staat Singapur mit diesen sogenannten Sand-Schmugglern nicht geradezu Handel treiben *muss*: Es ist so, als müsse der Staat jenen ursprünglichen Landraub wieder und wieder begehen.[39] Die Gründung eines Hoheitsgebietes muss außergewöhnlich sein, denn Herrschaft ist nie selbstverständlich – sie muss dauernd wiedererlangt werden. Falls es so ist, dass eine politische Gründung eine konstitutive Lüge braucht, stünde die Sejahat-Boje dafür, dass wir in unseren Anfängen vom Verschwinden bedroht waren.

Ein interessantes Detail ist, dass Sejahat auf Malaiisch *böse* bedeutet. Sejahat Island war wegen der gefährlichen Riffe in ihrem Umkreis so genannt worden oder wegen der Anwesenheit dunkler Geister. In gewisser Hinsicht kündigt das Verschwinden der Insel den Triumph säkularer Modernität an.[40] Keine Geister mehr in diesen Gewässern. Sand beschwört ein Bild der Reinheit herauf. Aber Landgewinnung hat auch den Aufstieg des Staates Singapur unterstützt, der auf territoriale Expansion und geheime Handelsstrategien setzt – das ist vielleicht eine andere Art des Bösen (oder besser: jenseits von Gut und Böse).

Für viele ist Lims Werk ein exemplarischer Versuch, für Singapur und Südostasien das Kuratorische zu denken. Aber das liegt weder an der monumentalen Größe der meisten seiner Ausstellungen, noch verdankt es sich dem Umstand, dass sie Südostasien zum Thema haben. Es liegt eher daran, dass diese Ausstellungen die Grenzen des Kuratierens als Prozess der Erkenntnisproduktion erweitern. Tatsächlich setzt Lim verschiedene Systeme maritimen Wissens ein-navigatorisches, kartografisches, ozeanografisches Wissen, Segelkunde-, um Ausstellungsstruktur und -prozess symbolisch darzustellen. Oft, wie etwa in dem Film *SEA STATE 6: Capsize* (2015), in dem Lim sein Segelboot immer wieder zum Kentern bringt, sind Theorie und Praxis verschränkt und bedingen sich gegenseitig. Aus der Praxis, in diesem Fall dem Kentern, entsteht Theorie. Viele der Stilmittel und Bilder in seinen Arbeiten stellen einen Lernprozess dar oder inszenieren eine Art von (möglichem) Scheitern. Lernen und Scheitern sind der Ausstellung und ihren Displays eingeschrieben. Die Ausstellung wird eher zu einer *Inszenierung* von verkörpertem Wissen als ein Leuchtfeuer der Gewissheit. Was wissen Artefakte schon? Lim's Ausstellungen sind von einem Gefühl der Gefährdung oder des bevorstehenden Untergangs charakterisiert. Es geht darum, die Unsicherheit und Zufälligkeit des Wissens zu betonen und weniger darum, eine dramatische Wirkung zu erzielen. Für Lim ist der Prozess der Erkenntnis und das Testen wesentlicher Bedingungen genauso wichtig wie das erworbene Wissen; tatsächlich eignet sich Lim auf prozesshafte Weise Wissen an, durch Vermittlung, theoretische Artefakte und reflexive Ausstellungen. Lims Methode würde ich nicht als *historisch* bezeichnen, sondern als Erweiterung von Wissen und Ausstellungskonventionen, die zwangsläufig Geschichte öffnet und der Vergangenheit erlaubt, sich der Gegenwart zu stellen.

Ich stelle mir vor, wie die Boje mit ihrem hypnotischen, wabernden Licht zu uns zurückschaut. Sie ist keine Sicherheitsvorrichtung von entscheidender Bedeutung mehr für Schiffe, die Gewässer der Region durchqueren wollen, sie wurde von einem größeren System maritimer Infrastruktur abgelöst. Was einst ein beruhigendes Licht für den einsamen Seemann war, ist heute der flackernde Leuchtimpuls am Kontrolltisch der Hafenbehörde. Wenn man vor langer Zeit Boote des Leids hinausschickte, geschah das, um die Götter gnädig zu stimmen. Die Moderne hingegen bringt mit sich, dass wir *uns selbst* als Götter bezeichnen-aber vielleicht sind wir am Ende die Betrogenen, weil das Risiko nur größer wird und immer mehr Systeme außer Kontrolle geraten. Die Sejahat-Boje, die ein gefährliches Gebiet kennzeichnete, erleichterte einst die Einfahrt in Singapurs Gewässer. Jetzt kann sie als Verweis auf eine geheime Geschichte staatlicher Expansion und Souveränität gesehen werden, und als Zeichen für eine nicht so erleuchtete Zukunft.

---

1   Vgl. James Frazer, *The Golden Bough*, London: Penguin, 1996, S. 42 (*Heinrich V.* nach A. W. Schlegel). Teile seines Buches beziehen sich auf Walter William Skeat (s. unten).

2   Vgl. Walter William Skeat, *Malay Magic. Being an Introduction to the Folklore and Popular Religion of the Malay Peninsula*, London: Macmillan and Co., 1900, S. 433-434.

3   Malaiisch für heiliger Ort, Pilgerstätte oder Tempel; nicht unbedingt ein Grab.

4   Skeat, op. cit., S. 68. Teile dieses Abschnitts stammen aus *The Selangor Journal: Jottings Past and Present*, Bd. 2, 1984, S. 90-92.

5   Im Laufe von rund anderthalb Jahrhunderten ist der Leuchtturm zu einem Forschungsgebiet für Meeresbiologen, einem Arbeitsplatz für Leuchtturmwärter und einem Paradies für Schatzsucher geworden. Das zwanzig Seemeilen weit sichtbare Signalfeuer des Leuchtturms wurde lange Zeit von Petroleumlampen gespendet und schließlich 1988 automatisiert. Mit der Automatisierung änderte sich die Rolle des Leuchtturmwärters, der seitdem eher als Hausmeister fungiert. Raffles Lighthouse ist einer von fünf

Leuchttürmen, die von der Maritime and Port Authority of Singapore unterhalten werden, und warnt Schiffe weiterhin vor felsigen Gewässern.

6 Diese geläufige Ansicht, dass Singapurs Geschichte als Hafenstadt 1819 begann, wird derzeit umgeschrieben: siehe John N. Miksic und Cheryl-Ann Low Mei Gek (Hg.), *Early Singapore 1300s–1819: Evidence in Maps, Text and Artifacts*, Singapur: Singapore History Museum, 2004; John N. Miksic, *Singapore and the Silk Road of the Sea, 1300–1800*, Singapur: NUS Press, 2013.

7 Zu Singapurs „Vergessen des Meers" siehe Paul Rae, „Singapore on Sea", in: *ISSUE: Art Journal*, Bd. 1: LAND, 2012, S. 46–50. Allan Sekulas *Fish Story* (1989–1995) bot ein exemplarisches Modell für Lims Praxis. Lim, der damals zur Gruppe Tsunami.net gehörte, stellte bei der documenta 11 (Kassel, 8. Juni–15. September 2012) zusammen mit Sekula aus.

8 Diese Aufklärung sollte man sich allerdings nicht analog zu einem älteren Modell vorstellen, das auf säkularer Rationalität und Wissenschaft beruht, sondern im Sinne eines neueren, in dem sich Vernunft, Unvernunft und das Unbewusste miteinander verbinden. In diesem neueren Modell sind Geist und Geschichte der Aufklärung auf Abweichung und Irrtum errichtet.

9 Zeitungsartikel weisen auf Picknicks für Schulkinder auf den Inseln in den Jahren 1954 und 1956 hin. (Dabei ist zu bedenken, dass für EinwohnerInnen Singapurs der Besuch der Inseln verboten war.)

10 Lim und Mustafa hatten sich zwar bei der Maritime and Port Authority of Singapore um eine Genehmigung für den Besuch des Leuchtturms bemüht, sie war ihnen aber nicht erteilt worden.

11 Der Swimmingpool lag im ehemaligen Country Club der Singapore Airlines in Changi.

12 James C. Scott, *Domination and the Arts of Resistance: Hidden Transcripts*, New Haven/London: Yale University Press, 1990, S. 19.

13 Z. B. „Es ist vom Autor beobachtet worden (S. 71, 153, 163), dass *kramat*-Tiere im Allgemeinen eine physische Eigentümlichkeit haben, wie beispielsweise einen geschrumpften Fuß oder einen verkümmerten Stoßzahn; es mag hinzugefügt werden, dass sie manchmal weiß sind [...] und sich daher von ihren Artgenossen durch die typische heilige Farbe abgrenzen. Ich erinnere mich, vor ein paar Jahren in der lokalen *Straits*-Zeitung gelesen zu haben, dass ein weißer Kleinkantschil, der irgendwo in Negeri Sembilan gefangen worden war, von den Malaien als *kramat* betrachtet wurde: Sehr bald, nachdem das Tier gefangen worden war, ich glaube am selben Abend, entkam es in der Nacht aus seinem Käfig, ein Umstand, der die Eingeborenen zusätzlich in ihrem Glauben an sein heiliges Wesen bestärkte." (Skeat, op. cit., S. 674)

14 Gespräche über dieses Projekt begannen beim Segeln vor Singapurs Südküste zwischen Lim, Mustafa und dem Autor im August 2014. Das Neue dieser Art des *Atelierbesuchs* besteht darin, dass Lim versucht, den Erkenntnisprozess zu inszenieren, selbst vor denjenigen, die mit ihm zusammenarbeiten.

15 Ein Ergebnis von Lims Maßnahme, in einem monatelangen Prozess die nachgebildete Boje mit Rankenfußkrebsen bewachsen zu lassen, besteht darin, dass dem Objekt die Zeit eingeschrieben ist. Die Rankenfußkrebse betten die Boje wieder in eine spezifische Zeit und einen spezifischen Ort ein, und wirken der Verlegung in einen eher virtuellen Ausstellungsraum entgegen. Mustafa hat darauf hingewiesen, dass die Temperatur der Gewässer um Singapur besonders geeignet ist für den Wuchs von Rankenfußkrebsen. Hier gibt es mehr Rankenfußkrebse auf Schiffsrümpfen als in jedem anderen Teil der Welt. Das derzeit eher ruhige Gewässer mit stabilen Temperaturen steht allerdings mit dem Mythos von rauen Wassern vor Singapurs Südküste im Widerspruch: Es wird gesagt, Sang Nila Utama habe seine Krone ins Meer geworfen und dadurch den Sturm bezwungen – um Singapura zu gründen. Die Sache mit dem „kabbeligen Wasser" stammt aus „THE GRID, intimations of a chart: Captain Wilson Chua in conversation with Charles Lim and Shabbir Hussain Mustafa", in: *SEA STATE 8 Seabook: An Art Project by Charles Lim*, Singapur: National Library Board, 2015.

16 Zu den entscheidenden Erfordernissen von Lims Verfahren, das Archivforschung, Recherchen nach Artefakten und Gespräche kombiniert, gehört ein *Testen* realer Bedingungen. Deshalb der Versuch, Rankenfußkrebse auf der Boje wachsen zu lassen, als eine Methode, tatsächliche Bedingungen von Umwelt und Geschichte innerhalb eines bestimmten Rahmens zu simulieren – und damit zu verstehen.

17 Chris Milton, „The Sand Smugglers", in: *Foreign Policy*, 4. August 2010, verfügbar unter http://foreignpolicy.com/2010/08/04/the-sand-smugglers, abgerufen am 20. Januar 2015.

18 Die Verschmelzung von *Casino* und *Wüste* in Marina Bay Sands – das, wie wir von seiner Webseite erfahren, „drei kaskadenförmige Hoteltürme unter einem außerordentlichen Himmelspark aufzuweisen hat, ‚schwebende' Kristallpavillons, ein lotusinspiriertes Museum, Einzelhandelsgeschäfte mit Spitzenlabels und internationalen Luxusmarken, schicke Restaurants mit Starköchen, Unterhaltung rund um die Uhr in Theatern, den heißesten Nachtclubs und einem Casino im Stil von Las Vegas" – ist kein Zufall: einer der Partner dieses „integrierten Bauprojekts" ist die Las Vegas Sand Corporation. *Wüste* (desert) dient als Metapher für eine *tabula rasa* oder Leerstelle und wird oft mit dem postmodernen Kapitalismus der

1970er bis 1990er Jahre assoziiert: siehe Robert Venturi, *Learning from Las Vegas: The Forgotten Symbolism of Architectural Form*, Cambridge, MA: MIT Press, 1977; Fredric Jameson, *Postmodernism, or, the Cultural Logic of Late Capitalism*, Durham, NC: Duke University Press, 1991. Die kritische Geschichte dieser Bauwerke des globalen Casino-Kapitalismus muss noch geschrieben werden; aber siehe für den Anfang Jeff Sallaz, *The Labor of Luck: Casino Capitalism in the United States and South Africa*, Berkeley, CA: University of California Press, 2009.

19  Siehe zum Beispiel Eric T. Jennings, „From Indochine to Indochic: The Lang Bian/Dalat Palace Hotel and French Colonial Leisure, Power and Culture", in: *Modern Asian Studies*, Bd. 37, Nr. 1, 2003, S. 159–194.

20  Milton, op. cit.

21  Es ist eine Frage, inwieweit diese *Schmuggler* nur Einzelpersonen sind, die versuchen, sich mühsam durchzuschlagen. *Illegal* sind sie nach Auffassung des Staates.

22  Joshua Comaroff berührt diesen Punkt in seinem Artikel „Built on Sand: Singapore and the New State of Risk", in: *Harvard Design Magazine*, Nr. 39, 2015, verfügbar unter http://www.harvarddesignmagazine.org/issues/39/built-on-sand-singapore-and-the-new-state-of-risk, abgerufen am 20. Januar 2015.

23  Zu einer Gegen-Geschichte des Landausbaus in Singapur vgl. Kevin Chua, „The Tiger and the Theodolite: George Coleman and the Dream of Extinction", in: *FOCAS: Forum on Contemporary Art and Society* 6, 2007, S. 124–149. Zur Geschichte der Einfriedung in Großbritannien, vgl. J. M. Neeson, *Commoners: Common Right, Enclosure, and Social Change in England, 1700–1820*, New York: Cambridge University Press, 1993.

24  Nicholas Tarling, *Piracy and Politics in the Malay World*, Melbourne: F. W. Cheshire, 1963, S. 11.

25  D. C. Boulger, *The Life of Sir Stamford Raffles*, London: Horace Marshall & Son, 1897, S. 272–273; zitiert nach Tarling, S. 16–17. Er fuhr fort: „Aber es gibt auch einen besonderen Umstand, der unsere unmittelbare Wachsamkeit erfordert. Eine umfangreiche Seestreitmacht wird in Batavia ausgerüstet, vorgeblich zur Unterdrückung der Piraterie. Wenn wir nicht Hand in Hand an der Aufrechterhaltung der *allgemeinen Sicherheit* des Ostindischen Archipels arbeiten und uns sogleich als interessierte Partei zeigen, um an der Wirkung teilzuhaben, die die Zurschaustellung dieser Aufrüstung in den Köpfen der eingeborenen Häuptlinge erzeugen soll, wird sie leicht zum Mittel gemacht, mit dessen Hilfe jene absolute Hoheitsgewalt über den Archipel wiedererlangt wird, die das Ziel der niederländischen Politik ist und die zu verhindern so äußerst wichtig für unsere Ehre und unsere Interessen ist." (Tarling, S. 17, Hervorhebung des Autors)

26  Fullerton: „es scheint mir, dass die Inseln im Süden der Straße von Singapur und innerhalb der politischen Grenzen der niederländischen Regierung Sitz und Zentrum des Unheils bilden." Minute, 22. Oktober 1823, *Straits Settlements Factory Records* S. 125, 3. November 1828, S. 157. Zitiert nach Tarling, S. 35.

27  Owen: „mit solchen Mitteln kann nur sehr wenig getan werden, um einer Praxis Einhalt zu gebieten, die so tief in den Gewohnheiten und den geschätzten Vorlieben dieser Menschen verwurzelt ist […]" Owen an Ibbetson, 24. Oktober 1830, Board's Collections 52586 (East India Company and India Board Records, Commonwealth Relations Office), S. 119. Zitiert nach Tarling, S. 53.

28  Owen an Ibbetson, op. cit.

29  Zu Gartenlogik s. Kevin Chua, „Simryn Gill and Migration's Capital", in: *Art Journal*, Bd. 61, Nr. 4, Winter 2002, S. 4–21. Zur Lücke im Gesetz siehe Tracy McNulty, „The Gap in the Law and the Border-Breaching Function of the Exception", in: *Konturen*, 2008, S. 1–26.

30  Hier ist eine *Tabula rasa*-Strategie am Werk, die für kolonialistische Ideologien sehr typisch ist – eine grundlegende Auslöschung der Tätigkeiten der beteiligten indigenen Gruppe(n).

31  Vgl. Jennifer L. Gaynor, „Piracy in the Offing: The Law of Lands and the Limits of Sovereignty at Sea", in: *Anthropological Quarterly*, Bd. 85, Nr. 3, Sommer 2012, S. 824; Laura Benton, „Legal Spaces of Empire: Piracy and the Origins of Ocean Regionalism", in: *Comparative Study of Society and History*, Bd. 47, Nr. 4, 2005, S. 700–724. Für neue Arbeiten zu Grotius siehe Martine Julia van Ittersum, *Profit and Principle: Hugo Grotius, Natural Rights Theories, and the Rise of Dutch Power in the East Indies, 1595–1615*, Leiden: Brill, 2006; und Peter Borschberg, *Hugo Grotius, the Portuguese, and Free Trade in the East Indies*, Singapur: NUS Press, 2011.

32  Die herrschende Denkweise in Systemen, wenn es um Infrastruktur geht, beschreibt Objekte wie etwa Straßen als Verteilungssysteme, bei denen die physische Präsenz der Infrastruktur ihrem größeren Zweck als Leiter von Güter- und Menschenströmen untergeordnet ist. Man liest Infrastruktur nicht als Objekt, sondern als System; nicht als Artefakt, sondern als Logik. Eine solche Art zu denken begann in der amerikanischen Architektur und Stadtplanung zu Beginn des 20. Jahrhunderts; in den Jahrzehnten nach dem Zweiten Weltkrieg begann Infrastruktur allerdings ihre eigene Form von negativen Rückwirkungen und Entfremdung zu produzieren. Das 21. Jahrhundert wird durch verschiedene Ansätze infrastrukturellen

Denkens charakterisiert: Einige ArchitektInnen und StädteplanerInnen ziehen es vor, die Stadt in die Infrastruktur statt die Infrastruktur in die Stadt zu stellen; andere vertiefen sich in eine zweite Ebene algorithmischer Prozesse, die in Infrastrukturen lauern. Z. B.: „Während Infrastruktur normalerweise Assoziationen mit physischen Netzwerken für Transport, Kommunikation oder die Versorgungswirtschaft hervorruft, umfasst sie zugleich gemeinsam genutzte Protokolle zur Formatierung aller möglichen Dinge von technischen Objekten über Führungsstile bis hin zu urbanen Räumen. Die normalerweise als geometrisch formale Objekte betrachteten Gebäudehüllen sind zu Infrastrukturen geworden – physische, räumliche Medien und Technologien, die sich als wiederholbare Phänomene durch die ganze Welt ziehen. Viele Infrastrukturen sind nicht mehr bloß das, was versteckt ist oder unter anderen urbanen Strukturen liegt, sondern sie *verkörpern* die urbane Formel." (Keller Easterling, „Disposition and Active Form", in: Katrina Stoll und Scott Lloyd (Hg.), *Infrastructure as Architecture: Designing Composite Networks*, Berlin: Jovis Verlag, 2010, S. 96.)

33  Zur Politik der Infrastruktur siehe Joseph W. Westphal, „The Politics of Infrastructure", in: *Social Research*, Bd. 75, Nr. 3, Herbst 2008, S. 793–804.

34  Siehe z. B. Anthony Reid, „Singapore between Cosmopolis and Nation", in: Karl Hack und Jean-Louis Margolin (Hg.), *Singapore from Temasek to the 21st Century: Reinventing the Global City*, Singapur: NUS Press, 2010, S. 37–54.

35  Eric Tagliacozzo, *Secret Trades, Porous Borders: Smuggling and States along a Southeast Asian Frontier, 1865–1915*, New Haven: Yale University Press, 2005. Zu Bojen und Leuchttürmen, s. S. 82ff.

36  Vgl. Tagliacozzo, op. cit., S. 88.

37  Zur Katastrophenpolitik vgl. Bonnie Honig, *Emergency Politics: Paradox, Law, Democracy*, Princeton, NJ: Princeton University Press, 2011; Carl Schmitt, *Der Begriff des Politischen*, Berlin: Duncker & Humblot, 1991 (1. Auflage 1932).

38  Zu Beginn des 20. Jahrhunderts „wurden Leuchttürme zu imposanten, leistungsfähigen Bauwerken, schwebende Panoptiken, in denen Besatzungen monatelang auf sich selbst gestellt bleiben konnten. Jetzt war es sehr viel schwerer, ungesehen nach Hinterindien zu kreuzen, weil eine Kette von Wachtürmen – die vollkommen in der Lage waren, auch bei Nacht zu sehen – sich über die ganze Grenze erstreckte." (Tagliacozzo, S. 84) Der Autor erwähnt auch „den ständigen auf Bewegungen der Handelsschifffahrt gerichteten Blick [...] besonders in den Grenz-Siedlungen." (S. 86) Vgl. auch Eric Tagliacozzo, „The Lit Archipelago: Coast Lighting and the Imperial Optic in Insular Southeast Asia, 1860–1910", in: *Technology and Culture*, Bd. 46, Nr. 2, April 2005, S. 306–328. Meine Formulierung beruft sich auf James C. Scott, *Seeing Like a State*, New Haven: Yale University Press, 1998.

39  Wie die Briten die lokalen malaiischen Fürsten überredet haben, ihnen die Insel Singapur zwischen 1819 und 1823 zu überlassen, ist wohlbekannt. Z. B.: „In den 1819 getroffenen Vereinbarungen hatten die malaiischen Häuptlinge nur die Einrichtung eines britischen Handelspostens gestattet, und Farquhar glaubte, malaiischem Brauch folgend, dass damit weder Grundeigentum noch das Recht übertragen wurde, Gesetze zu erlassen. [...] Danach gab Raffles jeden Versuch auf, die Häuptlinge und ihre Nachfolger in aufgeklärte Regierungspartner zu verwandeln. Er zahlte prompt ihre Vergütungen, und abgesehen davon, dass er ihre Anhänger entwaffnete, [...] ließ er sie in ihren privaten Enklaven ungestört, verdrängte sie aber allmählich aus dem öffentlichen Leben. Im Dezember 1822 änderte er all ihre Ansprüche auf einen Anteil an den öffentlichen Einnahmen in eine feste monatliche Zahlung um, und am Vorabend seiner endgültigen Abreise im Juni 1823 traf er eine Vereinbarung, ihnen ihre rechtsprechende Gewalt und Eigentumsrechte an Grund und Boden abzukaufen, abgesehen von den Gebieten, die speziell für sie bestimmt waren." C. M. Turnbull, *A History of Singapore 1819–1975*, London: Oxford University Press, 1977, S. 23.

40  All dies mag eine rassistische Komponente enthalten: Chinesisches Weiß (die Farbe von Sand) verdrängt eine Insel mit malaiischem Namen. Aber zu dieser Verdrängung von Malaien war es schon vorher gekommen: Während ihm die Neuerschaffung der einst bedeutenden Hafenstadt vorschwebte (deren große Zeit im 14. und 15. Jahrhundert gewesen war), drängte Raffles die realen Malaien, die in seiner Gegenwart auf Singapur lebten, ins Abseits. (Zu Raffles' Mythenbildung vgl. Christina Skott, „Imagined Centrality: Sir Stamford Raffles and the Birth of Modern Singapore", in: Hack, Margolin, op. cit., S. 155–184.)

41  Vgl. Jean-Paul Martinon (Hg.), *The Curatorial*, London/New York: Bloomsbury, 2013.

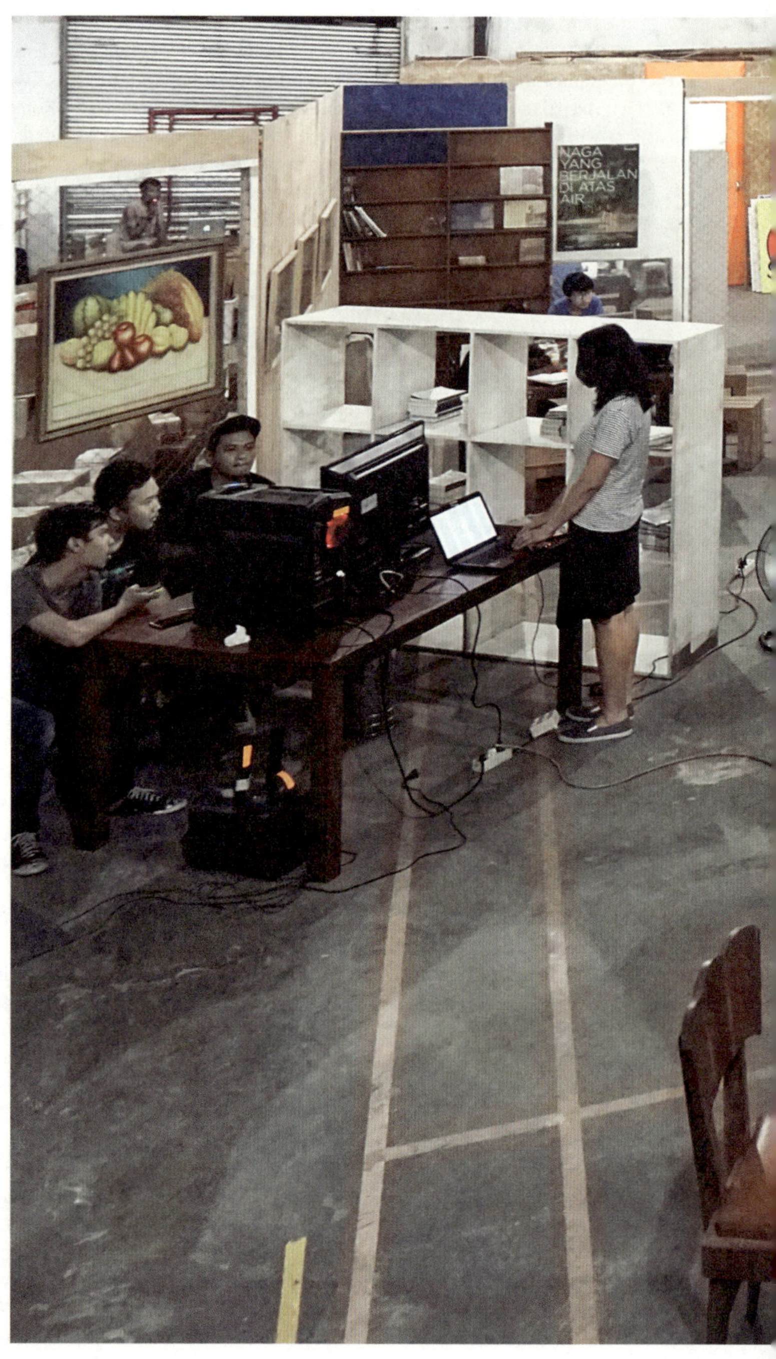

Ruangrupa
Gudang Sarinah Ekosistem
Jakarta, Indonesia

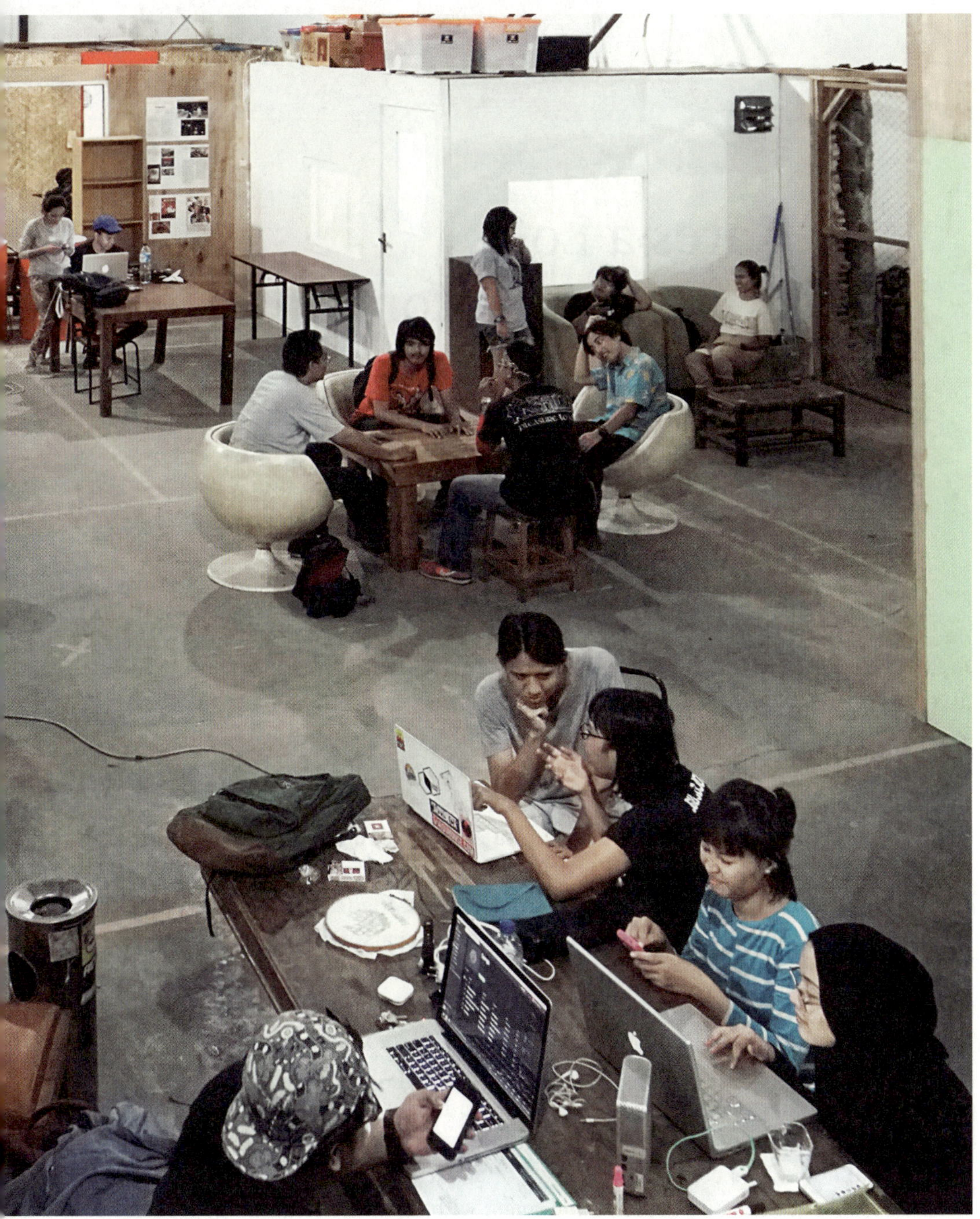

David Teh

# Who Cares a Lot?
# Ruangrupa as Curatorship

In 2011 Southeast Asia hosted two significant media art shows, both daring to juxtapose recent work from the region with seminal collections from the First World. In "Video, an Art, a History 1965-2010," the Singapore Art Museum (SAM) tentatively aired its nascent Southeast Asian collection alongside a roving blockbuster from the Centre Pompidou in Paris. At the National Gallery of Indonesia (Galnas), the Jakarta artists' collective Ruangrupa held the fifth installment of their video art biennial, "OK Video–Jakarta International Video Festival" featuring a curated selection from the catalogue of Electronic Arts Intermix in New York.[1] Both exhibitions were rare treats, featuring contemporary video works from Indonesia, Thailand, and Vietnam, side by side with works by Western artists, including Bill Viola, Dan Graham, VALIE EXPORT, and Vito Acconci–the first time this canon had alighted on the region en masse. In both exhibitions worlds came together, but they were worlds apart.

I found myself wondering what it would be like if these two worlds were swapped, if SAM were to take over the ageing halls of Galnas, and Ruangrupa the colonial nooks and crannies of SAM. For a start, we would see "OK Video" with fewer mosquitoes and comfortable seats; with an injection of Singaporean efficiency, Galnas would get a much-needed overhaul. SAM would meanwhile be unrecognizable, revived by a shot of the spontaneity and personality it lacks. Alas, it was wishful thinking. One can only dream of a day when the region's resources are effectively shared.

It could be objected that I am not comparing apples with apples. SAM is a well-funded public museum, with its own collection, but, like all of Singapore's institutions, it suffers from the overweening attentions of its bureaucratic parents.

Galnas, meanwhile, is a criminally neglected child—a "national" space for hire—and Ruangrupa, while by now a de facto institution, is an autonomous artists' collective with no collection and largely free from bureaucracy. Yet the comparison was telling: SAM balked at the task of integrating their works (either spatially or intellectually) with the visiting ones, leaving Southeast Asia a peripheral plug-in for the touring Euro-American canon. At "OK Video," the foreign material was not the main event; carefully selected to feed and challenge Indonesia's thriving video communities, it was not circumscribed architecturally in its own pavilion, but nested within a locally curated smorgasbord. The contrast was a stark demonstration of the raw value of curatorial vision, a value not proportional to budgets.

Context certainly helps. In Singapore's slick matrix of consumption, small curatorial fumbles will stick out like sore thumbs, while amidst the humming disorder of Jakarta—a city of some ten million souls, with a metropolitan population three times that—a little direction goes a long way. Yet the integration of local and international work was an important achievement, not least because the former draws upon, and critiques, the latter, but also because they are connected, whether consciously or unconsciously, through the history of the video medium itself, with shared formal parameters and shared referents in the world beyond the gallery. When it comes to exhibiting media art, it bears remembering that the museum itself is a medium, one to which a lot of media art is not native. The task of domesticating it is therefore fraught, especially in locations where institutions and curatorial practice are relatively young. So how is it that Jakarta, a chaotic mega-city with little infrastructure for contemporary art, has given rise to this sort of curatorial assuredness?

Site and Sound: Jakarta Calling (or, Karaoke as Method)
By far the most developed of Indonesia's 922 inhabited islands, Java is about half the size of the UK, with roughly twice the population. It dominates the national economy, and in creative industries increasingly casts a shadow over Indonesia's richer neighbors. Of its three artistic hubs, Bandung and Yogyakarta (Jogja) are the established centers of learning and production. Jakarta has long been the business hub, with the most commercial galleries. Given its strong non-commercial agenda, Ruangrupa might seem out of place in Jakarta—an hour's flight to the southeast, Jogja's cheap rents and slower pace make it an obvious base for collectives. But Ruangrupa is bound to Jakarta in every sense: physically, spiritually and conceptually, it is through and through a creature of the capital. This speaks volumes about the group's significance and the unique path it has taken in Indonesia's current contemporary art boom.

The collective was founded in 2000 by a group of young artists in a city then devoid of platforms for contemporary practice and collaboration. Their workshops and exhibitions fast became magnets for artists, designers, and researchers, eliciting broad-based community participation, distinguished by the group's knack for critical exploration of their urban surroundings. This urbanism has been their most consistent refrain. Though they have consistently worked with artists from elsewhere, Ruangrupa has made a profound commitment to Jakarta as both site and subject, to its people as both audience and authors. Since day one the group has taken the city itself–a noisy engine room of commerce and administration, not traditionally seen as a font of culture–as the primary protagonist of an epic adventure in collective storytelling. Heuristic as their approach may be, it is not without a certain realism, focused by an insistence upon the vitality of Jakarta's contemporary culture, as rooted not in some timeless past, but in a dense demographic and cultural stew of diverse and inextricable ingredients.

A pre-modern cosmopolitanism was forged here during the Srivijaya maritime empire that dominated the Malay world until the thirteenth century. Sunda Kelapa, as Jakarta was then known, had already long been a melting pot of regional and diasporic trading communities when the Dutch arrived in 1619. Renamed Batavia, the city was colonized and modernized, then nationalized as Jakarta. It is now being globalized, but this doesn't mean homogenization–rapid economic growth has come with an equally rapid dilation of the public sphere, and for a porous organization, the city's syncretic soil is fertile indeed. Such an environment puts a premium on openness; a trait Ruangrupa exhibits inside and out. While the founders may worry that a new crop of decision makers has been slow to emerge, a strong DIY ethos and a lack of hierarchy have been key to the group's sustainability. Their suburban headquarters in the south of the city boasts a well-used exhibition space, but it's more like a clubhouse: always open, always peopled–a studio, a library, a research lab, and a party venue, all in one. It would be lazy to call their collaborative house style "inclusive." Ruangrupa is shareware, their partnering indiscriminate–witness the soup of logos on their sponsor rolls. They tap every level of the institutional food chain, with a reach only possible in the last decade or so: from foreign NGOs and municipal and national governments, down to the humblest grassroots initiatives–a big tobacco company here, a national media network there, a small business around the corner.

According to Bandung-based curator Agung Hujatnikajennong, Indonesian contemporary art has seen two distinct phases. The first reflected civil society's atrophy under the authoritarian New Order (1965-98) of the country's second president, Suharto. The second, which is ongoing, reflects its flourishing and democratization since the wave of popular disgust (*reformasi*) that finally unseated that regime amidst regional financial crisis in 1998.[2] In the earlier period, the social conscience that had long been a cornerstone of national aesthetics–modern art's *sine qua non* since the independence struggle against the Dutch–found expression in a figurative modernism still loosely social realist in its scope. Its story remained that of nationhood, of the people (as, or against, nation), seasoned here and there with the "local" or the "traditional." Artists emerging since *reformasi*, however, are more playful and individualistic, enjoying the latitude of a liberalized public sphere, and the fruits of the country's steady rise in the global neoliberal pecking order. But while exemplary of this new generation, Ruangrupa strives to retain something of the representational logic of the old.

The result is a remarkably stable compound of activism and populism. The group's early embrace of lo-fi copy cultures and digital and open publishing models dovetailed with a neo-Situationism that was de rigueur at the couch-surfing stratum of global art in the early 2000s. Since 2000, Ruangrupa has published *Karbon*, a journal devoted to urban visual culture, which promotes criticism but also favors plain language. The biennial "Jakarta 32°C," which they have organized since 2004, brings students' work into the museum under the group's curatorial umbrella, democratizing the first steps to exhibition-making. Jakarta-based festivals like "OK Video," meanwhile, become launch pads for nationwide tours and workshops, as did their tenth anniversary festivities in 2010, held under the project banner "Decompression #10." And while in an earlier phase workshops were more hands-on and skills-based, as contemporary art production has flourished Ruangrupa's educational focus has sharpened around the critical faculties of writing and curatorship. The collective's prodigious capacity for outreach makes for an unruly aesthetic, encompassing everything from punk and street cultures, through documentary and ethnographic research, to conceptual and process-oriented experiments. Binding it all together is a firm conviction that the participants are agents in a living social history, one that is fundamentally urban and modern.

To profile Ruangrupa is to describe an event: time-based, immediate, and loosely structured; with a sense of purpose, yet more celebratory than agonistic. If one had to choose a single medium to characterize it, that medium would be karaoke. Indonesians love to sing, and a rich musical patchwork is an ever-present accompaniment to daily life. The refrains of old folk songs segue into distinctive modern genres like the racy *dangdut*, a hybrid of Malay, Indo-Arabic and 1970s rock sounds. A vivid medley of subcultures jostles with local and global pop, especially in the streets, where chronic traffic jams create a captive audience for wandering *ngamen* (buskers). It is no accident that live music and a certain chaotic, mob-karaoke ritual have become trademarks of the Ruangrupa experience. Indeed, this carnivalesque sonic profile betrays something of the group's curatorial program—it is prophetic in the sense Jacques Attali reserved for composition, presaging a new regime of cultural production that is live, open source, and, above all, poly-vocal.[3]

In his compelling account of Javanese modernity, anthropologist John Pemberton describes an extraordinary process whereby the island's eighteenth-century aristocracy, whose role was rapidly becoming ceremonial, re-encoded the technologies and trappings of Dutch colonial might.[4] The once terrifying sound of cannon fire, for instance, came to announce official diplomatic correspondence, or to mark a royal birthday or wedding; a hybrid pageantry was improvised, retrofitted, and elaborately codified. Pyrotechnics made for a spectacle of new order, distracting attention from the drastic defeat of the old. Pemberton also recalls how Suharto, going through the motions of electoral democracy during the Cold War, took these vestiges of contest and refurbished them once again, as tradition, in the name of another "new order." Ruangrupa, we might say, represents the opposite aural evolution. It is a stethoscope held to the rattling yet still growing chest of the metropolis, amplifying the hum of a popular sovereignty–long suppressed by colonialism and authoritarianism–over the ceaseless urban din.

## Ruangrupa as Curatorship?

In a recent essay on Ruangrupa, art historian Thomas Berghuis takes up some topical vocabularies for lassoing contemporary art's vast diversity of practices and newly integrated territories.[5] With nods to Nicolas Bourriaud's relational aesthetics and Terry Smith's reckoning with contemporaneity, he casts the group in the uncertain light of "the global," as a laboratory for an art to come. In the clamor of the Jakarta art world, many would say a breath of speculative air is just what the doctor ordered. But what is missing from this picture is a sense of the intense struggle–in this region, quite peculiar to Indonesia–over creative and intellectual labor. In this struggle the curatorial faculty is crucial, not only because curators are pivotal in capturing talent, but also because curatorial functions have long preoccupied many of the most talented. Some of Ruangrupa's core members exemplify this bind, but they stand out for having maintained both their independence from the market and their standing with respect to the curatorial cartel that serves it. They are not the only collective to have thrived since *reformasi*–there are dozens–but their endurance and success, at home and abroad, prompts the question: has it perhaps been by appropriating the function of curatorship that this independence has been secured?

As a vocation, curatorship in Southeast Asia is tenuous. But in Indonesia, where a bullish market has the profession in its clutches, it is the craft that is tenuous, not the worker. One much sought-after Jogja painter makes enough from the sale of a single picture to buy a large house. Curators have not missed out on the bonanza. This newly struck professional mold, still setting, is guarded by a small band of entrenched taste-makers. In a country where an ample meal can be had street-side for a dollar, they are well rewarded–an anomaly in the region–especially a senior cohort whose number may be counted on one hand. But most of the output is handled by a younger generation who came of age during *reformasi*.

At worst, their job entails the perfunctory anointment of new products for the market. For some, the whole process may be done on a smartphone: syncing calendars, browsing and selecting images, cutting and pasting together a recycled curatorial "essay," before parachuting into town for the opening reception. It's a well-oiled assembly line, by far the region's most efficient. The conscientious few will manage some conversation with the artist, maybe even write something new, but a backlog of shows leaves little time for research; the typical project-window lasts weeks, not months. It's a pity, for most were trained as artists and have a good grasp on matters of process; they speak persuasively of aesthetic currents, and artists' places within them. But for all their mobility, their horizons as curators are limited by a parochial market and a lack of credible institutional systems of validation and power.

If Asian modern art history has seldom ventured beyond national framings, this is not without reason. Rarely the product of organic urban fermentation, modern art has more often been a state-sanctioned project. But the unraveling of the Cold War has set the stage for a new mode of circulation and a new currency for the visual—a currency now called the contemporary. Gaining new patrons and markets, artists have filtered out certain modernist strains, and spun what's left in the direction of international trends. But curatorship, by contrast—at least, curatorship as we now know it, unhinged from the collection that once grounded the role—has more or less had to invent itself from scratch. In the first proper regional study on the subject, Patrick D. Flores confirms that the role has always been the province of discursively inclined artists, and not defined around collections. He identifies pioneers such as Apinan Poshyananda (a Thai) and Jim Supangkat (an Indonesian), who plugged Southeast Asian art into international circuits in the 1990s, as the key midwives of this contemporary.[6] Not incidentally, both were trained as artists; no less significantly, neither has ever taught curating, nor trained worthy successors. Entangled by bureaucratic and market strictures respectively, they seem to have accrued powers too precious to be handed down. Today's curators have inherited an invisible suit from these pathfinders, with little sense of professional continuity. And the corollary of this failure of professional memory is a failure to historicize exhibition making per se. Ruangrupa stands out here for having kept alive a parallel world for historically informed—if not always art historically informed—ways of working.

Getting Modernity

I recently asked an Indonesian curator—trained and still practicing as an artist—what he thought of the curatorial studies programs sprouting up around the world. If he were younger, where would he go to study this craft? His answer was revealing: "The Netherlands and Japan." For an emerging leader from the global periphery, the prospect of acquiring curatorial expertise in emerging territories remains dim. And it is more than ironic that he should nominate both of his country's former colonial masters, both wealthy nations with developed infrastructures for art, both steady fonts of the aid that has helped shape professional horizons in Indonesia. The pairing also serves to dramatize a certain historical polarity, perhaps collapsing now, between two very different demographic orders, as the vanguard cosmopolitanism of the Netherlands shrinks into something more akin to Japan's insular nationalism. But my friend was answering,

I suspected, with an eye on the past, not the future, which his explanation confirmed: "Because these two places really *got* modernity." The emphasis is his, and richly ambivalent–they "got it" in the sense of understanding it, but perhaps also in the sense of copping it, of being on the receiving end of some painful but irrevocable gift. "Getting" this most "contemporary" métier would thus entail getting a certain modernity first. Clearly we were no longer talking about modern art, about this or that modernism, but about a lived modernity. The key knowledge for curating in Indonesia would be found where an antecedent modernity had taken root, whence Indonesia's own modernity was grafted.

Upon reflection, this insistence on a source modernity also runs counter to the romantic nomadism that still pervades the curatorial discourse of a would-be "global" field.[7] Against the tide of this globalization wades the stubborn figure of the modern nation–nation as product of modernity and modernity as the flagship product of nation–a structure that seems almost archaeological amidst the recent vogue for fallen utopias.[8] But decaying though it may be, this concrete modernity in Indonesia's cities is by no means the picturesque relic of a bygone internationalism. It is the everyday built environment, still being refurbished, still humming with life. Thus are Bandung's colonial bungalows repurposed as factory outlets. The weary framework of Jakarta's Taman Ismail Marzuki, a public facility for modern culture inaugurated in 1968, is the subject neither of fond portraits nor of ideological ghost stories–it still functions as a rare and valued piece of public infrastructure.[9]

This unfinished modernity has done nothing to limit Ruangrupa's contemporary currency. For the dematerialization of art, too, is an incomplete project, and the "relational" turn, far from transcending it, has only upped the ante. As the artwork becomes activity (participation, social engagement, conviviality) the market moves to outflank it, at once celebrating the ephemeral and unreified spirit of the work, while perfecting its titration into parallel currencies. As a collective exhibiting internationally, whose core activity is the production and dissemination of knowledge rather than things, Ruangrupa is hardly immune. Indeed, the collective seems to exemplify that merger of artist and curator so often mooted in the ballooning discourse on exhibition making. In a recent edition of *Manifesta Journal* devoted to this subject, positions are staked around Walter Benjamin's 1934 lecture "The Author as Producer." We can hardly doubt the enduring relevance of this text in the post-industrial world, where museum may be likened to factory, and the mere prospect of collectivization, as John Roberts points out, no longer distinguishes artist from curator.[10] But these conditions are far from universal, and are by no means the manifest destiny of contemporary art in Asia. For Roberts, the curator unprepared to be an artist should step back into the wings and make way for those truly committed to thwarting art's instrumentalization. Such a synthesis has the whiff of an undead Hegelianism about it: the "artist-curator as producer" must finally take responsibility for his own philosophy of production, as Arthur Danto might have put it.

But if anything, Southeast Asian artist-curatorship ought to be read against the grain of this *telos*. Even for the region's most conspicuous trailblazers (Apinan and Supangkat), the outcome was precisely the opposite: a renewed separation of roles.

However, Ruangrupa might seem to embody the disciplinary merger, then, in attributing to the group the form of a curatorship to come, with or without the italics, we run the risk of mistaking tactical moves for a strategic program. And however appealing the image of their "contemporaneity," the group should first be seen in another light, a light in which modernity and nation still matter, and instrumentality is not (yet) the arch-enemy of art; a light in which artists make artworks and curators curate, and it is possible to do both. Perhaps Ruangrupa is more a spirit of curatorship—not limited to a single body, yet somehow tied to a place—that would defend the autonomy of artists, singular or plural, but not necessarily that of the artwork. For this spirit the audience, rather than the work of art, may be the ultimate object of curatorial care.

1   "Video, an Art, a History 1965-2010," co-curated by Christine van Assche and Patricia Levasseur de la Motte, Singapore Art Museum, June 10–September 18, 2011; and "OK Video FLESH: 5th Jakarta International Video Festival," curated by Hafiz, Agung Hujatnikajennong, Farah Wardani, Mahardhika Yudha, and Rizki Lazuardi, National Gallery of Indonesia, October 6–17, 2011.

2   Agung Hujatnikajennong, "Everything Melts onto the Screen: Video and Media Art in Indonesia," presentation at "Video Vortex #7," Kedai Kebun Forum, Yogyakarta, July 2011. See also his "The State and the Market: Two Decades of Indonesian Contemporary Art," in *Biennale Jogja XI–Equator #1*, exh. cat., (Yogyakarta: Yayasan Biennale Yogyakarta, 2011), 180–89.

3   See Jacques Attali, *Noise: The Political Economy of Music*, trans. Brian Massumi (Minneapolis: University of Minnesota Press, 1985).

4   See John Pemberton, *On the Subject of "Java"* (Ithaca, NY: Cornell University Press, 1994).

5   Thomas J. Berghuis, "Ruangrupa," *Third Text* 25, no. 4 (2011): 395-407.

6   Patrick D. Flores, *Past Peripheral: Curation in Southeast Asia* (Singapore: NUS Museum, 2008). Apinan, who left the biggest international footprint, was in fact the youngest of a regional cohort that included also Redza Piyadasa in Malaysia and Raymundo Albano in the Philippines. In the Indonesian context, it is worth noting the exceptional case of artist-couple Mella Jaarsma and Nindityo Adipurnomo, who founded the country's first contemporary art space, Cemeti Art House, in Jogja in 1988. Committed to artists' professional development and anything but parochial, Cemeti's legacy—art historical and curatorial—is hard to overstate.

7   I would not be the first to observe that this nomadism is often a smoke screen for the industrial and economic transmigration it quite faithfully maps. See Pascal Gielen, "Curating with Love, or a Plea for Inflexibility," *Manifesta Journal*, no. 10 (2010): 14-15.

8   See, for example, Guy Tillim's *Avenue Patrice Lumumba* (2007-8), or Cyprien Gaillard's *Desniansky Raion* (2007). Louidgi Beltrame's film *Brasilia/Chandigarh* (2008) even made it to Singapore with the Pompidou show. The appeal of this genre is apparently universal, although it might be interesting to compare the respective geographies of production and consumption.

9   The cultural center was built on the site of a public park established by Raden Saleh, Indonesia's first modern artist, during the Dutch East Indies era. In using this space for exhibitions and concerts, Ruangrupa continues a tradition of diverting art's resources towards the provision of public space. Patrick D. Flores deals specifically with the matter of incomplete modernities in "The Curatorial Turn in Southeast Asia and the Afterlife of the Modern" (2008), in Melissa Chiu and Benjamin Genocchio, eds., *Contemporary Art in Asia: A Critical Reader* (Cambridge, MA: MIT Press, 2011), 197-210.

10  John Roberts, "The Curator as Producer: Aesthetic Reason, Nonaesthetic Reason, and Infinite Ideation," *Manifesta Journal*, no. 10 (2010): 51-57. See also Hito Steyerl, "Is a Museum a Factory?" *e-flux journal*, no. 7 (2009), http://www.e-flux.com/journal/is-a-museum-a-factory/, accessed on April 23, 2012.

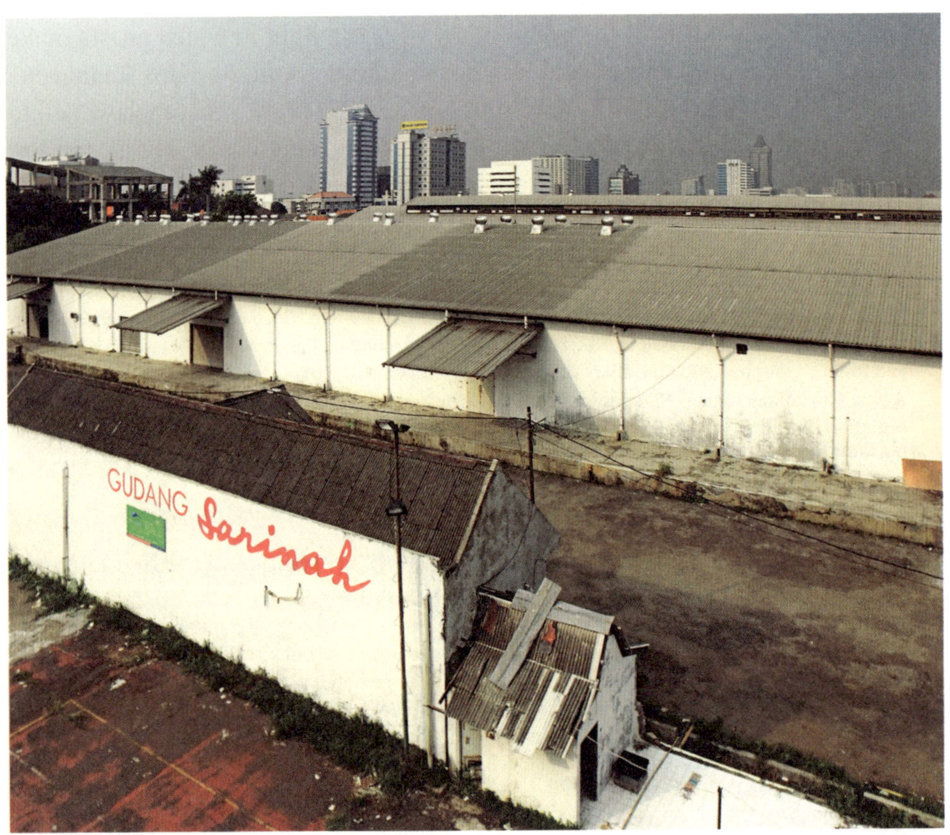


Ruangrupa
Gudang Sarinah Ekosistem
Jakarta, Indonesia

David Teh

# Wen kümmert es wirklich?
# Das Ruangrupa-Kollektiv
# als kuratorische Plattform

Im Jahr 2011 fanden in Südostasien zwei bedeutende Medienkunst-Ausstellungen statt, die sich zum Ziel gesetzt hatten, neue Arbeiten aus der Region neben wegweisenden Sammlungen aus der Ersten Welt zu präsentieren.[1]

Mit der Ausstellung *Video, an Art, a History 1965–2010* zeigte das Singapore Art Museum (SAM) zum ersten Mal seine gerade erst entstandene Südostasien-Sammlung, und zwar zusammen mit der Übernahme einer Blockbuster-Ausstellung aus dem Centre Pompidou. In der National Gallery of Indonesia (Galnas) veranstaltete das KünstlerInnenkollektiv Ruangrupa aus Jakarta zum fünften Mal seine Videokunst-Biennale *OK Video*, bei der auch eine kuratierte Auswahl aus dem Katalog der New Yorker Electronic Arts Intermix vorgeführt wurde. Beide Ausstellungen waren schon deshalb bemerkenswerte Ereignisse, weil sie zeitgenössische Videokunst aus Indonesien, Thailand und Vietnam sowie Arbeiten westlicher KünstlerInnen, darunter Bill Viola, Dan Graham, VALIE EXPORT und Vito Acconci, gleichberechtigt behandelten. Nie zuvor war diesem Kanon ein solcher Auftritt in Asien beschieden gewesen. Innerhalb der Ausstellungen kamen Welten zusammen und doch schienen die beiden Ausstellungsorte Lichtjahre voneinander entfernt zu sein.

Ich ertappte mich bei dem Gedanken, wie es wohl aussehen würde, wenn diese beiden Welten ihre Plätze tauschen würden. Wenn das SAM die altehrwürdigen Säle des Galnas übernähme und Ruangrupa die kolonialistischen Ecken und Winkel des SAM. Zunächst einmal hätte dies den Vorteil, dass man *OK Video* besuchen könnte, ohne von lästigen Moskitos umschwirrt zu werden – und komfortablere Sitzgelegenheiten gäbe es auch. Und andersherum könnte das Galnas – dafür würde die singapurische Effizienz schon sorgen – einer dringend nötigen Generalüberholung unterzogen werden. Das SAM im Gegenzug wäre kaum wiederzuerkennen, wenn die Spontaneität und Eigenwilligkeit, die dort fehlten, in seine Räumlichkeiten Einzug gehalten hätten. Natürlich hatte diese Tagträumerei rein gar nichts mit der Wirklichkeit zu tun. Der Tag, an dem in Südostasien über Ländergrenzen hinweg erfolgreich zusammengearbeitet wird, liegt nach wie vor in weiter Ferne.

Sicher könnte man sofort einwenden, dass in meinem Gedankenspiel Institutionen miteinander verglichen werden, die sich gar nicht vergleichen lassen. Das SAM ist ein finanziell recht üppig ausgestattetes öffentliches Museum, das über eine eigene Sammlung verfügt, doch wie alle Institutionen in Singapur unter der Einmischung von Behörden leidet. Das Galnas hingegen genießt einen größeren Spielraum und wird kaum bürokratisch gegängelt. Inzwischen ist das anonyme Kollektiv Ruangrupa zwar selbst zu einer Art Institution geworden, aber eine eigene Sammlung kann es nicht aufweisen. Und doch bin ich der Meinung, dass ein Vergleich zwischen beiden aufschlussreich ist. Das SAM scheiterte kläglich an der selbst gestellten Aufgabe, einen (räumlichen wie geistigen) Zusammenhang zwischen den eigenen Werken und den ausgestellten Leihgaben herzustellen. Die südostasiatische Kunst wirkte wie eine Zugabe aus der Peripherie, die niemand brauchte, und die neben den Werken der kanonischen Kunststars aus Europa und Amerika verblasste. Auf der Biennale *OK Video* waren die Arbeiten aus dem Ausland jedoch nicht das Hauptereignis. Sie waren vielmehr sorgfältig ausgewählt, um die Video-Communities Indonesiens zu bereichern und herauszufordern. Zudem waren die Arbeiten nicht architektonisch isoliert in einem eigenen Pavillon untergebracht, sondern eingebettet in eine nach lokalen Gesichtspunkten kuratierte Gesamtschau. In diesem Gegensatz kristallierte sich eine kuratorische Vision, die in keinem Verhältnis zu dem bescheidenen Budget stand, mit dem die Ausstellungsmacher auskommen mussten.

Sicherlich ist dabei auch der jeweilige Kontext wichtig. In Singapur mit seiner angepassten Konsumkultur muss man immer damit rechnen, dass kuratorische Experimente wie ein Fremdkörper wirken. Währenddessen stößt im flirrenden Chaos von Jakarta – einer Stadt mit zehn Millionen Einwohnern, die zu einem Ballungsgebiet gehört, in dem dreißig Millionen Menschen leben – schon ein kleiner, energischer Impuls auf eine große Resonanz. Die Verflechtung von lokaler und internationaler Kunst war nicht zuletzt deshalb eine bedeutsame Leistung, weil die indonesische Szene nicht nur stark vom Kunstgeschehen im Ausland beeinflusst wird, sondern an diesem auch Kritik übt. Zudem sind beide, ob nun bewusst oder unbewusst, ohnehin über die Geschichte des Mediums Video miteinander verbunden. Es gibt da jenseits der Ausstellungsräume gemeinsame formale Parameter und einen ähnlichen Zugriff auf die Welt. Wenn Medienkunst ausgestellt wird, kommt man nicht umhin, auch das Museum selbst als ein Medium zu erfahren, und zwar als ein Medium, in dem sich ein Großteil der Medienkunst gar nicht heimisch fühlt. Es ist deshalb eine äußerst schwierige Aufgabe, die Medienkunst zu domestizieren, insbesondere wenn es sich um Orte handelt, an denen Kunstinstitutionen und die kuratorische Praxis relativ neue Phänomene sind. Wie kommt es also, dass ausgerechnet Jakarta, diese unübersichtliche *Megacity*, die für zeitgenössische Kunst kaum gemacht scheint, ein derart bemerkenswertes kuratorisches Selbstbewusstsein an den Tag legt?

Der Klang des Ortes: Jakarta Calling (oder: Karaoke als Methode)
Java ist die mit Abstand dynamischste der 922 bewohnten Inseln Indonesiens. Obwohl sie nur halb so groß ist wie Großbritannien, wohnen dort mehr als doppelt so viele Menschen. Java dominiert die indonesische Wirtschaft, seine Kreativszene stellt die wohlhabenderen Nachbarstaaten zunehmend in den Schatten. Unter den drei Kunstmetropolen des Landes haben sich vor allem Bandung und Yogyakarta (Jogja) als Zentren der Kunstausbildung und -produktion hervorgetan. Als Wirtschaftsmotor des Landes bot Jakarta schon lange die meisten kommerziellen Galerien und damit auch die besten Geschäftsmöglichkeiten. Es mag zunächst verwundern, dass Ruangrupa, ein Kollektiv mit entschieden nicht-kommerzieller Ausrichtung, ausgerechnet in Jakarta zuhause ist. Nur eine Flugstunde weiter südöstlich locken bezahlbare Mieten und der entspanntere Rhythmus von Jogja. Doch Ruangrupa ist ganz und gar in Jakarta verwurzelt. In körperlicher, spiritueller, und konzeptueller Hinsicht ist es ein Geschöpf der Hauptstadt. Das sagt viel über die Bedeutung der Gruppe und über den einzigartigen Weg, den sie im derzeitigen indonesischen Kunstboom eingeschlagen hat.

Gegründet wurde das Kollektiv im Jahr 2000 von ein paar KunststudentInnen. Zu dieser Zeit suchte man in Jakarta vergebens nach Plattformen für zeitgenössische Kunst und kollaborative Praxis. Die Workshops und Ausstellungen der Gruppe entwickelten schon nach kurzer Zeit eine große Anziehungskraft auf KünstlerInnen, DesignerInnen und AkademikerInnen. Die verschiedenen Communities der Stadt waren zur Teilnahme aufgerufen und das Kollektiv verstand sich darauf, die unmittelbare urbane Umgebung zum Gegenstand kritischer Untersuchungen zu machen. Der Urbanismus wurde denn auch zu Ruangrupas Markenzeichen. Obwohl die Gruppe regelmäßig mit KünstlerInnen aus anderen Städten zusammenarbeitet, hat sie ihre tiefe Verbundenheit zu Jakarta nie in Frage gestellt. Jakarta war zugleich Ort und Thema, die Menschen der Stadt nicht nur Zuschauer, sondern immer auch Akteure. Vom ersten Tag ihres Bestehens an hat sich die Gruppe immer wieder mit der indonesischen Hauptstadt beschäftigt, diesem irrsinnig lauten Maschinenraum, von jeher Wirtschaftsmotor und Verwaltungszentrum, das bisher kaum durch kulturelle Glanzleistungen von sich reden gemacht hat. Ruangrupa hat diese Stadt zur Hauptfigur eines epischen Abenteuers in einer kollektiven Erzählung gemacht. Der Vergleich mag ein wenig manieriert erscheinen, ist aber einigermaßen treffend. Er betont die Vitalität von Jakartas Gegenwartskultur und verortet sie nicht in einer zeitlosen Vergangenheit, sondern in einem dichten demografischen und kulturellem Gefüge, das sich aus unterschiedlichen, miteinander verbundenen Komponenten zusammensetzt.

Allerdings existierte mit dem Seereich der Srivijaya, das die malaiische Welt bis zum 13. Jahrhundert beherrschte, schon vor der Neuzeit kosmopolitisches Leben in der Region. Damals hieß Jakarta Sunda Kelapa: ein Schmelztiegel, in dem die Handelsdiaspora eine Heimat fand, lange bevor die Holländer 1619 dort an Land gingen. Die europäischen Neuankömmlinge benannten die Stadt in Batavia um und modernisierten und kolonialisierten sie, bevor sie ihren heutigen Namen Jakarta erhielt. Die Hauptstadt des indonesischen Nationalstaates wurde schnell Teil des Globalisierungsprozesses, von Homogenisierung kann man jedoch nicht sprechen: Das rasante Wirtschaftswachstum geht einher mit einem ebenso beeindruckenden Niedergang der öffentlichen Sphäre. Doch die synkretistische Ausrichtung der Stadt erweist sich als fruchtbarer Boden, auf dem durchlässige Strukturen gedeihen können. Eine solche Umgebung begünstigt Offenheit, wie nicht zuletzt Ruangrupa bestätigt. Die Gründergeneration des Kollektivs zweifelte zwar kurz daran, ob Jüngere die Arbeit weiterführen würden, aber das *Do It Yourself*-Ethos und die flachen Hierarchien der Stadt sicherten das Fortleben der Gruppe. Ihre Räume im Süden der Stadt, in denen häufig Ausstellungen stattfinden, erinnern eher an ein Jugendzentrum. Die Türen sind immer offen, der Ort wird als Atelier, Bibliothek, Studienlabor und für Parties genutzt und steht niemals leer. Von Inklusion zu sprechen wäre noch untertrieben. Ruangrupa begreift sich als Shareware, jeder darf kommen, alle können mitmachen, wie die unzähligen Sponsorenlogos auf der Webseite zeigen. Das Kollektiv ist auf jeder Stufe der institutionellen Nahrungskette vertreten. Allein in den letzten zehn Jahren kam finanzielle Unterstützung von internationalen NGOs, dem indonesischen Staat, der Stadtverwaltung, aber auch von kleinen lokalen Initiativen. Zu den Förderern gehören neben kleinen Unternehmen aus dem eigenen Stadtviertel auch nationale Medienkonglomerate und internationale Tabakfirmen.

Der vor allem in Bandung tätige Kurator Agung Hujatnikajennong teilt die indonesische Gegenwartskunst in zwei Phasen ein. In der ersten Phase spiegelte sich das Siechtum der Zivilgesellschaft unter der autoritären Neuen Ordnung (1965–98) Präsident Suhartos auch in der Kunstwelt wider. Die zweite, gegenwärtige Phase verkörpert den Demokratisierungsprozess und das Aufblühen der Zivilgesellschaft, die nach einer Protestwelle (Reformasi) das Regime während der Asienkrise 1998 stürzte.[2]

In der ersten Phase fand das Nationalbewusstsein in einer Ästhetik Ausdruck, die als Grundpfeiler der Kunstproduktion des Landes seit dem Unabhängigkeitskampf gegen die Holländer gelten kann und vor allem einer gegenständlichen, im weitesten Sinne sozialrealistischen Moderne verpflichtet war. Im Kern ging es immer um die Nation, das Volk (der oder gegen die Nation), das je nach Bedarf mit ein wenig Lokalkolorit und Tradition angereichert wurde. Die KünstlerInnen, die seit den Reformasi-Protesten zum Zug kamen, sind dagegen verspielter und individualistischer. Sie profitieren von der Liberalisierung der Öffentlichkeit und dem Aufstieg Indonesiens in der neoliberalen Hackordnung der

Globalisierung. Ruangrupa ist der Inbegriff dieser neuen Generation, doch das Kollektiv hat die Logik der Repräsentation, wie der ersten Phase zugeschrieben, nicht völlig aufgegeben.

Daraus ist ein erstaunlich nachhaltiges Gemisch aus Aktivismus und Populismus entstanden. Die Anfänge der Gruppe zeichneten sich durch eine Nähe zur digitalen und Open Access-Kultur aus, die dem neo-situationistischen, couchsurfenden Zeitgeist der frühen Nullerjahre entsprach. Die erste Ausgabe der Zeitschrift *Karbon* erschien im Jahr 2000, thematisch setzte man auf die visuellen Kulturen der Stadt, sprachlich nahmen die Macher kein Blatt vor den Mund, das Ziel war Kritik. Zudem organisiert Ruangrupa seit 2004 die Jarkata 32 °C Biennale, bei der Arbeiten von Studierenden als Teil des kuratorischen Kollektivs ausgestellt werden, wodurch der Zugang zur ersten eigenen Ausstellung demokratischer ist. Festivals wie *OK Video*, die am Anfang nur in Jakarta stattfanden, machen mittlerweile in den großen Städten des ganzen Landes Station. Workshops werden in verschiedenen Städten veranstaltet, wie das zum Beispiel bei den Feierlichkeiten zum zehnten Geburtstag der Gruppe im Jahr 2010 der Fall war, der unter dem bezeichnenden Titel *Decompression #10* begangen wurde. In der Anfangszeit waren die Workshops praktisch orientiert und es ging eher um handwerkliche Fertigkeiten. Mit der Zeit–die Produktion zeitgenössischer Kunst in Indonesien hatte spürbar Fahrt aufgenommen–führten die Workshops zunehmend an einen kritischen Ansatz des Schreibens und Kuratierens heran. Dem Kollektiv gelingt es mit traumwandlerischer Sicherheit, das eigene Anliegen nach außen zu vermitteln. In diesem Orbit findet von Punk und Straßenkultur über Dokumentarfilme und ethografische Feldstudien bis hin zu prozessorientierter Konzeptkunst eigentlich alles seinen Platz. Der gemeinsame Nenner des Ganzen? Die feste Überzeugung, dass die TeilnehmerInnen die Geschichte der (urbanen und modernen) Gesellschaft, in der sie leben, aktiv mitgestalten.

Ruangruppa zu porträtieren heißt, ein Ereignis zu beschreiben. Für das Kollektiv ist der Zeitfaktor von entscheidender Bedeutung, Unmittelbarkeit spielt eine große Rolle und die zahlreichen Aktivitäten lassen sich nur schwerlich in eine feststehende Struktur einfügen. Die Gruppe ist zielstrebig, weiß, was sie will, setzt dabei jedoch mehr auf die mitreißende Kraft der Euphorie als auf Konfrontation. Im Grunde lässt sich Ruangrupa noch am ehesten mit Karaoke vergleichen. Indonesier singen gern und zu jedem Anlass. Ein feiner Klangteppich begleitet den Alltag. Die Refrains alter Volksweisen gehen fließend über in moderne Genres wie den rasanten Dangdut, ein Hybrid malaiischer, indoarabischer und rockiger Sounds. Auf den Straßen treffen verschiedenste Subkulturen mit lokalen und globalen Poptrends aufeinander. Im zähfließenden Verkehr Jakartas werden die Autofahrer, die im Stau stecken, zum Publikum für die Ngamen-Straßenmusiker. Nicht zufällig ist Ruangrupa für Livemusik und chaotische Karaokemobs bekannt. Dieses karnevaleske Soundprofil gehört zum kuratorischen Programm der Gruppe. Es vollzieht auf der Ebene der Kunst, was Jacques Attali für das Komponieren von Musik voraussagte. Ein neues Paradigma kultureller Produktion zeichne sich ab: Die Zukunft gehört Liveperformances, Open Source-Technologien und – buchstäblich wie im übertragenen Sinne – der Vielstimmigkeit.[3]

Der Ethnologe John Pemberton legt in seiner brillianten Studie zur javanesischen Moderne dar, wie die einheimische Aristokratie im 18. Jahrhundert begann, sich auf das Zeremonielle zu beschränkten und dadurch die Technologien und Verheißungen der holländischen Kolonialmacht neu kodierte.[4] Das Kanonenfeuer, das einst Angst und Schrecken verbreitete, stand nun im Dienste der Diplomatie und erklang zu wichtigen Anlässen wie königlichen Geburtstagen und Hochzeiten. Hybride Rituale wurden erdacht, in die Vergangenheit zurückprojiziert und mit einem komplexen Überbau versehen. Feuerwerke feierten die neue Ordnung und sollten die demütigende Niederlage gegen die Kolonialmacht vergessen machen. Pemberton erinnert daran, dass Suharto, als er während des Kalten Krieges den Anschein einer auf Wahlen beruhenden Demokratie um jeden Preis wahren wollte, sich diese Versatzstücke zu eigen machte, den Menschen als Landestradition verkaufte und dadurch seine Neue Ordnung zementierte. Ruangrupa versinnbildlicht eine dieser Vereinnahmung diametral entgegenstehende Klanggeschichte. Ruangrupa verstärkt die Bass-Sounds des demokratischen Souveräns, der so lange durch Kolonialismus und Autoritarismus unterdrückt wurde. Das Husten und Keuchen der Großstadtbewohner überlagert das weiße Rauschen der Macht.

### Ruangrupa als KuratorInnen?

In einem kürzlich erschienenen Essay wendet der Kunsthistoriker Thomas Berghuis das Vokabular zeitgenössischer Theoriediskurse auf diverse Praktiken in den neuen Territorien der globalisierten Kunstwelt an.[5] Er zitiert Nicolas Bourriauds relationale Ästhetik und Terry Smiths Abrechnung mit dem Begriff der Zeitgenossenschaft, um Ruangrupa im flimmernden Licht des *Globalen* erstrahlen zu lassen – für ihn stellt das Kollektiv ein Laboratorium der kommenden Kunst dar. Im Dickicht der Kunstszene Jakartas mag der frische Wind der Spekulation zwar wie gerufen kommen. Was bei Berghuis jedoch fehlt, sind die heftigen Kämpfe um kreative und intellektuelle Arbeit, die – in der gesamten Region, aber in besonderem Maße in Indonesien – ausgefochten werden. In dieser Auseinandersetzung ist die Bedeutung des Kuratorischen gar nicht hoch genug einzuschätzen, da KuratorInnen wichtige Akteure der Suche nach neuen Talenten sind, aber auch, weil die talentiertesten KünstlerInnen sich ausgiebig mit dem Kuratorischen beschäftigt haben. Einige der Gründungsmitglieder des Kollektivs stehen beispielhaft für diese Verflechtung. Was sie von anderen jedoch unterscheidet, ist ihre Unabhängigkeit vom Markt und die Integrität, auf die sie sich, anders als die etablierten Vertreter des Kuratorenkartells, berufen können. Ruangrupa ist natürlich nicht das einzige Kollektiv, das seit den Reformasi-Protesten entstand. Tatsächlich existierten mehr als ein Dutzend, aber die Hartnäckigkeit und der nationale und internationale Erfolg der Gruppe geben dennoch zu der Frage Anlass, ob es vielleicht die besondere Bezugnahme auf die Praxis und Theorie des Kuratierens war, die Ruangrupa diese Unabhängigkeit ermöglichten.

Kuratieren als Beruf(ung) bedeutet in Südostasien mitunter Prekarität. In Indonesien, wo die entfesselte Eigendynamik des Marktes längst die Kunstwelt erfasst hat, ist allerdings nicht der Arbeiter, sondern das Handwerk in Gefahr. In Jogja soll der Erlös aus dem Verkauf eines Gemäldes mittlerweile locker ausreichen, um ein großzügig angelegtes Grundstück zu erwerben. Auch KuratorInnen profitieren von dieser Goldgräberstimmung. Doch über die beruflichen Aufstiegschancen entscheidet letztlich eine kleine verschworene Gemeinschaft von Trendsettern. In einem Land, in dem Streetfood selten mehr als einen Dollar kostet, ist das Geschäft für diese Meinungsmacher äußerst lukrativ, was bei weitem nicht für alle südostasiatischen Länder gilt. In der älteren Generation lässt sich die Zahl der Trendsetter an einer Hand abzählen. Aber es sind die Jüngeren, die mit den Reformasi-Protesten groß wurden, die für den überwiegenden Teil der Kunstproduktion verantwortlich sind.

Im ungünstigsten Fall sind jüngere KuratorInnen Zulieferer für einen gierigen Markt, auf dem sie Produkte platzieren. Einigen genügt dafür schon ein Smartphone: ein flüchtiger Blick in den Terminplaner, ein paar Bilder von KünstlerInnen, die man im Internet findet, dazu ein recyceltes kuratorisches Essay, das mithilfe der Copy-and-Paste-Funktion erstellt wurde – und dann ab in die Stadt zur Vernissage. So sieht die neue Fließbandproduktion aus. Und sie funktioniert. Die Gewissenhafteren werden sich vielleicht noch um ein persönliches Gespräch mit dem Künstler bemühen und unter Umständen sogar etwas Selbstgedachtes zu Papier bringen, aber der eng getaktete Ausstellungsrhythmus lässt für ausführlichere Nachforschungen keine Zeit. Ein Projekt ist in der Regel auf Wochen, nicht auf Monate angelegt. Das ist umso bedauerlicher, da die meisten KuratorInnen eine künstlerische Ausbildung durchlaufen und ein solides Wissen erworben haben. Sie kennen die wichtigsten ästhetischen Strömungen und die Art, wie sich dieser oder jener Künstler zu ihnen verhält. Ungeachtet ihrer Mobilität bleibt ihre Perspektive jedoch provinziell. Ihre Augen sind auf den indonesischen Markt gerichtet, es fehlt an anderweitigen Systemen von glaubwürdiger Machtverteilung und institutioneller Anerkennung.

Die Geschichte der modernen Kunst Asiens spielt sich nach wie vor in einem nationalen Rahmen ab – und das hat seine Gründe. Moderne Kunst war nur selten das Produkt einer eigenständigen urbanen Dynamik. In der Regel war sie Staatskunst. Das Ende des Kalten Krieges bahnte neuen Formen der Zirkulation und einem neuen visuellen Paradigma den Weg. Wir nennen es zeitgenössisch. Neue Mäzene und Märkte taten sich auf, KünstlerInnen verabschiedeten sich von zahlreichen Spielarten des Modernismus und glichen das, was übrig blieb, mit internationalen Trends ab. Aber das Kuratorische (in der Bedeutung, die es heute besitzt: also losgelöst von den Sammlungen, die einst seine Existenz begründeten) musste sich mehr oder weniger neu erfinden. In der ersten ernsthaften Studie zum Thema, die ihr Hauptaugenmerk auf Südostasien richtet, weist Patrick D. Flores nach, dass die Rolle des Kuratoren immer schon theorieinteressierte KünstlerInnen angezogen hat. Über Sammlungen definierte man sich nur in Ausnahmefällen. Flores erkennt in Figuren wie dem Thailänder Apinan Poshyananda und dem Indonesier Jim Supangkat, die Südostasien in den 1990er Jahren auf die internationale Kunstlandkarte brachten, die Wegbereiter der Wende zum Zeitgenössischen.[6] Beide genossen eine künstlerische Ausbildung. Weder der eine noch der andere hielt jemals Hochschulvorlesungen über das *Kuratorische*. Folglich brachten sie auch keine SchülerInnen hervor, die in ihre Fußstapfen hätten treten könnten. Stattdessen sind sie in ein Geflecht aus Bürokratie und Markt verwickelt, das ihnen eine Machtposition verschafft hat, die sich nicht ohne weiteres an Jüngere vermachen lässt. Die KuratorInnen der Gegenwart stehen auf den Schultern dieser Giganten und trotzdem ist da kein Gefühl von Kontinuität. Wo man sich nicht an Vorgänger erinnert, kann man auch keinen historischen Sinn für Ausstellungen entwickeln. Ruangrupa hingegen gelingt es, sich immer wieder historisch verbürgte Arbeitsweisen zu vergegenwärtigen, ohne deswegen beim Geschichtskitsch zu landen.

## Getting Modernity

Vor kurzem fragte ich einen indonesischen Kurator, der zudem als Künstler tätig ist, was er von den *Curatorial Studies*-Studiengängen hält, die weltweit an Kunsthochschulen aus dem Boden schießen. Wo würde er sich einschreiben, wenn er etwas nochmal von vorn beginnen könnte? Seine Antwort war vielsagend: „In Japan oder den Niederlanden." Aussichten auf eine gute kuratorische Ausbildung in einem der Schwellenländer an der globalen Peripherie gibt es im Grunde nicht. Und es hat durchaus etwas Ironisches, dass er gerade die beiden ehemaligen Kolonialmächte als kuratorische Bildungsstätten wählte, reiche Länder mit hervorragender Infrastruktur und ausgezeichneten Kunstinstitutionen, die Indonesien nachhaltig finanziell unterstützen. Die beiden Staaten veranschaulichen darüber hinaus einen historischen Gegensatz zwischen zwei demografischen Strukturen, der sich allmählich aufzulösen scheint: auf der einen Seite die Niederlande als Wegbereiter des Kosmopolitismus, auf der anderen Japans insularer Nationalismus. Im Anbetracht der aktuellen Entwicklungen in Europa gewinnt man indes den Eindruck, dass auch die Holländer dabei sind, sich von der Welt abzukapseln. Aber die Antwort meines Freundes stand eher unter dem Eindruck der Vergangenheit, nicht der Zukunft, wie aus seinen weiteren Ausführungen deutlich wurde: „These two places really got modernity." Nur im Englischen kommt die ganze Doppeldeutigkeit dieser Bemerkung zum Vorschein. Japan und die Niederlande, so eine Lesart, haben wirklich verstanden, was es mit der Moderne auf sich hat. Oder meint „get" an dieser Stelle vielmehr „zuziehen", so wie man sich eine unangenehme Krankheit zuzieht, die man nicht mehr loswird? Ohne Moderne kein Kuratieren. Es ging also nicht mehr um moderne Kunst, um diesen oder jeden Modernismus, sondern um die Moderne als gelebte

Erfahrung. Um sich auf das kuratorische Arbeiten in Indonesien vorzubereiten, empfiehlt sich ein Aufenthalt an Orten, in denen eine andere Moderne Wurzeln schlug, die das gegenwärtige Antlitz Indonesiens zutiefst geprägt hat.

Ich musste lange über dieses Gespräch nachdenken, denn der Verweis auf eine frühere, ursprüngliche Moderne widerstrebt dem romantischen Nomadismus, der in Theoriediskursen vorherrscht, die ein „globales" Aktionsfeld postulieren.[7] Der Welle der Globalisierung widersteht der moderne Nationalstaat entschieden – der Nationalstaat als Produkt der Moderne und die Moderne als Produkt des Nationalstaats –, dieses altertümlich anmutende Artefakt, das neben der neuesten und schon gescheiterten Utopie natürlich überholt wirken muss.[8] Die indonesische Moderne, so ruinenhaft sie im Stadtbild der großen Metropolen des Landes auch erscheinen mag, ist keineswegs ein Relikt eines längst untergegangenen Internationalismus. Diese Moderne schlägt sich in der architektonischen Lebenswelt nieder, die man, so gut es geht, ein- und herrichtet und die auch heute noch sehr lebendig ist. So werden Bandungs Kolonialanwesen nun als Factory Outlets genutzt. Das heruntergekommene Taman Ismail Marzuki in Jakarta, das 1968 als öffentliches Zentrum für moderne Kultur eröffnet wurde, inspiriert wohl nicht dazu, sich als frisch verliebtes Pärchen davor fotografieren zu lassen. Aber es muss eben auch nicht für die ideologisch grundierte Zurschaustellung des Verfalls herhalten, sondern behauptet sich auch im 21. Jahrhundert als wichtiger Bestandteil der öffentlichen Kulturinfrastruktur.[9]

Der Bezug auf diese unvollendete Moderne ist Ruangrupas radikal zeitgenössischer Ausrichtung in keiner Weise abträglich. Schließlich sind auch die Entmaterialisierung der Kunst und der *relational turn* Projekte, die nicht abgeschlossen sind. Wenn die Aktivität selbst, ob nun unter dem Stichwort Partizipation, Engagement oder Konvivialität, das Kunstwerk ist, reagiert der Markt umgehend und feiert das Vergängliche und Unverdinglichte künstlerischer Arbeiten, um sie umso besser verwerten zu können. Auch Ruangruapa kann sich als Kollektiv, das international ausstellt und nicht etwa Dinge, sondern Wissen produziert und verteilt, diesem Sog nicht entziehen. Vielleicht hat die Gruppe die Fusion von Künstler und Kurator, die viele Theoretiker seit langem herbeisehnen, am konsequentesten vollzogen. Das *Manifesta Journal* hat diesem Thema jüngst sogar ein Sonderheft gewidmet, in dessen Mittelpunkt Walter Benjamins Vortrag „Der Autor als Produzent" aus dem Jahr 1934 stand. Dass dieser Text auch im postindustriellen Zeitalter relevant ist, daran kann es keinen Zweifel geben. Museen weisen mittlerweile frappierende Ähnlichkeiten zu Fabriken auf und der Begriff der Kollektivbildung trifft heutzutage, wie John Roberts überzeugend herausgearbeitet hat, genauso auf das Tun von KünstlerInnen wie auf das der KuratorInnen zu.[10] Aber das sind keine allgemeingültigen Gesetze, die überall auf der Welt gelten. Derartige Produktionsbedingungen müssen sich nicht zwangsläufig auch in Südostasien durchsetzen. Roberts geht so weit zu behaupten, dass KuratorInnen, die nicht gewillt sind, auch künstlerisch zu arbeiten, sich nicht darüber beschweren sollten, wenn sie von jenen verdrängt werden, die auch wirklich das Zeug dazu haben, der fortschreitenden Instrumentalisierung von Kunst endlich ein Ende zu setzen. Diese Haltung ist durchdrungen von einem zombiehaften Hegelianismus: Der „Künstler-Kurator als Produzent" ist für die Philosophie seiner eigenen Produktion verantwortlich, so ließe sich diese Entwicklung mit Arthur Danto resümieren. Doch Künstler-Kuratoren in Südostasien sollten sich auf dieses Ziel gar nicht erst einlassen. Denn selbst bei den bahnbrechendsten Figuren (wie Apinan und Supangkat) ließ sich vielmehr das Gegenteil beobachten: Eine neue Rollenteilung kam auf.

Auch wenn Ruangrupa an der Spitze einer Bewegung zu stehen scheint, die einige für die Zukunft des Kuratierens halten, sollte man taktische Erwägungen nicht als strategisches Programm fehldeuten. Die radikale *Zeitgenossenschaft* des Kollektivs fußt in einer Moderne, in der Nationalstaaten ihren Platz haben und die instrumentale Vernunft (noch) nicht automatisch der Erzfeind der Kunst sein muss. KünstlerInnen gehen ihrer künstlerischen Praxis nach, KuratorInnen kuratieren – und wer will, tut beides. Ruangrupa verkörpert einen gewissen kuratorischen Geist, der sich nicht auf einen einzelnen Körper beschränkt, sondern eher einem Ort verhaftet ist. Aus diesem Geist heraus lässt sich die Autonomie des Künstlers (oder der KünstlerInnen) verteidigen, aber nicht zwangsläufig die des Kunstwerks. In diesem Geist gilt die größte Aufmerksamkeit nicht dem Kunstwerk, sondern dem Publikum.


1   *Video, an Art, a History 1965-2010*, kuratiert von Christine van Assche und Patricia Levasseur de la Motte, Singapore Art Museum, 10. Juni-18. September 2011; *OK Video FLESH: 5th Jakarta International Video Festival*, kuratiert von Hafiz, Agung Hujatnikajennong, Farah Wardani, Mahardhika Yudha ud Rizki Lazuardi, National Gallery of Indonesia, 6.-17. Oktober 2011.

2   Agung Hujatnikajennong, „Everything Melts onto the Screen: Video and Media Art in Indonesia", Vortrag, gehalten im Rahmen der *Video Vortex #7*, Kedai Kebun Forum, Yogyakarta, Juli 2011. Siehe auch Hujatnikajennongs „The State and the Market: Two Decades of Indonesian Contemporary Art," in: *Biennale Jogja XI–Equator #1*, Ausst.-Kat., Yogyakarta: Yayasan Biennale Yogyakarta, 2011, S. 180-189.

3   Jacques Attali, *Noise: The Political Economy of Music*, ins Englische übersetzt von Brian Massumi, Minneapolis: University of Minnesota Press, 1985.

4   John Pemberton, *On the Subject of "Java"*, Ithaca, NY: Cornell University Press, 1994.

5   Thomas J. Berghuis, „Ruangrupa", in: *Third Text*, Bd. 25, Nr. 4, 2011, S. 395-407.

6   Patrick D. Flores, *Past Peripheral: Curation in Southeast Asia*, Singapur: NUS Museum, 2008. Apinan, der im Ausland wohl am bekanntesten ist, war der jüngste Vertreter einer Generation südostasiatischer KuratorInnen und KünstlerInnen, zu der auch Redza Piyadasa in Malaysia und Raymundo Albano auf den Philippinen gehörten. Im indonesischen Kontext sollte zudem das außergewöhnliche Künstlerpaar Mella Jaarsma und Nindityo Adipurnomo erwähnt warden, die 1988 Cemeti Art House, die erste ausschließlich auf zeitgenössische Kunst fokussierte Galerie des Landes in Jogja eröffneten. Der kuratorische und kunsthistorische Einfluss, den Cemeti Art House mit seiner Offenheit auf die Entwicklung von jungen KünstlerInnen hatte, war beträchtlich.

7   Ich wäre nicht der erste, der darauf hinweist, dass das nomadische Denken häufig als kulturelles Feigenblatt eingesetzt wird und dadurch genau die industriellen und ökonomischen Prozesse bemäntelt, denen es doch nachspüren wollte. Siehe Pascal Gielen, „Curating with Love, or a Plea for Inflexibility", in: *Manifesta Journal*, Nr. 10, 2010, S. 14f.

8   Siehe Guy Tillims *Avenue Patrice Lumumba* (2007-2008) oder Cyprien Gaillards *Desniansky Raion* (2007). Louidgi Beltrames Film *Brasilia/Chandigarh* (2008) schaffte es dank der Wanderausstellung des Centre Pompidou sogar nach Singapur. Die Anziehungskraft dieses Genres scheint universell, auch wenn es aufschlussreich wäre, die Produktions- und Rezeptionsgeografie dieser Arbeiten genauer herauszuarbeiten.

9　Das Kulturzentrum entstand auf dem Gelände eines öffentlichen Parks, den Raden Saleh, Indonesiens erster moderner Künstler, noch zur Zeit von Holländisch-Ostindien gestaltete. Wenn Ruangrupa diesen Ort nun für Ausstellungen und Konzerte nutzt, dann führen sie eine indonesische Tradition fort, die Kunst als Mittel versteht, öffentliche Räume zu schaffen. Patrick D. Flores geht dem Problem der unvollendeten Moderne nach in „The Curatorial Turn in Southeast Asia and the Afterlife of the Modern", in: Melissa Chiu and Benjamin Genocchio (Hg.), *Contemporary Art in Asia: A Critical Reader*, Cambridge, MA: MIT Press, 2011, S. 197–210.

10　John Roberts, „The Curator as Producer: Aesthetic Reason, Nonaesthetic Reason, and Infinite Ideation", in: *Manifesta Journal*, Nr. 10, 2010, S. 51–57. Vgl. auch Hito Steyerl, „Is a Museum a Factory?", in: *e-flux journal*, Nr. 7, 2009, http://www.e-flux.com/journal/is-a-museum-a-factory, abgerufen am 23. April 2012.

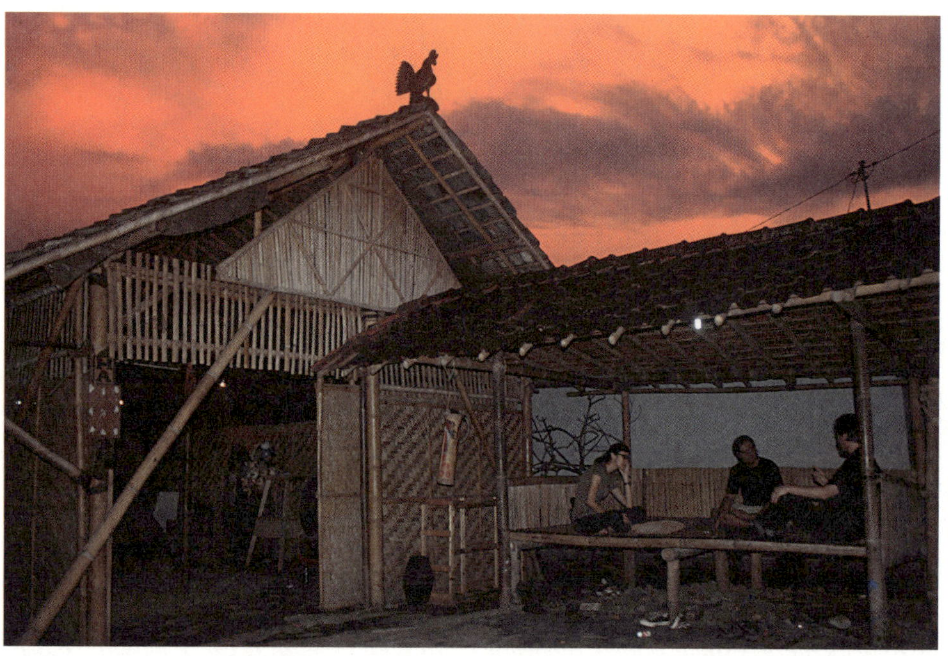

Eko Nugroho outside his studio, 2010
Yogyakarta, Indonesia

Tony Godfrey

# Tuesday in the Tropics

*Dear friends and colleagues,*

*It has for a long time irritated me that the art magazines publish so little on art in Southeast Asia where I now live. As they seem uninterested in running regular reviews or articles it seems the best I can do is, starting from today, send a weekly report. There are many good artists here that deserve some recognition.*

*I will try and keep it short, informative, and easy to read.*

*So long as there is something to report on I will send something every Tuesday morning so that those of you who work in the Northern climes can have a little bit of tropical sunshine at the start of the week.*

*Have a pleasant Christmas,*
*Tony*

December 23, 2014

I was in Yogyakarta from Tuesday to Wednesday of last week to do some interviews for my forthcoming book on Indonesian painting. Although I know most of these artists and their work well I want to be able to quote them as much as possible. Generally, in most of the writing about art in this region that I have read there are very few quotes from the artists, so, as a result, they remain strangely voiceless, especially when compared to artists in the West who are frequently interviewed and quoted. It is important for me that in a book that is very much about the artists as individuals you should hear their voice and get a sense both of their personality and their particular position on painting.

On the Tuesday as our plane was delayed I only met up with Handiwirman and Yunizar who rather than select images for the book and talk about them wanted to sit together and talk about their work generally. It was a good conversation in which we talked about the relationship between painting and sculpture (Handi is primarily a sculptor and Yunizar has recently been making sculptures). Also we talked about their relationship to the Jendela group (a group of five artists from Sumatra, all of whom stayed in Jogja after finishing college there—Jumaldi Alfi, Rudi Mantofani and Yusra Martunus are the other members). There are other important groupings such as Surrounded By Water in the Philippines—of which more next week. Handi and Yunizar said that when Jendela began they talked a lot about art, but now they are older they meet only occasionally and are more likely to ask each other how their children are doing. Their individual careers now have their own momentum and complexity. I guess most artists groupings (think of Die Brücke or CoBrA) are either short lived or, like this, become primarily social.

After we had finished and I had turned off my tape recorder, Handi asked, "What does drawing mean to you?" It is a good question: as we know the status of drawing is a complex one in contemporary art, and in Southeast Asia it is compounded by other issues. There are conservation issues because of the high humidity: the collectors are very obsessed with paintings as a medium. (As there are very few foundations and little state money collectors are very, very important in sustaining the art world.) Both Handi and Yunizar often do drawings before making a sculpture or painting but will then destroy them, not seeing them as finished or interesting as art works. For me they are often where you can see an artist thinking. I also said I was fascinated by how as we talked Yunizar would stack objects such as the ubiquitous pack of cigarettes and pens in different configurations and Handi, a man with large hands but the delicacy of a surgeon, would twist bits of wire. (I am afraid the only photo I took of this is a bit blurry [fig. 2]) This to me could be seen as a form of drawing too.

Drawing remains central to the work of Eko Nugroho who we visited the next morning. He has, he tells us, drawn every day of 2014. We looked at some of his recent sketchbooks: the words are always very important to him. As he said he began by being very much in love with cartoons.

Like many successful artists in Jogja he has built a large house and studio for himself and of course he has furnished it with his own fabrics, curtains and objects. His studio is on the ground floor but the living area is above so it can catch the breeze and have views out over the rice fields (fig. 5 and p. 190). It is a very different place from that where I first met him in 2010!

When I had first mentioned writing a book about painting in 2013 he had been very wary as he planned to do no paintings that year. By "paintings" he meant paint on canvas, but for me the temporary wall paintings he does for exhibitions are just as valid and interesting as those on canvas. Also, he is doing more embroideries than "paintings" at the moment but to me, as an art historian, these are not embroideries but tapestries which in previous centuries was a parallel form to painting (see Raphael, Rubens, etc.). The way he makes them is fascinating: he makes a painting on canvas (see attached image) and then gives it to some of the embroiderers he employs or gives work to. (They all lost their jobs when their factory got a computer driven machine. He is very committed to supporting and sustaining people who make things by hand.) They embroider or stitch directly into that canvas, periodically he will visit them and see how things are going, make adjustments, and changes. In effect the original painting is covered up or destroyed by the fabric. It is, of course, a unique object not a multiple.

After that my assistant and translator Theresia went to have lunch in a *Warung* (wayside stall). Chicken, rice, aubergine, green salad and *petai*–large green beans called "stink beans" in English served this time still in the long green pod. I really like them! (fig. 3)

En route to see S. Teddy we nipped into the shop DGMBT that Eko runs and where he sells T-shirts and objects by himself and others (fig. 1). There is a café and small exhibition space for young artists attached. It's a great place to buy Christmas presents!

With S. Teddy we mainly discussed his upcoming show in the project room at Equator Art Projects. He has the idea to make many paintings that look like red flags–each with a different emblem or image on. He is recovering from cancer: it was great to see him filled with enthusiasm and energy. I will tell you more about that show when we install it next month!

Wishing you all a very pleasant Christmas and a good 2015,

Tony

June 9, 2015

Dear friends and colleagues,

Art Jog. We call it an art fair, but its really a salon, like the Royal Academy. If that sounds stuffy—and it probably does—let's call it an annual art fair run by artists instead. There are no gallerists in nice suits or black dresses waiting in booths to sell you things. It is always a mix of old and young, established and "upcoming" artists.

It has changed since 2008 when it started, becoming even less like an ordinary art fair. It is now perhaps the "coolest" exhibition in Southeast Asia, the event people most want to be at.

This year I didn't go to the opening night. I was told 10,000 people had bought tickets for the evening and I couldn't face the crush. There is an astonishingly large audience for art in Indonesia—predominantly a young audience. As you can see from my snaps I went during the relatively sedate and uncrowded VIP preview beforehand. (BTW, It seems almost a tradition that not all the labels are up and work is still being installed during this preview. It is typical of the Jogja art world that it seems very improvised, chaotic and last minute—which it is!—but also in fact very professional. It is part of the charm that you can chat to the artists as they make some final adjustments.)

The organizers don't have to worry so much now about selling work: so many people go to it that they make a lot of money just on admission tickets. For the last three years it has been curated by Bambang "Toko" Witjaksono who has sought to make it not just a showcase for what is best in Jogja but a coherent exhibition—and a little international, with two artists from overseas: this year it is Mark Justiniani from Philippines and Yoko Ono—Japanese, I think?

Jogja has always been, not just an artist's town, but a painter's town, so it will come as a shock to many that Bambang "Toko" has included only one painting in this show of sixty or more artists. As someone who is finally finishing a book on Indonesian painting is this worrying to me? Am I writing about a peripheralized medium? No, not really. There seems a general concensus that the younger generation of painters are neither very original nor very good. Perhaps the presence of so many strong personalities in the two generations above is stifling. If there are no new good painters why show weak ones? Certainly the good paintings in past years had all been by the old guys. (Incidentally the best paintings on show in town at another exhibition curated by Enin Suprianto: three new works by Christine Ay Tjoe—one of the very few female artists in Indonesia with a strong profile).

I asked Bambang if that was his thinking and he laughed "yes!" the young painters are not coming forward, so let's focus on what is good—installations and participatory works. However apart from the maker of the token painter Masriadi five other artists I talk about in my painting book are here anyway: Entang Wiharso, Heri Dono, Eko Nugroho, Indieguerillas, Handwirman but with installations or sculptures. (Bambang Toko is in my book too for he is also a painter as well as curator.) Here painters are less canvas bound than in other cultures. Installation develops out of painting here in a way it has not in the West.

Which are the notable works? Mark Justiniani's vertigo inducing hole in the floor—all done with mirrors. Masriadi's painting. Installations by Eko and Heri, though not dissimilar from early work. Work in the entrance hall by Indieguerillas—customized becaks, (rickshaws used by hawkers) but selling psychological states rather than satay or ice cream (fig. 6). As so often here, they contain an in-joke: the memorable hair styles of Jogja artists Eddie Hara and Nasirun as well as those of Warhol and Basquiat (fig. 9).

There were some fun participatory art works: a shooting galley where you could defend the old, low rise town of Jogja against developers dropping, à la Space invaders, cranes and cement mixers from the sky; an immersive music machine by Rocka Radipa you could move your hands across to make different sounds.

One very in joke: the "Prison Art Lab" making works from any leaves you provide—many Jogja artists have been imprisoned recently for marijuana possession (fig. 8). As always, Handiwirman provided something that was both fun and slightly unsettling: some years ago he became fascinated in turning rubber toys inside-out. Here he has made a table like sculpture, coated it with rubber, then unpeeled it as if he is skinning an animal (fig. 4).

Art Jog has become such a big and well regarded event that a whole Jogja art week has built up around it with other exhibitions, events and openings popping up around the town. The best of them for me was a show at ARK by the redoubtable Freddie and Isabel Aquilizan. If nothing noteworthy turns up during the week I will tell you about it next Tuesday.


Wishing you all a jolly Tuesday,


Tony


PS. If you are in Singapore, nip over to NTU CCA at 7:30 pm: I am giving a lecture there on "Why I am not a Southeast Asian Specialist."

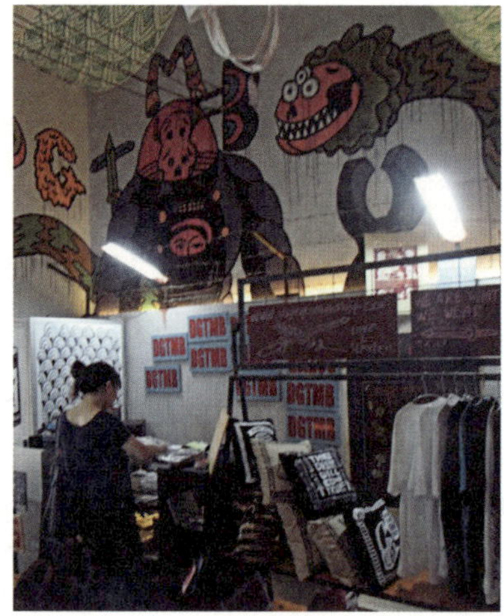

1

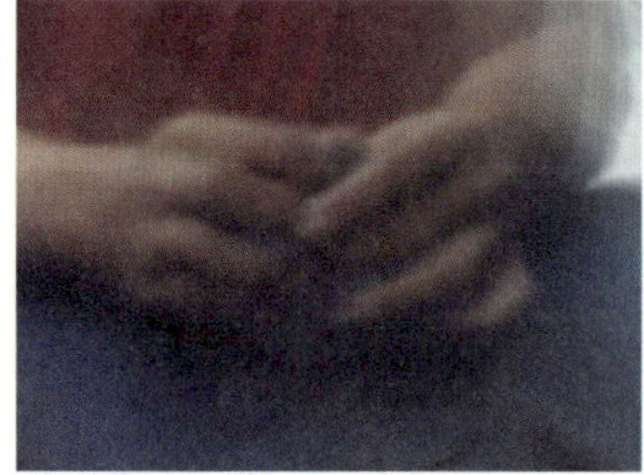

2

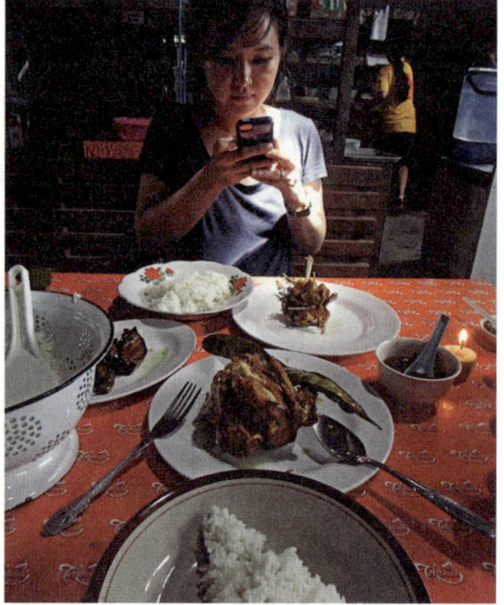

3

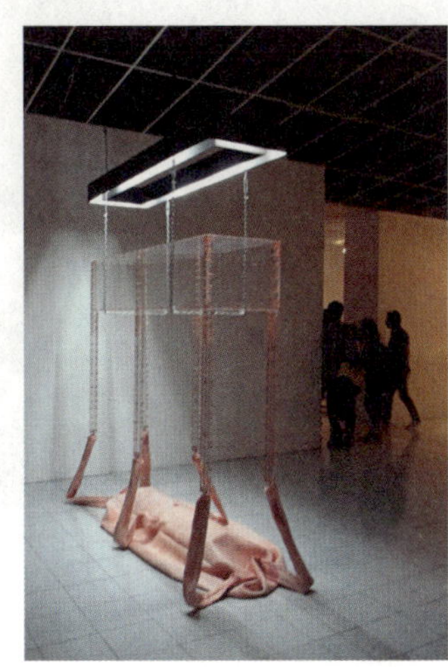

4

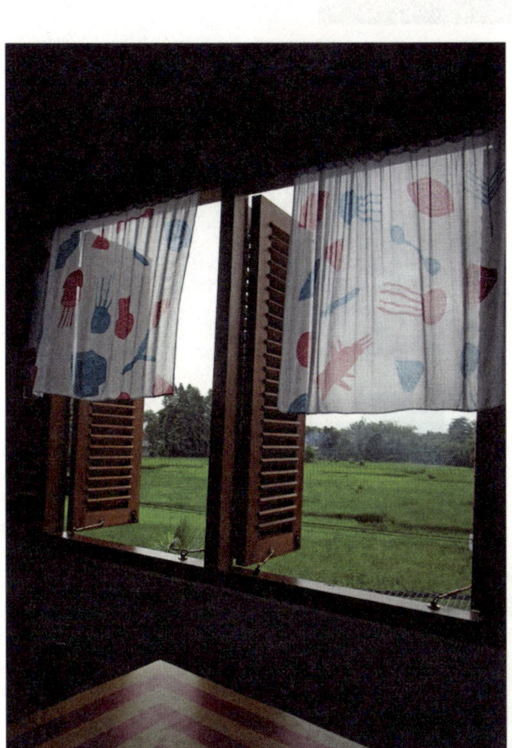

5

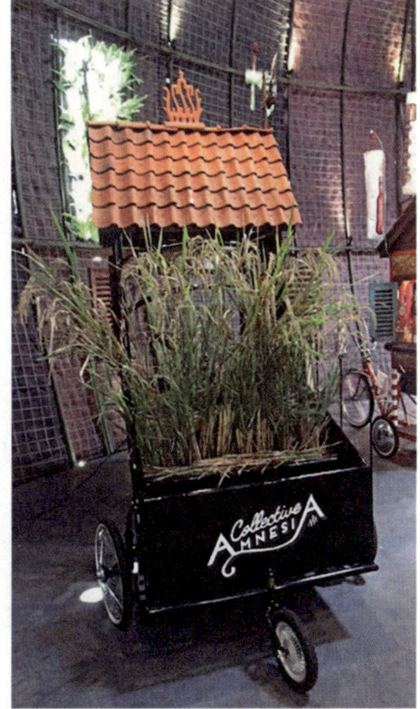

6

7

atas nama daun
WELCOME TO
PRISON ART LAB.
INSERT YOUR LEAVES HERE/
MASUK KAN DAUN MU DISINI.

8

TOP COLLECTION ARTISTS HAIR DO

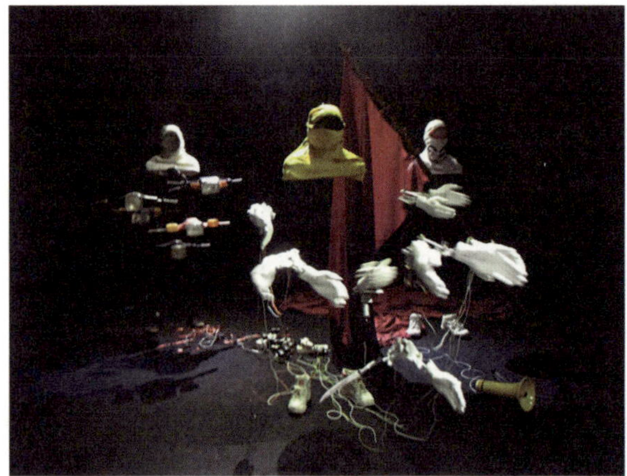

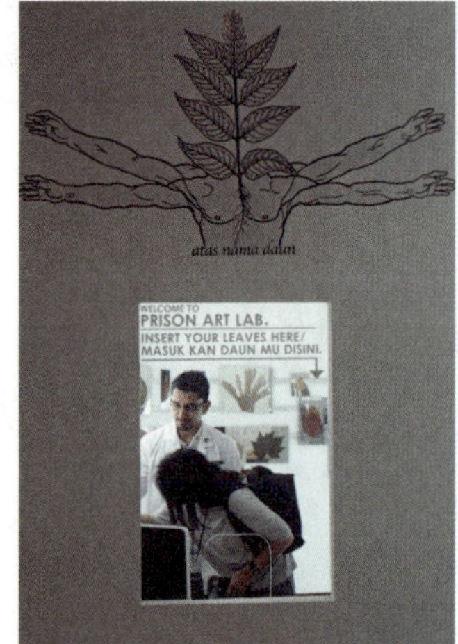

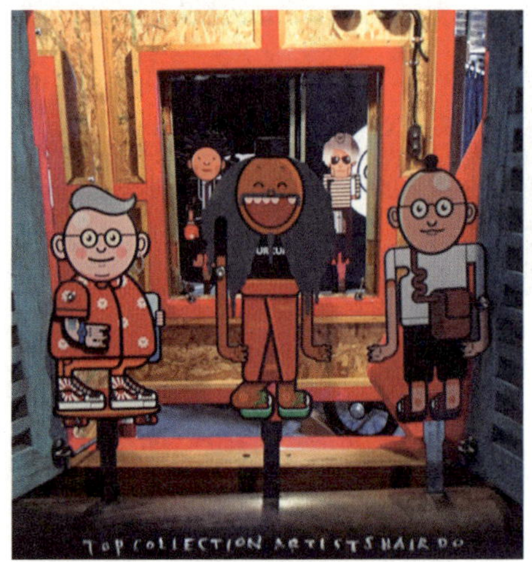

9

Tony Godfrey

# Dienstags in den Tropen

*Liebe Freundinnen und Freunde, liebe Kolleginnen und Kollegen,*

*ich finde es schon lange befremdlich, dass in Kunstzeitschriften so wenig über Kunst aus Südostasien, wo ich inzwischen lebe, publiziert wird. Da offensichtlich kein Interesse daran besteht, regelmäßig Besprechungen oder Artikel zu veröffentlichen, bleibt mir nur, ab heute wöchentlich Berichte zu schicken, denn es gibt hier viele gute KünstlerInnen, die Beachtung verdienen.*

*Ich werde versuchen, die Berichte so kurz, informativ und verständlich wie möglich zu halten.*

*Wenn es etwas zu berichten gibt, werde ich jeden Dienstagmorgen etwas schicken, damit diejenigen von Euch, die in nördlichen Gefilden arbeiten, zu Beginn der Woche ein wenig tropische Sonne genießen können.*

*Frohe Weihnachten,*
*Tony*

23. Dezember 2014

Am Dienstag und Mittwoch letzter Woche war ich in Yogyakarta, um einige Interviews für mein neues Buch über indonesische Malerei zu führen. Obwohl mir die meisten KünstlerInnen und ihre Arbeiten gut vertraut sind, möchte ich möglichst viele Originalzitate verwenden. Die meisten Texte, die ich über Kunst aus dieser Region gelesen habe, enthalten wenige Zitate von KünstlerInnen. Auf merkwürdige Weise bleiben die KünstlerInnen *stumm*, im Gegensatz zu Kolleg-Innen aus dem Westen, die oft interviewt und zitiert werden. Für mich ist es wichtig, dass in einem Buch über KünstlerInnen als Individuen die Stimmen dieser KünstlerInnen zu hören sind und die LeserInnen etwas über ihre Persönlichkeiten und künstlerischen Positionen erfahren.

Da unser Flug Verspätung hatte, konnte ich mich am Dienstag nur mit Handiwirman und Yunizar treffen. Statt Bilder für mein Buch auszusuchen und über sie zu sprechen, wollten die beiden lieber über ihre Arbeit im Allgemeinen diskutieren. Es war ein aufschlussreiches Gespräch, in dem es um das Verhältnis zwischen Malerei und Bildhauerei ging (Handi versteht sich in erster Linie als Bildhauer und Yunizar hat vor Kurzem begonnen, skulptural zu arbeiten). Wir sprachen auch über ihr Verhältnis zur Künstlergruppe Jendela (fünf Künstler aus Sumatra, die nach ihrem Studium in Jogja geblieben sind – außer ihnen gehören Jumaldi Alfi, Rudi Mantofani und Yusra Martunus dazu). Es gibt auch andere wichtige Künstlergruppen im südostasiatischen Raum wie *Surrounded By Water* auf den Philippinen, über die ich nächste Woche berichten werde. Handi und Yunizar erzählten, dass sie nach der Gründung von Jendela viel über Kunst gesprochen hätten, doch jetzt, wo sie älter seien, träfen sie sich nur noch gelegentlich und erkundigten sich mehr danach, wie es den Kindern gehe. Ihre jeweiligen Karrieren sind unterschiedlich verlaufen und jeder geht seinen eigenen Weg. Ich nehme an, die meisten Künstlergruppen (man denke an Die Brücke oder CoBrA) sind entweder von kurzer Dauer oder entwickeln sich zu einem lockeren Zusammenschluss.

Nachdem ich das Aufnahmegerät ausgeschaltet hatte, fragte Handi: „Was bedeutet Zeichnung für dich?" Das ist eine gute Frage, denn wie wir wissen, ist der Status von Zeichnungen in der zeitgenössischen Kunst komplex, und in Südostasien kommen noch andere Aspekte dazu. Die konservatorische Frage spielt wegen der hohen Luftfeuchtigkeit eine große Rolle, und SammlerInnen interessieren sich eher für Malerei. (Da es wenige Stiftungen und kaum staatliche Fördergelder gibt, sind SammlerInnen für die Kunstwelt extrem wichtig.) Sowohl Handi als auch Yunizar stellen oft Zeichnungen zur Vorbereitung ihrer Skulpturen oder Gemälde her, vernichten sie aber anschließend, da sie für sie keine autonomen oder interessanten Kunstwerke sind. Für mich bieten sie häufig die Möglichkeit zu sehen, wie ein Künstler denkt. Ich sagte auch, dass es mich faszinierte, wie Yunizar während unseres Gesprächs die Zigarettenpackungen und Stifte, die überall herumlagen, zu verschiedenen Anordnungen stapelte, und Handi, ein Mann mit großen Händen, die er aber feinmotorisch einsetzt wie ein Chirurg, kleine Drahtstücke drehte. (Leider ist das einzige Foto davon etwas unscharf, Abb. 2) Für mich ist das auch eine Form des Zeichnens.

Zeichnungen spielen eine zentrale Rolle in der Arbeit von Eko Nugroho, den wir am nächsten Morgen besuchten. Er erzählte uns, er hätte 2014 an jedem Tag gezeichnet. Wir sahen uns einige seiner jüngsten Skizzenhefte an: Worte sind für Eko immer sehr wichtig. Er sagte, alles habe damit angefangen, dass er seine Leidenschaft für Comics entdeckte.

Wie viele erfolgreiche KünstlerInnen in Jogja hat er sich ein großes Haus mit Atelier gebaut, natürlich mit eigenen Textilien, Vorhängen und Gegenständen ausgestattet (Abb. 5 und S. 190). Sein Atelier ist im Erdgeschoss, der Wohnbereich aber darüber, damit eine frische Brise hineinwehen und man die Aussicht über Reisfelder genießen kann. Das Haus ist ganz anders als das, in dem ich ihn 2010 kennengelernt habe!

Als ich 2013 das erste Mal erwähnte, dass ich ein Buch über Malerei schreiben wollte, war er sehr zurückhaltend, da er nicht vorhatte, in diesem Jahr Bilder zu malen. Mit „Bilder" meint er Farbe auf Leinwand. Für mich zählen die temporären Wandgemälde, die er für Ausstellungen anfertigt auch dazu und sie sind genauso interessant. Zudem produziert er zurzeit mehr Stickereien als „Bilder", doch für mich als Kunsthistoriker sind es keine Stickereien, sondern Tapisserien, die in vergangenen Jahrhunderten eine parallele Form zur jeweiligen Malerei bildeten (wie Raffael von Urbino im Renaissance-Zeitalter, Peter Paul Rubens im Barock und ähnliche). Eko stellt sie auf faszinierende Weise her: Zuerst malt er ein Bild auf Leinwand, das er dann den Stickerinnen gibt, die er beschäftigt. (Sie alle haben ihre Arbeit verloren, als in der ortsansässigen Fabrik eine computergesteuerte Maschine angeschafft wurde. Es liegt dem Künstler sehr daran, handwerklich arbeitende Menschen zu unterstützen.) Sie sticken oder nähen dann direkt auf die Leinwände. Gelegentlich besucht er sie, um zu sehen, wie sie weiter kommen und um Dinge anzupassen oder Veränderungen vorzunehmen. Am Ende des Prozesses wird das Originalgemälde vom Stoff bedeckt oder zerstört. Es sind natürlich Unikate und keine Multiples.

Danach aß meine Assistentin und Übersetzerin Theresia zu Mittag in einem *Warung* (Imbiss am Straßenrand). Hühnchen, Reis, Auberginen, grüner Salat und *Petai*-große grüne Bohnen, die auf Englisch *stink beans* genannt werden und hier in der langen grünen Hülse serviert werden. Ich mag sie sehr! (Abb. 3)

Auf dem Weg zu S Teddy hielten wir kurz bei DGMBT, Ekos Laden, in dem er T-Shirts und Objekte von sich und anderen verkauft und an den auch ein Café und ein kleiner Ausstellungsraum für junge KünstlerInnen angeschlossen sind (Abb. 1). Ein wunderbarer Ort, um Weihnachtsgeschenke einzukaufen!

Mit S Teddy sprachen wir hauptsächlich über seine bevorstehende Ausstellung im Projektraum von Equator Art Projects. Er will zahlreiche Gemälde, die wie kleine rote Fahnen aussehen, malen – jeweils mit einem anderen Emblem oder Bild darauf. Er erholt sich von einem Krebsleiden, und es war schön, ihn so voller Enthusiasmus und Energie zu sehen. Ich werde mehr über die Schau berichten, wenn wir sie nächsten Monat installieren!

Ich wünsche Euch allen frohe Weihachten und alles Gute für 2015,

Tony

9. Juni 2015

Liebe Freundinnen und Freunde, liebe Kolleginnen und Kollegen,

Art Jog – wir nennen es eine Kunstmesse, doch eigentlich handelt es sich um einen Salon, wie die Royal Academy. Wenn sich das muffig und bieder anhört – und das tut es vermutlich –, nennen wir sie stattdessen eine jährliche, von KünstlerInnen organisierte Kunstmesse. Es gibt dort keine GaleristInnen in schicken Anzügen oder schwarzen Kleidern, die euch Dinge an Messeständen verkaufen wollen. Art Jog bietet immer eine gute Mischung aus Jung und Alt, etablierten und aufstrebenden KünstlerInnen.

Seit der ersten Ausgabe 2008 hat sich vieles verändert; die Veranstaltung ähnelt noch weniger einer herkömmlichen Kunstmesse. Heute ist sie vielleicht die coolste Ausstellung in ganz Südostasien, ein Ereignis, an dem fast alle teilnehmen wollen.

In diesem Jahr bin ich nicht zum Eröffnungsabend gegangen. Mir wurde erzählt, 10.000 Menschen hätten Karten für den Abend gekauft, und ich wollte mich diesem Gedränge nicht aussetzen. Es gibt in Indonesien ein erstaunlich großes Kunstpublikum – meist junge Menschen. Wie man auf meinen Schnappschüssen sieht, besuchte ich die Schau während der relativ ruhigen und nicht überlaufenen VIP-Preview. (Es scheint, nebenbei bemerkt, fast schon Tradition zu sein, dass während der Preview noch nicht alle Schildchen angebracht sind und noch aufgebaut wird. Das ist typisch für die Kunstwelt in Jogja, die viel improvisiert, chaotisch ist und unter Zeitdruck zu stehen scheint. Zugleich ist sie aber auch sehr professionell. Es macht den Reiz aus, dass man mit den KünstlerInnen sprechen kann, während sie noch letzte Veränderungen an ihren Werken vornehmen.

Die VeranstalterInnen müssen sich inzwischen keine großen Gedanken mehr machen, wie sie ihre Kunst verkaufen können: Es kommen so viele Menschen, dass sie alleine mit dem Verkauf von Eintrittskarten viel Geld verdienen. In den letzten drei Jahren ist Bambang „Toko" Witjaksono der Kurator gewesen, dem es nicht nur darum geht, die beste Kunst aus Jogja zu zeigen, sondern eine überzeugende Ausstellung zu präsentieren – die auch ein bisschen international sein darf. Dieses Jahr waren es zwei ausländische KünstlerInnen: Mark Justiniani von den Philippinen und Yoko Ono – sie ist Japanerin, oder?

Jogja war schon immer eine Stadt nicht nur der KünstlerInnen, sondern vor allem der MalerInnen. Daher wird es womöglich viele schockiert haben, dass Bambang „Toko" nur ein einziges Gemälde in einer Ausstellung mit mehr als sechzig KünstlerInnen zeigte. Sollte das mich, als jemand, der gerade an einem Buch über indonesische Malerei arbeitet, besorgt machen? Schreibe ich über ein ins

Abseits gedrängtes Medium? Nein, nicht wirklich. Es scheint Konsens zu sein, dass die jüngere Generation von MalerInnen weder sehr originell noch sehr gut ist. Vielleicht ist die Präsenz so vieler starker Persönlichkeiten aus den beiden Generationen davor erdrückend. Wenn es keine guten neuen MalerInnen gibt, warum sollte man schwache zeigen? Die besten Gemälde der letzten Jahre stammen alle von den älteren Semestern. (Übrigens ist die beste Malerei, die zurzeit in der Stadt zu sehen ist, in einer anderen Ausstellung zu finden, die Enin Suprianto kuratiert hat: es handelt sich um drei neue Arbeiten von Christine Ay Tjoe – eine der sehr wenigen profilierten Künstlerinnen in Indonesien).

Ich fragte Bambang, ob das seine Gedanken waren, und er lachte, „Ja!" Die jungen MalerInnen zeigen sich nicht, also konzentrieren wir uns auf das, was gut ist – auf Installationen und partizipative Arbeiten. Dennoch sind zusätzlich zu dem Alibimaler Nyoman Masriadi fünf weitere KünstlerInnen vertreten, über die ich in meinem Buch schreibe: Entang Wiharso, Heri Dono, Eko Nugroho, Indieguerillas und Handwirman, allerdings mit Installationen oder Skulpturen. (Auch Bambang kommt in meinem Buch vor, denn er ist nicht nur Kurator, sondern auch Maler.) Die MalerInnen beschränken sich hier weniger auf die Leinwand als in anderen Kulturen. Aus der Malerei entwickeln sich auf andere Weise Installationen als das im Westen der Fall ist.

Welche bemerkenswerten Arbeiten sind auf der Messe zu sehen? Mark Justinianis schwindelerregendes Loch im Boden – nur mithilfe von Spiegeln erzeugt. Die Malerei von Masriadi, Installationen von Eko und Heri – obwohl ihre Arbeiten an frühere Werke erinnern. Dann ist da noch die Arbeit von Indieguerilla in der Eingangshalle – sie präsentieren speziell angefertigte *Becaks* (Rikschas, die von Straßenhändlern benutzt werden), aus denen statt wie üblich Satay oder Eis emotionale Zustände zum Verkauf angeboten werden, Abb. 6. (Wie so oft hier, enthalten sie Insiderwitze: Anspielungen an die unvergesslichen Frisuren der Jogja-Künstler Eddie Hara und Nasirun wie auch von Warhol und Basquiat (Abb. 9).

Es gibt mehrere lustige partizipative Arbeiten: ein Schießstand, an dem man das alte Jogja mit seinen niedrigen Häusern gegen Bauunternehmer, die wie Eroberer aus dem Weltraum Baukräne und Zementmischer von Himmel abwerfen, verteidigen muss oder eine Musikmaschine von Rocka Radipa, die zur Versenkung einlädt, mit der man durch Handbewegungen verschiedene Klänge erzeugen kann.

Ein wirklicher Insiderwitz: Das Prison Art Lab erzeugt Kunstwerke aus Blättern unterschiedlichster Pflanzen, die man mitbringt – viele KünstlerInnen aus Jogja saßen in letzter Zeit im Gefängnis, weil sie mit Marihuana erwischt wurden (Abb. 8). Wie immer zeigt Handiwirman eine lustige und zugleich leicht beunruhigende Arbeit: vor einigen Jahren fing er an, sich für Gummispielzeuge zu begeistern, die er von innen nach außen stülpte. Hier hat er eine tischartige Skulptur gebaut, sie mit Gummi überzogen und das Gummi dann abgeschält, so, als würde er ein Tier häuten (Abb. 4).

Art Jog ist zu so einer großen und vielbeachteten Veranstaltung geworden, dass eine ganze Jogja-Kunstwoche sich um sie herum entwickelt hat, mit Ausstellungen, Veranstaltungen und Eröffnungen in der ganzen Stadt. Die beste Ausstellung war für mich die der beeindruckenden KünstlerInnen Freddie und Isabel Aquilizan bei ARK. Falls ich auf weitere interessante Dinge stoße, berichte ich nächsten Dienstag davon.

Einen vergnügten Dienstag wünscht Euch

Tony

P.S. Falls du in Singapur bist, schau doch um 19.30 Uhr im NTU CCA vorbei: Ich halte dort den Vortrag „Warum ich kein Südostasienexperte bin".

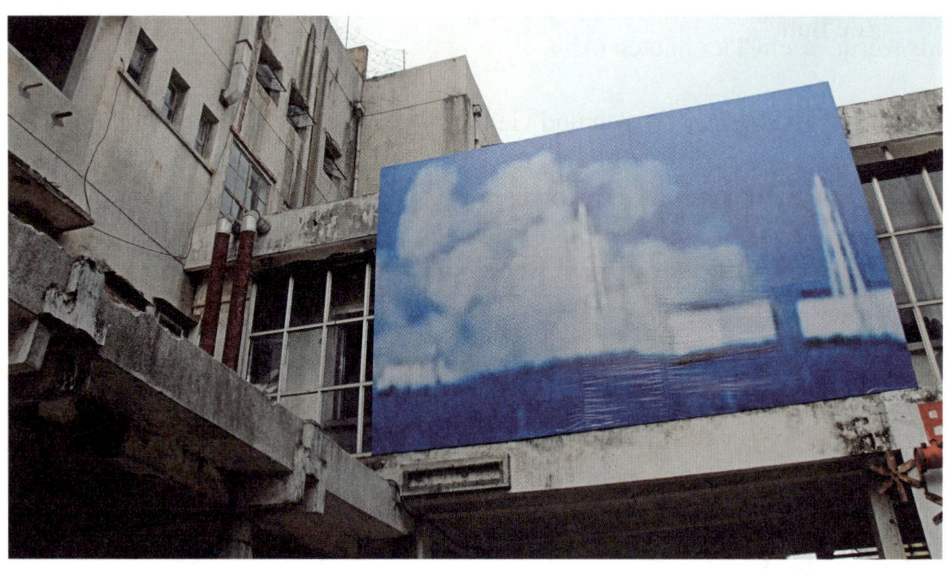

Hyoungsang Yoo, *Destruo*, 2013
Nhà Sàn Collective, Hanoi, Vietnam

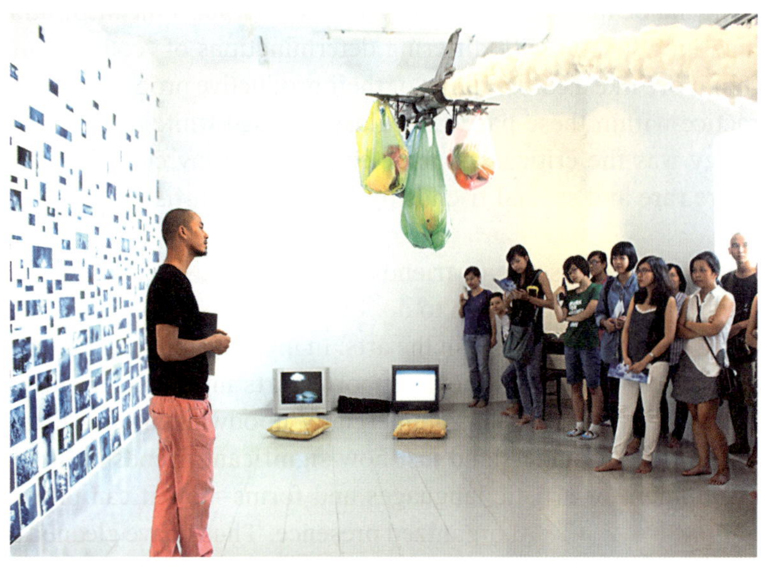

Artist talk by Tuan Mami
"The Clouds Will Tell," 2014
Nhà Sàn Collective, Hanoi, Vietnam

Zoe Butt

# Practicing Friendship: Respecting Time as a Curator

Every day I take a moment to quietly reaffirm my motivations for working in the arts, for I've got to be frank, I once nearly quit on my passion. Utterly. At a too-early point in my career, I had grown oh-so-tired of the way neoliberal systems of institutional approval were dictating how artistic innovation was allowed to take form and be interpreted—a stance touted to respect the inspiration of artists from far-flung locales with differing determinations of "contemporaneity," but sadly felt more like a colonization of their productive processes. What sustained my practice within these particular glass-encased white cube bureaucracies of museology was the critical intimacy cultivated in my curatorial department[1]— these were rare and special friendships of regional artistic knowledge. Indeed, management was wary of our closeness.

Ever since, the presence of friendship in my field has been of key consideration in the work I have chosen to do. I value this space of intimacy as the most discerning base of knowledge in the arts. In my decision to exit the "professionalized" landscape of government-supported arts infrastructure in Australia for the ideologically monitored, commercially hoodwinked terrain of China and Vietnam, I came to understand just how significant friendship is to sustaining the development of artistic languages and forms—how it can provide political autonomy with a powerful organized presence. Thus I have gleaned much about the purpose of art and its relevance from the social spaces of artists; indeed, these domestic environments of friendship crucially shape my work.

And what is this "work"? It's the building of care towards independent houses of culture that are rooted in the formal and vernacular artistic languages of their localities today. They are immaterial and concrete, often small in size yet holding dreams as vast as the sky, whose charge of memory is grasped as living souls that count for a collective consciousness—a never-ending social network of differing pulse whose objects and ephemerality deserve constant re-categorization. I'm talking particularly about houses of culture built by artists that dwell together in landscapes of psychological pain and political poverty; where to be visible and publicly interactive is to incur possible conflict; where the power in friendship is an alliance, a crucible of remembering and resilience; where the power in friendship becomes the means to politically challenge those who seek to define you.

My work is referred to as "curating," for me it is the dialogical intertextuality of engaging artists and their art to create encounters between aesthetics and politics[2]—it's about facilitating time, performing time, imprinting time, and, dare I say, producing time. It is about caring for the way memory is locally visualized and responsibly provoked; it's about interpreting, describing, and collecting the adhesive presence of time between memory and emotion, between form and its political legitimacy, between shadows opaque, liquid, and porous. Time that only those in friendship can truly critically understand. For it is within friendship that the *production* of representation—the journey towards that final destination called an artwork by an artist—is able to remain nameless. I say nameless for it is in naming that we are coded, thus presumed spoken for. I say nameless for it is in friendship (that code, that bond, beyond law) that the face[3] of the artist, the author, is permitted the space to be. It is within this space of friendship— the qualities of respect, trust, reliability, credibility, constancy, openness—that namelessness can look with unconditioned eyes on its surroundings, can learn of its interdependency on the facts and legends of its people (perhaps the Filipina would call it *kapwa*[4]), allowing the idea to learn how to breathe, to figure its own relationship to the world, to beg friendship to make introduction to discursiveness sturdier, to come up with a name that reflects the dreams inherent to its conjuring, to hope that its eventual interface does not enter the aesthetic regime with only one stride.

But this profession of mine is a deeply uneven one in definition and practice, and ultimately hinges on the geographies and social networks with which we live and devote. In this wondrous calamity of difference, I believe the context of art and culture must be facilitated, and I believe such facilitation requires physical and psychological space that is carefully weighted between local and global meaning. Some curators believe their key task to contribute to a history of exhibitions; in an ecology of cultural lack, however, I believe my key task is to sustain critically thinking creative communities of friendship.

But let's revisit time. If I click "yes" on a friendship request on Facebook, am I thus now a "friend"? If I set up an art project in Saigon as a social enterprise engaging victims of human trafficking along the border region with China, yet I've never spent time with such a victim, do I truly believe in my work? If I curate an art exhibition in London of Syrian contemporary art with artists I don't even physically recognize, am I demonstrating care in knowing the depth of my naming their dreams into words has consequence, particularly considering the global depravity of their ongoing civil war? How important is the investment of shared experiential time to build interpersonal networks that responsibly define who we are and what we do as curators working transnationally in the twenty-first century?

In speaking of this occupation of mine—curating—I'd like it to invest more "time" in understanding an artist and the conditions with which their art is given meaning, presence, and value in the sites that gave birth to its existence. With the current speed of the global systematization of art, and its palate to collect and showcase the "global" within museum and biennial platforms, I think it crucial that such systems care about the impact of its tourism on local communities struggling to sustain criticality with their own cultural knowledge. The attitude with which we produce, display, consume, and interpret contemporary art should be supportive of sustaining its diversity in production and meaning.

And here I must return to friendship, for it is sadly not the acclaimed venue notches of an artist's curriculum vitae that a depth of exchange with artistic sites of production is practiced—not the likes of MoMA or the Tate; not the Venice Biennale, nor Art Basel. Their showcase-driven, marketable (and thus time-tabled) arms hold the interface (the artwork) aloft from the context of its production as opposed to considering how to give those arms increased dimension, to give physical articulation to such context. It is rather within the smaller, grass-roots, guerilla-like, "alternative" collective spaces of action, at the local level, that arms and hands are found in provocative swat and caress, where time is of currency in encouraging patient constructive thinking.

If only these two planets of social capital could sit at a regular table and share a meal of time, perhaps then we could discuss the impact of shifting the situatedness of an exhibition;[5] or perhaps better implement a research strategy for collecting art by which knowledge networks from the local ecologies' major museums seek to acquire are integrated as friendships into departmental structures of museum life.[6] I must emphasize here again why I say "friendships," as opposed to "professional appointments"; for friendship demands a respect for time, a deference for the longterm in building social forms of knowledge, a respect for the role of honor in failure while searching for success. In contexts of suppressed psychological pain and political poverty particularly—think Syria with Doxbox; think Cuba with Immigrant International; think Congo with Studio Kabako; think Cambodia with SaSa Art Projects; think Vietnam with Sàn Art; think Sri Lanka with Sri Lanka Archive of Contemporary Art, Architecture, and Design and so many more—it is the silken thread of friendship that sustains, gives purpose, and ultimately breeds a respect for knowledge and memory that is nurturing and under constant re-evaluation. The physical walls of these houses of culture are often crumbling, contested, mobile, virtual, or publicly inaccessible and thus trust is of urgency to ensure survival.

This is not to say that professional appointments are void of such bonds, and I am sure I will find readers thinking I am overly idealistic with my romance of friendship in the context of art and its production/facilitation here, but what I am trying to say is that a curatorial address book needs to remember the impact of context on human intelligence and its cultural underpinnings. Speed dating parachute meetings by visiting curators turn art into a factory of showcase with no depth, and I have witnessed first-hand just how many of these visits critique and leave young artists utterly gutted, confused, and helpless. We need to practice friendship across our transnational planets of differing understandings of time to give structures of social capital the chance to interlock.

"Only primary friendship is stable (*bebaios*), for it implies decision and reflection: that which always takes time [...]," Derrida says.

> A decision worthy of the name–that is a critical and reflective decision– could not possibly be rapid or easy, as Aristotle then notes, and this remark must receive all the weight of its import.[7]

I wonder what Derrida would say if tasked to comment on the interpersonal networks of "*guanxi*," for it is in this system of social reciprocity and mutual benefit in China and Vietnam–an interpersonal network of friendship anchored in nurturing *long-term* exchange[8] that I have witnessed respect and knowledge expand, opportunities facilitated, and contacts of social currency gained. I am speaking particularly of my experiences in China and Vietnam, these countries that were violently thrown into a globalizing industrial competition, where local "culture" has been systematized by paranoid political surveillance mechanisms who argue patriotism, nationalism, and profit as key determinants of approval. In such environs (and there are many other similar landscapes of cultural control–think the divisive and brutal religious doctrines that have mired Afghanistan, India, and Myanmar, for example), the infrastructure for the arts is incredibly lacking in funds, facilitation, and space, and it is thus the interpersonal networks of artistic friendships that enable and innovate this lack, who invoke historical consciousness embedded within artistic languages "[...] by courting, by creating [...] that *begging bowl* to which the gift is drawn."[9]

Of course the instrumentalization of such a "begging bowl" can be dark, intelligibly limiting, and hauntingly violent (corruption in business; cronyism in politics), but that is where the agency of such networks has been foiled by ego, and where reciprocity has lost its mindfulness. Yes, I say "mindfulness" as opposed to "utility," and now perhaps we have Buddha sharing a cup of tea with Aristotle in this little duel, but I say mindfulness for its being "present," for its acknowledgment of interconnected cyclical dependencies and, thus, the interwoven urgency to be held responsible for its cause and effect. Friendships can be useful in practice—we take advantage of what the Other can provide—social introductions to beneficial people, sharing of skills, a sage for advice, but friendships are also virtuous bound beyond profit, beyond "use."

I may be impractical in my plea for time, for friendship, to be respected within the showcase and collection of art, but I think in the increasing entertainment frenzy of event management and a rationalized capitalistic system of cultural accountability, we must remember "[t]he mode of production of material life conditions the social, political, and intellectual life process in general. It is not the consciousness of men that determines their being, but, on the contrary, their social being that determines their consciousness."[10]

1   I refer to my time working at the Curatorial Department of Contemporary Asian and Pacific Art at Queensland Art Gallery, Brisbane, Australia from 2001 to 2007.

2   "Politics revolves around what is seen and what can be said about it, around who has the ability to see and the talent to speak, around the properties of spaces and the possibilities of time," Jacques Rancière and Gabriel Rockhill. *The Politics of Aesthetics: the Distribution of the Sensible* (London: Continuum, 2004). (Loc 278, Kindle).

3   "Is relationship with Being produced only in representation, the natural locus of evidence? Does objectivity, whose harshness and universal power is revealed in war, provide the unique and primordial form in which Being, when it is distinguished from image, dream, and subjective abstraction, *imposes itself* on consciousness? Is the apprehension of an object equivalent to the very movement in which the bonds with truth are woven?"; "A relation whose terms do not form a totality can hence be produced within the general economy of being only as proceeding from the I to the other, as a *face to face,* as delineating a distance in depth—that of conversation, of goodness, of Desire [...]," Emmanuel Lévinas, *Totality and Infinity: An Essay on Exteriority* (Pittsburgh: Duquesne University Press, 1969), 24, 39.

4   "*Kapwa*" is an indigenous Filipino (Tagalog) term of psychology whose root is anchored in pre-Hispanic, pre-colonial thinking, a cultural ethnic attitude of "the self in the other." This is a relational attitude between generations where each individual acknowledges their relevance and responsibility to carry forward their ancestral collective significance, in particular respect to their local community and natural environment, http://glossary.mg-lj.si/referential-fields/subjectivization/kapwa, accessed October 23, 2015.

5   For example, to study the impact of Carolyn Christov-Bakargiev's dOCUMENTA (13) in her extending the exhibition presence to Kabul with her "Kabul-Bamiyan: Seminars and Lectures" program; to better understand the impact of such global surveys on the sites in which its thematics are inspired, to beg the question, "how can such showcase platforms be continuous and long-term in their critical cultural exchange?"

6   The Tate Modern has curatorial adjunct appointments that allow these individuals to remain in the contexts they specialize, live, and work (José Roca and now Inti Guerrero as Estrellita B. Brodsky Adjunct Curator of Latin American Art); it also possesses an "Asian Acquisitions Committee" of rotating expertise and social status within the region it claims to care. How can such models of curating and collecting be better discussed in impact and formation so as to improve its work and relevancy, in order for other institutions of enabling capacity to learn and innovate?

7   Jacques Derrida, *Politics of Friendship* (London: Verso, 1997), 15.

8   Xiaoying Qi, "Guanxi, Social Capital Theory and Beyond: Toward a Globalized Social Science," *The British Journal of Sociology* 64, no. 2 (2013).

9   Lewis Hyde, *The Gift: Creativity and the Artist in the Modern World (25th Anniversary Edition)* (New York: Vintage Books, 1983), 186.

10   https://www.marxists.org/archive/marx/works/1859/critique-pol-economy/preface-abs.htm, accessed October 23, 2015.

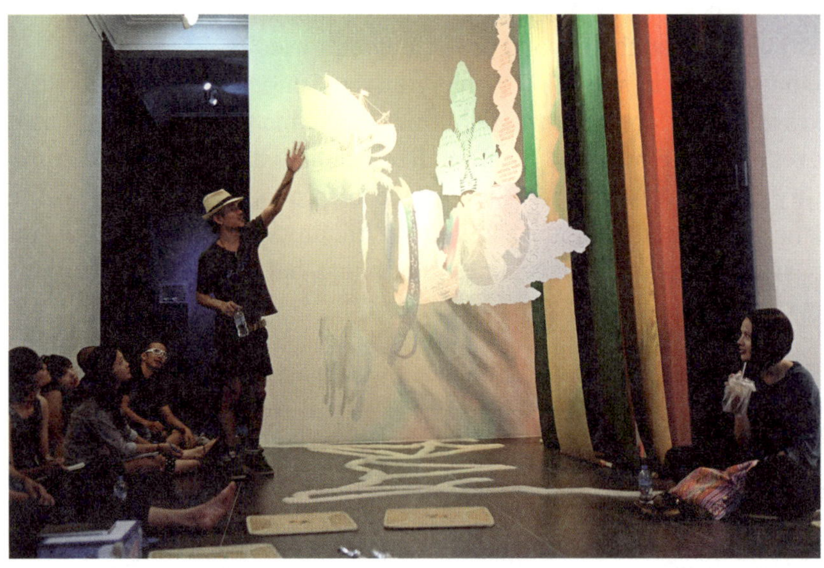

Artist talk by Rudy Atjeh
"Jeumpa," 2014
Sàn Art, Ho Chi Minh City, Vietnam

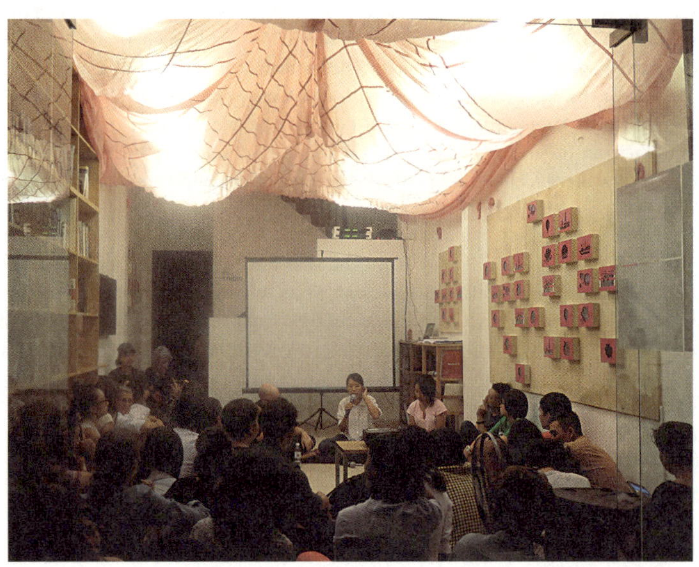

Artist talk by Nguyen Thi Thanh Mai
"Day by Day," 2015
Sàn Art, Ho Chi Minh City, Vietnam

Zoe Butt

# In Freundschaft arbeiten.
# Zeit im kuratorischen Prozess

Jeden Tag nehme ich mir kurz Zeit, um mich der Gründe zu vergewissern, warum ich überhaupt noch im Kunstbereich arbeite – denn es gab, ehrlich gesagt, einen Moment, in dem ich meinen Enthusiasmus fast völlig verloren hätte. Viel zu früh in meiner Laufbahn war ich es leid zu beobachten, dass neoliberale Systeme institutioneller Anerkennung festlegen, auf welche Weise sich künstlerische Innovation manifestieren darf und wie sie bitte zu interpretieren sei. KünstlerInnen aus entlegenen Regionen erfahren vermeintlich Anerkennung, indem ihre Arbeit aus unterschiedlichen Motiven als *zeitgenössisch* gelobt wird. Trauriger Weise fühlt es sich aber eher an wie die Kolonialisierung ihrer Produktionsprozesse. Was mich dazu bewegte, weiterhin in diesen *White-Cube*-Bürokratien der Museologie zu arbeiten, war das von Diskussion und Nähe geprägte Klima, das in der Abteilung herrschte, in der ich kuratorisch tätig war.[1] Wir waren auf eine Weise befreundet, wie es nur selten vorkommt. Unsere Basis war ein gemeinsames Wissen über die Kunst der Region. Diese Verbundenheit wurde von unseren Vorgesetzten nicht ohne Skepsis zur Kenntnis genommen.

Seitdem ist für mich Freundschaft das wichtigste Kriterium bei der Suche nach einem neuen Job. Ich schätze diesen Raum der Vertrautheit als die anspruchsvollste Basis des Wissens im Kunstbereich. Meine Entscheidung, die *professionelle* Sphäre der staatlich geförderten Kunstinfrastruktur in Australien zu verlassen und mich dem ideologisch kontrollierten und kommerziell korrumpierten Terrain Chinas und Vietnams zuzuwenden, machte mir klar, wie wichtig Freundschaft für die Entwicklung künstlerischer Sprachen und Formen ist – wie sie politische Autonomie erzeugen kann, die mit strategischer Stärke auftritt. Ich habe in befreundeten KünstlerInnenkreisen sehr viel über Zielsetzungen und die Relevanz von Kunst gelernt; tatsächlich wird meine Arbeit wesentlich von diesem familiären Umfeld der Freundschaft geprägt.

Und worin besteht meine *Arbeit*? In der Unterstützung unabhängiger Kunsträume, die mit den künstlerischen Sprachen der jeweiligen Regionen verwurzelt sind – virtuelle Orte und auch reale Räume, die meistens eher klein sind, deren Träume und Visionen aber größer nicht sein könnten. Würde man sich die unzähligen Erinnerungen, die uns umgeben, als lebendige Seelen vorstellen, wären sie es, auf die es ankäme, damit ein kollektives Bewusstsein entsteht. Sie bilden ein unendliches soziales Netzwerk, das sich aus unterschiedlichen Impulsen speist und deren Verhandlungsgegenstände in ihrer Flüchtigkeit immer wieder neu eingeordnet werden müssen. Ich meine hier insbesondere Kulturräume, die von Künstlerinnen und Künstlern gegründet wurden, die sich gemeinsam in einer Landschaft mentalen Schmerzes und politischer Armut zusammenfinden, in der es bereits zu Konflikten führen kann, wenn man sichtbar ist und öffentlich in Erscheinung tritt. Es geht um Räume, in denen Freundschaft Bündnisse schafft, in denen die Bereitschaft des Erinnerns auf ein Klima des Durchhaltens trifft, an denen die Freundschaft zu einem Mittel wird, diejenigen politisch herauszufordern, die über uns bestimmen wollen.

Meine Arbeit nennt man *Kuratieren*, doch für mich geht es um eine dialogische Intertextualität. Ich lade KünstlerInnen ein, um die Möglichkeit zu schaffen, dass sich Ästhetik und Politik begegnen.[2] Es geht darum, Zeit zur Verfügung zu stellen, Zeit zu gestalten, Zeit zu prägen, ich möchte sogar sagen, Zeit zu schaffen. Wir versuchen einen behutsamen Umgang damit zu pflegen, wie Erinnerungen an einem bestimmten Ort in Bilder übertragen und wie sie beim Betrachter verantwortungsvoll hervorgerufen werden können; es geht um das Interpretieren, Beschreiben und Sammeln der an uns haftenden Gegenwart, der Zeit zwischen Erinnerung und Empfindung, zwischen der Form und ihrer politischen Legitimität, zwischen den Schatten und Schattierungen, die mal undurchsichtig, mal flüchtig oder brüchig sind. Dabei ist es wichtig miteinander Zeit zu verbringen, für die nur miteinander befreundete Menschen ein wirklich kritisches Verständnis haben können. Denn nur in der Freundschaft kann die *Produktion* von Repräsentation – die Reise zu einem Ziel, das Kunstwerk genannt wird – namenlos bleiben. Ich sage namenlos, denn durch die Benennung werden wir kodiert, wird mutmaßlich in unserem Namen gesprochen. Ich sage namenlos, denn nur in der Freundschaft (dem Code, der Bande jenseits des Gesetzes) wird der KünstlerIn, der AutorIn Raum gewährt, sich von Angesicht zu Angesicht zu begegnen.[3] Innerhalb dieses Raums der Freundschaft – des Respekts, des Vertrauens, der Zuverlässigkeit, der Glaubwürdigkeit, der Konstanz, der Offenheit – kann die Namenlosigkeit mit einem unvoreingenommenen Blick ihre Umgebung wahrnehmen, etwas über die Wechselbeziehung von Fakten und Fama erfahren, von denen die Menschen umgeben sind (eine Filipina würde es *kapwa*[4] nennen). Die Idee kann dadurch lebendig werden und herausfinden, wie sie sich auf die Welt bezieht; sie kann Freundschaft stützen, um Diskursivität solider zu gestalten;

damit schließlich ein Name gefunden werden kann, der die Träume auch wirklich widerspiegelt, die sie hervorruft. So lässt sich hoffen, dass die noch im Entstehen begriffene Schnittstelle der Idee, das Kunstwerk, nicht zu schnell in das Regime der ästhetischen Einordnung gerät.

Allerdings weicht die Definition meines Berufs sehr von der Alltagspraxis ab und hängt letztlich von den Geografien und sozialen Netzwerken ab, in denen wir leben und denen wir uns widmen. In dieser unakzeptablen Ungleichheit der Bedingungen, muss meiner Meinung nach der künstlerische und kulturelle Kontext gefördert werden, und hierfür ist ein physischer und psychologischer Freiraum nötig, der vorsichtig abwägt, welche Bedeutung die Arbeit auf lokaler und welche sie auf globaler Ebene hat. Manche KuratorInnen glauben, ihre Hauptaufgabe läge darin, mit ihren Ausstellungen Kunstgeschichte zu schreiben. Doch in einer Ökologie des kulturellen Mangels besteht die Hauptaufgabe, glaube ich, eher darin, kritisch denkende, kreative, freundschaftlich verbundene Gemeinschaften zu fördern.

Aber zurück zum Thema Zeit. Wenn ich auf Facebook bei einer Freundschaftsanfrage auf „Ja" klicke, bin ich dann eine *Freundin*? Wenn ich in Saigon ein Kunstprojekt kuratiere, bei dem es um Opfer des Menschenhandels an der Grenze zu China geht, und ich das als soziale Initiative konzipiere, aber nie Zeit mit einem der Opfer verbracht habe – glaube ich dann wirklich an meine Arbeit? Wenn ich in London eine Ausstellung zeitgenössischer, syrischer Kunst mit KünstlerInnen mache, die ich nicht einmal vom Sehen kenne, zeige ich dann, dass ich mich mit den Konsequenzen beschäftige, die meine Benennung ihrer Träume mit sich bringen, besonders in Anbetracht der Abscheulichkeit des nicht endenden Bürgerkriegs in ihrem Land? Wie wichtig ist es, in eine geteilte Zeit der Erfahrung zu investieren, um Netzwerke zu bilden, die auf verantwortungsvolle Weise definieren, wer wir sind und was wir als transnational arbeitende KuratorInnen im 21. Jahrhundert tun?

Wenn ich über meine Tätigkeit – das Kuratieren – spreche, möchte ich, dass dabei mehr *Zeit* investiert wird, um die KünstlerInnen besser zu verstehen und auch die Bedingungen zu begreifen, unter denen ihrer Kunst Bedeutung, Präsenz und Wert verliehen wird; dass auch mehr Zeit investiert wird in das Verständnis der Orte, die für die Entstehung der Kunstwerke bedeutend sind. Angesichts der derzeitigen Geschwindigkeit, mit der die Kunst global systematisiert wird und sich angleicht, und angesichts der Tendenz, das *Globale* in Museen und Biennalen zu sammeln und auszustellen, sehe ich es kritisch, dass sich solche Systeme zwar für die Auswirkungen des so entstehenden Tourismus auf die lokalen Gemeinschaften interessieren, weniger aber dafür, dass diese Gemeinschaften versuchen, ihre Kritikfähigkeit mit ihrem eigenen kulturellen Wissen aufrechtzuerhalten. Die Haltung, mit der wir zeitgenössische Kunst produzieren, ausstellen, konsumieren und interpretieren, sollte unterstützen, dass ihre Vielfalt in der Produktion *und* in ihrer Bedeutung bewahrt wird.

Und an dieser Stelle muss ich wieder über Freundschaft sprechen, weil es trauriger Weise nicht die gefeierten Ausstellungsorte in der Vita einer KünstlerIn sind, an denen ein intensiver Austausch mit den Orten der künstlerischen Produktion stattfindet – nicht im MoMA oder in der Tate; nicht auf der Venedig Biennale oder der Art Basel. Die ausgestreckten Arme greifen nach ausstellbarer, vermarktbarer Kunst (sind also von einem Zeitplan getrieben) und halten mit aller Kraft die Schnittstelle (das Kunstwerk) so weit wie möglich von seinem Produktionskontext fern, statt darüber nachzudenken, wie diese Arme größer und stärker gemacht werden könnten, um diesen Produktionskontexten mehr Sichtbarkeit zu geben. Es sind eher die kleineren lokalen, basis-orientierten, Guerilla-artigen, alternativen Kunstorte, wo einem mal auf die Finger gehauen wird und dann wieder auf die Schulter geklopft, und in denen Zeit die Währung ist, mit der geduldiges, konstruktives Denken unterstützt wird.

Wenn sich diese beiden Universen des sozialen Kapitals regelmäßig gemeinsam an den Tisch setzten und sich Zeit nähmen, dann wäre es vielleicht möglich, darüber zu diskutieren, wie es sich auswirkt, wenn man die Grundvoraussetzungen von Ausstellungen verändert.[5] Oder vielleicht wäre es noch besser, Strategien zu entwickeln – wie das zum Teil schon große Museen tun, die Kunst aus bestimmten Zusammenhängen sammeln wollen – Wissensnetzwerke lokaler Ökologien in die Abteilungen des Museumsbetriebs *freundschaftlich* zu integrieren.[6] Ich muss nochmals betonen, warum ich hier von *Freundschaften* spreche und nicht von *professionellen Stellen*: Freundschaft erfordert Respekt vor der Zeit und die Achtung des Langfristigen beim Aufbau gesellschaftlicher Formen des Wissens. Freundschaft ist auch der Garant für Respekt vor der Würde beim Scheitern auf der Suche nach Erfolg. In Kontexten unterdrückten emotionalen Schmerzes und politischer Armut (man denke an Syrien mit Doxbox; Kuba mit Immigrant International; Kongo mit Studio Kabako; Kambodscha mit SaSa Art Projects; Vietnam mit Sàn Art; Sri Lanka mit Sri Lanka Archive of Contemporary Art, Architecture, and Design und viele andere), ist es der seidene Faden der Freundschaft, der Unterstützung gibt, Sinn verleiht und schließlich Respekt vor dem Wissen und der Erinnerung bewahrt, der Dinge gedeihen lässt und einer ständigen Neubewertung aussetzt. Die physischen Mauern dieser Kulturhäuser bröckeln oft. Die Orte sind unter Beschuss, sie haben wechselnde Standorte, manchmal sind sie auch nur virtuell oder nicht öffentlich zugänglich. Daher ist Vertrauen dringend notwendig, um überhaupt ihr Bestehen zu sichern.

Das heißt nicht, dass es bei professionellen Stellen keine freundschaftlichen Verbindungen gäbe, und ich bin mir sicher, dass manche LeserInnen mich aufgrund meiner emphatischen Auffassung von Freundschaft im Kunstzusammenhang – ihrer Entstehung und Förderung – zu idealistisch finden werden. Doch was ich sagen möchte ist, dass sich KuratorInnen sehr bewusst darüber sein sollten, wie stark der Kontext auf die menschliche Intelligenz und ihre kulturellen Bedingungen einwirkt. Ein Speed-Dating mit kurz vorbeischauenden KuratorInnen verwandelt Kunst in eine Ausstellungsfabrik ohne Tiefgang, und ich habe selbst erlebt, wie bei vielen solcher Besuche junge KünstlerInnen erst hart angegangen und danach vollkommen enttäuscht, verwirrt und hilflos zurückgelassen wurden. Wir müssen – über unsere transnationalen Universen hinaus, in denen Zeit sehr unterschiedlich aufgefasst wird – Freundschaft praktizieren, um den Strukturen des sozialen Kapitals die Chance zu geben, ineinander zu greifen.

„Einzig die Erste Freundschaft ist gefestigt oder stabil (*bebaios*), da sie die Entscheidung und die Überlegung einschließt, also etwas, das stets Zeit braucht", schreibt Derrida.

> Eine ihres Namens würdige, also kritische, überlegte, reflektierte Entscheidung darf daher weder überstürzt noch leichtfertig getroffen werden, Aristoteles merkt es eigens an – und die Anmerkung muss in ihrer ganzen Tragweite und in ihrem ganzen Gewicht bedacht werden.[7]

Ich frage mich, was Derrida zu den Netzwerken von *guanxi* gesagt hätte, denn in diesem System sozialen Austauschs und gemeinsamen Nutzens, das in China und Vietnam praktiziert wird und das auf der *Langfristigkeit des Austauschs basiert,* habe ich erlebt, wie sich Respekt und Wissen ausbreiten, sich neue Handlungsmöglichkeiten entwickeln und zunehmend Kontakte als Währung des Sozialen kursieren.[8] Ich spreche insbesondere von meinen Erfahrungen in China und Vietnam, in den Ländern, die gewaltsam in einen Globalisierungswettbewerb geworfen wurden, bei dem die lokale Kultur durch paranoide politische Überwachungsmechanismen systematisiert worden ist und das mit dem Argument rechtfertigt wird, Patriotismus, Nationalismus und Profit seien die bestimmenden Faktoren von Anerkennung. In solchen Umgebungen – und es gibt viele ähnliche Landschaften kultureller Kontrolle – man denke etwa an die polarisierenden und brutalen religiösen Doktrinen, die Länder wie Afghanistan, Indien und Myanmar in ernste Schwierigkeiten bringen – fehlt es der künstlerischen Infrastruktur an finanziellen Mitteln, Chancen und Freiräumen. Daher sind es die Freundschaften zwischen KünstlerInnen mit ihren Netzwerken, die innovativ mit diesen Mängeln umgehen, die sich auf das historische Bewusstsein der jeweiligen künstlerischen Sprachen berufen, „[...] indem sie diese *Bettelschale*, zu der das Geschenk hingezogen wird, aufspüren und hervorbringen".[9]

Natürlich kann die Instrumentalisierung einer solchen Bettelschale finster, geistig einschränkend und auf gespenstische Weise gewalttätig sein (Korruption in der Wirtschaft; Nepotismus in der Politik), aber nur dort, wo die Wirkkraft dieser Netzwerke durch Egoismen vereitelt wird und der gegenseitige Austausch nicht mehr sorgsam ist und an Achtsamkeit verliert. Ja, ich sage *Achtsamkeit* und nicht *Nutzen* – und jetzt trinkt Buddha vielleicht mit Aristoteles eine Tasse Tee in diesem kleinen Duell – doch ich sage *Achtsamkeit*, weil es genau darum geht, dass sie vorhanden ist, denn durch sie wird gewährleistet, dass der Austausch zyklisch stattfindet; dass es um eine Dringlichkeit geht, die mit Vielem verwoben ist; die um ihre Verantwortung für Ursachen und Wirkungen weiß. Freundschaften können sehr nützlich sein – wir profitieren davon, was der Andere zu bieten hat: ein nützlicher Kontakt, ein kluger Rat … Doch Freundschaften führen über das hinaus, was nützlich und profitabel ist.

Es klingt vielleicht praxisfern, wenn ich in Bezug auf das Ausstellen und Sammeln von Kunst für Zeit, Freundschaft und Respekt plädiere, aber ich finde, wir müssen uns angesichts des zunehmenden Entertainment- und Event-Wahnsinns in der Kunstwelt und angesichts des rationalisierten kapitalistischen Systems, das die Kultur den Regeln der Gewinnoptimierung unterwirft, an folgendes erinnern: „Die Produktionsweise des materiellen Lebens bedingt den sozialen, politischen und geistigen Lebensprozess überhaupt. Es ist nicht das Bewusstsein der Menschen, das ihr Sein, sondern umgekehrt ihr gesellschaftliches Sein, das ihr Bewusstsein bestimmt."[10]

1   Ich beziehe mich hier auf die Jahre 2001 bis 2007, als ich im Curatorial Department of Contemporary Asian and Pacific Art at Queensland Art Gallery, Brisbane, Australien gearbeitet habe.

2   „Die Politik bestimmt, was man sieht und was man darüber sagen kann, sie legt fest, wer fähig ist, etwas zu sehen und wer qualifiziert ist, etwas zu sagen, sie wirkt sich auf die Eigenschaften der Räume und die der Zeit innewohnenden Möglichkeiten aus." Jacques Rancière, *Die Aufteilung des Sinnlichen. Die Politik der Kunst und ihre Paradoxien*, Berlin: b_books, 2008, S. 26.

3   „Ereignet sich die Beziehung zum Sein allein in der Vorstellung, dem natürlichen Ort der Evidenz? Stellt die Objektivität, deren Härte und universelle Macht der Krieg offenbar macht, die einzige Form und die ursprüngliche Form dar, in der sich das Sein, wenn es sich vom Bild, vom Traum, von der subjektiven Abstraktion unterscheidet, dem Bewusstsein *aufnötigt*? Ist die Auffassung eines Gegenstandes gleichbedeutend mit dem Faden, der die Bande der Wahrheit knüpft?" Ibid., S. 24.

4   *kapwa* ist ein Begriff indigener Filipino (Tagalog), dessen Wurzeln im prähispanischen, präkolonialen Denken liegen. Er bezeichnet eine kulturell-ethische Vorstellung, die das „Selbst im Anderen" bezeichnet. Es ist eine relationale Haltung zwischen den Generationen, bei der jedes Individuum seine Relevanz und seine Verantwortung dafür anerkennt, die kollektive Bedeutung der Vorfahren weiterzuführen, was besonders im Respekt vor der lokalen Gemeinde und der natürlichen Umwelt zum Ausdruck kommt. http://glossary.mg-lj.si/referential-fields/subjectivization/kapwa, abgerufen am 23. Oktober 2015.

5   Hier könnte man beispielsweise darüber diskutieren, welche Auswirkungen die Erweiterung von Carolyn Christov-Bakargievs dOCUMENTA (13) mit ihrem Programm „Kabul-Bamiyan: Seminars and Lectures" auf Kabul hatte; man könnte besser verstehen, welche Konsequenzen diese Art von globalen Überblicksausstellungen auf die Orte haben, die thematisiert werden; es wäre interessant, die Frage zu stellen: „Wie können solche Ausstellungsplattformen kontinuierlich und langfristig zu einem kritischen kulturellen Austausch führen?"

6   Bei Tate Modern gibt es kuratorische „Adjunct"-Stellen, die es ermöglichen, dass die Personen in den Kontexten, auf die sie spezialisiert sind und in denen sie leben und arbeiten, bleiben können (José Roca ist Estrellita B. Brodsky Adjunct Curator of Latin American Art). Das Museum hat auch ein Asian Acquisitions Committee mit wechselnden Experten in der Region, die es fördern möchte. Wie können solche Modelle des Kuratierens und Sammelns wirksamer und besser durchdacht werden, um zur Erneuerung anderer Förderinstitutionen beizutragen?

7   Jacques Derrida, *Politik der Freundschaft*, Frankfurt am Main: Suhrkamp, 2002, S. 37f.

8   Xiaoying Qi, „Guanxi, Social Capital Theory and Beyond: Toward a Globalized Social Science", in: *The British Journal of Sociology*, Jg. 64, Nr. 2, 2013.

9   Lewis Hyde, *The Gift: Creativity and the Artist in the Modern World (25th Anniversary Edition)*, New York: Vintage Books, 1983, S. 186.

10  Karl Marx, „Zur Kritik der Politischen Ökonomie", in: Karl Marx und Friedrich Engels, *Werke*, Berlin: Dietz Verlag, Band 13, 7. Auflage 1971, unveränderter Nachdruck der 1. Auflage 1961, Berlin/DDR, S. 8–9.

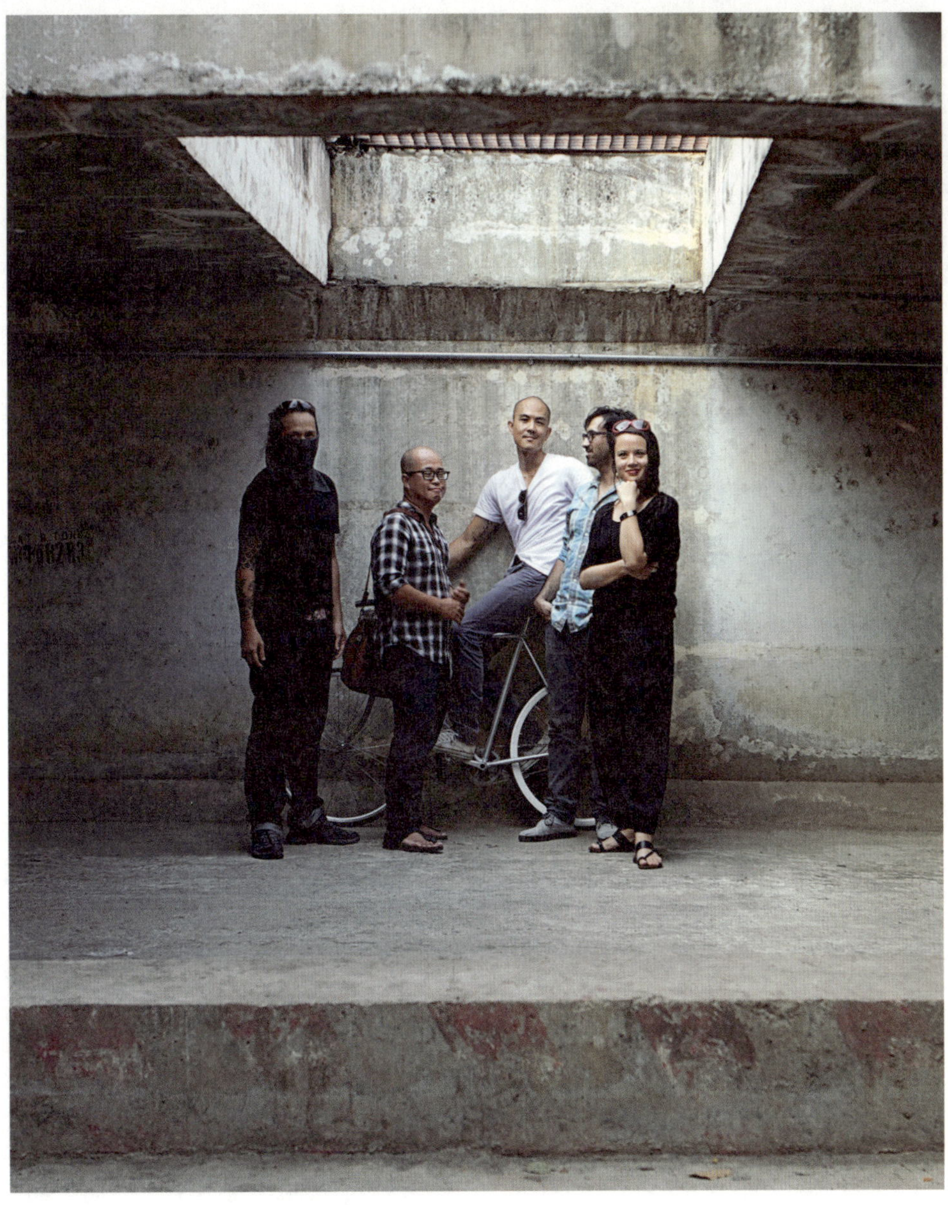

Members of the curatorial board of Sàn Art, 2013
Phunam, Dinh Q Le, Tuan Andrew Nguyen, Matt Lucero, and Zoe Butt, director
Ho Chi Minh City, Vietnam

Simon Soon

# Rethinking Curatorial Colonialism

This cursory essay is not so much an attempt to provide some far-reaching insight into knowledge production via the rubric that we have come to call "the curatorial," rather than an opportunity to rethink the parameters of the currency in which the curatorial is imbricated with the political.[1] By this I refer to the increasing currency in which the term "the curatorial," in instances that have been used by writers/curators like Maria Lind or the Goldsmiths College Curatorial/ Knowledge program, have come to anxiously represent a rhetorical form of interdisciplinary knowledge mapping and discursive performance.[2] In more recent parlance, it is also described as a kind of "commoning."

This is in contrast to the idea of curating solely as an activity or a practice of putting together an exhibition or even the pre-contemporary art role of a curator as a caretaker of a collection. Instead, the emphasis on the curatorial is primarily centered on the activation of sites of discourse that purport to be socially and philosophically transformative. Such a claim is problematic, especially if we consider the kind of institutional networks that support this form of performative thinking. As a discursive spectacle that emerged from the 1990s onwards, the curatorial as the epistemological handmaiden of advanced capitalism that continues to align itself within the paradigm of reason along the tradition of the Enlightenment meant that certain blind spots continue to exist even if curatorial discourse makes bold critical claims towards discursive reflexivity.

It is the aim and motivation of the curatorial, when directed at art and activism emerging from "other" parts of the world, that I would like to try to discuss here as a problem area. The very encompassing notion of the curatorial has inadvertently carried within its thinking process an unintended colonizing framework.

I believe this has to do with how the notion of the curatorial continues to frame and transform specific urgencies into a form of knowledge that is largely generated within a specific reflexive, promotional, and pedagogical mechanism. In this act of knowledge construction, third world art and activism achieves contemporaneity by becoming an archive, pressed into the service of institutional critique in the first world.

One generous view is that this line of inquiry could help resist the uncritical adoption of a hegemonic and dominant form of curatorial forms of inquiry, as well as its attendant institutional standards, from being replicated uncritically elsewhere outside of Euro-America. This is what I took from Irit Rogoff's lecture in Hong Kong at the Asia Art Archive Symposium "Sites of Construction."[3] Her strongest argument undoes the presumption that cultural infrastructure and support automatically guarantees superior culture. In its place, she offered a tentative but by no means exhaustive list of artist initiatives, including Raqs Media Collective, Collectivo Situaciones, Tucuman Arde, Oda Projesi, and X-Urban. These are artist initiatives that either take the form of social practice or proceed as engagements with critical theory. Though different in textures and responses, they exist primarily as local enterprises that respond to specific socio-political contexts, and have been clustered by Rogoff under the umbrella of art and activism.

In this manner, the notion of contemporaneity is also framed differently. It is not seen simply as a historical period but as multiple sets of shifting "urgencies" whereby the relationship of contemporary art with the past is defined by its use value for the present political/ideological struggles and critique. Even so, in one fell swoop, the enumerated list of collectives and art practices, collected and abstracted, are constellated within a framing device that renders them objects of study for a different purpose. Here, creative activism is transformed into an archive towards an enterprise whose sole aim is to unpack existing, presumably Western, institutional modes and models of curating as determining what are successful ways of discourse production. Who really cares about the sweat and tears, meat and grit of context when one is removed from the grinding reality of conflicts and negotiations, the actual pedagogical process that goes into shaping specific engagement, when this can be theorized in London?

### Southeast Asia as Curatorial Conceit

If one assumes this is strictly an East/West division, let me provide an example of how such curatorial process and thinking can also emerge in other parts of the world by attending to a specific case study.

Take the recent political situation in Thailand as an example since it represents a scenario and a series of evolving and shifting political battle lines that is not entirely black and white. Suffice it to say, the complex political scenario suggests that the typology of mass movement, which we so often take to represent the people as a kind of political force, does not always align with democratic processes, even if it claims to.

Ironically, just as the anti-government protest was taking place out on the streets, right outside the doorsteps of the Bangkok Art and Culture Centre (BACC), a survey exhibition "Concept Context Contestation: Art and the Collective in Southeast Asia" was being held inside it. The exhibition attempted to bring into discussion art practices that demonstrated "locally-rooted conceptual thinking used to actively engage audiences [...] CCC investigates the close connection between conceptual approaches and social ideologies in Southeast Asian contemporary art of the last four decades."[4]

The antinomies between the kind of struggle that was taking place outside on the street and the abstracted grounds of contestation drawn out inside the gallery, where social justice calls the artist activist/conceptual figure into being, could not have been more stark. The exhibition constellates a group of conceptual artworks from "Southeast Asia" and presents them as both an archive and social critique.

Besides the fact that most of the artists showcased are in fact household names in the art collector circuit, the curatorial premise that argues that a significant feature of Southeast Asian conceptual practice is colored by a political commitment is extremely vague to the point of uselessness.[5] How this is political is not enumerated other than facile artistic engagement with notions of history, memory, and politics.

It seems that in this instance, the curatorial has signaled the ever-present possibility in which institutional discourse subsumes radical politics. While the curatorial premise held out some posture of reflexivity by considering the region as a comparative frame in order to postulate a shared history over and beyond the silos of national art histories, it is achieved at the expense of addressing certain blind spots within its own discursive mechanism.

In the case of the exhibition, not only are specific positions and histories abstracted through the conceit of the comparative, in comparison with the energy on the street outside of the BACC, what the curatorial did was to flatten the texture of protest, its motivation, context, and concept–even as it claims to recover these potentialities as strategic archives.

## The Artful and the Artless

The comparison above therefore brings to the fore the question about whether "contemporary art" as an ecology and institution really has any special purchase on the present. The following discussion attempts to address this through a number of case studies. In an Art Basel Hong Kong's talk program some years ago, an interesting observation was made during the launch of a newly released monograph on the late Tsang Tsou Choi, the mad graffiti calligrapher, who is better known as the King of Kowloon.[6]

What piqued my interest was that during the talk the Chinese cultural critic Ou Ning took the opportunity to draw parallels between Tsang's practice and a relatively young figure in Hong Kong's activism scene, Joshua Wong. Prior to the umbrella movement,[7] the then fifteen-year-old Joshua Wong was already seen as a kind of boy wonder figure who founded a movement called Scholarism (學民思潮) in 2011, where he managed to mobilize a group of secondary school students to oppose the Moral and National Education (德育及國民教育) school curriculum introduced by the Hong Kong Education Bureau.

The new school curriculum sought to revise how Hong Kong history is being taught. This change was perceived by the youth of Hong Kong to be ideologically skewed in what it says about Chinese sovereignty over Hong Kong, even under the "one nation, two system" arrangement, Hong Kong was handed back to the Chinese government in 1997 under the promise that the island would retain a large measure of internal autonomy, including universal suffrage, which the country still, debatably, does not enjoy today. Here, it is significant to highlight how Ou Ning had managed to connect these two phenomena together.

Now I want to compare Ou Ning's statement to a statement made by Ili Farhana, a Malaysian writer and activist. Farhana noted on her blog:

> Up until today, involvement between art and activism in Malaysia is still a rare occurrence. Not to say it doesn't exists, but it is rare. Protests in Malaysia if compared to those that took place in other countries, lack color. It is often about speeches and heated admonition that at the end of the day weakens the momentum of the masses if it is the only thing that is being offered to the masses. We do not ask to be entertained but to seek the intersection between the artistic/cultural and the mass movement, that should come together to bring about change in the country.[8]

On the one hand, we have in the Malaysian case an anxiety that social protest in and of itself is insufficient if it does not possess a creative element–elements I presume that are meant to add a little creative spark to the protest, to make it exceed the dullness and tedium of politics. In doing so, not only does it seek to transform the terms of art, it also seeks to quite naively rethink politics as possibly more creative. While on the other hand, you have someone like Ou Ning, who has no desire at all to seek out that "creative element" or spark within a social protest movement. So it's almost as if the entire protest form itself, without any form of creative additives, was sufficiently artful on its own terms and that what art or culture (or the sphere we operate within as historians, curators, artists) needs to do, is to make a claim of this discourse. We don't really have anything to add to this space really, all we have to do is to consume it and make it part of our own "cultural discourse."

I find both examples interesting in their desire to bridge this almost unbridgeable chasm between the larger political issue and the location of the creative and the aesthetic within this space. Our desire to fetishize mass movement and energies is apparent: think of Egypt, Taksim Gezi Park, Istanbul, Syria, Bangkok, and Taiwan. We search for a creative sign of life within turmoil, but what exactly are we in fact searching for?

In recent years, I find myself following some of the most artless controversies that have visited Asia. For example, Alvin Tan and Vivian Lee, or known collaboratively as Alvivi until their recent breakup, was best known for sharing their sex videos online. They also ran a confessional and bare all sex confession channel on YouTube in 2012 that has made both Singaporeans and Malaysians recoil in horror at their antics and derring-dos.

The other personality that has made recent headlines is Singaporean rabble-rouser Amos Yee, who incidentally calls himself an "artist" on his Facebook page. Though he started making YouTube videos at the age of thirteen, which ranged from a review of *Moby Dick* to homemade movies, his claim to notoriety can be attributed to a video that lambasted both the Christian Right and Lee Kuan Yew, shortly after the latter's passing in 2015.

What do these YouTube personalities have in common? In a sense, their deep-seated distrust towards cultural norms is expressed through a refusal to play by the rules of the system, harboring a deep suspicion for any systematized and industrialized forms of pedagogy. Unlike Simon Castets's and Hans Ulrich Obrist's search for post-1989 digital natives who still operate within the glib performance of civil discourse, Alvivi and Amos Yee are decidedly belligerents in their refusal to even be civil or governable through the regulatory and spectacle power of discursive performance.[9]

Is it therefore not surprising that in within a kind of curatorial ecology that increasingly prizes curatorial education in centers such as Bard College, Goldsmiths, and de Appel that a certain discursive density emerges from which the above "artists" cannot be assimilated or tamed due to their belligerence? Ultimately, this leads me to the question: are there phenomena out there that resist the curatorial? If we assume that the curatorial owes some of its operative logic to the faculty of reason of the Enlightenment and yet is a thinking process that has emerged specifically in the era of late capitalism, can there be a space where we can escape from the curatorial? What happens to things that you cannot explain away by reason and discourse?

Now, I am not going to be like Ou Ning to say that what Alvivi and Amos Yee did constitute a kind of cultural practice (let alone "art") that suddenly needs to be framed in relation to some kind of curatorial knowledge about the contemporary condition/culture or art. I don't want to colonize what they are doing into our knowledge, whether this is art historical or curatorial. Including them in a story about Singaporean and Malaysian visual cultural history, or exhibiting them, doesn't seem to do justice to it.

What I want to suggest here is the incommensurable gulf between what Alvivi and Amos Yee are doing as a possible space for activism that exceeds what we are trying to frame or discuss when we try to understand the precarious and slippery concept of art and activism combined. In fact, I want to hold them up as a mirror of the kind of conceptual blind spot on our part to recognize the limits of the curatorial as a field. A field that continues to call itself progressive still believes that it is trendy, liberal, forward thinking, yet at the same time seeks out the entirely formulaic and repetitive. Do we then need to revise the terms of our engagement?

## Curiosity

Where do we go from here? There is really no new method that I want to suggest here. I would only tentatively suggest what has been understood by most if not all curators, yet this is something that is often held up as more of an ideal than a necessity or a precondition for any form of work that one does. One must work from a genuine compulsion to know, driven by curiosity rather than urgency.

It calls for a kind of anthropology of sustained inquiry. This means that one does not treat the curatorial simply as a deconstructive paradigm. One's research needs to proceed from a genuine unpacking of assumptions rather than navel-gazing at the epistemological processes that inform the curatorial.

Proceeding from the above, an understanding of the world does not stem from the violent enterprise of mapping. It has less to do with how many disciplinary terrains, knowledge domains, and geographic localities one can traverse and bind together through the stagecraft of the curatorial or what kind of descriptive paradigm one can summon to bring the world into relief. Instead, a turn towards curiosity calls for a genuine desire to know another through experience, so that the other does not only become valuable and urgent, solely when it becomes an archive for those in a privileged position to critique their own institutional procedure.

As an example I will not turn to an exhibition but to a film, and one that embodies such an expanded notion of curatorial knowledge. This suggests I am not so much against this expansion of the curatorial as a form of knowledge and practice than the specific vectors that such discussions have so far engendered. This is also in keeping with the spirit of the curatorial to dislodge the exhibition space and practice as the primary site in which the curatorial could manifest itself. I refer here to Tan Pin Pin's documentary film *Invisible City*, in which she catalogued the obsessions that the world at large might not deem to be significant, but nevertheless resonate with those individual actors who have lived through a certain moment in Singapore's history.

Reflecting on the documentary, Tan notes: "I decided to seek out people who, like me, choose Singapore as the topic of their work. I don't mean where Singapore is the setting for their work, but where Singapore is the main subject."[10]

Her film explores Singapore through the viewpoints of four idiosyncratic but highly colorful residents who have lived through Singapore at the cusp of her independence. They are Ivan Polunin who produced numerous films of native communities in Singapore and Malaya in the 1950s; Marjorie Doggett, who has a collection of photographs she took from the 1950s of old buildings that are now demolished; Han Tan Juan, a student activist who showed a collection of photographs connected to the Chinese middle school student riots; Lim Chen Sian, an archaeologist excavating a sixty-year-old military bunker on Sentosa island. These are personal obsessions, traumas, and memories at best, but stitched together with their voices ricocheting against the other they offer a vision of the island-city through the lens of social and cultural history that is vastly different in tone and texture from that of Singapore's political history.

This catalogue of obsessions is fascinating to me on two counts. All our talks of a transnational turn have occluded those committed to localities. The focus in this instance demonstrates a stubborn refusal to speak of the global only from one particular vantage, from one particular frame of mind. Does digging up a fifty-year-old Coke bottle in a Singapore army bunker, in the annals of archaeology, have any global resonance? However, the film-making methodology as a curatorial device here takes the risk of translating one archaeologist's obsession, compelling the filmmaker to take responsibility in the way we read the other instead of abnegating this responsibility in favor of solipsistic critique of the very enterprise of curating.

In doing so, the film is also committed to a trenchant refusal towards parity or a sense of coexistence that has been taken as a hallmark of contemporaneity. Rather than pit the global as a circuit against the national, the local offers other historical frames of reference that are equally significant and that are equally multitudinous in their ability to challenge official national history. In this argument against the coexistence of concepts, one turns against the desire to catch up with the world and instead argues for a speaking to the world from other positions. The history of the world can be shaped through other visions and locales outside of putative centers.

In a wonderful exchange where director Tan Pin Pin is interviewing Ivan Polunin, a medical officer who shot color footage of native communities in his study of tropical diseases in the 1950s, reached a kind of impasse when confronted by a subject who reflected on her curatorial gaze.

> Off camera: Can I ask you …
> Ivan: You can definitely ask me, but whether you get an answer is another matter.
> Off camera: I'll try any way.
> Ivan: Whether you get a satisfactory answer is very much another matter.

This leads me to the second point. The above exchange demonstrates a struggle on the part of the director to come to grips with her subject and in that scenario it also shows us something akin to curatorial sincerity when one is summoned to the task of interpretation.

In what Tan does, her curiosity does not merely become a catalogue of obsession in order to deconstruct disciplinary thinking, but extends beyond the need to address the anxiety of genuine political transformation, to manifest and give the very obsession of her subjects a voice in their particularities. In this way, the film does not need to anxiously declare its relevance as an emancipatory space of the political, since the curiosity of the other that drives Tan's filmmaking is already transparent. The question of ethical sympathy is less of a sleight of hand than a willingness to listen. So too, I think, should be the curatorial.

1    The ideas expressed in this essay have previously been presented on two occasions. This was first presented in a panel discussion at Art Stage Singapore in 2013. The preliminary concept was expanded and then presented as "Resisting Curatorial Colonialism" in a one-day symposium, "Practicing Resistance," at Perth Institute of Contemporary Art in 2014.

2    See "Maria Lind on the Curatorial," *Artforum*, October, 2009. Goldsmiths College website further notes, "The conjunction of the title 'Curatorial/Knowledge' implies an understanding of curating as the production of and engagement with knowledge. Thus 'knowing' is not the absorption of information and materials, and neither simply analysis and interpretation, but rather something we actively produce through our various practices." Available at: http://www.gold.ac.uk/pg/mphil-phd-curatorial-knowledge/.

3    See Irit Rogoff, "The Expanding Field," *Yishu* (March/April 2014).

4    "Concept Context Contestation: Art and the Collective in Southeast Asia," 2014. Available at http://edm.bacc.or.th/edm/201402/eng.html; See also *Concept Context Contestation: Art and the Collective in Southeast Asia*, ed. Iola Lenzi (Bangkok: Bangkok Art and Culture Centre, 2014).

5    In fact, one of the curators is a collector of a number of the artists featured in the exhibition. The ethical quandary here relates to what extent the curator needs to declare his or her self-interest. This is especially pertinent when the exhibition prides itself as canon-making and the selection is an attempt at writing a kind of "art history."

6    Art Basel Hong Kong, Salon 25, May 2013. Available at: https://www.youtube.com/watch?v=DLl3IHM3n6A.

7    Umbrella Revolution was the name given to protests against a decision of the Standing Committee of the National People's Congress in Beijing made in August 2014 to have the candidates for the Hong Kong Executive first be elected by a committee before presenting them to the people of Hong Kong. The protests lasted until December 2014. In 2016, Joshua Wong was found guilty by a court as the leader of the demonstrations (Editor's note).

8    Ili Farhana, "Adakah Seni Kita Sedari?," *Pohon Bintang*, January 2, 2014, https://pohonbintang.wordpress.com/2014/01/02/adakah-seni-kita-sedari/. "Hingga ke hari ini, penglibatan seni dan aktivisma di Malaysia masih dilihat sangat kecil, bukan tidak ada, tetapi kecil. Protest-protest di Malaysia jika dibandingkan di negara-negara lain masih kurang warnanya, dan hanya tentang ucapan-ucapan atau pesan-pesan amarah yang akhirnya akan melemahkan momentum massa jika hanya itu saja yang mampu ditawarkan pada massa. Kita bukannya minta untuk dihiburkan tetapi mengakrabkan gerakan massa dengan hal-hal kesenian dan budaya yang seharusnya berjalan sejajar dalam menuntut perubahan negara."

9    89 Plus is a long-term research project that began in 2014. See: http://www.89plus.com.

10   Tan Pin Pin, "Director's Note," *Invisible City* (2007), http://www.tanpinpin.com/invisiblecity/IC%20SYNOPSIS%20BIO%206.4mb.pdf.

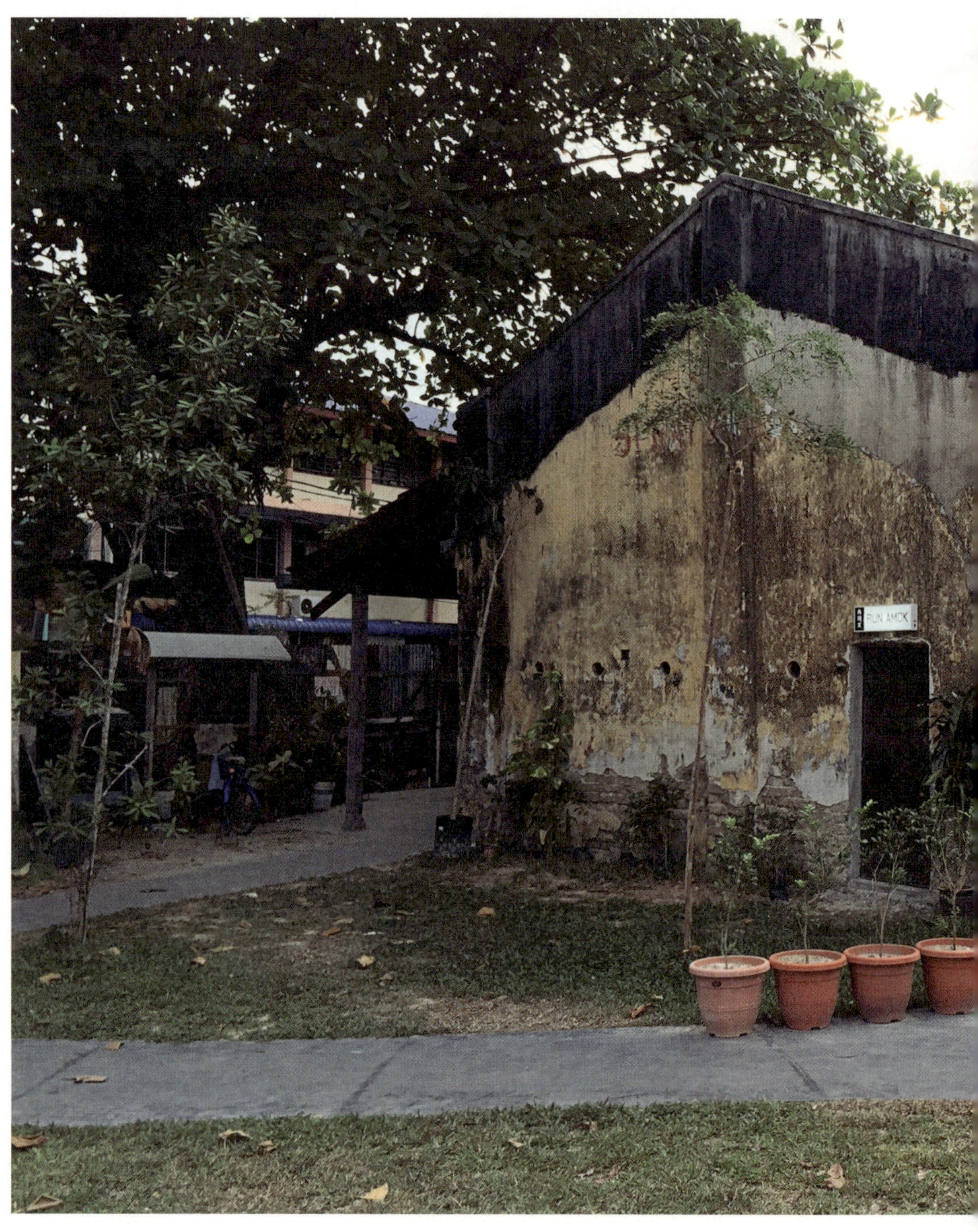


Run Amok Collective
Penang, Malaysia

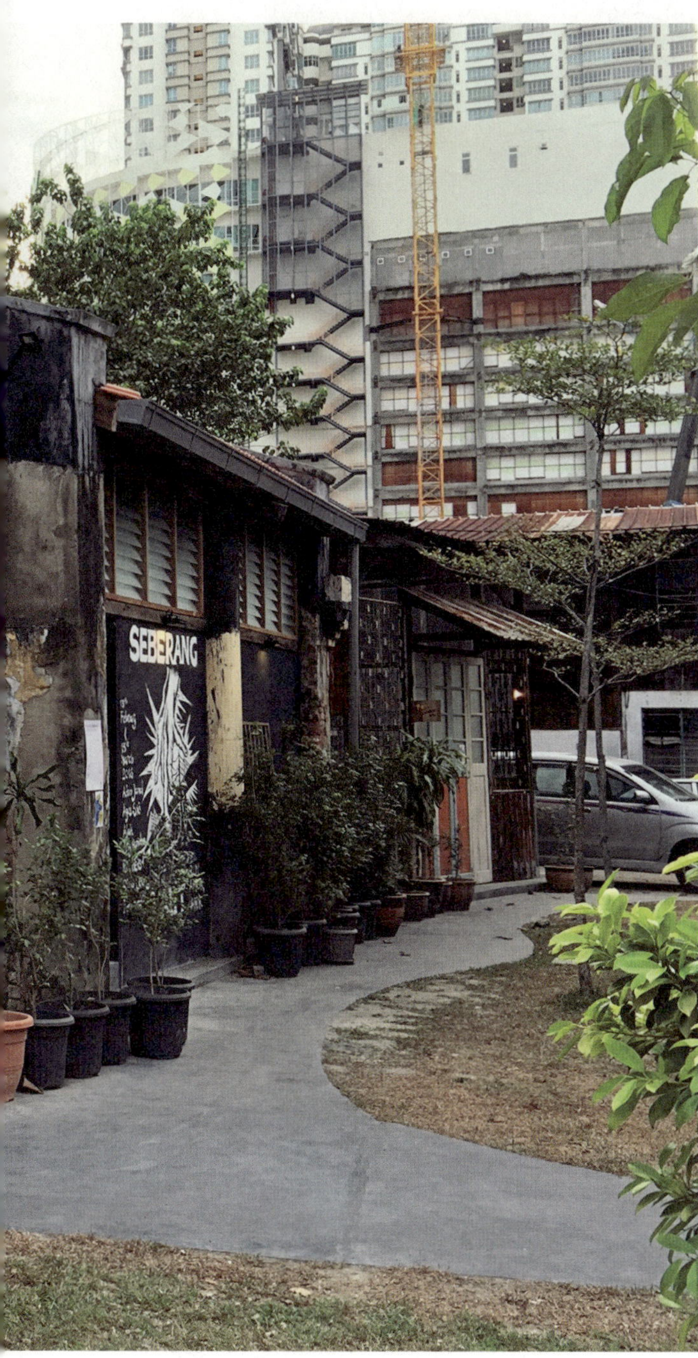

Simon Soon

# Ein anderer Blick auf den kuratorischen Kolonialismus

Der vorliegende Essay versteht sich nicht als groß angelegter Versuch, tiefe Einblicke in die Mechanismen der kuratorischen Wissensproduktion zu geben, sondern als erster Schritt, um einen anderen Blick auf das Kuratorische und sein Verhältnis zum Politischen zu gewinnen.[1] Zahlreiche AutorInnen und KuratorInnen wie Maria Lind oder die MacherInnen des Studiengangs *Curatorial/ Knowledge* am Goldsmiths College berufen sich auf den viel zitierten Begriff des *Kuratorischen*, der als rhetorische Figur für einen Diskurs und eine Kartografie des Wissens steht, deren Konturen genauso unklar bleiben wie das *Commoning*, mit dem das Kuratorische oft in Verbindung gebracht wird.[2]

Diese Entwicklung steht im Widerspruch zum üblichen Verständnis des Kuratierens als Organisieren einer Ausstellung, aber auch dem noch älteren Bild der KuratorIn als VerwalterIn und PflegerIn einer Kunstsammlung. Wenn man heute vom Kuratorischen spricht, ist damit etwas anderes gemeint: die Schaffung diskursiver Orte, die sich als Vektor gesellschaftlicher und philosophischer Veränderung verstehen. Eine solche Behauptung erscheint allerdings problematisch, sobald man den Blick auf die institutionellen Netzwerke richtet, die dieses performative Denken ermöglichen. Als diskursives Spektakel leistet das Kuratorische seit den 1990er Jahren epistemologische Schützenhilfe für den fortgeschrittenen Kapitalismus und verortet sich gleichzeitig in der Tradition aufklärerischer Vernunft. Das Kuratorische gibt zwar vor, eine kritische Form diskursiver Reflexivität zu sein, ist aber nicht in der Lage zu erkennen, was es dabei übersieht.

Ich möchte hier vor allem untersuchen, was passiert, wenn die Ziele und Motivationen des Kuratorischen auf die Kunst und den Aktivismus der nichteuropäischen Welt treffen. Das Theorieparadigma, das dieser weit gefasste Begriff verkörpert, ist trotz bester Absichten von einer kolonialisierenden Grundhaltung geprägt. Meiner Ansicht nach stülpt das Kuratorische dringlichen Problemen eine eigene Agenda über und verwandelt diese dadurch in ein Wissen, das größtenteils aus einer bestimmten reflexiven, pädagogischen und auf Öffentlichkeit basierten Struktur heraus erzeugt wird. Dieser Akt der Wissensproduktion gesteht der Kunst und dem Aktivismus der sogenannten Dritten Welt eine Zeitgenossenschaft nur insofern zu, als dass beide der Institutionskritik in der Ersten Welt dienlich sein könnten.

Diesem Ansatz ließe sich zugutehalten, dass er helfen kann, die hegemoniale beziehungsweise etablierte Auffassung der kuratorischen Praxis und die damit einhergehenden institutionellen Standards nicht blindlings zu reproduzieren, sondern sich zu widersetzen, wenn diese Haltung außerhalb Europas und der USA unkritisch übernommen wird. So zumindest habe ich den Vortrag verstanden, den Irit Rogoff im vorigen Jahr im Rahmen des Symposiums *Sites of Construction* am Asia Art Archive in Hongkong gehalten hat.[3] Ihr stichhaltigstes Argument wandte sich gegen die Annahme, dass eine kulturelle Infrastruktur und finanzielle Fördersysteme ausreichten, um eine gehaltvolle Hochkultur hervorzubringen. Dies unterlegte sie mit einer Aufzählung künstlerischer Initiativen, die keinen Anspruch auf Vollständigkeit erhebt, darunter das Raqs Media Collective, das Collectivo Situationes, Tucuman Arde, Oda Projesi und X-Urban. Gemeinsam sind ihnen die Hinwendung zu gesellschaftlicher Praxis und der Bezug auf die kritische Theorie. Trotz ihrer höchst unterschiedlichen Ausrichtung und Struktur gruppiert Rogoff diese überwiegend lokalen Projekte, die aus ganz bestimmten soziopolitischen Kontexten heraus entstehen, unter dem Banner „Kunst und Aktivismus".

Damit fasst Rogoff Zeitgenossenschaft neu: nicht länger als historischen Moment, sondern als multiple Abfolge sich ständig verändernder Dringlichkeiten, anhand derer das Verhältnis zur Vergangenheit durch den Gebrauchswert bestimmt wird, den diese für den politisch-ideologischen Kampf in und die Kritik an der Gegenwart hat. Handstreichartig stellt sie die besagten Kollektive und Initiativen in einen Rahmen, der sie umgehend in einen Untersuchungsgegenstand verwandelt und einem ganz anderen Zweck dienen soll. In der Folge wird künstlerischer Aktivismus zu einem Archiv, das einzig darauf ausgerichtet ist, institutionelle Funktionsweisen und Formen des Kuratierens im Hinblick darauf zu dekonstruieren, wie *westliche* Diskursproduktion abläuft. Wen kümmern die Tränen und all die Mühsal dieser lokalen Kämpfe? Was zählt, ist, dass irgendjemand, der mit der Wirklichkeit dieser Konflikte und Probleme, also mit den maßgeblichen Prozessen, die dem Engagement vor Ort eine Prägung geben, nichts zu tun hat, in London dazu eine Theorie parat hat.

### Südostasien als Kunstgriff

Dieses Spannungsverhältnis lässt sich nicht auf das vermeintliche Problem westlicher Denkmuster reduzieren, sondern begegnet uns ebenso in anderen Teilen der Welt, wie einige kurze Fallstudien verdeutlichen sollen.

Man braucht nur einen Blick auf die Geschehnisse in Thailand zu werfen, die auch deshalb ein interessantes Beispiel sind, weil sich die dortigen politischen Fronten ständig verschieben und nicht ohne weiteres in ein Schwarz-Weiß-Raster fügen. Die Unübersichtlichkeit der Situation in Thailand lässt es ratsam erscheinen, von einer liebgewonnenen und weithin akzeptierten Typologie Abschied zu nehmen, die dazu tendiert, Massenbewegungen reflexartig für einen Stellvertreter des Volkes zu halten. Die Masse steht nicht immer auf Seiten der Demokratie, auch wenn sie vorgibt, dies zu tun.

Es war bezeichnend, dass, während draußen regierungskritische Proteste tobten, im Bangkok Art and Culture Centre die thematische Ausstellung *Concept Context Contestation: Art and the Collective in Southeast Asia* stattfand. Die Ausstellung wollte Kunstpraktiken in Frage stellen, die sich „eines an lokalen Gegebenheiten orientierten Begriffsdenkens" bedienten, „um die Zuschauer aktiv miteinzubeziehen". *Concept Context Contestation* setzte sich zum Ziel, „die enge Verbindung zwischen konzeptuellen Ansätzen und gesellschaftlichen Ideologien in der südostasiatischen Gegenwartskunst der letzten vierzig Jahre zu untersuchen".[4]

Der Gegensatz zwischen den Straßenkämpfen und dem abstrakten Protest im Kulturzentrum, wo Fragen sozialer Gerechtigkeit sofort die AktivistenkünstlerIn und begriffliche Konstellationen auf den Plan rufen, hätte größer nicht sein können. Die Ausstellung präsentierte Konzeptkunst aus Südostasien, sie wollte beides sein: Archiv und Gesellschaftskritik.

Ganz abgesehen von der Tatsache, dass die meisten der KünstlerInnen unter SammlerInnen bereits eine gewisse Bekanntheit erlangt hatten, war die kuratorische Prämisse der Ausstellung – südostasiatische Konzeptkunst als Form politischen Engagements – so vage, dass man sich fragen mußte, ob sie ihrem eigenen Anspruch dadurch nicht eher schadete als nützte.[5] Denn was genau an der Ausstellung politisch gewesen sein soll, wurde nicht weiter ausgeführt. Man bekam lediglich die übliche Kunst-Kost zu Großthemen wie Geschichte, Erinnerung und Politik.

An diesem Beispiel wird deutlich, dass das Kuratorische ständig Gefahr läuft, radikale Politik einem institutionellen Diskurs unterzuordnen. Das Versprechen von Reflexivität, das im komparatistischen Fokus auf eine Region und ihre Geschichte aufscheint, wo andere sich in die Bunker der nationalen Kunstgeschichte zurückgezogen hätten, wird nur teilweise gehalten. Der diskursive Mechanismus der Ausstellung birgt tote Winkel. Singuläre Positionen und Geschichten verschwinden hinter dem komparativen Ansatz, der sich letztlich als bloßer Kunstgriff entpuppt und im Vergleich zur Energie der Straßenproteste ziemlich blass wirkt. Widerstand wird einförmig, platt, seine Struktur, der Kontext, in dem er sich Bahn bricht, und die Begriffe, die sich die Beteiligten von ihm machen – sie alle werden geglättet, auch wenn das Kuratorische sich auf die Fahnen geschrieben hat, diese widerständigen Potenziale als strategisches Archiv fruchtbar zu machen.

## Das Kunstvolle und das Kunstlose

Ob die zeitgenössische Kunst als Institution und Netzwerk sich einer besonders großen Nähe zur Gegenwart rühmen darf, kann also bezweifelt werden. Es bleibt allerdings offen, welche Konsequenzen daraus zu ziehen sind, wie ich anhand einiger weiterer Beispiele darlegen werde. Vor ein paar Jahren wurde während einer Podiumsdiskussion auf der Art Basel Hongkong ein posthumes Werk des verstorbenen Tsang Tsou Choi vorgestellt, ein verrückter Graffitikalligraph, den viele als King of Kowloon kennen.[6]

Meine Aufmerksamkeit war geweckt, als der chinesische Verleger, Aktivist und Kurator Ou Ning in seinem Vortrag eine Parallele zog zwischen der künstlerischen Praxis Tsangs und Joshua Wong, einem relativ jungen Vertreter der Hongkonger Aktivistenszene, der während der sogenannten Regenschirm-Revolution[7] von sich reden machte. Wong, so könnte man zusammenfassen, ist ein 15-jähriges Wunderkind, das 2011 die soziale Bewegung *Scholarism* (學民思潮) ins Leben rief. Er mobilisierte eine Gruppe von OberschülerInnen, um gegen den Lehrplan (德育及國民教育) aufzubegehren, den die Schulbehörde in Hongkong gerade eingeführt hatte. Vorwürfe wurden laut, dass der Lehrplan ein revisionistisches Geschichtsbild verfechte, von dem viele BürgerInnen Hongkongs dachten, es sei genau auf die ideologischen Bedürfnisse der Kommunistischen Partei Chinas zugeschnitten. Die Maßnahme schien dem „Eine Nation, zwei Systeme"-Arrangement zuwiderzulaufen, das Hongkong nach der britischen Übergabe der Staatshoheit an die Volksrepublik China im Jahre 1997 einen Großteil seiner inneren Autonomie zusichern sollte. Dazu gehörte auch das allgemeine geheime Wahlrecht, das den DemonstrantInnen zufolge noch immer nicht gilt. Mich interessiert, welche Verbindung Ou Ning zwischen dem Künstler und dem Aktivisten herstellte.

Ein Vergleich bietet sich an zu einem vor ein paar Monaten geposteten Blogeintrag der malaiischen Künstlerin und Aktivistin Ili Farhana:

> Bis heute bleibt es höchst selten, dass Kunst und Aktivismus sich in Malaysia überschneiden. Nicht, dass es in der Richtung gar nichts gäbe, aber es kommt nur selten vor. Im Vergleich zu anderen Ländern fehlt es den Protesten in Malaysia oft an Strahlkraft. Sie erschöpfen sich in der Regel in endlosen Reden und inbrünstigen Mahnungen, die, wenn nichts anderes aus ihnen erwächst, letztlich die Initiative der Massen schwächen. Wir wollen nicht einfach unterhalten werden, sondern auf die Zusammenführung von Kunst und Kultur auf der einen und Massenbewegungen auf der anderen Seite hinarbeiten – nur so können wir das Land wirklich verändern.[8]

Einerseits also das Beispiel aus Malaysia, wo vor allem die Befürchtung zum Ausdruck kommt, dass sozialer Protest nicht ausreicht, solange er kein schöpferisches Element enthält. Damit ist wohl gemeint, dass Kunst dem Protest das gewisse Extra gibt, um über die Mühsal und Langeweile von Politik hinauszugelangen. Dabei ist nicht nur eine Umdeutung des Kunstbegriffs zu beobachten, sondern es kommt auch die – meiner Ansicht nach – naive Vorstellung zum Vorschein, Politik müsse in gewisser Weise kreativer, schöpferischer sein. Aber schon Walter Benjamin hat vor den Folgen einer Ästhetisierung der Politik gewarnt.

Andererseits gibt es da jemanden wie Ou Ning, der überhaupt kein Bedürfnis hat, das schöpferische Element oder den kreativen Funken politischer Proteste ausfindig zu machen. Der Protest genügt sich als kunstvolle Form selbst, auf kreative Zusätze ist er nicht angewiesen. Alles, was Kunst und Kultur (beziehungsweise die Sphäre, in der sich HistorikerInnen, KuratorInnen und KünstlerInnen bewegen) zu tun brauchen, ist, sich in diesen Diskurs einzuklinken. Dem Raum des Protests ist eigentlich nichts hinzuzufügen, wir müssen ihn nur in uns aufnehmen – gleichsam konsumieren – und in unseren eigenen kulturellen Diskurs integrieren.

Ich finde die beiden Beispiele äußerst aufschlussreich: Sie sind angetrieben vom Wunsch, die beinahe unüberwindbare Kluft zwischen knallharter Politik und künstlerischer Praxis zu überbrücken. Ob in Ägypten, im Istanbuler Gezi-Park, in Syrien, Bangkok oder nun auch in Taiwan – wir fetischisieren die Masse, ihre Energie und Antriebskraft und suchen nach einem schöpferischen Lebenszeichen inmitten des Tumults. Aber wonach suchen wir eigentlich wirklich?

Ich muss zugeben, dass ich mit einigem Interesse die Skandale verfolgt habe, die in Asien Aufsehen erregten und mit Kunst im engeren Sinn gar nichts zu tun hatten. Sie waren buchstäblich kunstlos. Alvin Tan und Vivian Lee, die bis zu ihrer Trennung gemeinsam als Alvivi auftraten, haben sich mit Internet-Sexvideos einen Namen gemacht. Sie betrieben darüber hinaus einen vor freimütigen sexuellen Bekenntnissen strotzenden YouTube-Kanal, der in Singapur und Malaysia Entsetzen angesichts der Eskapaden und Kapriolen des Paares auslöste.

Auch Amos Yee, ein *enfant terrible* aus Singapur, der sich auf seiner Facebookseite eher beiläufig als Künstler bezeichnet, landete jüngst in den Schlagzeilen. Schon mit dreizehn Jahren begann er, eigene Videos auf YouTube zu veröffentlichen, deren Spektrum von selbstproduzierten Filmen bis zu Besprechungen von Melvilles *Moby Dick* reichte. Berühmt und berüchtigt wurde er allerdings mit einem Video, das kein gutes Haar an christlichen Rechten und Lee Kuan Yew ließ – und das kurz nach dem Tod dieses ersten Premierministers von Singapur im Jahr 2015.

Haben diese YouTube-Ikonen überhaupt irgendetwas gemeinsam? Sie teilen eine tiefsitzende Skepsis gegenüber kulturellen Normen, sie weigern sich, sich an die von oben verordneten Spielregeln zu halten, sie misstrauen jeder systematischen Massenpädagogik. Simon Castets und Hans Ulrich Obrist beschreiben die nach 1989 geborenen *Digital Natives* mit den herkömmlichen Mitteln eines aalglatten zivilgesellschaftlichen Diskurses. Aber Alvivi und Amos Yee sind auf Streit aus, sie sind respektlos und unregierbar, sie entziehen sich dem Diskursspektakel.[9]

Es überrascht nicht, dass ein kuratorisches Ökosystem, das zunehmend Wert auf die richtige Ausbildung an Institutionen wie dem Bard College, dem Goldsmiths College und de Appel legt, mit diesen *KünstlerInnen* wenig anzufangen weiß. Ihre Streitlust lässt sich nicht beschwichtigen. Woran sich unmittelbar die Frage anschließt: Gibt es Phänomene, die sich dem Kuratorischen widersetzen? Gehen wir davon aus, dass die operative Logik des Kuratorischen einer aufklärerischen Vernunft entspringt, die ihre spezifische Ausprägung im Spätkapitalismus gefunden hat: Kann man dem Kuratorischen dann überhaupt entkommen? Wie gehen wir mit alldem um, das sich nicht mit dem Hinweis auf die (selbstkritische) Macht der Vernunft wegdiskutieren lässt?

Ich habe nicht vor, wie Ou Ning das vielleicht getan hätte, Alvivis und Amos Yees Aktivitäten als, wenn nicht gleich Kunst, dann zumindest kulturelle Praxis zu deuten, die am ehesten zu begreifen ist, wenn sie in ein Verhältnis zur gegenwärtigen Lage von Kunst und Kultur gesetzt wird. Ich will vermeiden, dass ein kunsthistorisches oder kuratorisches Wissen sich das Tun der beiden gleichsam kolonialistisch erschließt und einverleibt. Sie in eine längere Geschichte singapurischer und malaiischer Bildkultur einzuschreiben oder schlicht als Teil einer Ausstellung zu präsentieren, wäre unangemessen und würde ihnen nicht gerecht.

Von Bedeutung ist gerade die unüberwindbare Kluft zwischen Alvivis und Amos Yees Internetaktivitäten und dem Versuch, dieses Tun auf den Begriff zu bringen, indem man es schlicht unter der Rubrik Kunst und Aktivismus verbucht. Sie sind der konzeptuelle blinde Fleck, der verhindert, dass wir uns die Grenzen des Kuratorischen vergegenwärtigen. Die Sphäre der Kunst nimmt für sich in Anspruch, progressiv, trendy, permissiv, der Zukunft zugewandt zu sein. Doch gleichzeitig wirkt sie unglaublich repetitiv und formelhaft. Ist es daher an der Zeit, unsere Praxis einer gründlichen Revision zu unterziehen?

## Neugier

Was tun? Ich werde hier nicht auf ein grundlegend anderes Vorgehen drängen. Ich möchte lediglich hervorheben, was den meisten KuratorInnen ohnehin bewusst ist, auch wenn sie darin eher ein Ideal und nicht so sehr eine Notwendigkeit oder eine Vorbedingung unserer Arbeit sehen. Der Wille zum Wissen ist unabdinglich, und wird nicht so sehr von bloßer Dringlichkeit befeuert, sondern von *genuiner Neugier*.

Mein Vorschlag zielt auf eine Anthropologie, die nicht länger bloß als Zielscheibe der Dekonstruktion herhalten muss, sondern ein dauerhaftes Engagement erfordert. Es reicht nicht, sich einzugestehen, dass man den Anderen niemals kennen kann und jeder Versuch, sich ihn vorzustellen, von Anfang an zum Scheitern verurteilt ist. Alle Vorannahmen gehören auf den Prüfstand, ohne dabei in eine selbstverliebte Nabelschau zu verfallen, bei der sich wieder alles nur um die Eigenarten des Kuratierens als Disziplin dreht.

Um die Welt zu verstehen, genügt es nicht, sie zu kartografieren. Sie ist mehr als die Summe der Orte, Themen und Bereiche, die das kuratorische Handwerk (oder deskriptive Paradigmen, die uns die Welt näherbringen sollen) zu einem kohärenten Ganzen zu bündeln vermag. Nur durch Neugier können wir einander und unsere Erfahrungen besser begreifen, sonst wird das Andere nur dann dringlich und wertvoll, wenn es zugleich als Archiv für diejenigen taugt, die sich aus einer privilegierten Position heraus damit begnügen, ihre eigenen institutionellen Verfahren einer kritischen Prüfung zu unterziehen.

Als Beispiel für diese Neuausrichtung soll mir nicht etwa eine Ausstellung, sondern ein Film dienen, der diesen erweiterten Begriff kuratorischen Wissens verkörpert. Das Ziel besteht nämlich nicht darin, gegen die Erweiterung des Kuratorischen als Wissens- und Praxisform zu polemisieren, sondern dessen bisherige Stoßrichtung zu hinterfragen. Insofern fühle ich mich dem Kuratorischen durchaus verpflichtet, denn es hat stets versucht, Galerien und Ausstellungsräume hinter sich zu lassen und der Praxis selbst den Vorzug zu geben. In ihrem Dokumentarfilm *Invisible City* katalogisiert Tan Pin Pin eine Obsession, für die viele möglicherweise wenig übrig haben, die jedoch all diejenigen teilen dürften, die die Geschichte Singapurs selbst erlebt haben.

„Ich wollte Leute finden", so Tan, „die wie ich Singapur selbst zum Thema ihrer Arbeit machten. Damit meine ich nicht Singapur als Arbeitsplatz, sondern als Sujet."[10] In ihrem Film trifft man dann auch vier schillernde ProtagonistInnen, die in Singapur lebten, als der Stadtstaat unabhängig wurde: Ivan Polunins Filmaufnahmen alteingesessener Bevölkerungsgruppen in Singapur und Malaysia aus den fünfziger Jahren des vergangenen Jahrhunderts; Marjorie Doggett, die seit mehr als sechzig Jahren alte, mittlerweile längst abgerissene Gebäude fotografiert; Han Tan Juan, ein Student und Aktivist, der sich auf Fotos der Unruhen an chinesischen Schulen spezialisiert hat; Lim Chen Sian, ein Archäologe, der sechzig Jahre alte Militärbunker auf der Insel Sentosa ausgräbt. Es sind persönliche Obsessionen, Traumata und Erinnerungen – nicht mehr und nicht weniger. Doch zusammengenommen bilden sie einen Resonanzraum für die einzelnen Stimmen. Sie eröffnen einen sozial- und kulturhistorischen Blick auf den Inselstaat, der sich mit dem Tonfall und dem Inhalt der offiziellen Geschichtsschreibung Singapurs nicht in Übereinstimmung bringen lässt.

Tans Katalog der Obsessionen finde ich aus zwei Gründen spannend. Durch das Gerede von einer transnationalen Wende haben wir all diejenigen aus dem Blick verloren, die sich für eine spezifische Lokalität einsetzen. Tans Arbeit verweigert sich stur einer Rhetorik des Globalen, die nur ihre eigene Sichtweise und Geisteshaltung gelten lässt. Schlägt die Ausgrabung einer Cola-Flasche, die seit fünfzig Jahren in einem alten Armeebunker in Singapur verschüttet war, globale Wellen? Im Sinne des Kuratorischen Filme zu machen, heißt, Risiken einzugehen, wenn man sich mit einem einzelnen Archäologen beschäftigt und dessen Obsessionen in das Medium des Films übersetzt. Die Filmemacherin übernimmt die Verantwortung dafür, wie sie den anderen deutet, anstatt wie das viele tun, diese Verantwortung von sich zu weisen und sich in der Rolle der solipsistischen Kritikerin des Kuratorischen zu gefallen.

Die Dokumentation erteilt dem Paritätsdenken und der Gleichzeitigkeit eine Absage, die von anderen als Inbegriff der Zeitgenossenschaft gefeiert werden. Tan spielt das Globale nicht gegen das Nationale aus. Sie arbeitet heraus, dass das Lokale als historischer Bezugsrahmen ein genauso schlagkräftiger und vielgestaltiger Widersacher der offiziellen nationalen Geschichtsschreibung sein kann. Die Abwendung von der Gleichzeitigkeit setzt dem Wunsch, weltweit auf dem neuesten Stand zu sein, Grenzen. Andere Blickwinkel auf die Welt werden möglich. Auch jene Perspektiven, die nicht im vermeintlichen Zentrum des Geschehens stehen, können dazu beitragen, eine Weltgeschichte zu schreiben.

Es gibt eine herrliche Szene, in der Tan den Mediziner Ivan Polunin interviewt, den Tropenmediziner, dem wir wichtige Farbfilmaufnahmen indigener Gemeinschaften aus den 1950er Jahren verdanken. Die Filmemacherin sah sich mit einem Gegenüber konfrontiert, das den kuratorischen Blick umdrehte und auf sie zurückwarf.

> – Darf ich Sie etwas fragen?
> Ivan: Natürlich dürfen Sie, aber ob Sie eine Antwort bekommen …
> – Okay, ich versuch's einfach mal.
> Ivan: Ob Sie eine zufriedenstellende Antwort erhalten, ist wirklich eine andere Frage.

Dieser kurze Dialog bringt mich zu einem letzten Punkt. Er verdeutlicht, dass die Regisseurin alle Kräfte aufbieten muss, um ihrem Sujet gerecht zu werden. Genau darin besteht kuratorische Aufrichtigkeit angesichts der einschüchternden Aufgabe der Weltdeutung. Tans Neugier wird eben nicht zu einem Katalog der Obsessionen, der einzig im Dienste der Dekonstruktion und der Sorge um grundlegende politische Veränderungen steht. Sie geht weit darüber hinaus und überlässt es ihrem Gegenüber, die eigenen Obsessionen in all ihren Absonderlichkeiten zu schildern. Tans Dokumentation hat es gar nicht nötig, die eigenen emanzipatorischen Ansichten und den Stellenwert des Politischen ständig an die große Glocke zu hängen. Die Neugier, die ihr Filmprojekt antreibt und ihm zugrunde liegt, ist in jeder Szene offensichtlich. Sie spricht für sich. Tan begegnet ihrem Sujet zugleich mit großer Sympathie. Aus der Bereitschaft zuzuhören, entsteht ein ethisches Band zwischen beiden. Das Kuratorische könnte sich dort einiges abschauen.

1  Die Grundideen für diesen Aufsatz konnte ich im Rahmen von zwei Veranstaltungen weiterentwickeln. Die erste war eine Podiumsdiskussion auf der Art Stage Singapore 2014. Den Leitbegriff des kuratorischen Kolonialismus habe ich in dem Vortrag „Resisting Curatorial Colonialism", den ich 2014 während des eintägigen Symposiums *Practicing Resistance* am Perth Institute of Contemporay Art gehalten habe, umfassend problematisiert.

2  Maria Lind, „The Curatorial", in: *Artforum*, Nr. 103, Oktober 2009. Auf der Webseite vom Goldsmiths College ist darüber hinaus zu lesen, dass „der titelgebende Zusammenschluss „Curatorial/Knowledge" bereits nahelegt, dass Kuratieren bedeutet, Wissen zu produzieren und sich mit ihm auseinanderzusetzen. Wissen heißt weder Informationen und Kursmaterialien auswendig zu lernen, noch etwas zu analysieren

und zu deuten, sondern verweist auf etwas, das wir durch diverse eigene Praktiken hervorbringen." http://www.gold.ac.uk/pg/mphil-phd-curatorial-knowledge, abgerufen am 31. Juli 2016.

3 Irit Rogoff, „The Expanding Field", in: *Yishu Journal of Contemporary Chinese Art*, Bd. 13, Nr. 2, März/April 2014.

4 Siehe den Begleitband Iola Lenzi (Hg.), *Concept Context Contestation: Art and the Collective in Southeast Asia*, Bangkok 2014. http://edm.bacc.or.th/edm/201402/eng.html, abgerufen am 31. Juli 2016.

5 Tatsächlich gehört einer der Kuratoren zu den Käufern und Förderern gleich mehrerer der ausgestellten Künstler. Es stellt sich die Frage, die im Grunde ein ethisches Dilemma ist, inwiefern ein Interessenkonflikt vorlag. Das scheint mir umso wichtiger, da die Ausstellung für sich beansprucht, einen neuen Kanon zu etablieren und mit ihrer Auswahl Kunstgeschichte zu schreiben.

6 „Salon", Art Basel Hongkong, 25. Mai 2013, https://www.youtube.com/watch?v=DLl3IHM3n6A

7 Die sogenannte Regenschirm-Revolution bezeichnet Proteste, die sich gegen einen Beschluss des Nationalen Volkskongresses in Peking richteten, der im August 2014 vorgab, den Verwaltungschef von Hongkong zunächst von einem Komitee wählen zu lassen, bevor das Volk darüber abstimmen kann. Die Proteste dauerten bis Dezember 2014 an. Joshua Wong wurde als verantwortlicher Anführer der Demonstrationen von einem Gericht 2016 für schuldig erklärt. (Anm. der Hg.)

8 Ili Farhana, „Adakah Seni Kita Sedari?", in: *Pohon Bintang*, 2. Januar 2014, https://pohonbintang.wordpress.com/2014/01/02/adakah-seni-kita-sedari/, abgerufen am 31. Juli 2016.

9 Castets und Obrist tauften ihr Projekt dann auch *89 Plus*, http://www.89plus.com.

10 Tan Pin Pin, „Director's Note", *Invisible City*, 2007. http://www.tanpinpin.com/invisiblecity/IC%20SYNOPSIS%20BIO%206.4mb.pdf, abgerufen am 31. Juli 2016.

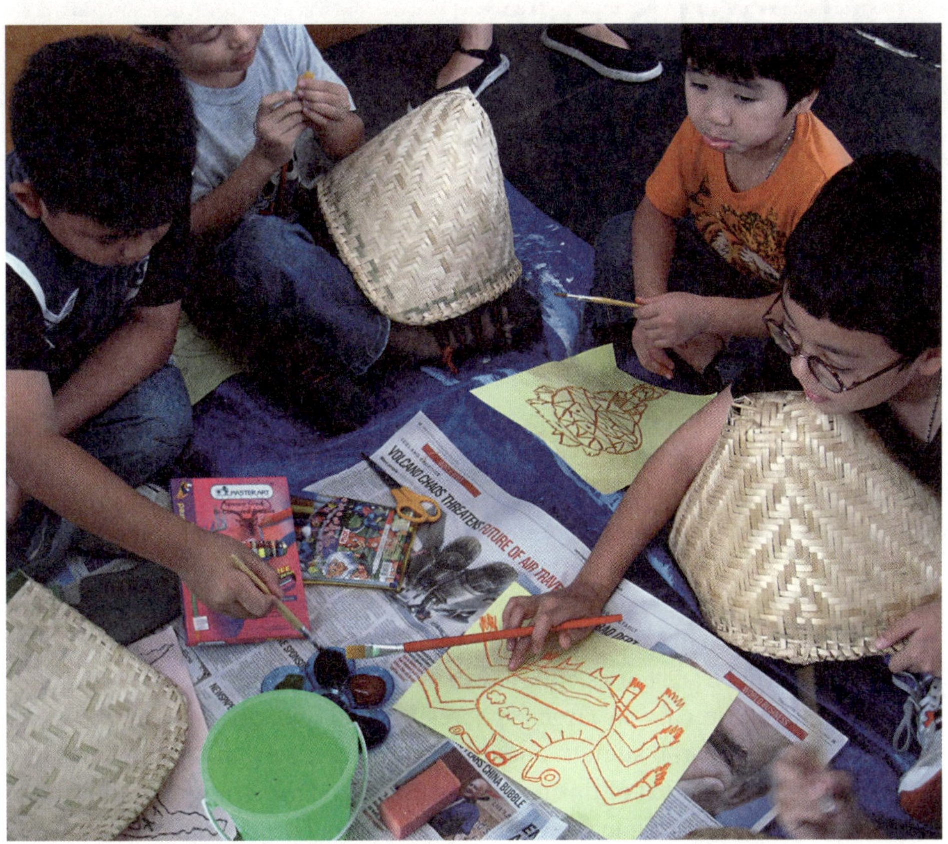

Childrens' workshop as part of the exhibition
"The Tropics," 2010
The Jim Thompson Art Center, Bangkok, Thailand

Eileen Legaspi-Ramirez

# Southeast Asia in a Crawl Space: Tempering Curatorial Hubris

I must confess that this text emerges from a rising discomfort over what I fear are growing complicities from a recent past, and an increasingly ominous trail of failed international engagements of an arguably unsatisfying nature. Globally, while curatorial studies may have indeed shifted to, or at least opened up to a discursive front across several platforms, I hazard that the purported dispersal of cores of knowledge-generating structures and vaunted departures from much-critiqued tropes of nationality, singular notions of modernism, and caricaturist senses of difference are not as entrenched as the "curatorium" is wont to claim. Arguably this is the case in larger spheres beyond and often even within the gated world of curatorial studies, and particularly in regard to Southeast Asia.

The immediate context of this text is an unevenly sensed frenzy to which academics and artists working in Southeast Asia are being drawn and perform within. That project cuts across art and cultural institutions, with their circuits of scholars and creative agents called up to actively conjure Asia in light of exchanges spurred by the onset of the ASEAN Economic Community (AEC)—only one of many intra-regional and transregional trade blocs that have emerged over decades of trying to tend to the problematics of the market by sidestepping state regulation of the movement of people and goods across borders. The AEC touts ten country players (Brunei, Cambodia, Indonesia, Laos, Malaysia, Myanmar, the Philippines, Singapore, Thailand, and Vietnam), which are supposed to stand to gain some US\$ 2.6 trillion as mobility of resources is made possible, and that encompasses 622 million people "traded" in an integrated zone of presumably converging interests over a massive aggregated scale of goods, services, capital, and labor.

ASEAN itself has often been called out on its non-punitive, purely conciliatory manner of forging a largely ceremonially united front. Alongside this state of affairs comes the quick realization that even the most seductive of globally trafficked epistemological shifts do not always travel so neatly in all-or-nothing packages that easily get taken up by the next curatorial venture embarking on the regional sphere. The underlying premise is that channels of exchange and mediation engendered by globalized economic transactions merely need to be greased up by culture, and this avowedly includes the tactical instrumentalization of art famously described in the 1996 Asia Society *Traditions/Tensions* exhibition-publication. The Thai artist-curator (and since turned state agent) Apinan Poshyananda organized the exhibition-publication, wherein these titular tropes were outrightly pegged as slippery lubricants. Fast forwarding to 2016, a good two decades after: How are we as individuals caught up in the whirlwind of the AEC and other bloc platforms stepping up to, or subverting that task of smoothing out the diplomatic bumps and bruises? Let it be said that my framing this within the always moving parameters of performance is not an attempt to interminably align the work of art historians, curators, and artists with a notion of performance as sheer pretense or superfluous staging, but rather, as perhaps defensive subjectification, or at least a contingent mode of self-identification. This is often as visceral as it is also subtly sensed.

When I walk into conferences or even in much more modest gatherings where Asia or Southeast Asia is on the table, I find that the rituals of introductions inevitably include some reference to where one works and how art figures in the particular imagination of the socio-political context we're perceived to be navigating. These days, it has indeed become much more fashionable to wager representations with a veneer of independence, and so we chuck citizenship for professional affiliation right down to registration forms and conference directories, as if this actually disentangles us from the impositions of otherwise disavowed agendas and structural dysfunctionalities by way of class, race, ethnicity, gender, creed, and so on. And so what I think has been happening in the continually being written art history of the modern and contemporary of Southeast Asia is precisely that: a trading of identity that is not entirely disposable but is also chimeric. Performing Southeast Asia has become this approximation of a chemistry of selves that while possibly toxic, can be momentarily potent.

The movement of bodies, our bodies, coming to meetings, project-pegged conferences, exhibitions, and so on hinges upon a willingness to stir up these possible collisions and/or sometimes yielding of essences and sewn-up agendas. Each initiative at addressing the region is to some degree a reaffirming of someone or some territory's bragging rights to hub status, which in turn could come across as anything from wholesale agreement, a modest hack, or the eroding of fragile channels through which scholars' and artists' paths inevitably get intertwined even if interventions fall short of getting embodied, with overtures unrequited. The primary assumption here is that the circulations and continued making of Asia requires the sublimating of certain aspects of subjectivity in deference to the contingencies of staking a claim in whichever conversation is at hand. This often requires the occupying of a tactical position that privileges certain aspects like difference and affinities, but downplays others that may not be the discourse trend of the moment or that might be too polarizing to serve up as a viable talking point. In the spirit of affirming the skepticism that Melani Budianta brought up at the recent conference, Making Southeast Asia: From Region to World, much of what I have to say here is grounded in a less than triumphalist rhetoric about this region which appears to perceptibly narrow and broaden from much more mercenary rather than symbiotic impulses. This contingent neighborliness in navigating between antinomies bridged by discursive elbow room among these congregations of individuals whose internal dissonance gets papered over by perceived as but not necessarily operative allegiances is something that gets taken for granted if at all recognized.

## Shifting Logics of Participation

What this text modestly asks the reader to consider is to look at how ephemeral networks of fluid relations play a critical role in the construction of a region through creative and discursive practice. In looking at how these figure alongside the more overtly political and economic negotiation of the shaping of that construction, the essay hopes to demonstrate how agents in the artworld participate in this mapping and remapping through institutional, quasi- and counter-institutional routes. Taking its cue from the Cambodia-based academic Roger Nelson's essay, "Pathways in Performance: In and Around Cambodia?," the essay also attempts to approximate an account of some selected "performances."[1] With these performances artists and cultural agents coast across by submitting wholly or tactically, or attempt to pose a challenge to totalizing logics that at least in rhetoric pose as critical of a still under-problematized idea of a region of resemblances. While anchored on specific sites with their own nuanced pasts, Nelson's text graphically articulates his notion of "performed diplomacy" with its tactical sublimation of discomfort. He focuses on how this was perpetuated in the context of Norodom Sihanouk's regime, but his articulation also finds resonances in the way Filipino artists, historians, curators, and theorists under the Marcoses and periods onward, are counted upon to enflesh a face-mask-body construction of compliant sameness or at the very least cleverness towards sites and modalities through which culture is trafficked. The assertion is that the surfacing of gnawing distinctions and contestations amidst these performances of nationalism and regionalism is seen as necessary foil to the effacing of skewed conditions in relational encounters with "others" from this imagined region. This is this research's bottom line, but also hopefully propels questions about efficacy and ethicality as areas for more deepened inquiry.

As an initial signpost, I proffer the state-engineered performance of history and grandeur called *Kasaysayan ng Lahi* (History of the Race) staged at the opening of the Folk Arts Theater in the Philippines in 1974.[2] I cite this specifically in that it vividly demonstrates the Marcosian state's desire for engagements within Asia and beyond, and how the meticulous crafting of aspirations we might now call curation centrally plays in the staging of such positionalities.

Case 1: *Kasaysayan ng Lahi:* Choreographed Relations (1974)
Following a two-hour parade on the Manila bay front lined by bused-in school-children, this mural turned tableau with a mammoth cast of 3,000 chorally enacted the birth of the Philippines from the Stone Age to Marcos's New Society. This extravaganza, coming after another elaborate launching (of the Cultural Center of the Philippines), occasioned the descending upon the country of figures such as the Mexican artist Rufino Tamayo, only one of many flown in to be given people's awards at the Folk Arts Center. Still another key guest of the period was the Yogyakarta-based Affandi brought over by the First Lady, Imelda Marcos, after she had herself spent five days touring Borobudur. The centrality of perfor-mance to her taking on the cultural portfolio is revealed as such:

> Through the centuries the Filipino has been putting on a mask in order to confound his conquerors. When the time came for him to take off the mask because it was no longer needed, he found that it had become part of his face. This is the commanding image of our crisis of identity. [...] For centu-ries these remembered passions have been in exile, buried beneath the shell of borrowed forms.[3]

Then Foreign Secretary Carlos P. Romulo, in turn, sealed this pronouncement with his own universalist and populist inflection in what I would argue is a defen-sive stance in light of the Philippines' inability to tout temple complexes as grand and imposing as its neighbors:

> Here on this modern Acropolis by the sea, a new Parthenon has arisen. From this new dwelling of the maiden shall issue forth today the procession that shall convey Athena's robe to the nation. It is a thing of beauty that is also a permanent joy to the beholder. Like Minerva's Temple, let it distill the wisdom and the culture of the many–peoples inhabiting these fair isles, and bequeath them to the ages. Let these peoples, who yesterday wrote on water and built on sand, henceforth build enduring spires on this bedrock. We have a New Society to erect; we have a new civilization to build.[4]

Case 2: documenta 12, Asia Speaks Up, Kassel (2007)
From the above cast of thousands we shift to a tiny gathering of editors of South-east Asian magazines and journals assembled in 2006 conjoined with an unfor-tunately stalled regional initiative called Comparative Contemporaries at The Substation Singapore. This Singapore meeting was the first of several lead up

events to documenta 12, which came with a parallel documenta magazines platform. My participation came by way of the journal called *Pananaw, Philippine Journal of Visual Arts* as it was invited unto a series of editors' meetings (Singapore, New York, Kassel) for the Magazines Project that at least on the surface appeared as a comparatively more inclusive platform vis-a-vis the largely Eurocentric Kassel-wide exhibition. This Southeast Asia contingent variably consisted of editors from such publications as the webzine-portals *Kakiseni, Talawas, Ctrl+P,* and *Midnight University,* Indonesia's *Kalam, Karbon, Kunci,* and at one point, Cemeti Art Foundation, Malaysia's *Sentap* and *Off the Edge,* Singapore's *FOCAS* and *Vehicle,* and curiously, China's *Dushu* which did not figure in the earlier meetings but made a fleeting appearance in Kassel itself. These meetings were loosely themed but essentially served as occasions for talking shop amidst the spectrum of ground conditions we all gingerly sought to comprehend all the way through a final round in Kassel during the 100 days run of documenta itself.

*d12 Magazines* was touted as a magazine of magazines with the added twist that each participant could, in principle instigate conversations with other participating magazines whose editors could "curate" from the shared platform content bound to documenta's leitmotifs of bare life, education (what can be done?), and lastly, is modernity our antiquity? How did we find ourselves in this company and at this platform of Babel proportions? And note there was no budget to enable translations. My suspicion was that it had to do with several earlier initiatives that took place in Singapore just past 2000, organized by The Substation, wherein the IFIMA meeting on Socially Engaged Art Practices and Comparative Contemporaries conferences were launched in 2002 and 2003.

Often enough, particularly in the case of undertakings organized from Europe, Asia still comes across as a tabula rasa and the organizer attempting an aspirational spread that passes muster diversity-wise counts on the magnanimity of peers to accomplish an often well-intended but usually erratically diffused opportunity to engage. The potential network, as it is being brought into shape per project/venture as such is profiled as primarily critical of some strain of neo-liberalism and at least on the surface, conversant with a modicum of ideas, language, and fields to which resources aiming to bring people together have gravitated. And so for regulars in the conference circuit, that may mean anything from skewing presentations toward Jacques Rancière one year, Nicolas Bourriaud/Grant Kester/Claire Bishop and the antagonisms of collective enterprises, and the expanding and contracting sphere of the commons and the Anthropocene in the very recent past. In our specific case throughout the Magazines Project series of meetings, we seemed to have constantly been trying to locate points from which we could launch future conversations given that this chance to breach country spaces had come so belatedly and so strangely having to come under documenta's largesse. In that vacuum of unfamiliarity, unfortunately the clichés (e.g., is the Philippines's postcolonial American hangover inevitably what sets it apart from the rest of Asia?) still become the most accessible push buttons, and notwithstanding the few but precious sustained partnerships that came forth eventually, exchanges still remained at hit and miss.

But we did get those handshakes going, very often for the very first time across dash lines and protected zones. Let me say that in as far as the d12 project went, we were certainly not a naive lot, though in the very first meeting in Singapore, our Myanmar colleague from *Staintet* was visibly on edge and would not, if he could help it, take to the microphone or allow any documentation that could be used to prove he had managed to get outside of Myanmar at the time. What I would say was definitively accomplished in these small meetings was the birthing of an informal, albeit inchoate, circle of voices. At the very end of the process, we were, for about a week, literally holed up in an inner room at documenta-Halle only to be publicly presented to d12's luncheon audience in a public event delimited by the contours of a dysfunctional human rights-scape, in a session on censorship called Asia Speaks Up. Speaking of crawl spaces, there was very little room to maneuver art into that frame but we did all give it a fair shot.

Since documenta 12, the editors from the Chiang Mai-based *Midnight University* had been hushed up, charged with lèse-majesté leading up to and all through the aftermath of martial law in Thailand. This reminds me of how Joan Kee, writing on Hans-Ulrich Obrist's "New Utopia" in 2004, mentions how artists like Lee Bul and Mariko Mori have parlayed criticism about failing to be exemplars of their national origins while at the same time also being seen as playing up to or playing with the narratives circulating in the global arenas that enable their mobility across these spaces. In this case of our motley crew of editors convening at documenta, we may have dutifully called out our governments in regard to the iron fists that sought to keep us in check, but personally, years down the line, one still suffers this gnawing feeling we may have not put in all that we could to do right by the artworlds we presumably came to speak from. The stark reality of regimes of censorship could hardly be argued with for instance, but it remains an uphill battle trying to dislodge organizer mindsets insistent on reducing Asia to a mere hotbed of human rights violations and not much else. The begging question remains: just how agentive could we have aspired to get under such fraught circumstances where attempts at visibility might be seen as cutting corners?

Case 3: "WE=ME Plus: A Malleable Asia," Bangkok (2013)
Not too long after, another fairly modest, but this time unabashedly more officious venture with the tagline: "WE=ME, Appreciate Difference" came into play at Silpakorn University Art Centre curated by Paramaporn Sirikulchayanont. This ASEAN exhibition/conference assembled artists, curators, art students, and educators from Brunei, Cambodia, Indonesia, Laos, Malaysia, Myanmar, the Philippines, Singapore, Vietnam, and Thailand, with China again as SEA plus one. While the awkward, catch-all tone may not have directly played out in the work shown; Imhathai Suwattanasilp's photographs amidst intricately crocheted hair strand constructions for instance lent a whimsical enough flair to an otherwise

reductively identity-laden reading. Still, the overwhelmingly feel-good tenor sent clear signals this was not a place in which the intolerances in the region's contested seas were to be summoned with any earnestness. While this framing may have merely been a function of mistranslation, it was also symptomatic of the feeble posture of commonality aspired to in a project where "one's culture will be the culture of all." This proposed utopic route became even more spotlighted once the casual discussions in the conference got underway, one of the most poignant moments for me being when one senior Thai artist equivocally set off to differentiate "their" art from what they derisively called "Chatuchak art" (with all the inferred dismissiveness he could muster of "affordable art" venues that have sprung up in Asia as a way for young artists to slip into visibility). So much for the long-term avant-garde charge to wear down the art and life divide. So goes too that impassioned charge to break down art-craft binaries. I bit my tongue and quietly just went along.

I must confess again I had not so fully realized till then just how effectively sublimated antagonisms strewn across those panels actually were.  By the time I had gotten a better grasp of the tenacity of such hierarchical thinking, an unexpected comment from an Australian expatriate pointed too to how the wider Asia-Pacific trope was foreclosed in this event as she asked about where they were in this conversation.  Where such contemporaneities are apparently being summoned out of necessity rather than emanating from any inviolably nurtured kinships, one is tempted to cast hope on much more informal channels of affinities.  This was certainly one take-away from David Teh's recent lecture, "Whither art history?  Institutions, curatorship and the undead nation state" delivered at Green Papaya Art Projects in Manila.[5] Given these primarily artist-driven channels where the vetting is accomplished with a lot less vigilant gatekeeping, I came away provisionally agreeing that the backroads could be a mitigating and countervailing context simply because, in the more fluid tiers of the artist-organizer, there are simply more agents to contend with, in more dispersed sites, to be navigated through in much more variable modalities.

Case 4: "Concept, Context, Contestation," Bangkok (2013–14)

The recourse to foregrounding and perceived localisms however brings its own risks it seems. In less than a year, I was to return to Bangkok to participate in the collateral symposium for "Concept, Context, Contestation: Art and the Collective in Southeast Asia," a project curated by Iola Lenzi, Agung Hujatnikajennong, and Vipash Purichanont for and at the Bangkok Art and Culture Centre (BACC). The press narrative was clear-cut enough about how this exhibition would "defend the idea that conceptual approaches used in contemporary art of Southeast Asia are not necessarily imported but rather can find their source in home culture." It was a defensive stance I found myself musing over as I came along wondering if we had set upon yet another compromised proposition. After all, there we were, another motley crew (this time from Singapore, Indonesia,

Thailand, Myanmar, Cambodia, Malaysia, and Vietnam) gathered amidst the supreme irony of making an argument for a notion of the collective just as the red and yellow shirts had drawn dividing lines around the exteriors of the building we were at, causing this BACC public program to be put on hold for an extended period before the occupiers were persuaded to move elsewhere. Nevertheless, and quixotically as it may have seemed, I made a pitch for individual as opposed to purely individualist latitude, for a more deeply considered look at these claims over dangerously essentialized perceptions of collective spirit and reductionist politics. In light of the heavy edits my catalogue essay baring these points were subjected to, the nagging fear remained I was not only speaking to the void but also in default mute mode. The impassioned curatorial insistence on conjuring Asia as embodying a specific imagination of what constituted the social undeniably underpinned the project. And yet, in affirmation again of Budianta's invoking of agency amidst the incidental, we put ourselves in harm's way and wager that the risks are commensurate to what might be forsaken in the process.

<u>Reprising Nation: Inscapes and Wading through Curatorial Rhetoric</u>
Given such hindsight, I would say that there remain certain critical vanguard positions in the staking of Southeast Asia so coveted from within and without, that these are not easily yielded nor always subject to pretenses to generosity. By invoking C. J. Wee's essay, "We Asia?," we might recount how Japan Foundation organized, by the turn of the twenty-first century "another part of what was 'under construction': a [curatorial] network-in-progress, transcending the geographical framework known as 'Asia' and continuing to expand on a global scale." Forming a multicultural Asian "curatorium" was a step toward polycentric global connectivity.[6] In effect, what seemed to be on the table then was the purposive supplanting of what were perceived to be exterior structures variably ignoring or summoning Asia for their own defined ends. Apparently, the idea then was precisely to build regional muscle, to vet from within the claimed site that is Asia. This brings up questions about how these "peer structures" continue to take shape: what kind of disenfranchisements and/or privileging of logics continue to happen even if the telling emanates from within? Taken in this critical light, it is not at all surprising that the "curatorium" now figures prominently in the self-perpetuating circuits of perennials, triennials, biennials, and the global art fair franchises where expert referrals take the place of ground research in the mapping and surfacing of practices and discourse. These short-circuited channels, innocuously enough come framed within such pedantic strictures as must-see, must-speak to lists where the exigencies of time and tour outcomes appear to engender herd behavior. Joan Kee, writing in 2004 discerned "the implicit formation of an overclass of Asian artists monopolizing a finite amount of critical visibility."[7] Yet alongside this, what generally does not get called out is the overclass of exemplar curator-critic-historians that rein within the narrow confines of the artworld that, no matter how it might try to present itself as transnational,

still often lapses into tropes of nation and pseudo-territory often as ruse for guarding professional terrain. One can keep looking at the manifestations of this web of relationships, but one need not look too far to see how the networks are zealously policed. The originating discomfort that I found also ringing through Nelson's essay is something that I would locate in these relational contexts that seem to be temporally curated rather than cultivated for the long haul via grassroots research that might at least put up some healthy challenges to the operative monopolies of power. But really, must the region-making interminably surrender to this speed dating as opposed to drawn out encounters wherein defenses and hesitations are worked through with circumspection and untidiness?

Returning to Joan Kee's "Twenty Questions," we might again ask if the diffusion of authority in terms of both "narratives and authors"[8] has come to any degree of fruition since then, or whether we have succumbed to trading one overclass for another in entanglements with the hegemonic parades of soft power. Put another way, and in the specific case of the Philippines, has the state and its artworld agents gone for broke at the expense of spread and a healthy dissensus? As we supposedly arrived in Venice in 2015 for instance, after a half-century of non-participation, at what cost did that come? By seizing space in order to remake the worlds we look at so forlornly as dysfunctional, how much of the colonizing fervor is imbibed in this churning of occupied space?

Concretely for the Philippines, in evoking a "worldscape" through its pavilion housing "Tie a String Around the World" one might read against the grain and point to how it unwittingly plays at what it presumably challenges, for one thing, the foregone conclusion of Venice still remaining prime gatekeeper and site to be mastered if one is to count for anything. The main state backpeddler of the enterprise, perilously puts it as lodging the Philippines in the Olympics of the artworld.[9] Tragically, no curatorial contrapunto sought to finesse that pronouncement. And so, notwithstanding the cunningly framed rhetoric of staging a conversation about the reconfigurations of the global, the project's critical charge dangerously gets blunted by the logistical and political machinery that insists that this is indeed a national ticket for the global arriviste, reams and reams of text on the fraught imperial roots of the nation-state notwithstanding. Thus, as much as Manuel Conde's film *Genghis Khan*[10] summons transcendent registers beyond state territory, rituals of national ascendance continue to be enacted in Venice. Before the eyes of the world, one wears traditional Philippine dress, to the excitement of the toniest and least conscience-laden of Filipino glossies—the same *Tatler* franchise that glammed up the Marcoses' eldest, Imee Marcos, in brazen red gown. Discursively framed in the vernacular and local, as opposed to the earlier impetus to "internationalize," this Philippine Pavilion certainly cannot be faulted for facile reductionism. Take for instance curator Patrick D. Flores's conjuring Salvatore Scarpitta's work referenced by Jose Tence Ruiz's velvet textile membrane stretched across and around his room-busting installation. Causing a spectral presence of a sentry called Shoal, Ruiz's work makes up one of the two artist's projects in the pavilion. Flores notes how the folksy but luxuriant velvet "strips of cloth pass through holes in other pieces, creating a tension that widens the slit-shaped wounds." My sense, however, is that this aspired for tension invoked by alluding to the non-places of Ayungin and the Kalayaan Island Group[11] (in the case of the second project by Manny Montelibano) remains elusive. This is despite the brave charge to have the over-spill of spatial and aural encounter defy the limits of dashed lines and other constructed fortifications. The proposition of a pavilion in which Montelibano, through his overlaying of journeys taken through the Kudaman epic chant and ambient radio frequencies within range in Bataraza, harvests an otherwise un-heard soundscape off southernmost Palawan is potentially poignant. Perhaps even more so since the province has turned into a key staging point of Filipino-American training and muscle-flexing military exercises. Flores describes how Montelibano's multi-channel video, *A Dashed State*, "subtly stirs up another rip-ple in this discourse." So one tries to overlook the fact that the most fervent senatorial mediator behind the representation is the same media hound whose large scale wardrobe of indigenous weaves is rivaled only by a consistent pen-chant for switching political parties as the popular tides shift–pun very much intended. Still in his Venice Biennale catalogue essay, "All Over," curator Flores sums up the venture thus: "These artists have invested in an art practice rooted in a modernity at once worldly and committed to an ebullient locality, suffering no neurosis of the outside and not belaboring the authentic that is supposedly im-manent." Undeniably eloquently put, this however still sets off a scent of the culturati cloaking and uncloaking themselves in the robes of nation and/or re-gion whenever needed and however inconsistently with their publicly projected rhetorical sympathies. This happens elsewhere of course, and is certainly no monopoly of the artworld. Yet this doffing of hats in the direction where doors can be pried open if one agrees to place oneself in shady company to undertake validation rituals that enable a ravenously capital intensive venture that these flashy platforms have become has tragically become par for the course. While invoking China as locus of overdetermined capital, such ventures fail to reckon with how the amassed cultural capital behind the sending comes with its own soddy footprints amidst the internal wrangling for power positions in the local artworld.

Fast forward to 2016 when ASEAN through the ten-country Film Asean Foun-dation and through the triumphalist words of filmmaker and Film Development Association of the Philippines head, Briccio Santos, sets the stage for the craft-ing of narratives that "depict the ways of life of the Asean communities." Predict-ably premised on the logic of shared costs, how might such a clunky regional body actually navigate through the choppy waters that literally flow through Asia? Given ASEAN's consistently non-committal, take-it-elsewhere stance for instance on the multi-country wrangling over the South China (our West

Philippine) sea, will China's remaining regional allies in ASEAN craft space for the counter-narratives of less militarily mighty and certainly lower rung trade partners? How compelling and nuanced could an ASEAN-collaborated film, for instance, become in light of this prevalent tiptoeing over national and regional economic futures? How might this further the momentum of the first-off Martin Gropius Bau venue at the European Film Market that is part of the Berlinale? Santos still longingly looks to Cannes as the next site to stage this rose-colored imaginary, seemingly impervious to the undeniably fierce and escalating jostling for position, resources, and patrimony in the imagined zone of détente that is Asia. Rather than leave you with the sense that this story begins and ends with the Marcoses and other sordid alignments, I would say that I do hope that I am mistaken about perceiving these alliances as mere means to completing transactions that dangerously teeter toward recolonizing rather than decolonizing privileged sites where we only delude ourselves into thinking we are much more benign than we really are. When the "curatorium," however poignantly and intelligently, engages in world-making with nary a regard of its own hubris and savvy pontifications spewed inwardly and outwardly, which quarters in the shrinking commons would summon the gall to speak? Perhaps those of us repeatedly implicated in the contested spaces wherein our work proceeds might step off the milk train a bit, readily accept how less than invincible we actually are, and then at least attempt to account for how the predatory structures of making art have forged our contaminated existences within the layered skirts of critical practice.

1   Roger Nelson, "Pathways in Performance (in and around Cambodia)?" in "The Place of Performance," ed. Hendrik Folkerts and Sophie Berrebi, special issue, *Stedelijk Studies*, no. 3 (2016).

2   Reference to the 1974 launching of the Folk Arts Center in Manila is taken from the archives of the Kalaw Ledesma Foundation, Manila.

3   Excerpt from Imelda Marcos's speech delivered at the Folk Arts Theater inaugural; text published in the *Daily Express*, July 9, 1974.

4   Excerpt from Carlos P. Romulo's speech, *Daily Express*, July 9, 1974.

5   Talk delivered at Green Papaya Art Projects, May 17, 2016.

6   C. J. Wee Wan-ling, "We Asians? Modernity, Visual Art Exhibitions and East Asia," *Boundary* 2 (Spring 2010): 23, 120.

7   Joan Kee, "Twenty Questions" in *Positions: East Asia Cultures Critique* 12, no. 3 (2004): 604.

8   Ibid., 609.

9   See http://lorenlegarda.com.ph/after-51-years-phl-returns-to-art-worlds-olympics-venice-biennale/; a press story subsequently reprinted in Philippines mainstream networks.

10  The entire Philippine presentation consisted of the film *Genghis Khan* by National Artist Manuel Conde alongside installations by Jose Tence Ruiz and Manny Montelibano. The film itself was proffered as the center of the installation.

11  These are among the Philippine islands in the midst of contending claims between China and the Philippines.

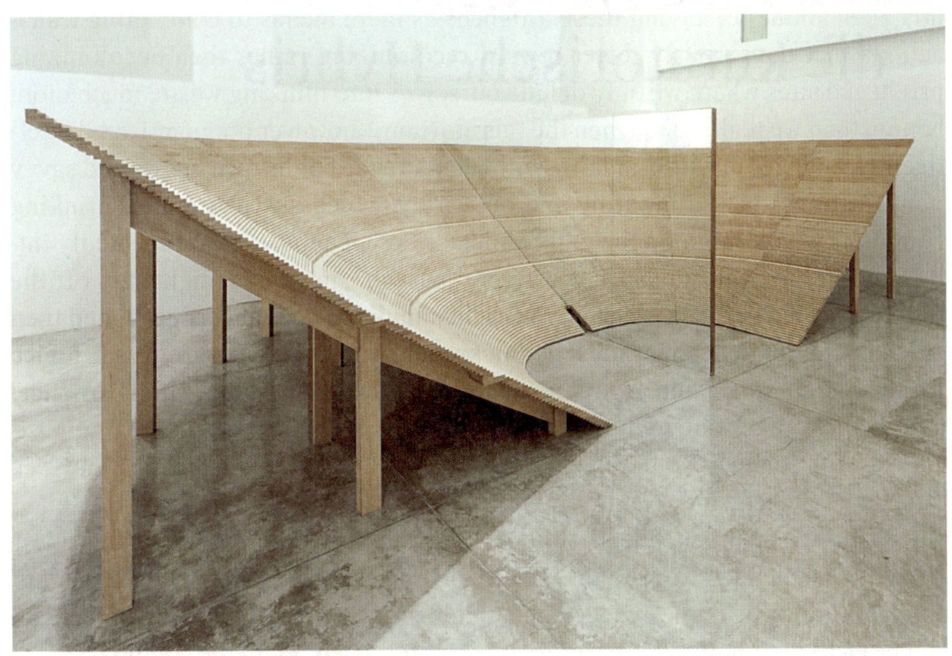

Paul Pfeiffer
*Vitruvian Figure*, 2015
Museum of Contemporary Art and Design
Manila, Philippines

Eileen Legaspi-Ramirez

# Südostasien im Zwischenboden.
# Ein Plädoyer gegen die kuratorische Hybris

Dieser Text, das will ich gleich vorausschicken, ist dem wachsenden Unbehagen geschuldet, das ich angesichts der besorgniserregenden Kontinuitäten einer Vergangenheit empfinde, von der man sich in der Kunstwelt ständig lossagt, und das ich angesichts der Leute habe, die trotz der zahlreichen Kongresse und internationalen Konferenzen zum Thema südostasiatische Kunst auf der Strecke geblieben sind. Natürlich haben die Curatorial Studies global gesehen ein paar vielversprechende Diskursfronten aufgemacht oder sich zumindest einigen bestehenden zugewandt. Dennoch würde ich behaupten, dass – anders als das Kuratoriat immer wieder behauptet – in den meisten Bereichen jenseits (aber auch innerhalb) dieser in sich geschlossenen Welt die Demokratisierung wissensproduzierender Strukturen und der vermeintliche Abschied von der Nationalstaatsform, der künstlerischen Moderne und dem Fetisch Differenz eher Wunschbild als Wirklichkeit sind.

Es gehört zum unmittelbaren Entstehungszusammenhang dieses Essays, dass es seit ein paar Jahren einen gewissen (recht unterschiedlich wahrgenommenen) Hype um AkademikerInnen und KünstlerInnen aus und in Südostasien gibt. Dieses Phänomen umfasst sämtliche Kunst- und Kulturinstitutionen und läuft oft darauf hinaus, dass von ForscherInnen und Kreativen erwartet wird, sich doch bitte mit Asien auseinanderzusetzen, gerade jetzt, da sich im Rahmen der ASEAN-Wirtschaftsgemeinschaft alle Mitgliedsstaaten den Austausch groß auf die Fahnen geschrieben haben. Die ASEAN ist einer der vielen regionalen und überregionalen Wirtschaftsblöcke, die in den letzten Jahrzehnten entstanden sind, um Handelsbeschränkungen abzubauen und nationalstaatliche Einmischung in den grenzüberschreitenden Personen- und Güterverkehr weitgehend zu unterbinden. Die zehn Mitgliedstaaten der ASEAN (Brunei, Kambodscha, Indonesien, Laos, Malaysia, Myanmar, die Philippinen, Singapur, Thailand, Vietnam) versprechen sich durch den besseren Ressourcenfluss Mehreinnahmen in Höhe von 2,6 Billionen US-Dollar. Man geht wie selbstverständlich davon aus, dass die Einzelinteressen in dieser Freihandelszone konvergieren werden, damit 622 Millionen Menschen ein riesiges Volumen an Gütern, Dienstleistungen sowie Kapital hin- und herschieben und sich selbst beziehungsweise ihre Arbeitskraft zu Markte tragen können.

Man hat der ASEAN immer wieder vorgeworfen, sie sei letztlich ein zahnloser Tiger, da sie über keinerlei Sanktionsmacht verfüge und vor allem damit beschäftigt sei, den größtenteils illusionären Eindruck von Geschlossenheit zu vermitteln. Innerhalb der KuratorInnenszene hat sich zudem herausgestellt, dass auch in Zeiten der Globalisierung epistemologische Verschiebungen nicht ohne weiteres Grenzen überwinden, auch wenn viele der Versuchung erliegen, ganze Weltregionen dem interessierten Publikum als All-Inclusive-Paket zu verscherbeln. Dahinter steht die Vorstellung, dass die Kanäle, über die die globalisierten ökonomischen Transaktionen laufen, sich problemlos für die Kulturvermittlung nutzen lassen. So wird Kunst instrumentalisiert, wie beispielsweise der Katalog zur Ausstellung *Traditions/Tensions*, die 1996 von der Asia Society organisiert wurde, eindrücklich zeigt. Treibende Kraft hinter der Ausstellungspublikation war der thailändische Künstler-Kurator Apinan Poshyananda, der mittlerweile ganz offiziell als Staatsdiener auftritt. Die Ausstellung (mitsamt ihrem begrifflichen Überbau) hat sich als perfektes Schmiermittel für diese Karriere erwiesen. Knapp zwanzig Jahre danach hat die Frage, wie wir als Individuen der ASEAN begegnen und ob wir es als unsere Aufgabe betrachten, gleichsam Kunst zu diplomatischen Zwecken einzusetzen oder vielmehr jeden Versuch in diese Richtung vereiteln sollten, nichts von ihrer Aktualität verloren. Wenn ich mich bei der Erörterung dieser Frage immer wieder auf das Performanz-Paradigma beziehe, dann soll das keineswegs heißen, dass ich die Arbeit von KunsthistorikerInnen, KuratorInnen und KünstlerInnen als bloßen Vorwand abtue oder ihr eine reine Feigenblattfunktion zuschreibe. Für mich verweist die Art der Inszenierung vielmehr auf eine behutsame Form der Subjektivierung und eine kontingente Art der Selbstidentifikation. Bisweilen wird sie als markerschütternd erlebt, dann wieder nur unterschwellig.

Wenn ich auf Tagungen oder kleinere Konferenzen zum Thema Asien oder Südostasien gehe, fällt mir auf, dass zu den Höflichkeitsritualen mittlerweile auch gehört, ein paar knappe Angaben zur eigenen Herkunft zu machen und grob einzuordnen, welche Rolle Kunst im jeweiligen gesellschaftspolitischen Kontext und der sozialen Vorstellungswelt spielt. Heutzutage gibt man sich gern unabhängig, die eigene Staatsangehörigkeit wird heruntergespielt, das sei doch lediglich ein Verwaltungsakt, eine Information, die im Pass verzeichnet ist und die man vielleicht noch im Programm der Konferenz der Vollständigkeit halber erwähnt. Man tut so, als ließe sich die Staatsangehörigkeit einfach abschütteln und vergisst darüber geflissentlich die eigene Verwicklung in strukturelle Probleme wie Klasse, Ethnie, Geschlecht, Religion. Bei vielen, die an der Geschichte der modernen und zeitgenössischen Kunst in Südostasien fortwährend mitschreiben, hat man das Gefühl, sie halten Identität, wenn nicht für ein Wegwerfprodukt, so doch für einen Mantel, den man bei Bedarf abstreifen kann, da es sich im Grunde um ein Hirngespinst handelt. Stattdessen *performt* man lieber Südostasien, ein identitäres Gemisch, das kurzfristig berauschend wirkt, aber langfristig durchaus toxische Effekte haben kann.

Körper, unsere Körper, sind in Bewegung, sie gehen auf Veranstaltungen, auf Konferenzen, die aus irgendwelchen Projekten hervorgehen, sie besuchen Ausstellungen. Für dieses Spiel muss man gewappnet sein, immer wieder kommt es zu Kollisionen, man legt andere auf ihre Positionen fest oder enthüllt eine versteckte Agenda. Der Wunsch, sich ausführlicher einer Region zu widmen, geht nicht selten mit dem großspurigen Anspruch einher, eine Person oder ein Gebiet zum nächsten großen Ding hochzujubeln. Das kann sich ganz verschieden äußern. Wie reagiert man darauf? Pauschale Übereinstimmung, stilles Mitläufertum, Sabotage all der Netzwerke, die dem Austausch unter KünstlerInnen und AkademikerInnen dienen können, aber nicht müssen – oder lässt man die Annäherungsversuche der Großregion schlicht unerwidert? Die Kreisläufe, die Asien performativ hervorbringen sollen, beruhen auf der Forderung, gewisse Aspekte von Subjektivität zurückzufahren, sonst ist man bei den wirklich interessanten Debatten der Gegenwart schnell außen vor. Aus taktischen Gründen werden bestimmte Gesichtspunkte und theoretische Wahlverwandtschaften – Stichwort: Differenzdenken – hervorgehoben, während andere, die sich nicht so leicht mit dem Diskurs der Stunde in Übereinstimmung bringen lassen oder als Gesprächsthemen zu polarisierend sind, heruntergespielt werden. Melani Budianta brachte diesbezüglich während eines auf der Konferenz Making Southeast Asia: From Region to World gehaltenen Vortrages ihre Skepsis zum Ausdruck, der ich nur zustimmen kann. Vieles von dem, was ich hier sagen möchte, ist denkbar ungeeignet für die triumphalistische Rhetorik, die man in der südostasiatischen Kunstwelt derzeit vernimmt. Letztere scheint ohnehin weniger symbolischen als pekuniären Bedürfnissen zu entspringen. Auf gutnachbarschaftliches Verhalten können sich alle einigen, gerade wenn es gilt, als Individuum unter Einsatz der eigenen Ellbogen seinen Platz in einem gut gefüllten diskursiven Raum zu finden, in dem jede Meinungsverschiedenheit, wenn sie denn überhaupt als solche benannt wird, schnell hinter dem *Cordon sanitaire* einer vermeintlichen, immer wieder beschworenen, aber nicht unbedingt funktionierenden Interessengemeinschaft verschwindet.


## Die Wandlungen der Partizipationslogik

Wir denken zu wenig darüber nach, wie flüchtige Netzwerke hochgradig fluider, auf kreativer Praxis basierender Beziehungen die diskursive Konstruktion einer Region ganz wesentlich beeinflussen. Der vorliegende Beitrag untersucht, wie die AkteurInnen der Kunstwelt parallel zum politischen und wirtschaftlichen Einigungsprozess Südostasiens an dieser regionalen Neuvermessung auf institutionellen, aber auch quasi- und gegeninstitutionellen Wegen mitwirken. „Pathways in Performance: in and around Cambodia?", ein Essay des in Kambodscha arbeitenden Kurators und Kunsttheoretikers Roger Nelson, hat für ein solches Vorgehen einen wichtigen Grundstein gelegt.[1] Nelson befasst sich darin mit einigen ausgewählten Projekten von KünstlerInnen und Kulturschaffenden, die sich der totalisierenden Logik regionaler Konstruktionsprozesse völlig unterordnen, sich zwischenzeitlich mit ihr arrangieren oder sie offen in Frage stellen und zumindest versuchsweise die nur selten problematisierte Vorstellung einer Region der Ähnlichkeiten kritisieren. Nelsons Essay, der sich nuanciert mit der Geschichte und Eigendynamik der Orte, auf die er sich bezieht, auseinandersetzt, versinnbildlicht nichtsdestotrotz eine „Diplomatie-Performanz", die ihr eigenes Unbehagen verschweigt, wenn es nur der guten Sache dient. Er konzentriert sich vor allem auf das Regime des kambodschanischen Monarchen Norodom Sihanouk (1922–2012), aber man würde zu ähnlichen Ergebnissen kommen, wenn man sich genauer ansähe, wie philippinische KünstlerInnen, HistorikerInnen, KuratorInnen und TheoretikerInnen unter dem Diktator Ferdinand Marcos, eine maskenhaft-gefällige Konformität zu verkörpern und sich raffiniert in das Spiel mit der Kultur einzufügen hatten. Für Nelson sind es die kleinen Unterschiede und Abweichungen in diesen „Performances" von Nationalismus und Regionalismus, die als notwendiges Korrektiv zur vermeintlichen Abschaffung der Ungleichheit in den Begegnungen mit den „Anderen" aus dieser imaginierten Region gesehen werden müssen. Nelsons Studie konfrontiert uns mit Fragen zur Wirksamkeit der Ethik und der Ethik der Wirksamkeit, die – an anderer Stelle – einer eingehenderen Untersuchung bedürften.

Als erste Fallstudie möchte ich *Kasaysayan ng Lahi* (Geschichte der Rasse) heranziehen, eine staatlich orchestrierte Performance historischer Grandeur, die zur Eröffnung des philippinischen Folk Arts Theater 1974 aufgeführt wurde.[2] Sie veranschaulicht nicht nur, wie ernst es dem Marcos-Regime mit seinem gesamtasiatischen Engagement war, sondern zeigt auch, wie akribisch und anspruchsvoll dieses Engagement in Szene gesetzt – wir würden heute sagen: kuratiert – wurde.

### Erster Fall: *Kasaysayan ng Lahi*: Choreografie der Beziehungen (1974)

Die Schulkinder wurden extra mit Bussen angekarrt, damit sie der zweistündigen Parade, die entlang der Bucht vorbei zog, aus nächster Nähe beiwohnen konnten. Sie sahen ein gigantisches Spektakel, eine Mischung aus Historienpanorama und Tableau vivant, in dem 3000 Menschen die Geschichte der Philippinen von der Steinzeit bis zu Marcos' neuer Gesellschaft nachstellten. Zu jener Zeit folgte eine pompöse Veranstaltung der nächsten, man denke nur an die aufwendige Eröffnung des Cultural Center of the Philippines. Berühmte Persönlichkeiten wie der mexikanische Künstler Rufino Tamayo wurden ins Land geholt, einer von vielen, die mit einem Preis im Folk Arts Center ausgezeichnet wurden. Ein weiterer hochrangiger Gast war der in Yogyakarta lebende Affandi, den die First Lady Imelda Marcos persönlich eingeladen hatte, noch ganz unter dem ästhetisch inspirierenden Eindruck einer fünftägigen Reise zu den Tempelanlagen von Borobudur. Performance stand im Zentrum ihres frisch entdeckten Interesses für Kultur, wie sie selbst einräumte:

> Der Filipino trug über Jahrhunderte eine Maske, um seine Eroberer zu verwirren. Als die Zeit kam, die Maske abzunehmen, weil sie nicht mehr gebraucht wurde, bemerkte er, dass sie zu einem Teil seines Gesichts geworden war. Es ist das wohl eindrücklichste Bild unserer Identitätskrise [...] Wir erinnerten uns zwar noch an die Leidenschaften, aber diese lebten seit Jahrhunderten im Exil, sie gingen verschütt unter der Hülle geborgter Formen.[3]

Der damalige Außenminister Carlos P. Romulo wiederum gab dieser Erklärung eine ganz eigene, universalistische und populistische Wendung, sie war nun – wie ich meine – Ausdruck einer Abwehrhaltung, eines Minderwertigkeitskomplexes in Anbetracht der Tatsache, dass die Philippinen keine Tempelanlagen vorzuweisen haben, die so komplex und imposant wären wie die der Nachbarvölker:

> Hier auf dieser modernen Akropolis am Meer ist ein neuer Parthenon entstanden. Möge durch diese jungfräulichen Gefilde ein Festzug wandern, der das Gewand der Athene der [philippinischen] Nation übergibt. Möge dieser von atemberaubender Schönheit sein und dem Betrachter fortwährend Freude bereiten. Möge in diesem Land, dem Tempel der Minerva gleich, die Weisheit und Kultur der Vielen zusammenkommen – all der Völker, die diese liebreizenden Inseln bewohnen und sie der Ewigkeit vermachen. Lasst diese Völker, die gestern noch auf Wasser schrieben und auf Sand bauten, von nun an feste Türme auf diesem Fundament erbauen. Es gilt, eine neue Gesellschaft zu errichten; es gilt, eine neue Zivilisation zu erschaffen.[4]

## Zweiter Fall: documenta 12, Asia Speaks Up, Kassel (2007)

Nach dieser Massenveranstaltung möchte ich nun auf ein kleines Treffen von RedakteurInnen südostasiatischer Magazine und Zeitschriften zu sprechen kommen, die sich 2006 im Rahmen der regionalen Initiative Comparative Contemporaries zusammengetan hatten (leider ist diese Initiative inzwischen etwas eingeschlafen). Dieses Treffen fand im Kunstraum The Substation in Singapur statt und war eine von zahlreichen Veranstaltungen, die im Vorfeld der documenta 12 auf der documenta Magazines-Plattform auf die Beine gestellt wurden. Ich nahm als Redakteurin der Zeitschrift *Pananaw. Philippine Journal of Contemporary Arts* teil, die zu einer Reihe von internationalen kunstjournalistischen Veranstaltungen (in Singapur, New York und Kassel) eingeladen worden war. Die Kollaboration zwischen internationalen Kunstmagazinen sollte wenigstens oberflächlich den Anschein von Inklusivität erwecken, den man bei den überwiegend eurozentrischen Ausstellungen in Kassel ansonsten vermisste. Die südostasiatische Abordnung bestand aus Publikationen wie den Webzine-Portalen *Kakiseni, Talawas, Ctrl+P* und *Midnight University, Kalam, Karbon, Kunci* und der *Cemeti Art Foundation* aus Indonesien, *Sentap* und *Off the Edge* aus Malaysia, *FOCAS, Vehicle* aus Singapur und *Dushu* aus China, dessen Team bei den früheren Treffen nicht anwesend war, aber einen kurzen Auftritt in Kassel hatte. Es gab eine grobe Themenvorgabe, doch letztendlich diente sie vor allem dazu, sich darüber klar zu werden, was in der Schlusssitzung in Kassel während der 100-tägigen documenta auf uns zukommen würde.

*d12 Magazines* wurde als Magazin der Magazine angekündigt. Alle Teilnehmer-Innen wurden dazu ermuntert, Kontakte mit anderen teilnehmenden Magazinen anzubahnen. Auf Grundlage dieser Plattform konnten die RedakteurInnen Inhalte „kuratieren", die sich an den Leitthemen der documenta – das nackte Leben, Bildung (was kann getan werden?) und schließlich der Frage, ob die Moderne unser Altertum ist – orientierten. Wie konnten wir in diesem babylonischen Gewusel überhaupt zueinander finden (denn es gab kein Geld für Dolmetscher)? Derartige Projektideen lassen sich bis zum Beginn des Jahrtausends zurück-verfolgen, als The Substation 2002 und 2003 die IFIMA-Konferenzen (International Forum for InterMedia Art) zu sozial engagierter künstlerischer Praxis und vergleichenden Studien des Zeitgenössischen ins Leben rief.

Auf europäischen Veranstaltungen wird Asien häufig als *Tabula rasa* wahr-genommen. Die OrganisatorInnen bemühen sich wacker um eine gewisse Band-breite unter den TeilnehmerInnen, die den Anforderungen der *Diversität* genüge tun soll. Sie sind jedoch auf gut gemeinte Hinweise von ein paar KollegInnen angewiesen, damit es zu einem – planlosen und wie zufällig zustande gekom-menen – Austausch kommen kann. Das Netzwerk, das für diese Unterfangen aktiviert wird, soll möglichst kritisch gegenüber allen möglichen Facetten des Neoliberalismus sein. Grundkenntnisse all der Ideen und Thesen, die für das Ge-lingen dieser Zusammenkünfte beitragen könnten, sind ausdrücklich erwünscht. Wer regelmäßig an diesen Konferenzen teilnimmt, weiß, dass es manchmal mit einer Präsentation zu Rancière schon getan ist. Im nächsten Jahr bietet sich viel-leicht etwas zu Bourriaud, Kester oder Bishop an. Wie wär's mit folgender Frage: Welchen Widersprüchen sind kollektive Initiativen heute ausgesetzt? In jüngster Zeit waren Allgemeingut (*Commons*) und das Anthropozän ziemliche Kassen-schlager. Die am Magazines-Projekt beteiligten MitarbeiterInnen waren ständig darauf bedacht, den Gesprächsfaden auch in der Zukunft nicht abreißen zu lassen. Schließlich war es erst die documenta, die uns alle an einen Tisch ge-bracht hatte. Es bot sich die Gelegenheit, die Grenzen des Nationalen endlich hinter sich zu lassen. In dieser Atmosphäre der Unvertrautheit gediehen die Diskussionen immer dann prächtig, wenn sie von typischen Klischees ausgingen (Prägt das imperiale amerikanische Erbe auch die postkolonialen Philippinen?).

Aus diesem Austausch gingen ein paar wenige, aber umso wertvollere und anhaltende Partnerschaften hervor, anderes wiederum hätte man sich komplett sparen können.

Zum ersten Mal erfolgte so etwas wie eine Annäherung über Länder- und Institutionengrenzen hinweg. Wir im d12-Projekt waren keine politischen Naivlinge. Beim allerersten Treffen in Singapur war unser Kollege von *Staintet* aus Myanmar sichtlich nervös und vermied es tunlichst, das Wort zu ergreifen – aus Angst, jemand könnte mitschreiben. Denn es durfte nicht publik werden, dass er das Land verlassen hatte. Ein informeller und in vielerlei Hinsicht unfertiger und vielstimmiger Kreis fand sich. Am Ende dieses Prozesses haben wir uns etwa eine Woche lang in einen Innenraum der documenta-Halle buchstäblich verkrochen, um schließlich dem Publikum eines öffentlichen d12-Luncheons vorgeführt zu werden. Die Veranstaltung hieß Asia Speaks Up, auf der Tagesordnung standen die nach wie vor unsichere Menschenrechtslage in einigen Ländern und das Problem der Zensur – das war der thematische Zwischenboden, der für Südostasien vorgesehen war und in dem es für Kunst kaum Platz gab. Wir versuchten trotzdem unser Bestes.

Die documenta 12 war zu Ende. Kurze Zeit später wurden RedakteurInnen der Midnight University in Changmai zum Schweigen gebracht und mithilfe des in Thailand verhängten Kriegsrechts wegen Majestätsbeleidigung angeklagt. Ich musste an Joan Kees' Text zu Hans Ulrich Obrists *New Utopia* aus dem Jahr 2004 denken, in dem sie beschreibt, wie sich die Künstlerinnen Lee Bul und Mariko Mori die ihnen gegenüber vorgebrachte Kritik, sie seien alles andere als mustergültige Staatsbürgerinnen, zu eigen machten, um sich in der globalen Diskursarena umso besser positionieren zu können. Sie spielten mit einem Raum, der ihnen eine neue Mobilität gestattete – oder war das schon Anbiederung? Der zusammengewürfelte Haufen von KunstredakteurInnen, die sich auf der documenta trafen, hat pflichtgemäß Position gegen das Gesetz der eisernen Faust bezogen, auf dessen Grundlage unsere PolitikerInnen regieren und uns klein halten wollen, doch noch Jahre später bleibt das ungute Gefühl, womöglich nicht alles getan zu haben, um der Welt der Kunst, in deren Namen wir ebenso sprachen, zu ihrem Recht zu verhelfen. Gegen die rigorose Zensur konnten wir praktisch nichts ausrichten. Einer anderen Sisyphusarbeit sollten wir uns allerdings nicht verweigern. Wir müssen den vorgefassten Meinungen von KuratorInnen und AusstellungsmacherInnen etwas entgegensetzen, wenn sie Asien reflexhaft auf das Problem der Menschenrechtsverletzungen reduzieren. Bleibt die Frage, welchen Bewegungsspielraum wir in einem öffentlichen Raum haben, wo jeder mit fraglichen Mitteln versucht, sich einem westlichen Publikum anzubiedern?

Dritter Fall: *WE=ME* oder: Bau' dir dein Asien, Bangkok (2013)
Kurze Zeit später fand eine andere, ziemlich bescheidene, doch dieses Mal ungeniert offiziöse Veranstaltung am Silpakorn University Art Centre statt. Das Motto lautete: *WE=ME, Appreciate Differen.ce* Bei dieser von Paramaporn

Sirikulchayanont kuratierten ASEAN-Ausstellung mit begleitender Konferenz kamen KünstlerInnen, KuratorInnen, Kunststudierende und-dozentInnen aus Brunei, Kambodscha, Indonesien, Laos, Malaysia, Myanmar, von den Philippinen, Singapur, Vietnam, Thailand und-als einziger Nicht-ASEAN-Staat-China zusammen. Während der etwas peinliche thematische Slogan sich in den ausgestellten Werken nicht direkt widerspiegelte (Imhathai Suwattanasilps Fotos, die, um nur ein Beispiel zu nennen, von aufwendig gehäkelten Haarbüscheln umgeben waren, injizierten dankenswerterweise eine gehörige Dosis Skurrilität in das ansonsten dominierende und gelegentlich überladene Identitätsthema), ließ sich nicht leugnen, dass sich eine gewisse Wohlfühlstimmung in den Ausstellungshallen breitmachte. Das Signal war deutlich genug zu vernehmen: Das hier ist nicht der Ort, um Intoleranz, geopolitische Instabilität oder umstrittenen Ansprüche auf Seegebiete zu diskutieren. Inwieweit diese Atmosphäre den Intentionen des Ausstellungsmachers entsprach, weiß ich nicht, aber sie war symptomatisch für die lustlos vorgetragenen Pathosformeln, die Gemeinsamkeit beschwören sollten und ein politisches Projekt-das der ASEAN-verfolgen, in dem „die eigene Kultur zur Kultur aller wird". Die Schattenseiten dieses utopischen Fahrplans Richtung Zukunft kamen zum Vorschein, als auf der Konferenz die informellen Diskussionen begannen. Es war für mich eine einschneidende Erfahrung, als ein älterer thailändischer Künstler „seine" Kunst von dem, was er verächtlich Chatuchak-Kunst nannte (und in seinem Tonfall schwang Verachtung mit für die jungen, noch nicht arrivierten KünstlerInnen, so als ob sie ihre „erschwinglichen Werke" feilböten), unterschieden wissen wollte. Das war also übriggeblieben vom Traum der Avantgarde, die Trennung von Kunst und Leben in die Geschichtsbücher zu verbannen. Das war also übriggeblieben vom inspirierenden Versuch, den Gegensatz von Kunst und Kunsthandwerk zu überwinden. Ich biss mir auf die Zunge und verließ schweigend den Raum.

Ich muss gestehen, dass mir bis dahin gar nicht bewusst war, wie effizient Konflikte und Kontroversen auf diesen Podiumsdiskussionen tatsächlich verdrängt werden. Eine in Asien tätige australische Journalistin legte ebenfalls den Finger in die Wunde, als sie sich öffentlich wunderte, wie es denn bei dieser Veranstaltung um den asiatischen-pazifischen Raum stehe, denn Australien wurde mit keinem Moment erwähnt. In der Psychoanalyse würde man von einer Verwerfung sprechen. Solche räumlichen Zeitgenossenschaften lassen sich möglicherweise am ehesten auf informellem Wege herstellen, im offenen Austausch und aus wechselseitiger Sympathie. Das zumindest schien David Teh in seinem Vortrag „Whither art history? Institutions, curatorship and the undead nation state" nahezulegen, den er kürzlich am Green Papaya Art Projects in Manila hielt.[5] In Zusammenhängen, die sich eher über Netzwerke von KünstlerInnen ergeben, sind die Zugangskontrollen weniger hart. Dass das interessante Nebenwege eröffnet leuchtet mir ein, weil es im kleineren Maßstab viel mehr barrierefreie Zonen gibt, mehr MitstreiterInnen, mehr Orte und viel mehr Möglichkeiten zu navigieren und sich einzubringen.

Vierter Fall: *Concept, Context, Contestation*, Bangkok (2013–2014)

Doch der Rückzug ins Lokale und die Betonung vermeintlicher örtlicher Eigenarten bergen neue Risiken. Im Jahr darauf kehrte ich nach Bangkok zurück, um an einem Symposium teilzunehmen, das im Rahmen der Ausstellung *Concept, Context, Contestation: Art and the Collective in Southeast Asia* stattfand, die von Iola Lenzi, Agung Hujatnikajennong und Vipash Purichanont im Bangkok Art and Culture Centre (BACC) kuratiert wurde. Der Pressetext ließ keine Zweifel daran, dass die Macher der Meinung waren, „dass die Begrifflichkeit der zeitgenössischen südostasiatischen Kunst nicht zwangsläufig importiert ist, sondern ihren Ursprung in der heimischen Kultur haben kann". Ich dachte über diese rückwärtsgewandte Haltung nach und fragte mich, ob derartige Behauptungen nicht genauso problematisch sind wie die gefällige Kunstwelttheorieprosa, die sie kritisiert. Die Truppe war so bunt wie stets (mit Gästen aus Singapur, Indonesien, Thailand, Myanmar, Kambodscha, Malaysia und Vietnam). Man stritt für eine neue Idee des Kollektivs, während draußen vor der Tür die Rot- und Gelbhemden um jeden Meter Straße kämpften. Das BACC sah sich aufgrund der Blockade gezwungen, sein Programm solange auszusetzen, bis die Besetzer-Innen ihren Widerstand aufgaben. Ich gab mir alle Mühe, den Wert des Individuums, das nicht mit dem Individualismus identisch ist, gegen essenzialistische Verklärungen des Kollektivs und den daraus resultierenden verengten Politikbegriff zu verteidigen – es war ein Kampf gegen Windmühlen. Es gab beträchtliche redaktionelle Eingriffe in meinen Katalogtext. Meine Worte verhallten nicht nur ungehört, man wollte mich gänzlich zum Verstummen bringen, zumindest war das die Angst, die ich verspürte, als ich die Kürzungen das erste Mal sah. Ich kann der leidenschaftlich verfochtenen Grundidee des Projekts durchaus etwas abgewinnen: Asien steht für eine spezifische Vorstellung des Sozialen. Aber mir geisterten noch Budiantas Überlegungen zum Handeln unter Bedingungen der Kontingenz im Kopf umher. Wer sich auf diese Weise auf Asien beruft, setzt einiges aufs Spiel, ohne sich dessen unbedingt bewusst zu sein.

Zurück zur Nation: Innenansichten der kuratorischen Rhetorik

Es gibt nach wie vor kritische, avantgardistische Positionen, die sich auf das Hype-Thema Südostasien beziehen, ohne dass man deswegen gleich Ausverkauf schreien müsste, auch wenn diese Leute um ihre Abhängigkeit von gewissen Gönnern wissen. Liest man C. J. Wees Essay „We Asia?", kann man nachvollziehen, wie um die Jahrtausendwende die Japan Foundation „einen anderen Einigungsprozess" organisierte: „ein im Entstehen befindliches [kuratorisches] Netzwerk, das über den als ‚Asien' bekannten, geografischen Rahmen hinausgeht und weltweit Mitglieder hinzugewinnt." Dieses multikulturelle, asiatische Kuratorium war ein Schritt hin zu einem polyzentrischen, globalen Zusammenhalt.[6] Man wollte Strukturen abschaffen, die als rein äußerlich betrachtet wurden und Asien entweder völlig ignorierten oder es für ihre eigenen Zwecke einspannten. Offensichtlich bestand die Idee darin, regionale Kräfte zu bündeln, um von innen heraus diesen sagenumwobenen Ort namens Asien unter die Lupe zu nehmen. Welche „Peer-Strukturen" bilden sich dabei heraus? Wer kommt zum Zug, wer wird an den Rand gedrängt? Diese Fragen stellen sich auch und gerade, wenn die Innenperspektive eingenommen wird. So überrascht es nicht, dass dieses Kuratoriat zu einer wichtigen Größe geworden und auf zahlreichen Ausstellungen, Triennalen, Biennalen und auf der ganzen Welt verteilten Kunstmessen-Ablegern präsent ist. ExpertInnen entscheiden über den Zutritt, KennerInnen der lokalen Szene sind ins Hintertreffen geraten. Es gibt Vorgaben, Listen von Kunstwerken, die man gesehen, und Menschen, mit denen man gesprochen haben muss. Zeit- und Erfolgsdruck verstärken den Herdentrieb. 2004 beobachtete Joan Kee „die implizite Bildung einer [neuen] Oberschicht asiatischer Künstler, die kritische Aufmerksamkeit, eine begrenzte Ressource, für sich allein in Beschlag nimmt."[7] Doch daneben gibt es die oft übersehene Oberschicht der KuratorInnen-KritikerInnen-HistorikerInnen, die im kleinen Königreich der Kunstwelt herrschen und denen – ungeachtet des transnationalen Gehabes – niemand erklären muss, wie sich nationale Strukturen für den Kampf um Diskursterritorien und symbolisches Kapital nutzen lassen. Sie haben ein dichtes Beziehungsnetzwerk gesponnen, bei dem man schnell feststellt, dass nicht jeder dazugehört. Das Unbehagen darüber zieht sich auch durch den eingangs zitierten Essay von Nelson. Beziehungen werden eine Zeit lang kuratiert und kultiviert. Langfristige Bemühungen um den Aufbau horizontaler Strukturen, welche die Machtmonopole in der Kunstwelt aufbrechen könnten, sucht man vergebens. Aber mal ehrlich, um eine regionale Identität zu schaffen, braucht es mehr als professionelles Speed-Dating. Wären nicht längerfristige Treffen geeigneter, bei denen Abwehrhaltungen und Unsicherheiten umsichtig und vorurteilsfrei diskutiert werden könnten?

Um noch einmal auf Joan Kees „Twenty Questions" zurückzukommen, ließe sich fragen, ob „die Aussaat von Autorität über Erzählungen und Autoren" seitdem irgendwelche Früchte getragen hat, oder ob wir durch eigene Verstrickungen und angesichts der endlosen Inszenierungen von Soft Power lediglich eine Oberschicht durch eine andere ersetzt haben.[8] Im Hinblick auf die Philippinen heißt das: Haben der Staat und seine Repräsentanten in der Kunstwelt alles auf eine Karte gesetzt und darüber die Vielfalt und eine lebhafte Kultur des Dissens geopfert? 2015 war das Land nach einem halben Jahrhundert das erste Mal wieder in Venedig vertreten – doch zu welchem Preis? Wir erobern uns einen Platz zurück, um der westlichen Öffentlichkeit mit fast schon kolonialistischem Eifer zu zeigen, wie dysfunktional die Räume sind, in denen man unsere Herkunft verortet.

So könnte man die „Weltlandschaft" in *Tie a String Around the World*, die im philippinischen Pavillon ausgestellt war, entgegen der von ihr bekundeten Absichten lesen und herausarbeiten, wie sehr sie unwillentlich dem, was sie ablehnt, in die Hände spielt. Venedig hat nach wie vor eine wichtige Gatekeeper-Funktion. Dort muss man präsent sein, um als etwas zu gelten. Die staatliche

Verantwortliche für den Auswahlprozess sprach dann bezeichnenderweise auch von den „Olympischen Spielen der Kunstwelt".[9] Leider gab es keinen kuratorischen Kontrapunkt, der auf diese Bemerkung reagierte. All die Schaumschlägerei, all das Geschwätz von globaler Neuausrichtung, all die Hinweise auf die kritische Haltung des Kunstwerkes werden übertönt vom Lärm einer logistischen und politischen Maschinerie, die sicherstellt, dass hier gerade einem nationalen Emporkömmling Zugang zur Weltbühne verschafft wird (woran die zahlreichen gut gemeinten Texte über die imperialen und imperialistischen Ursprünge des Nationalstaats nichts ändern). In Venedig werden nationale Aufstiegsfantasien ausagiert, da mag Manuel Condes Film *Genghis Khan* noch so eindrücklich auf Politik jenseits staatlicher Territorien dringen.[10] Vor den Augen der Weltöffentlichkeit trägt man traditionelle philippinische Kleidung, übrigens zum Entzücken des philippinischen *Tatler*, einem reißerischen und gewissenlosen Hochglanzmagazin, das auch der ältesten Marcos-Tochter Imee die Ehre erwies und sie im eleganten roten Kleid zeigte. Einige waren empört, doch diese Dynastie scheint definitiv über dem Gesetz zu stehen. Der philippinische Pavillon machte zwar ein paar unbeholfene Versuche, sich für Lokales und das Alltagsleben zu öffnen, wo man früher konsequent auf „Internationalisierung" gesetzt hätte. Man denke nur an Jose Tence Ruiz' Hommage an Salvatore Scarpitta, die der Kurator Patrick D. Flores präsentierte. Eine Membran aus samtenem Stoff legte sich über eine Installation, die die Dimensionen des Ausstellungsraumes zu sprengen schien. Daneben gab es klare Bezüge zu *Shoal*, der zweiten Arbeit des Künstlers im Pavillon, die auf einen Territorialdisput anspielte: Die BRP Sierra Madre ist ein abgewracktes Geisterschiff, das von der philippinischen Regierung als Vorposten im Südchinesischen Meer eingesetzt wird. In seinem Begleittext beschreibt Flores, wie die zugleich volkstümlichen wie luxuriösen Samtstreifen „durch Öffnungen in andere Werke hineingezogen werden und die einmal geschlagenen Wunden noch weiter aufreißen". Ich hatte jedoch eher den Eindruck, dass die Spannung, die mit dem Hinweis auf die zu den Spratly-Inseln gehörenden Nichtorte wie Ayungin und Kalayaan (im Falle des zweiten Projekts von Manny Montelibano) erzeugt werden sollte, nie wirklich aufkam.[11] Das Vorhaben, sich durch eine heftige Konfrontation räumlicher und akustischer Elemente willkürlich gezogenen Landesgrenzen und territorialen Setzungen entgegenzustellen, fand ich aber durchaus gewagt. Montelibanos Soundtrip führt durch den epischen Kudaman-Gesang, der immer wieder von Radiofrequenzen überlagert wird, die in Bataraza empfangen werden können. Es ist ein ungewöhnliches und ergreifendes Klanggemälde dieses südlichsten Zipfels der Provinz Palawan. Dazu muss man wissen, dass die Provinz regelmäßig für philippinisch-amerikanische Militärübungen herhalten muss, wenn es gilt, Stärke zu demonstrieren. Flores meint schließlich aber allen Ernstes, dass Montelibanos multimediale Mehrkanal-Videoinstallation *A Dashed State* „weite Wellen im Diskursmeer schlagen wird". Ich zwinge mich, die Tatsache auszublenden, dass der leidenschaftlichste Förderer dieses Projektes im Senat eine absolut mediengeile

Person ist, deren umfangreiche Garderobe indigener Kleidung nur von ihrem grenzenlosen Opportunismus übertroffen wird. Je nachdem, wie die Stimmung im Volk ist, wird auch die Parteizugehörigkeit gewechselt. In Flores' Essay „All Over", den er für den Katalog der Venedig Biennale verfasst hat, liest man stattdessen: „Diese Künstler haben sich einer Kunstpraxis verschrieben, die in einer Moderne wurzelt, die zugleich weltzugewandt und einer quirligen lokalen Identität verpflichtet ist. Sie wenden sich weder neurotisch dem Außen zu, noch versteifen sie sich auf eine Authentizität, die es tief im Inneren zu entdecken gäbe." Das mag durchaus eloquent formuliert sein, in der Sache spricht hier jedoch ein Kulturbegeisterter, der sich immer dann auf Nation und/oder Region beruft, wenn es ihm passt – auch wenn es seinen öffentlich verlautbarten globalen Sympathien zuwiderläuft. So etwas geschieht überall und beschränkt sich nicht auf die Kunstwelt. Respekt wird genau an den Stellen bekundet, wo berufliche Türen aufgehen könnten; man begibt sich in zweifelhafte Gesellschaft, um die Anerkennung zu bekommen, die diese kapitalintensiven Kunstprojekte mit sich bringen – all das ist traurige Normalität geworden. China wird als Ort des imperialen Kapitals an den Pranger gestellt und man unterschlägt dabei das gierig akkumulierte kulturelle Kapital, das man im Gerangel um die Machtpositionen in der lokalen Kunstwelt der Philippinen angehäuft hat – in der Hoffnung, es vielleicht einmal nach Venedig zu schaffen.

Jetzt also das Jahr 2016. Die ASEAN hat einen Filmableger gegründet, die aus zehn Mitgliedsstaaten bestehende Film Asean Foundation, die, so der sichtlich euphorisierte Filmemacher und Leiter der Film Development Association of the Philippines, Briccio Santos, endlich den Weg freimache für die großen Erzählungen, die „die Lebensstile in den ASEAN-Ländern abbilden". Wie soll eine solch schwerfällige regionale Körperschaft durch die buchstäblich rauen geopolitischen Gewässer Asiens navigieren? Die ASEAN predigt beim internationalen Gezerre um das Südchinesische (für uns Westphilippinische) Meer Zurückhaltung, will mit der Sache am liebsten gar nichts zu tun haben. Werden Chinas verbleibende ASEAN-Verbündete es zulassen, dass auch weiterhin Gegennarrative aus militärisch schwächeren und ökonomisch zweitrangigen Ländern kommen? Wie muss man sich das Modell der Film-Koproduktionen vorstellen, das der ASEAN vorschwebt? Schon jetzt versucht man, Konflikten möglichst aus dem Weg zu gehen; was zählt, ist nationales und regionales wirtschaftliches Potenzial. Hofft man, als regionaler Block besser auf dem *European Film Market* dazustehen, dem im Martin-Gropius-Bau stattfindenden Businessforum der Berlinale, den Berliner Filmfestspielen, die zunehmend nach Asien blicken? Santos selbst träumt wahrscheinlich von einem Auftritt in Cannes: die perfekte Bühne für dieses Fantasie-Asien, in dem es eigentlich nur Entspannungspolitik gibt. Vom zunehmend eskalierenden Wettstreit um Rohstoffe, Macht und Geld in der Region will man nichts hören. Mir ist es selbst unangenehm, dass dieser Essay mit der Marcos-Dynastie und anderen zwielichtigen Gestalten beginnt und endet. Vielleicht irre ich mich auch, aber mich beschleicht manchmal das ungute Gefühl, regionale Bündnisse wie die ASEAN, die wir leichtfertig gutheißen, stellen nicht den Endpunkt der Dekolonisierung dar, sondern begünstigen Formen der Rekolonialisierung. Wenn das Kuratoriat – auf mitunter äußerst kluge und berührende Weise – sich eine eigene Welt schafft, ohne die eigene Hybris mit zu bedenken, sondern vielmehr permanent scheinheilige Platituden nach innen und außen absondert, wie soll man da erwarten, dass irgend jemand den Mut aufbringt, um für das Gemeinwohl und gegen Marktinteressen die Stimme zu erheben? Vielleicht sollten diejenigen von uns, die sich in diesem Milieu bewegen, von der ganzen Absahnerei etwas Abstand nehmen und akzeptieren, dass auch wir nicht unbesiegbar sind. Wir sollten zumindest versuchen, Rechenschaft darüber abzulegen, wie die rücksichtslosen Strukturen des Kunstschaffens unsere beschädigten Existenzen in der Peripherie der kritischen Praxis geprägt haben.

1   Roger Nelson, „The Place of Performance", in: Sonderausgabe der *Stedelijk Studies*, Mitherausgeber Hendrik Folkerts und Sophie Berrebi, Heft 3, 2016.

2   Der Hinweis auf die Eröffnung des Folk Arts Center in Manila im Jahr 1974 stammt aus den Archiven der Kalaw Ledesma Foundation, Manila.

3   Auszug aus Imelda Marcos' Rede bei der Eröffnung des Folk Arts Theater. Der Text wurde im *Daily Express* vom 9. Juli 1974 veröffentlicht.

4   Auszug aus der Rede des Außenministers Carlos P. Romulo beim selben Anlass, veröffentlicht im *Daily Express* vom 9. Juli 1974.

5   Vortrag bei Green Papaya Art Projects, 17. Mai 2016.

6   C. J. Wee Wan-ling, „'We Asians?' Modernity, Visual Art Exhibitions and East Asia", in: *Boundary* 2, Frühjahr 2010, Bd. 37/1, S. 23, S. 120.

7   Joan Kee, „Twenty Questions", in: *Positions: East Asia Cultures Critique*, Jg. 12, Heft 3, S. 604.

8   Ibid., S. 609.

9   http://lorenlegarda.com.ph/after-51-years-phl-returns-to-art-worlds-olympics-venice-biennale/, ein Pressebericht, der anschließend in den philippinischen Mainstream-Medien nachgedruckt wurde, abgerufen am 31. Juli 2016.

10  Der Auftritt der Philippinen bestand aus dem Film *Genghis Khan* des Staatskünstlers Manuel Conde und installativen Arbeiten von Jose Tence Ruiz und Manny Montelibano. Der Film stand im Zentrum der Inszenierung.

11  Die Inseln liegen zwischen den philippinischen Inseln. China und die Philippinen erheben Besitzansprüche und befinden sich darüber im Konflikt.

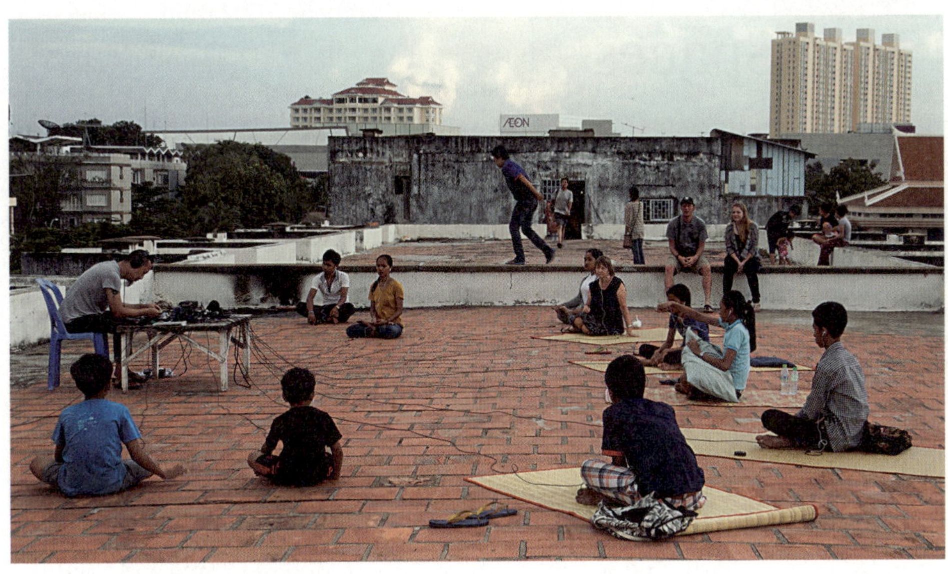

Yan Jun, *Noise Hypnotizing*, 2015
Sa Sa Art Projects, Phnom Penh, Cambodia

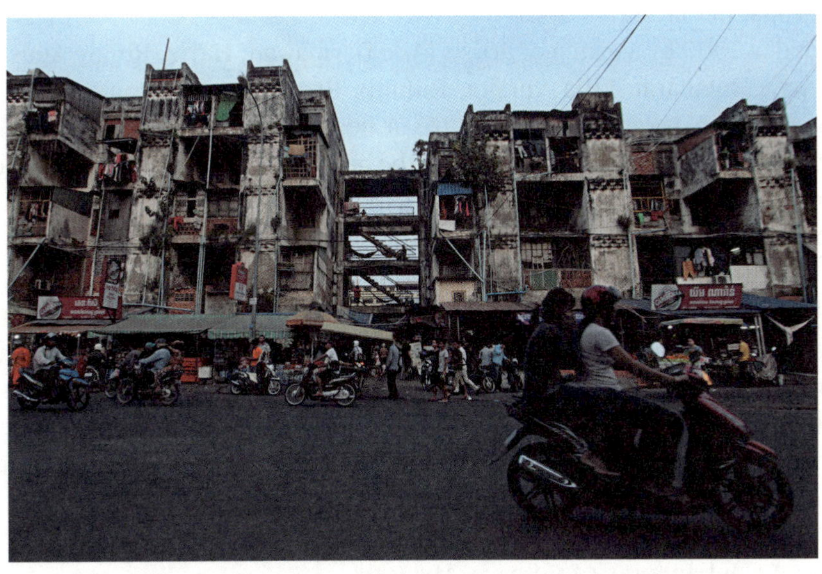

Sa Sa Art Projects
The White Building, Phnom Penh, Cambodia

# Art Spaces

### Sa Sa Art Projects, Cambodia
Phnom Penh's only not-for-profit artist-run space dedicated to experimentation and collaboration is Sa Sa Art Projects. Founded in 2010 by Cambodian arts collective Stiev Selapak, it is located in a historic apartment complex known as the White Building. Sa Sa Art Projects engages with Cambodian and visiting artists, creative individuals and groups, students, and the White Building's residents to realize art projects and events that are accessible to and enjoyable by everyone.

### Cemeti Art House, Indonesia
Founded in Yogyakarta, Indonesia in 1988 by artists Mella Jaarsma and Nindityo Adipurnomo, Cemeti Art House has been actively involved in engaging and promoting contemporary Indonesian art. Through exhibitions, residency programs, and talks, Cemeti Art House continues to serve as an important research and cultural center in Indonesia and the region. Cemeti Art Foundation, today Indonesian Visual Art Archive (IVAA), evolved from this art space.

### Ruangrupa, Indonesia
Founded in 2000 by a group of artists (Ade Darmawan, Hafiz, Ronny Agustinus, Oky Arfie Hutabarat, Lilia Nursita, Rithmi), Ruangrupa is a contemporary art organization in Jakarta, Indonesia. As a nonprofit organization, it works to advance art ideas in urban contexts and the broad scope of culture through exhibitions, festivals, an art laboratory, workshops, research, and book, magazine, and online journal publications.

### Run Amok Collective, Malaysia
Founded by artist Hoo Fan Chon in 2013, Run Amok Collective positions itself as an alternative platform within the existing local and regional art ecosystem. Based in Penang, Malaysia, it collaborates with art and cultural practitioners to respond to current socio-political conditions through a language that is relevant to contemporary locality and everyday experiences.

### Lostgens' Contemporary Art Space, Malaysia
Established in 2004 by artist and curator Yeoh Lian Heng, based in Kuala Lumpur, Malaysia, this self-managed experimental space aims to encourage originality, creativity and individuality, as well as to promote contemporary arts and community art projects. It provides an alternative space for budding innovative

exhibitions and performances. More than just a place that brings together artists, it also provides a platform for a dynamic growth of multi-layered artistic culture.

## Jorge B. Vargas Museum, Philippines

Located in Quezon City, Philippines, Vargas Museum was inaugurated in 1987. It is the primary modern and contemporary art museum of the Philippines, focusing primarily on research, exhibition, and education. Its permanent collection consists of paintings, sculptures, drawings, covering Philippine artistic creativity from the 1880s to the 1960s.

## Museum of Contemporary Art and Design, Philippines

Housed within the College of Saint Benilde's School of Design and Art (SDA) in Manila, Philippines, the Museum of Contemporary Art and Design (MCAD) operates as an international contemporary art space. MCAD's contemporary exhibitions and programs are produced through collaboration with local and international artists and curators.

## The Substation, Singapore

Singapore's first independent contemporary arts center, The Substation was established in 1990 by the late Kuo Pao Kun, it is known for its pioneering and experimental arts programming. Over the years, The Substation has worked with some of Singapore's most critically acclaimed artists, writers, and intellectuals, including Ong Keng Seng, Alvin Tan, and Ivan Heng.

## NTU Centre for Contemporary Art Singapore

The national research centre of Nanyang Technological University is located at the Gillman Barracks, a former British Military Camp redeveloped into an international arts cluster. The NTU Centre for Contemporary Art Singapore is unique in its constellation of international exhibitions and residencies, research and academic education. Thinking in new ways of Spaces of the Curatorial in Southeast Asia and beyond, the center positions itself as a space for critical discourse and diverse modes of knowledge production through art.

## National Gallery Singapore

Opened in 2015, National Gallery Singapore oversees the largest public collection of modern art in Singapore and Southeast Asia. Occupying two national monuments, the former Supreme Court and City Hall, the Gallery reflects Singapore's unique heritage and geographical location. The Gallery features Singapore and Southeast Asian art in its long-term and special exhibitions. It also works with leading museums worldwide to co-present Southeast Asian art in a wider context, positioning Singapore as a regional and international hub for the visual arts.

## The Jim Thompson Art Center, Thailand

Located in the heart of Bangkok, Thailand, The Jim Thompson Art Center is situated in the same compound as the Jim Thompson House. Completed in 1959 as the residence of American entrepreneur James H. W. Thompson, it serves as a haven for Bangkok's local and international arts and cultural communities as a place to mingle, interact, and exchange dialogues. In conjunction with its exhibitions, the Center's activities include events, seminars, lectures, and workshops.

## Nhà Sàn Collective, Vietnam

Founded in Hanoi by artists Nguyen Manh Duc and Tran Luong, Nhà Sàn Studio operated between 1998 and 2011. It re-established itself as Nhà Sàn Collective in 2013. As an artist-run art space and collective, its mission is to promote contemporary art in Vietnam. Working with exhibitions, collaborative projects, education, and cultural exchanges, Nhà Sàn Collective seeks to examine traditional, local, and global socio-political contexts and history.

## Sàn Art, Vietnam

Established in 2007 by Dinh Q. Lê, Tuan Andrew Nguyen, Phu Nam Thuc Ha, and Tiffany Chung, Sàn Art is an artist-initiated, nonprofit contemporary art organization committed to the exchange and excavation of cultural knowledge within an interdisciplinary community. It seeks to promote, facilitate, and showcase contemporary art through production, exhibition, residency, talks, and education. Sàn Art is based in Ho Chi Minh City, Vietnam.

# Kunsträume

Sa Sa Art Projects, Kambodscha
Der Kunstraum wurde 2010 vom kambodschanischen Künstlerkollektiv Stiev Selapak gegründet und befindet sich im White Building, einem bekannten, historischen Wohnkomplex. Sa Sa Art Projects ist Phnom Penhs einzige gemeinnützige Produzentengalerie für experimentelle und kollaborative Projekte und entwickelt mit KünstlerInnen aus Kambodscha und dem Ausland, mit Einzelpersonen und Gruppen, mit StudentInnen und BewohnerInnen des White Buildings Kunstprojekte und Veranstaltungen, die für alle Bevölkerungsgruppen Kambodschas offen sind.

Cemeti Art House, Indonesien
1988 gründeten die KünstlerInnen Mella Jaarsma und Nindityo Adipurnomo in Yogyakarta, Indonesien, das Cemeti Art House. Es widmet sich der Förderung zeitgenössischer indonesischer Kunst. Mit seinen Ausstellungen, Residenzprogrammen und Diskussionsveranstaltungen ist Cemeti Art House ein wichtiges Forschungs- und Kulturzentrum für Indonesien und die Region. Die Cemeti Art Foundation, kürzlich umbenannt in Indonesian Visual Art Archive (IVAA), ging aus diesem Kunstraum hervor.

Ruangrupa, Indonesien
Die gemeinnützige Organisation für zeitgenössische Kunst wurde im Jahr 2000 von einer Gruppe von KünstlerInnen (Ade Darmawan, Hafiz, Ronny Agustinus, Oky Arfie Hutabarat, Lilia Nursita, Rithmi) im indonesischen Jakarta, Indonesien, gegründet. Ruangrupa arbeitet an der Verwirklichung künstlerischer Ideen in urbanen Kontexten und agiert als kuratorische Plattform für Ausstellungen, Festivals, Workshops, Forschungsprojekte sowie die Veröffentlichung von Büchern, Zeitschriften und Onlinepublikationen.

Run Amok Collective, Malaysia
Das Run Amok Collective wurde 2013 vom Künstler Hoo Fan Chon gegründet und positioniert sich als alternative Plattform innerhalb der bestehenden lokalen und regionalen Kunstlandschaft. Das in Penang, Malaysia, ansässige Kollektiv setzt sich gemeinsam mit anderen Kunst- und Kulturakteuren mit den gegenwärtigen gesellschaftspolitischen Zuständen auseinander und entwickelt dafür eine Sprache, die für die heutigen Bedingungen vor Ort und die Alltagserfahrungen der Menschen relevant ist.

Lostgens' Contemporary Art Space, Malaysia
Der selbstverwaltete, experimentelle Raum in Kuala Lumpur in Malysia wurde
2004 vom Künstler und Kurator Yeoh Lian Heng gegründet. Er realisiert zeitgenössische und kommunale Kunstprojekte und möchte damit vor allem Origi-
nalität, Kreativität und Individualität fördern. Lostgens' Contemporary Art Space
bietet einen alternativen Raum für Ausstellungen und Performances junger, auf-
strebender KünstlerInnen und ist eine Plattform für die dynamische Entwicklung
einer vielschichtigen künstlerischen Kultur.

Jorge B. Vargas Museum, Philippinen
Das Vargas Museum wurde im Jahr 1987 in Quezon City auf den Philippinen
eröffnet. Es ist das wichtigste Museum für moderne und zeitgenössische Kunst
der Philippinen und gehört zur University of the Philippines. Seine Schwerpunk-
te sind Ausstellungen, Forschung und Bildung. Die ständige Sammlung umfasst
Malerei, Skulpturen und Papierarbeiten vorwiegend philippinischer Künstler-
Innen von den 1880er bis in die 1960er Jahre.

Museum of Contemporary Art and Design, Philippinen
Das Museum of Contemporary Art and Design (MCAD) ist ein Ort für internationale zeitgenössische Kunst und befindet sich im College of Saint Benilde's
School of Design and Art (SDA) in Manila, Philippinen. Die Ausstellungen und
das Vermittlungsprogramm des MCAD entstehen in Zusammenarbeit mit lokalen
und internationalen KünstlerInnen und KuratorInnen.

The Substation, Singapur
Der Kunstraum ist Singapurs erstes unabhängiges Zentrum für zeitgenössische
Kunst. The Substation wurde 1990 von dem inzwischen verstorbenen Kuo Pao
Kun gegründet und ist bekannt für sein wegweisendes und experimentelles Pro-
gramm. Über die Jahre hat The Substation mit vielen, von der Kritik gefeierten
KünstlerInnen, SchriftstellerInnen und Intellektuellen Singapurs zusammen-
gearbeitet, darunter Ong Keng Seng, Alvin Tan und Ivan Heng.

NTU Centre for Contemporary Art Singapore
Das Forschungszentrum der Nanyang Technological University befindet sich in
den Gillman Barracks, einer ehemaligen Kaserne der britischen Armee, die sich
zu einem internationalen Kunstquartier entwickelt hat. Das NTU CCA Singapore
verschränkt internationale Ausstellungen und Residenzen, Forschung und akademische Bildung. Es positioniert sich durch neue Denkansätze und über Räume
des Kuratorischen in Südostasien als Zentrum kritischer Diskurse und unterschiedlicher Formen von Wissensproduktion durch Kunst.

National Gallery Singapore
Die 2015 eröffnete National Gallery Singapore verfügt über die größte öffentliche Sammlung moderner Kunst in Singapur und Südostasien und ist in zwei palastartigen, denkmalgeschützten Gebäuden untergebracht, dem ehemaligen Obersten Gerichtshof und dem Rathaus. Die Gebäude verweisen auf das besondere Erbe und die hervorgehobene geografische Lage Singapurs. Die National Gallery Singapore arbeitet regelmäßig mit führenden internationalen Museen zusammen, um südostasiatische Kunst in einem breiteren Kontext zu zeigen und Singapur als ein regionales und internationales Zentrum der bildenden Kunst zu positionieren.

The Jim Thompson Art Center, Thailand
Das Jim Thompson Art Center ist ein Teil des Jim Thompson House und befindet sich im Zentrum der thailändischen Hauptstadt Bangkok. Es wurde 1959 als Wohnsitz des amerikanischen Unternehmers James H. W. Thompson erbaut und dient heute lokalen und internationalen Kunst- und Kultur-Communities als Ort der Interaktion und des Austauschs. Das Zentrum organisiert neben Ausstellungen auch Veranstaltungen, Seminare, Vorträge und Workshops.

Nhà Sàn Collective, Vietnam
Das von den Künstlern Nguyen Manh Duc and Tran Luong in Hanoi, Vietnam, gegründete Nhà Sàn Studio existierte von 1998 bis 2011. Im Jahr 2013 nahm es unter dem Namen Nhà Sàn Collective seine Aktivitäten wieder auf. Dem von KünstlerInnen betriebenen Kunstraum und Kollektiv geht es um die Förderung zeitgenössischer Kunst in Vietnam. Mit Ausstellungen, Kooperationen und Austauschprogrammen erkundet das Nhà Sàn Collective traditionelle, lokale und globale gesellschaftspolitische Zusammenhänge.

Sàn Art, Vietnam
Die gemeinnützige Organisation für zeitgenössische Kunst Sàn Art wurde 2007 von Dinh Q. Lê, Tuan Andrew Nguyen, Phu Nam Thuc Ha und Tiffany Chung in Ho-Chi-Minh-Stadt, Vietnam, gegründet. Die Gruppe arbeitet interdisziplinär und widmet sich der Verbreitung kulturellen Wissens. Sàn Art fördert zeitgenössische Kunstproduktionen, stellt sie aus und bietet Residenzen für KünstlerInnen an. Sàn Art lädt regelmäßig zu Diskussionsveranstaltungen ein.

# Authors

Ute Meta Bauer is a curator and, since 2013, the Founding Director of the NTU Centre for Contemporary Art Singapore and a Professor at the School of Art, Design and Media, Nanyang Technological University (NTU). In 2015, she co-curated with Paul C. Ha, Director of the MIT List Visual Arts Center, the US Pavilion at the 56th Venice Biennale presenting artist Joan Jonas.

Zoe Butt is Executive Director and curator of Sàn Art until December 2016 and Designated Director of Factory Contemporary Arts Centre, both in Ho Chi Minh City, Vietnam. After eight years of co-producing the "Asian Pacific Triennial of Contemporary Art," Australia, she has led artist-initiated organizations in China and Vietnam. She is a regular contributor to *Art Asia Pacific, Dispatch: Independent Curators International, Artlink, Printed Projects,* and *Realtime.*

Lee Weng Choy is an art critic, writer, and the President of the Singapore Section of the International Association of Art Critics (AICA). He is a part-time consultant with the National Gallery Singapore and a regular collaborator of the NTU Centre for Contemporary Art Singapore. His essays have been published in *Contemporary Art in Asia* (MIT Press, 2011) *Modern and Contemporary Southeast Asian Art* (Cornell University Press, 2012), and *Theory in Contemporary Art since 1985* (Wiley-Blackwell, 2012).

Kevin Chua is an Associate Professor of Art History at Texas Tech University, USA. He specializes in the history of 18th- and 19th-century European art as well as modern and contemporary art in Southeast Asia. Chua has published essays on Simryn Gill, Ho Tzu Nyen, Donna Ong, the Migrant Ecologies Project, 1950s Nanyang painting, and the politics of animality in 19th-century Singapore.

Patrick D. Flores is a Professor of Art History and Criticism at the Department of Art Studies, University of the Philippines, Quezon City, where he is also the curator of the Jorge B. Vargas Museum. In 2015, he curated the Philippine Pavilion at the 56th Venice Biennale. Recent publications include "Contemporaneity and Art in Southeast Asia," a special issue of *Third Text* (2011), co-edited with Joan Kee, and *Past Peripheral: Curation in Southeast Asia* (NUS Museum 2008).

Gridthiya Gaweewong is a curator and the Artistic Director of The Jim Thompson Art Center and the co-founder of the nonprofit art space Project 304, both in Bangkok, Thailand. Recent projects include *Unreal Asia: Oberhausen International Short Film Festival* (2009), Germany, and "Apichatpong Weerasethakul: The Serenity of Madness" (2016), the inaugural exhibition of the MAIIAM Museum in Chiang Mai, Thailand.

Tony Godfrey is an art historian and curator who teaches at LASALLE College of the Arts, Singapore, Ateneo University, Manila, Philippines and the University of Plymouth, United Kingdom. His most recent curatorial collaborations include "Between the Street and the Mountain" (2016), Arario Gallery, Shanghai, China and "Life Jacket Under the Seat," Langgeng Art Foundation, Yogyakarta, Indonesia (2016). Since 2014, he has been publishing *Tuesday in the Tropics*, an online-distributed illustrated weekly letter.

Yin Ker is an Assistant Professor at the School of Art, Design and Media, Nanyang Technological University, Singapore. As an art historian, her most recent work focused on Myanmar's pioneer modern painter, Bagyi Aung Soe (1923–1990). Her research interests include "art" and "art history" as variable constructs, the intersections of ancient and modern methods of knowledge- and image-making, and ways of telling (hi)stories of Buddhist art.

Eileen Legaspi-Ramirez is a faculty member of the Department of Art Studies of the University of the Philippines, Quezon City. Her work spans curation, publishing, and art education. She is a committee member of Another Roadmap School, and part of the editorial collective *Southeast of Now: Directions in Contemporary and Modern Art*, a peer review journal published by NUS Press.

Brigitte Oetker was a Professor for Creative Processes at KMM, Institut für Kultur- und Medienmanagement, Hamburg, Germany, from 2008 to 2016. She has been the editor of *Jahresring–Annual of Fine Arts* since 1989. Since 1988 she has been member of the board of Villa Romana Residency in Florence, which gives grants to young artists.

Isabel Podeschwa is an editor. Publications she has worked on recently include *The Pantry* (Jap Sam Books/argobooks, 2012) and *Jahresring 62: Toward an Aesthetics of Living Beings* (Sternberg Press, 2015). She is currently working on a monograph on Amelie von Wulffen.

Seng Yu Jin is a Senior Curator at The National Gallery Singapore. He previously taught at LASALLE College of the Arts in the MA Asian Art Histories and BA Fine Arts programs. Seng's research interests cover regional art histories focusing on Southeast Asia in relation to the history of exhibitions and artist collectives in the region.

Simon Soon is a Senior Lecturer in the Visual Art Department, Cultural Centre, University of Malaya, Malaysia. His research focuses on 20th-century art in Southeast Asia. He is a member of the editorial collective of *Southeast of Now: Directions in Contemporary and Modern Art*, a peer review journal published by NUS Press.

Nora A. Taylor is the Alsdorf Professor of South and Southeast Asian Art at the School of the Art Institute of Chicago, United States. She is the author of *Painters in Hanoi: An Ethnography of Vietnamese Art* (University of Hawaii Press, 2004, and NUS Press, 2009) and co-editor of *Modern and Contemporary Southeast Asian Art: An Anthology* (Cornell SEAP, 2012).

David Teh is a writer, curator, art advisor, and researcher based at the National University of Singapore (NUS), specializing in Southeast Asian contemporary art. His writings have appeared in *Third Text, Afterall, LEAP Magazine, Art Asia Pacific, artforum.com,* and *The Bangkok Post*. His book *Thai Art: Currencies of the Contemporary* will be published in 2017 by MIT Press.

# Autorinnen und Autoren

Ute Meta Bauer ist Kuratorin und seit 2013 Gründungsdirektorin des NTU Centre for Contemporary Art Singapore sowie Professorin an der School of Art, Design and Media an der Nanyang Technological University (NTU). 2015 kuratierte sie zusammen mit Paul C. Ha, Direktor des MIT List Visual Arts Center, den US-amerikanischen Pavillon der 56. Venedig Biennale, mit einer Ausstellung von Joan Jonas.

Zoe Butt ist Direktorin und Kuratorin von Sàn Art und designierte Direktorin des Factory Contemporary Art Centre, beide in Ho-Chi-Minh-Stadt, Vietnam. Nachdem sie acht Jahre lang die Asian Pacific Triennial of Contemporary Art in Australien mitorganisiert hatte, leitete sie von KünstlerInnen initiierte Kunsträume in China und Vietnam. Sie schreibt regelmäßig für *Art Asia Pacific*, *Dispatch: Independent Curators International*, *Artlink*, *Printed Projects* und *Realtime*.

Lee Weng Choy ist Kunstkritiker, Schriftsteller und Präsident der singapurischen Sektion der International Association of Art Critics (AICA). Er berät die National Gallery Singapore und ist regelmäßiger Mitarbeiter des NTU Centre for Contemporary Art Singapore. Seine Essays sind in *Contemporary Art in Asia* (MIT Press 2011), *Modern and Contemporary Southeast Asian Art* (Cornell University Press 2012) und *Theory in Contemporary Art since 1985* (Wiley-Blackwell 2012) erschienen.

Kevin Chua ist Dozent für Kunstgeschichte an der Texas Tech University, USA. Seine Forschungsschwerpunkte sind die europäische Kunstgeschichte des 18. und 19. Jahrhunderts sowie die moderne und zeitgenössische Kunst Südostasiens. Er hat Essays zu Simryn Gill, Ho Tzu Nyen, Donna Ong, dem Migrant Ecologies Project und zur Malerei der 1950er Jahre in Nanyang sowie über die Politik der Animalität im Singapur des 19. Jahrhunderts veröffentlicht.

Patrick D. Flores ist Professor für Kunstgeschichte und Kunstkritik am Department of Art Studies, University of the Philippines, Quezon City, wo er auch als Kurator des Jorge B. Vargas Museums tätig ist. 2015 kuratierte er den philippinischen Pavillon der 56. Venedig Biennale. Seine jüngsten Veröffentlichungen: „Contemporaneity and Art in Southeast Asia", eine mit Joan Kee herausgegebene Sonderausgabe von *Third Text* (2011), und *Past Peripheral: Curation in Southeast Asia* (NUS Museum 2008).

Gridthiya Gaweewong ist Kuratorin und künstlerische Leiterin des Jim Thompson Art Center und Mitbegründerin des gemeinnützigen Kunstraums Project 304, beide in Bangkok, Thailand. Projekte u.a.: *Unreal Asia, Internationale Kurzfilmtage Oberhausen* (2009) und *Apichatpong Weerasethakul: The Serenity of Madness* (2016), die Eröffnungsausstellung des MAIIAM Museums in Chiang Mai, Thailand.

Tony Godfrey ist Kunsthistoriker und Kurator und lehrt am LASALLE College of the Arts, Singapur, an der Ateneo University, Manila, Philippinen, und der University of Plymouth, Großbritannien. Jüngste kuratorische Zusammenarbeiten u.a.: *Between the Street and the Mountain* (2016), Arario Gallery, Shanghai, China, und *Life Jacket Under the Seat* (2016), Langgeng Art Foundation, Yogyakarta, Indonesien. Seit 2014 veröffentlicht er „Tuesday in the Tropics", einen Online-Newsletter.

Yin Ker ist Assistant Professor an der School of Art, Design and Media, Nanyang Technological University, Singapur. Zurzeit beschäftigt sich die Kunsthistorikerin mit Myanmars wegweisendem, modernen Maler Bagyi Aung Soe (1923–1990). In ihrer Forschung befasst sie sich mit Kunst und Kunstgeschichte als variable Konstruktionen, mit den Schnittstellen zwischen historischen und modernen Methoden der Wissens- und Bildproduktion sowie mit Geschichte(n) buddhistischer Kunst.

Eileen Legaspi-Ramirez ist Fakultätsmitglied am Department of Art Studies der University of the Philippines, Quezon City. Sie arbeitet als Publizistin und Kuratorin und ist im Bereich der Kunstausbildung tätig. Sie ist Gremiumsmitglied der Another Roadmap School und Mitglied des Redaktionskollektivs der Fachzeitschrift *Southeast of Now: Directions in Contemporary and Modern Art* (NUS Press).

Brigitte Oetker war von 2008 bis 2016 Professorin für Kreative Prozesse in der Bildenden Kunst am KMM – Institut für Kultur- und Medienmanagement, Hamburg. Seit 1989 ist sie Herausgeberin des *Jahresring – Jahrbuch für Kunst*, seit 1988 Mitglied des Vorstands der Villa Romana, einem Künstlerhaus in Florenz, das jährlich Arbeitsstipendien vergibt.

Isabel Podeschwa ist Lektorin und Redakteurin und arbeitete in den letzten Jahren unter anderem an den Publikationen *Vorratskammer/Pantry* (Jap Sam Books/ argobooks 2012) und *Jahresring: Zu einer Ästhetik des Lebendigen* (Sternberg Press 2015). Aktuell arbeitet sie an einer Monografie über Amelie von Wulffen.

Seng Yu Jin ist Senior Curator an der National Gallery Singapore. Zuvor lehrte er am LASALLE College of the Arts Asiatische Kunstgeschichte und Bildende Kunst. Seng forscht zu regionaler Kunstgeschichte mit Schwerpunkt auf der Geschichte von Ausstellungen und Künstlerkollektiven in Südostasien.

Simon Soon ist Senior Lecturer im Visual Art Department des Cultural Centre, University of Malaya, Malaysia. Sein Forschungsschwerpunkt ist die südostasiatische Kunst des 20. Jahrhunderts. Er ist Mitglied des Redaktionskollektivs der Fachzeitschrift *Southeast of Now: Directions in Contemporary and Modern Art* (NUS Press).

Nora A. Taylor hat die Alsdorf Professur für Süd- und Südostasienstudien an der School of the Art Institute of Chicago, USA inne und ist Autorin von *Painters in Hanoi: An Ethnography of Vietnamese Art* (University of Hawaii Press 2004 und NUS Press 2009) sowie Mitherausgeberin von *Modern and Contemporary Southeast Asian Art: An Anthology* (Cornell University Press 2012).

David Teh ist Schriftsteller, Kurator, Kunstberater. Er forscht an der National University of Singapore (NUS) mit Schwerpunkt auf südostasiatischer Gegenwartskunst. Er schreibt Beiträge für *Third Text, Afterall, LEAP Magazine, Art Asia Pacific*, artforum.com und *The Bangkok Post*. Sein Buch *Thai Art: Currencies of the Contemporary* erscheint 2017 bei MIT Press.

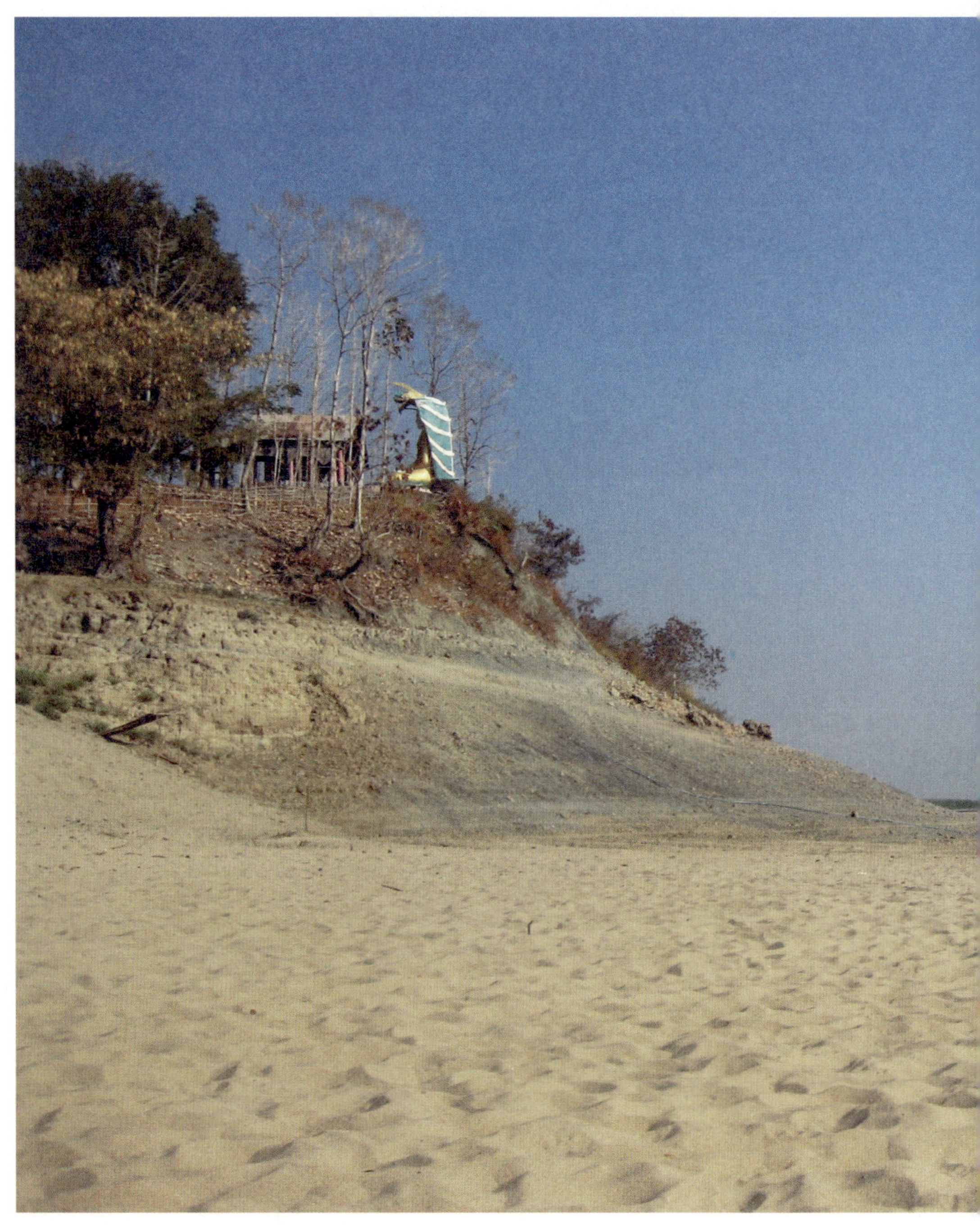

Min Thein Sung
*Holiday*, 2010
Performance
Myoutbak Village, Myanmar

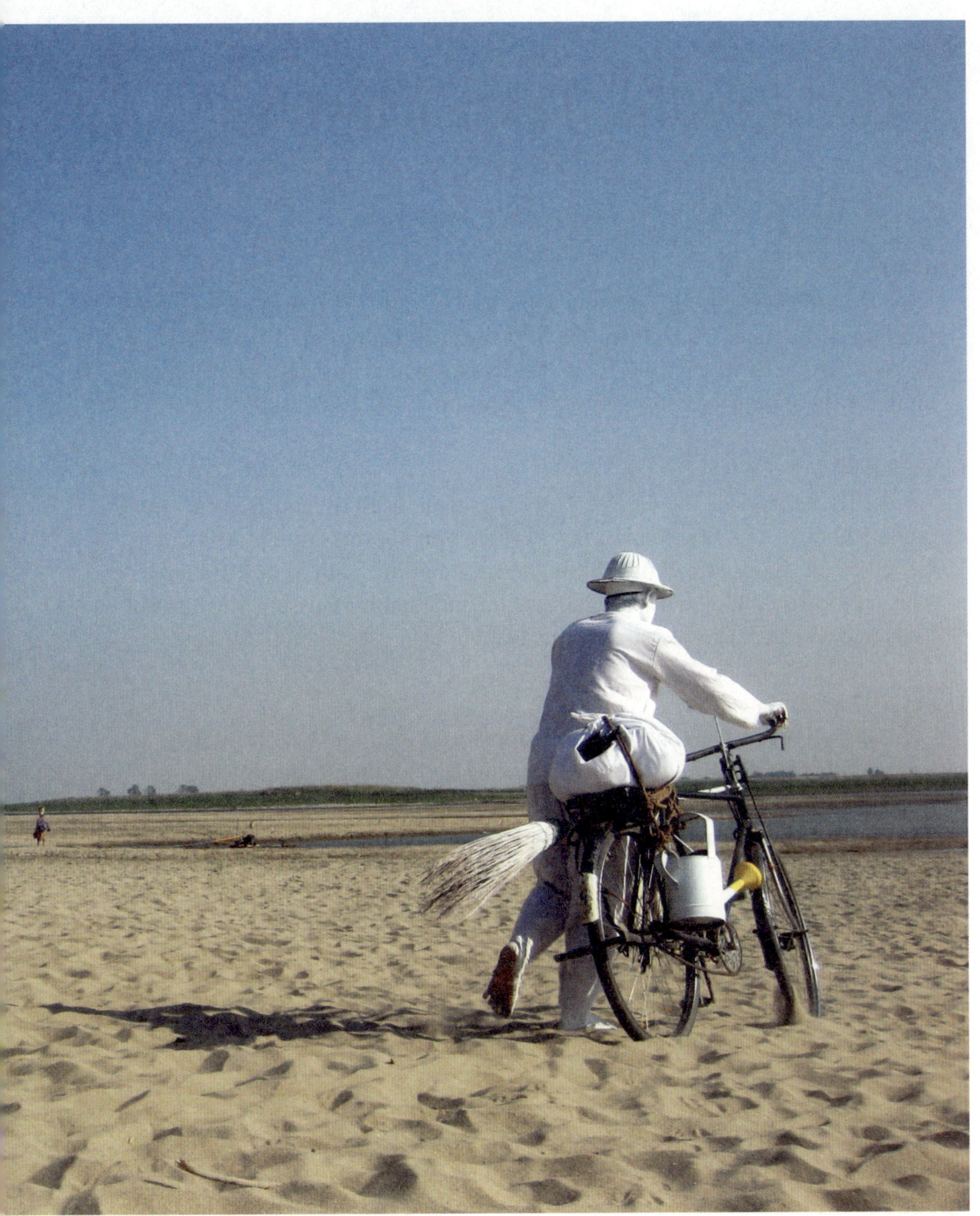

# Text Credits/Textnachweis

**Butt, Zoe**

"Practicing Friendship: Respecting Time as a Curator" is reprinted with permission of the Asia Art Archive. The text was a contribution to the fifth issue of Asia Art Archive's online blog *Field Notes* which marked the fifteenth anniversary of the Hong Kong based institution. © 2015 Zoe Butt, Saigon.

**Chua, Kevin**

An earlier version of the essay "The Curatorial as Buoy and Beacon" was published in *SEA STATE: Charles Lim Yi Yong*, Singapore: National Arts Council, 2015, on the occasion of the Singapore Pavilion, 56th Venice Biennale. The author would like to thank Charles Lim and Shabbir Hussain Mustafa for assistance on an earlier version of this essay.

**Flores, Patrick D.**

"Within and Across: Troublesome Propositions" was originally written as a paper titled "Collection/Collective: Tracing the Southeast Asian Contemporary," delivered at the CIMAM conference in Shanghai, China, 2010; and for an event of the tenth anniversary of Ruangrupa in 2010 in Jakarta.

**Gaweewong, Gridthiya**

"The Mekong as a Site of Artistic Production" is an essay adapted from a lecture for the symposium "The Geopolitical and the Biophysical: A Structured Conversation on Art and Southeast Asia in Context, Part II" that took place at the NTU Centre for Contemporary Art Singapore, June 2016.

**Godfrey, Tony**

"Tuesday in the Tropics" is an illustrated weekly letter that Tony Godfrey has sent to his friends and colleagues by e-mail since 2014. It is first published in this volume.

**Ker, Yin**

"Why Play? An Outsider's Point of View on Making & Seeing Art in Myanmar Today" is an unpublished essay originally written for the exhibition catalogue to "plAy: Art from Myanmar Today," Osage Gallery, Singapore, 2010, curated by Yin Ker and Isabel Ching.

Seng Yu Jin

"Framing Contemporary Art in Southeast Asia through Exhibitionary Discourses" refers to an earlier version of this essay with the title "The Primacy of Exhibitionary Discourses: Contemporaneity in Southeast Asian Art, 1992–2002," in *Intersecting Histories: Contemporary Turns in Southeast Asian Art*, School of Art, Design and Media, Nanyang Technological University, Singapore, 2012.

Teh, David

The essay "Who Cares a Lot? Ruangrupa as Curatorship" was first commissioned by and published in *Afterall*, no. 30 (Summer 2012). Reprinted in this volume with kind permission of the University of Chicago Press.

All texts are printed with kind permission of the authors./Der Abdruck der Texte erfolgt mit freundlicher Genehmigung der Autorinnen und Autoren.

# Image Credits/Bildnachweis

5
Moelyono Moel and Lostgens' Contemporary Art Space, Kuala Lumpur, Malaysia

12
Phu Luc and Nhà Sàn Collective, Hanoi, Vietnam

20/21
Timoteus Anggawan Kusno and Cemeti Art House, Yogyakarta, Indonesia

30
Jorge B. Vargas Museum, University of the Philippines, Quezon City, Philippines

42
Museum of Contemporary Art and Design, Manila, Philippines

56/57, 69
The National Gallery Singapore

82/83
Bui Cong Khanh and Sàn Art Art, Ho Chi Minh City, Vietnam

92, 93, 286
Apichatpong Weerasethakul and Kick the Machine, Chiang Mai, Thailand

104, 114/115
Min Thein Sung

126
NTU Centre for Contemporary Art Singapore

134/135
Koh Nguang How

144
Charles Lim Yi Yong and Future Perfect, Singapore

155
Charles Lim Yi Yong

168/169, 178
Panji Purnama Putra

190, 196
Tony Godfrey and Eko Nugroho

197
Tony Godfrey, Eko Nugroho, Handiwirman Saputra, and Indieguerillas

198
Tony Godfrey, Jompet Kuswidananto, Indieguerillas, and Prison Art Lab

206
Nhà Sàn Collective, Hanoi, Vietnam

212
Sàn Art, Ho Chi Minh City, Vietnam

219
Nguyen Nhat Nam

228/229
Run Amok Collective, Penang, Malaysia

239
Gridthiya Gaweewong

251
At Maculangan and Museum of Contemporary Art and Design, Manila, Philippines

265
above: Sa Sa Art Projects, Phnom Penh, Cambodia
below: Sok Chanrado

278/279
Min Thein Sung

All images are reprinted with kind permission of the photographers and institutions mentioned above./Der Abdruck der Bilder erfolgt mit freundlicher Genehmigung der genannten Fotografen und Institutionen.

Village cinema program, 2016
Sa Sa Art Projects
Phnom Penh, Cambodia

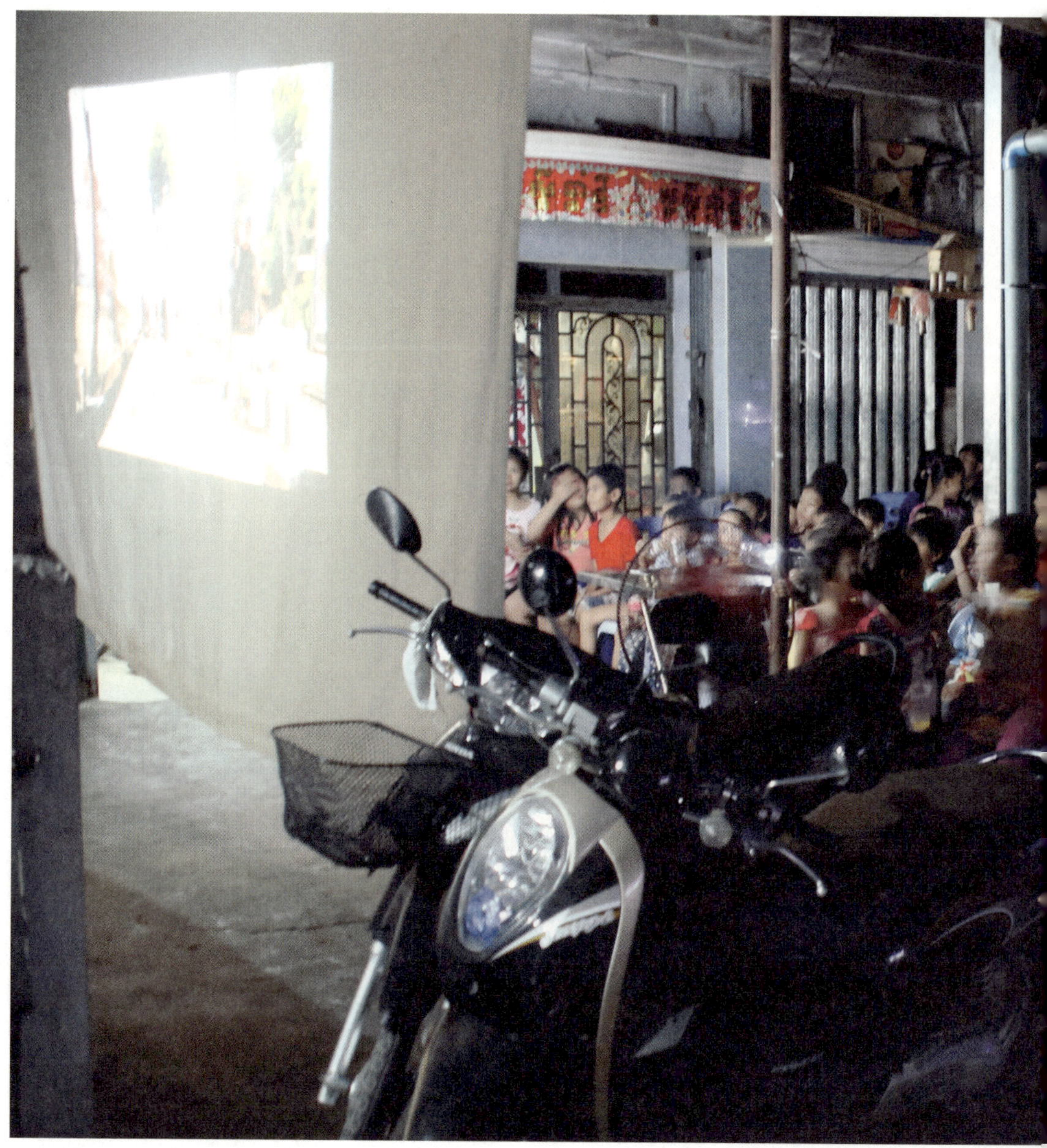